Politics and Public Policy

Politics and Public Policy

Third Edition

Carl E. Van Horn
John J. Heldrich Center for Workforce Development,
Rutgers University

Donald C. Baumer
Smith College

William T. Gormley Jr.
Public Policy Institute, Georgetown University

CQ PRESS
A Division of Congressional Quarterly Inc.
Washington, D.C.

CQ Press
A Division of Congressional Quarterly Inc.
1414 22nd St. N.W.
Washington, DC 20037

(202) 822–1475; (800) 638–1710

www.cqpress.com

⊚ The paper used in this publication meets the minumum requirements of the American National Standards for Information Sciences—Permanence of Paper for Printed Library Materials, ANSI Z39.48-1992.

Printed in the United States of America
05 04 03 02 01   5 4 3 2 1

Library of Congress Cataloging-in-Publication Data
In process.

ISBN 1-56802-483-5

FOR
Ben and Maggie Baumer
B.J. and Ken Gormley
Evan and Ross Van Horn

whose support and encouragement made this
work possible

Contents

Tables, Figures, and Boxes

Preface

Why do policymakers select certain problems for attention and ignore others? How do policymakers design and implement policies? How do those policies ultimately influence the nation? These questions are the focus of this book. The practice of politics and policymaking is complicated, involving thousands of people in government institutions and the private sector, but it can be understood by those who are willing to make the effort.

In *Politics and Public Policy* we go beyond conventional analyses that focus narrowly and exclusively on presidents and members of Congress to offer a comprehensive and realistic view of policymaking in the United States. Laws, regulations, administrative rulings, and corporate decisions ensue from the efforts of judges, bureaucrats, corporate officials, journalists, and voters as well as from those of legislators and chief executives. Moreover, state and local governments play an important and expanding role in the design and conduct of public policies.

In *Politics and Public Policy* we use a unique framework to explore the roles of the various people and institutions that make public policy. Differences in the politics within these arenas result in different policies and outcomes. To facilitate an understanding of such variations, we describe six domains of public policy:

1. *Boardroom politics:* decisions by business leaders and professionals that have important public consequences
2. *Bureaucratic politics:* rule making and adjudication by administrators who consider the interests of clients, legislators, and the chief executive, in addition to using their own professional judgment
3. *Cloakroom politics:* lawmaking by legislators who weigh the competing demands of constituents, interest groups, and presidents or governors
4. *Chief executive politics:* decision making dominated by presidents, governors, mayors, and their advisers
5. *Courtroom politics:* court orders by judges, influenced by interest groups and their competing adversaries
6. *Living room politics:* the consequences of public opinions expressed by and through grassroots movements, political activists, voters, and the mass media

We prefer the "policy domain" approach over the traditional "policy process" approach, with its focus on the stages of agenda setting, policy formulation, implementation, and evaluation. We should emphasize, however, that the two approaches are not incompatible. Although this book was designed to stand on its own in public policy and American government courses, many of our colleagues tell us that they use it in conjunction with a more traditional policy process text to broaden students' perspectives on the politics of policy-making in the United States.

What we offer is a road map for negotiating the twists and turns of the public policy landscape. We hope readers will come away with a better understanding of how policies are made and implemented, who is powerful and who is not, and how public policies influence American citizens. We also hope readers will be better equipped to judge the performance of their nation's political institutions and their leaders.

The book integrates discussions of policymaking with a look at real policies and their effects. How policies are chosen and implemented is important, but so is what is decided and what those decisions mean for citizens and society. Policymakers are constantly faced with difficult and unpleasant choices. Tax policy, entitlement programs, global warming, conflicts in the Middle East, and a plethora of other problems pose severe tests for political institutions and their leaders. Understanding more about how institutions process decisions and make policy will help readers better evaluate their leaders' performance on issues that matter most to them.

This third edition of *Politics and Public Policy* includes some important changes that have been made to incorporate new scholarship and to strengthen arguments made in the last two editions. The entire book has been updated to reflect issues facing political institutions and policy leaders in the early years of the twenty-first century.

The first two chapters introduce the actors and institutions that shape policies and the distinctively American context in which those public solutions to problems are demanded. These chapters also identify for students some of the normative concerns to which we return in the concluding chapters. In Chapters 3 through 8 we apply our unique approach to understanding public policy through the perspective of the six policy domains; each domain has different power centers, different arenas for struggle, different participants, and often different outcomes.

After describing and analyzing the policy domains, we turn to more normative and evaluative concerns in Chapters 9 and 10. These chapters assess American political institutions and evaluate progress on broad goals of public policy.

We appreciate the support and encouragement we have received from many people in the production of this book. Those who helped with earlier editions have been acknowledged in those editions. We are pleased to recognize several others who have helped us prepare the third edition—Ken Gormley, Joel Grossman, Jack Hoadley, Doug Reed, and Ruth Simmons. We received excellent research support from Denise Balik, a Ph.D. student in the political science department at Rutgers University.

We are especially appreciative of CQ Press for its continuing support of this book through its three editions. Brenda Carter was helpful in encouraging us to undertake another edition. This edition also reflects the careful attentions of Joanne S. Ainsworth, the manuscript editor who saw the book through the editing process.

Finally, we are most grateful to our families for their continued support and encouragement.

Politics and Public Policy

Chapter 1 **American Politics and Public Policy**

The winner of the 2000 presidential election, which had been held on November 7, was finally determined thirty-five days later, when the U.S. Supreme Court halted a recount of disputed ballots in Florida. The Court's 5–4 decision ensured that Texas governor and Republican candidate George W. Bush would become the forty-third president of the United States by securing him Florida's 25 electoral votes, for a total of 271 electoral votes, enough for victory. By overturning a 4–3 Florida Supreme Court decision ordering a statewide recount, the U.S. Supreme Court dashed the hopes of Vice President Al Gore, the Democratic standard bearer, who won the popular vote by a margin of more than 500,000 and garnered 266 electoral votes.

It was an extraordinary ending to one of the closest elections in U.S. history. Never in U.S. history had the final result been determined by a direct confrontation between the U.S. Supreme Court and a state supreme court. Not since 1888, when Benjamin Harrison defeated Grover Cleveland, had a president been elected without winning the popular vote. And President George W. Bush's margin of victory in the electoral college was the closest since 1876, when Rutherford B. Hayes beat Samuel J. Tilden by one electoral vote.

To observers of American politics and public policy, the bitter, drawn-out presidential election of 2000 offers another, extraordinary example of the public policy process in the United States. It is a process, established by the U.S. Constitution more than 200 years ago, that fragments power between federal, state, and local officials and across legislative, executive, and judicial institutions. Americans could follow the protracted post–election day struggle on television, which offered round-the-clock coverage of judicial hearings, the ballot recounts, and the comments of the candidates, their staffs, and lawyers. Some important lessons about the political and policy process were brought into sharp relief by these events:

- Local government officials administer federal, state, and local elections. They design the ballots, decide what kind of voting machines to purchase, and determine whether and how to count disputed ballots.
- State administrative officials—the director of elections or secretary of state— oversee local elections, which are governed by state laws enacted by the legislature and the governor. State election officials interpret these statutes and ultimately certify the final results of elections.

1

- Courts at the local, state, and federal levels resolve disputes over the administration and interpretation of election laws. First-level trial court decisions are reviewable by state appellate courts. State Supreme Court decisions are reviewable by the U.S. Supreme Court. Judges on these courts, by choosing which facts to accept and ignore, and how to read the meaning of federal and state statutes and constitutions, are often the ultimate makers of public policy.
- The mass media not only communicates information about unfolding events but also shapes public views about the fairness of the electoral process, the relative merits of the arguments by opponents, and the motivations and behavior of the candidates, their supporters, and government officials.
- Wealthy contributors provided millions of dollars to support the legal and public relations strategies during the post-election battle.

In this book, we attempt to explain public policy by focusing on political institutions as critical but changing elements of the policymaking process. As seen in Table 1-1, American public policy and politics have undergone significant changes in the last decade. Helping the reader understand those changes and, more important, how they came about is a core objective of this book. We develop a balanced view of political feasibility, stressing both constraints and opportunities. In addition, we move beyond the politician-centered view so often found in textbooks on American politics. Indeed, we extend our institutional analysis beyond the traditional branches of government—the executive, legislative, and judicial—to encompass corporate executives at one end and ordinary citizens and the mass media at the other. In doing so, we advance a broader view of what constitutes public policy.

All of this confirms E. E. Schattschneider's observation that the choice of conflicts is critical to the determination of political success or failure.[1] But we need a better understanding of how policy domains differ, how settled or unsettled they are, and how they shape the choices we face.

Our primary aim in this book is to develop a conceptual framework for thinking about the relationship between politics and public policy. That framework stresses the importance of political institutions, which we have defined broadly to include structures and norms associated with different policymaking settings. Such a perspective yields six policy domains that form the core of the discussion in this book. Although we generalize about different political institutions, we also emphasize that political institutions can be changed. We cite examples of such changes and spell out their implications for public policy. We have tried to move away from the view that policymaking is a sequential, linear process. We have also eschewed the perspective that voters and public officials are profit maximizers whose behavior can be predicted on the basis of rational expectations. Thus our approach to the "new

Table 1-1 The Changing Context of Politics and the American Economy, 1990–2000

Factor	1990	2000
Unemployment	6 percent (high of 7.8 percent in 1992)	4 percent
Deficit (-) / surplus (+)	-$290 billion (1992)	+$124 billion
Cost of congressional campaigns	House and Senate candidates spent a total of $368 million in 1990	House and Senate candidates spent a total of $650 million in 2000
Divided government: composition of Congress	Republican president; Democratic majority in Congress	Republican president; Republican majority in House of Representatives; Senate split evenly between parties
Internet access	11 percent (1994)	48 percent (2000)
Number of welfare cases	11,460,382	6,603,607 (Sept. 1999)
Gross domestic product (GDP)	$5,738.4 billion	$9,571.9 billion

Sources: Unemployment: Bureau of Labor Statistics, "Labor Statistics from the Current Population Survey," online at http://www.stats.bls.gov/eag/eag/map.htm, July 5, 2000; deficit/surplus: *Economic Report of the President* (Washington, D.C.: Government Printing Office, 2000); cost of congressional campaigns: Common Cause, "Overall Campaign Spending at the Federal Level," 1999, online at http://www.commoncause.org/publications/cycle_total_cycle_facts.html, August 15, 2000; welfare cases: U.S. Department of Health and Human Services, Administration for Children and Families, "Change in TANF Caseloads," 2000, online at http://www.acf.dhhs.gov/news/stats/caseload.htm, August 10, 2000; GDP: Executive Office of the President, Office of Management and Budget, *Budget of the United States Government, Fiscal Year 2001* (Washington, D.C.: Government Printing Office, 2000), 170–171.

institutionalism" is to stress the importance of political institutions without reducing them to quantities in abstract mathematical formulas. The world of politics is messier than all that, but it is not so chaotic as to preclude some generalizations.

This book is organized so that the connection between politics and public policy remains in view. It is important to be able to see the forest *and* the trees. To that end, this chapter introduces several important themes and perspectives. We begin with a discussion of the public officials authorized by the national and state constitutions to make policy. Next, we turn to the subject of how governments interact with other governments in a federal system. Then the influence of lobbyists and journalists on public policy is examined. We subsequently illustrate the remarkable elasticity of policy-making in the United States by focusing on the two ends of the policy-making spectrum: private decision making and public decision making. Last, we introduce the six policy domains and attempt to show how complex and interdependent the process is. The six policy domains will be explored in depth in Chapters 3 through 8.

Policymakers

At all levels of American government, power over public policy is shared by different institutions—legislatures, chief executives, and courts. The U.S. Constitution gives Congress the authority to make laws, the president the responsibility to administer them, and the Supreme Court the right to interpret and enforce them. The separation of powers is designed to make each institution independent of the others. Each delegation of authority is qualified by other constitutional provisions, however, so that legislative, executive, and judicial powers are shared to some extent. The same phenomenon is apparent at the state and local levels. Government institutions are as interdependent as they are independent.

The functioning of these institutions over time has accentuated this sharing and interdependence, although a considerable degree of separateness and independence still exists. In addition, a variety of bureaucratic institutions has been created that, independently, wield substantial power over public policy. In subsequent chapters it will be demonstrated that there is more to public policy than public officials. Here, however, the focus is on legislators, chief executives, bureaucrats, and judges.

Legislators

Under the Constitution and its state-level counterparts, legislators are the principal lawmakers in the political system. To become a law, a proposal, in the form of a bill, must be approved by Congress, a state legislature, or a city council. Approval depends on coalition building, the aim of which is to obtain the support of a legislative majority. Without legislative approval, no taxes can be raised, no money can be spent, and no new programs can be launched. The constitutional assumption is that the people's elected representatives should play the leading role in making public policy.

To ensure a high degree of responsiveness, legislators are accountable to the electorate every two, four, or six years. In practice, however, electoral accountability does not always result in the adoption of policies favored by the voters. One reason is that individual legislators can escape responsibility for policies adopted or not adopted by the legislature as a whole. Through casework, or constituency service, legislators can cultivate a hard core of grateful constituents who will support their legislator because he or she has performed some useful service for them, such as expediting the delivery of a Social Security check or arranging a tour of the Capitol. These norms enable legislators to pursue their own preferred policies, subject, of course, to certain constraints. A senator from a tobacco state probably would not tempt fate by leading the fight against tobacco advertising.

Legislative observers would find this mode of behavior more acceptable if legislators were responsive to the chief executive or to legislative party leaders, who may take a broader view. Such responsiveness could help to integrate legislative policymaking. But legislative bodies are notoriously decentralized and fragmented, at least in the United States. In western Europe, it is common to find parliamentary systems, in which the chief executive is also the leader of the parliament or legislative body, and "responsible party" systems, in which legislative members of the same party vote together on major issues. The United States, in contrast, has separate legislative and executive branches, weak political parties, and legislators with king-sized and queen-sized egos. Legislators in the United States enjoy a freewheeling, swashbuckling style that makes legislative coalition building difficult.

Another problem confronting legislative coalition builders is the concentration of power in legislative committees. Often referred to as "little legislatures," committees are the legislative workshops, where bills are hammered out, amendments are drafted, and deals are struck. But here, too, many ideas are condemned to the dustbin of history. For that reason, committees are known as legislative graveyards; most bills die in committee without coming to the floor for a vote.

Despite these obstacles, legislators pass an amazing number of measures. Every year, for example, state legislatures in the United States approve about 40,000 bills.[2] In general, legislative bodies prefer to pass bills that distribute benefits rather than bills that impose penalties or bills that redistribute the wealth across social classes.[3] Legislative bodies prefer bills that delegate authority to the chief executive or the bureaucracy, although they may complain about executive "usurpation." By delegating authority to others, legislators escape responsibility for difficult policy problems and for solutions that upset people. Delegation has become rampant since Franklin Roosevelt's New Deal, when the Supreme Court allowed Congress to delegate considerable authority to the executive branch. This has led some observers to wonder whether a system of checks and balances has in fact become a system of blank checks.

Chief Executives

With individual legislators marching to their own drumbeats, chief executives face a formidable task when they engage in the politics of lawmaking. Legislative deference to chief executives is far from automatic. Legislative resistance is especially likely when the legislative and executive branches are controlled by different political parties. During the last fifteen years, more than half of the states have had divided control of government, where at least one chamber of the legislature is controlled by the opposite party of the governor. In the 1998 elections, divided control in state government dropped slightly to twenty-three states. At the national level, at least one chamber of Congress has been controlled by a party different from the president's for thirty-four of the last forty-eight years.[4] The 2000 elections complicated matters even further in the Senate, in which the Republicans and Democrats each held fifty seats.

Regardless of which party controls the legislative branch, chief executives cannot take legislative cooperation for granted. Even under the best of circumstances, the chief executive's power is the "power to persuade."[5] Chief executives cannot simply tell legislators what to do. Rather, they must wheedle and cajole, relying on good ideas, political pressure, personal charm, public support, and a touch of blarney. Some chief executives, such as Ronald Reagan, have made the most of the power to persuade, at least for a time. Others, such as Jimmy Carter, were far less effective at speech making and personal appeals. Bill Clinton was quite adept at mobilizing pubic opinion to advance his initiatives in the face of an opposing Congress.

If wit and wisdom facilitate persuasion, chief executives also possess other important resources that come with the office. Perhaps the most important of these resources is visibility. When the president of the United States catches cold, it makes national news. A gubernatorial runny nose is less newsworthy, but governors and mayors have no difficulty making headlines. Because of this visibility, chief executives have emerged as the leading agenda setters within the government. Along with the mass media, they help to determine which issues the public thinks about and which issues the government will address. Some formal vehicles for this agenda-setting role are the president's State of the Union address and a governor's State of the State address. But chief executives can command an audience at any time, especially in time of crisis.

Despite their best efforts, chief executives lose many legislative battles. For example, the legislature may adopt a bill, as requested by the chief executive, but one with so many amendments that it is unacceptable. When this happens, the chief executive may veto the bill, in which case the legislature may vote to override. In many states, governors have what is known as the line-item veto for budget bills. This enables governors to delete particular line items or programs from the budget without vetoing the entire bill—a formidable power that some presidents have coveted. Even line-item vetoes may be overridden, however.

When chief executives get sufficiently frustrated with the legislative branch, they may resort to questionable means to pursue policy goals. For example, Arizona governor Bruce Babbitt issued an executive order declaring Martin Luther King Day a state holiday after the state legislature failed to enact equivalent legislation. Babbitt's successor, Evan Meeham, promptly rescinded the holiday, also by executive order.[6] Both actions illustrate the breakdown of executive-legislative cooperation. To the dismay of congressional Republicans, President Clinton issued more than 450 executive orders while in office. For example, in June 2000 Clinton announced that states could pay unemployment benefits to parents who take time off from work after childbirth. He also expanded environmental protection of federal lands in several western states and imposed inspections and gun-tracing requirements on gun dealers.[7]

There are, however, perfectly legal ways for chief executives to have an impact on public policy when legislative cooperation diminishes.[8] As the legislative branch has delegated more authority to the bureaucracy, chief executives have recognized that they can make policy as effectively through their influence on management as through legislation. By appointing loyal, capable cabinet and subcabinet officials, they can influence bureaucratic policymaking. According to one observer, governors now spend more time managing state government than they do working with the state legislature.[9] Some presidents have also demonstrated keen interest in the management side of policymaking. Nixon attempted to create an "administrative presidency" with high-level bureaucrats who followed the president's lead on major issues. Nixon's administrative presidency was derailed by the Watergate affair, but the strategy was used effectively by Reagan.[10] Bush arranged his White House staff hierarchically with chief of staff and former governor John Sununu at the top. Clinton, in contrast, organized his staff in such a way that several senior staffers had access to him and he thus remained involved in the development and technical details of proposals.

Bureaucrats

The bureaucracy's size, power, and discretion to make decisions have grown enormously. Since 1969 state bureaucracies have increased more than 60 percent to 4.7 million people, and local bureaucracies have expanded more than 45 percent to 10.5 million people.[11] Although the size of the federal bureaucracy has been more stable during this period, its influence has grown as it dispenses larger amounts of federal money. Federal bureaucrats have ample opportunities to structure the behavior of state and local governments by awarding or withholding federal grants-in-aid. Bureaucrats at all levels of government also award contracts to private sector firms for goods or services supplied to the government. There can be little doubt that the bureaucracy constitutes a "fourth branch of government."

One of the bureaucracy's jobs is to implement policy by designing programs to carry out laws. The Internal Revenue Service (IRS) implements policy when it designs tax forms to conform with congressional intent. Similarly, the Immigration and Naturalization Service (INS) implements policy when it warns employers not to hire illegal immigrants. If statutes were clear and airtight, the implementation of policy would be fairly routine, but few statutes fit that description.

The importance of the bureaucracy in policy implementation sometimes distracts attention from the role the bureaucracy plays in policymaking. Many laws are in fact drafted by bureaucrats or by legislative aides with substantial assistance from bureaucrats. In addition, bureaucrats make policy openly and directly through what is known as administrative rule making. For example, the Federal Communications Commission (FCC) voted in 1996 to strengthen the Children's Television Act of 1990, which requires television networks to provide educational programs for children. This policy, in the form of an administrative rule, was adopted without an explicit mandate from Congress.

The FCC is one of the independent regulatory commissions—multimember bodies that operate relatively independently of the chief executive. The president appoints the regulatory commissioners, but they serve until their terms expire. Independent regulatory commissions are responsible for licensing nuclear power plants, resolving labor relations disputes, regulating the money supply, and setting the rates charged by public utilities.

In contrast to independent regulatory commissions, most bureaucracies are nominally accountable to the chief executive, who has the power to appoint and to fire the top officials. Most bureaucrats, however, are civil servants with considerable job security. As a general rule, they are less committed to the president's policies than are cabinet and subcabinet officials. Moreover, agencies develop strong symbiotic relationships with constituents and client groups. The Agriculture Department may be more sympathetic to farmers than to a president who wants to reduce farm price supports. In addition, chief executives do not appoint all agency heads. In state government, the people elect some agency heads, which may include the attorney general, the treasurer, the secretary of state, the auditor, and the superintendent of education. Finally, bureaucrats are accountable to other public officials, including legislators and judges. It is fair to say that the bureaucracy has many masters.

Judges

When legislators, chief executives, and bureaucrats cannot agree on appropriate public policies, the controversies often must be settled in the courts. In the American system of government, judges are the ultimate arbiters of policy disputes. They decide whether a law is constitutional and whether an administrative rule is legal. They decide when the federal government may tell state and local governments what to do. They decide the meaning of phrases such as equal protection, freedom of speech, separation of powers, and due process of law.

Judges, particularly federal judges, play a central role in the policy process. Federal judges are not passive arbiters of narrowly defined disputes but active architects of public policy. They immerse themselves in the details of technology, methodology, and administration. Increasingly, they have moved from procedural reasoning to substantive reasoning, at times functioning as legislators and managers. In specific cases, federal judges have seized control of state prisons, mental health facilities, and public schools. In addition, they have directed state legislatures to spend more money on underfunded programs. Judge Frank Johnson required a host of costly reforms at Alabama's mental hospitals, on the grounds that under the Fourteenth Amendment the rights of patients and inmates were being violated.[12] Similarly, Judge Arthur Garrity took over much of the management of the Boston public schools to ensure that his school desegregation orders were faithfully carried out.[13] Judge Orrin Judd took control of Willowbrook, a New York state mental facility for children, demanding increased activity for the residents, repairs to the institution, and other significant changes.

Decisions by federal district court judges may be reversed by U.S. circuit courts of appeals or by the U.S. Supreme Court. Appellate judges, as they are sometimes called, generally defer to trial judges, such as federal district court judges, however. They also defer to judges who preceded them on the bench. It is rare for the Supreme Court to reverse an earlier Supreme Court decision, even if today's justices would have decided the case differently. This informal norm is known as the doctrine of *stare decisis*, or adherence to precedent, from the Latin phrase meaning, "let the decision stand."

Despite stare decisis, courts move in new directions as new problems, such as AIDS, arise and as society takes note of changes, such as the growing number of working women. Indeed, in many policy domains, judges have been the principal trailblazers in government. The Supreme Court under Chief Justice Earl Warren took the lead in securing rights for persons accused of a crime.[14] The Court under Chief Justice William H. Rehnquist, although widely viewed as conservative, has taken steps to ensure affirmative action and to limit sexual harassment. For example, in *Johnson v. Santa Clara County*, the Rehnquist Court upheld a local government decision promoting a qualified woman ahead of a qualified man, even though the man was slightly better qualified.[15]

The Rehnquist Court has been continuously innovative in the area of federalism. During the 1990s a majority of justices overruled federal law in favor of state statutes. For example, the Rehnquist Court declared unconstitutional a federal law that would have required state and local officials to do background checks of gun dealers in *Printz v. U.S.* (1997).[16]

When the U.S. Supreme Court interprets the Constitution, that interpretation is binding in other courts. State supreme courts usually are the ultimate arbiters of disputes covered by state constitutions, however. If the Supreme

Court allows searches and seizures under certain circumstances, a state supreme court may strike down the same kinds of searches and seizures, based on its reading of the state constitution. As the Supreme Court has once again become more conservative on the subject of criminal justice, state supreme courts have found civil rights for criminal defendants in state constitutions.[17]

The vagueness of phrases such as *equal protection* and *due process of law* permits courts wide leeway and discretion. Constitutions constrain the behavior of judges but do not determine their behavior. Richard Neely, chief justice of the West Virginia Supreme Court, said:

> Since there is hardly any question which cannot be framed in such a way as to assume "constitutional" dimensions, for all intents and purposes every conceivable question of public policy is up for review by the courts. Vested with this power to determine what is and what is not within the purview of their authority, courts can at will substitute their judgment for that of all the other agencies of government.[18]

Judges, however, cannot act unless a case is brought before them by litigants. Furthermore, appellate judges must reach a consensus before they can speak. But this process is far less complex for a panel of three judges or nine justices than it is for a legislative body consisting of dozens or hundreds of individuals who represent diverse constituencies. As a result, when legislators reach an impasse on controversies such as abortion, school busing, and capital punishment, judges are in a position to fill this power vacuum.

A Federal System

Federalism

Washington, D.C., has no monopoly over the making of public policy in the United States. State and local governments are policy institutions within the federal system of government and in their own right. They are responsible for implementing most federal domestic programs, which typically leave many basic aspects of policy to the discretion of state and local decision makers.

The United States has a truly multigovernmental system. For many issues, state governments are virtually immune from federal supervision and control. Banking regulation, insurance regulation, and occupational licensing remain firmly in the hands of state administrative agencies. Questions concerning divorce and child custody are handled almost exclusively by state courts. Even public utility regulation is controlled largely by the states, despite sharp increases in utility bills and growing public concern.

Considerable autonomy is also exercised at the local level. Zoning decisions, which shape the character of neighborhoods and the quality of everyday life, are made by local governments, without so much as a raised eyebrow from state government officials or federal court judges. Inspections of housing, restaurants, and buildings, all of which are necessary for public health, are controlled by local governments with little input from other levels of government.

Intergovernmental Relations

Despite the considerable discretion exercised by state and local governments, the federal government has extended its control over them by offering the "carrot" of federal grants-in-aid in return for certain concessions. President Lyndon Johnson's War on Poverty relied heavily on such grants-in-aid. President Nixon used a different approach, which he called the new federalism. Under Nixon, the flow of federal dollars increased dramatically, whereas federal restrictions were loosened somewhat. President Reagan also voiced support for a new federalism, but his version combined sharp cutbacks in federal support with new responsibilities for state governments. President Bush continued the Reagan approach, calling for less aid for transportation projects, for example, but new mandates in other areas.

The enactment of welfare reform during the Clinton presidency is a perfect example of this surge in federalism. The 1996 law continued funding to states for welfare programs at the previous fiscal year's level but empowered states to decide how those funds would be spent. States submitted their individual plans to the federal government for approval but had very few and very broad federal guidelines to follow.

About 84 percent of the federal aid to state and local governments comes in the form of categorical programs, which have narrowly defined objectives, distinct statutory and budget identities, detailed planning and operational requirements, and defined target populations.[19] Prior to 1996 the nation's principal income support strategy for the poor, Aid to Families with Dependent Children, was a categorical grant program. AFDC's purpose was to help poor families with children maintain a minimal standard of living. Cash assistance was provided to families if they met explicit statutory and administrative standards and obeyed certain regulations. Even though the states funded one-half of the cost of AFDC, federal law governed its fundamental rules. With the passage of the Personal Responsibility and Work Opportunity Reconciliation Act in 1996, welfare was transformed from a categorical grant into a block grant. This change removed the guarantee of cash assistance to low-income parents caring for young children. States have wide discretion in determining eligibility and allocating aid. When a state's block grant runs dry, the state has the option to fund assistance out of the state budget, but there is no federal requirement to do so. Despite proposals to transform Medicaid, the primary national health insurance program for the needy, into a block grant during the welfare reform debates, it remains one of the largest categorical grants today.

Block grant programs—the balance of federal aid—give states and localities money for broad purposes, such as health, housing, education, and employment, but do not require that all recipients offer a specific set of programs and services. State and local governments have wide discretion to invest federal dollars as they see fit, but the federal government remains responsible for ensuring that the funds are spent for their intended purpose. For example, under the Community Development Block Grant program, mayors, governors, and their staffs may select a mix of housing services that seems well suited to the particular needs of their community.

Categorical programs still predominate, but Presidents Nixon and Reagan accomplished a shift away from categorical programs and toward greater reliance on block grants.[20] The reliance on block grants continued to expand under Clinton's administration, as the transformation of welfare, previously the largest categorical grant, exemplifies. A parallel shift took place in regulation, from direct orders and mandates to more indirect forms of federal control, such as partial preemptions and crossover sanctions. An example of a partial preemption is the Surface Mining Control and Reclamation Act of 1977, which grants states the option of running their own strip-mining program, provided that federal standards are accepted. If a state refuses the option, the federal government exercises full preemption, running the program out of a regional office. Examples of crossover sanctions include the federal government's ability to withhold highway funds from states that refuse to set the drinking age at twenty-one years or to conform to a certain maximum highway speed limit. The federal government usually bargains with the states in the hope of achieving federal objectives.

Policy Influences outside Government

Interest Groups and Political Parties

The fragmented, decentralized policy system described so far is highly permeable by groups outside of government. Private interest group involvement in public policy is a widely recognized and long-standing fact of American government. Interest groups work closely with legislators and bureaucrats to develop mutually beneficial policies. The specialized committee structure of Congress, which is mirrored in most state legislatures, enables interest groups to focus their efforts on the individuals and groups with power over the issues of greatest concern to them.

Clusters of people interested in the same issue—members of legislative committees and subcommittees, bureaucratic agencies that administer the policies formulated by a committee, and the groups that are most directly affected by such policies—are often called subgovernments or issue networks. These networks wield considerable influence over many policy domains, such as the financial industry, agriculture, public works, and defense contracting. Interest groups are full-fledged partners in major policymaking circles.[21]

The number and variety of interest groups in the United States are enormous. Although no one has been able to count all of them, various sources provide a rough estimate of the size of the interest group population, which has grown rapidly since the 1960s. A study of the interest groups in 1998 produced the following findings:

- The number of registered lobbyists grew 37 percent between September of 1997 and June 1999 from 14,946 lobbyists to 20,512;
- There were more than 38 registered lobbyists and $2.7 million in lobbying expenditures for every member of Congress in 1998;
- Insurance interests, pharmaceuticals and health products, telephone utilities, and tobacco were the top four industries represented in Washington, spending about $286 million combined.[22]

Given the strong representation of private economic interests, it is not surprising that citizen groups have gotten into the act. More than 1,200 citizen groups are represented in Washington. Environmental groups, civil rights organizations, antipornography groups, and gun-owner organizations are all examples of such groups. Thousands of additional groups may be found in state capitals and other communities.

State and local government officials also hire staffs to represent them in Washington. The National Governors' Association, National Conference of State Legislatures, National League of Cities, U.S. Conference of Mayors, National Association of Counties, and other organizations actively lobby the national government on matters of concern to states and localities. They also press legislators and administrators to act favorably on requests for financial assistance and regulatory decisions.

There is tremendous diversity in the size, resources, leadership, cohesiveness, and prestige of interest groups that participate in the policy process. Those with substantial money, committed members, strong leadership, and a favorable reputation exert considerable influence. All other things being equal, having a large membership is desirable because a group's political clout is enhanced if it speaks for many voters. But large groups have difficulty maintaining a unified membership and directing their activity toward policy goals that excite members. Therefore, small, intense, single-issue groups may be more successful than large groups.

An interest group with few members but a good deal of clout is the Business Roundtable—an organization of a few hundred top corporate executives. Although its membership is small, the enormous wealth it represents enables it to compete effectively in policy arenas with labor unions, such as the American Federation of Labor-Congress of Industrial Organizations (AFL-CIO), which represents nearly 13 million workers.

When interest groups approach elected officials and government administrators, they are lobbying for help either to get something done to benefit them or to stop something from happening that adversely affects them. Many people equate lobbying with corrupt contributions or pressure tactics of one sort or another. Although some of these practices do go on, the normal situation is considerably more complicated than that.

Effective lobbying rests on the use of information and money. When lobbyists meet with members of Congress, they supply facts about issues and political intelligence about the positions and strategies of others in Congress and the executive branch. Lobbyists testify at congressional hearings, observe committee deliberations, and perform other services for their clients. Groups sponsor professional and social gatherings to which elected officials are invited—and often paid a fee for appearing—to cement relationships. Interest groups may conduct public relations campaigns to persuade voters in the member's district to support their cause. Advertising, press releases, and letter-writing campaigns are all used to build a climate of support for their positions and to secure favorable treatment from legislators. And, of course, groups contribute to congressional election campaigns—nearly $220 million in 1998.[23]

Interest groups also lobby executive agencies. Bureaucratic agencies are responsive to interest groups because they need political allies to advance their policy goals and to protect them from legislators or chief executives who may dislike their programs and policies.[24] Lobbying bureaucratic agencies generally entails using the same techniques used with legislators, except that campaign contributions apply only to elected officials. All major agencies have one or more constituent groups with which they maintain close and mutually beneficial alliances.

Interest groups are active within the judicial arena, although there they are less visible. The direct contribution of money is rare because it is illegal to bribe judicial officials. But interest group budgets can be used to back legal cases that have policy significance. Suits seeking to overturn legislative or administrative decisions are a common outcome of practically all important policy disputes. These challenges come not just from businesses trying to protect their financial interests; civil rights groups and environmentalists have successfully pursued legal strategies that have advanced their causes. Even the selection of judges is not beyond the reach of interest groups. They lobby executives and legislators on behalf of certain court nominees, and in some states and localities interest groups try to influence election contests between candidates for the bench.

As interest groups have become more numerous and influential, political parties have declined in importance as "linkage mechanisms" between citizens and government. Political parties continue to play a vital role in recruiting candidates for office; they also provide cues to voters that continue to matter, especially in elections where other information is scarce. But party organizations lack the technical expertise that interest groups possess—a key weakness in complex policy debates. And candidates for office rely less and less on parties to bring their message to voters. Instead they have turned increasingly to the mass media to play that important role.

The Mass Media

Perceptions of public officials, public policies, and governments are shaped significantly by the mass media, especially television and newspapers. By focusing obsessively on the "horse race" aspects of presidential campaigns, the media do not give voters enough real help in their efforts to evaluate the candidates' issue positions. By devoting more attention to national and local politics than to state politics, the media limit public awareness of state politics. By oversimplifying and sensationalizing certain policy controversies, the media discourage rational decision making. On the positive side, the media can be credited with exposing public problems and errant public officials. Political scientists and other observers are devoting increased attention to the role of the media in politics, especially their impact on election campaigns. The outcome of electoral contests often ushers in a new administration, with a new vision for the future. By influencing the outcome of elections, the media indirectly influence public policy as well.

Clearly, the media influence public perceptions of the candidates' character traits and thereby shape campaign issues. Election results frequently hinge on how well each side presents its case to the media or through the media. Jimmy Carter was unable to overcome a perceived lack of leadership ability in 1980, but Ronald Reagan did not seem to be hurt by reports that he invented or distorted facts in his political speeches. President Clinton continued to score high in the public opinion polls even after the unflattering portrayal of him in the media coverage of the various scandals during his term. In his concession speech following an overwhelming defeat at the polls in 1984, Walter Mondale admitted that he was an anachronism—a candidate who felt uncomfortable on television in a television age. The presidential campaign of former senator Gary Hart in 1988 was abruptly interrupted when newspapers ran stories suggesting marital infidelity. Sen. Joseph Biden also withdrew from the presidential race following press accounts of plagiarism. For some candidates, character is the issue.

The media have increasingly examined the private lives of political candidates. During Clinton's campaigns in 1992 and 1996 as well as during his tenure in office, the American people were treated to frequent media investigations into his private financial, social, or marital life. The 2000 presidential election campaign produced the same phenomena. The private lives and pasts of George W. Bush and Al Gore were featured prominently in the media's coverage of the campaign.

The media's influence on politics and public policy extends well beyond the electoral arena. It is pervasive, reaching citizens in the nation's heartland and the powerful in Washington. Ironically, the media's influence is often so strong and ubiquitous that it is not noticed. The readers of the *Tri-City Herald* live near a nuclear power plant and a high-level nuclear waste disposal site in Hanford, Washington. This newspaper, which has long promoted nuclear power, runs numerous stories about the safety, reliability, and economy of nuclear power and few stories about the dangers and unanticipated costs of nuclear energy. Stories have carried headlines such as "Radiation Linked to Good Health" and "A-Plants Don't Taint Environment." The paper's editors refer to nuclear "storage sites" rather than nuclear "dumps."[25] Exposure to such pronuclear sentiment on a regular basis means that local citizens are primed to view nuclear power favorably. Unless local newspapers fairly present both sides of an issue, citizens will lack one source of information they need to make intelligent decisions.

In contrast, many newspapers encourage investigative reporting, much of it very thorough and effective. The *Washington Post*'s persistent investigation of the Watergate break-in helped bring about the resignation of President Nixon and ushered in a new era in campaign finance. The *Chicago Sun-Times*'s 1978 series on the bribes, kickbacks, and payoffs accepted by city building inspectors, health inspectors, and fire inspectors had a major impact on city practices. In its zeal to catch greedy inspectors, the *Sun-Times* purchased a tavern dubbed The Mirage, operated it for several months, and documented numerous instances of corruption. Following the publication of the series, the Chicago Fire Prevention Bureau created an internal investigations unit to monitor the quality of fire inspections; the city initiated team inspections by building, fire, and health inspectors to discourage shakedown attempts; the U.S. Justice Department added new lawyers to deal with findings concerning tax fraud; the IRS assigned additional agents; and the Illinois Department of Revenue created a permanent task force, the "Mirage Unit," for systematic audits.[26]

Although the media's ability to shape public policy is rooted in the ability to shape public opinion, the elite media—the major television networks, the preeminent newspapers, and the weekly news magazines—shape public policy directly. Chicago's public officials reacted swiftly to the *Sun-Times*'s series on corruption, rather than waiting for public outrage to mount. One often sees the same phenomenon following reports on *60 Minutes* or, in some instances, in anticipation of such reports. As a public relations exercise, public officials often react to an investigative report rather than face the fire storm of public criticism it is expected to trigger. In the process, media influence is magnified. The mere threat of a public outcry may be sufficient to alter public policy.

The Scope of Conflict

In most textbooks on American politics and public policy, the United States is described as a "representative democracy" in which citizens elect representatives—legislators and chief executives—who in turn make public policy. Elected representatives, taking the public's views into account, pass laws and make other authoritative decisions. They also appoint bureaucrats and judges, who adopt rules and adjudicate disputes. But representative democracy is only part of the picture. Many decisions of the utmost importance are made by corporate elites who do not have to answer to the American people. Although nominally accountable to boards of directors or stockholders (or both), corporate managers are in fact free to make many decisions as they see fit. These decisions—concerning plant location, production, marketing, jobs, and wages—are private.

At the other end of the policymaking spectrum, some decisions are made not by public officials but by the people. This is literally true when voters participate in "issue elections." It is also true, for all intents and purposes, when public opinion becomes so aroused that public officials are compelled to defer to citizens and their preferences.

What exists in the United States, therefore, is not representative democracy but "elastic" democracy. When the scope of conflict is exceedingly narrow, representative democracy gives way to private decision making, such as corporate governance. When the scope of conflict is exceedingly broad, representative democracy gives way to public decision making in the form of direct democracy (Table 1-2). The policymaking process can be thought of as a kind of rubber band, which stretches well beyond the original contours of representative democracy.

Private Decision Making

Although it is useful to view business groups as lobbyists or intervenors in the policymaking process, it is necessary to view them as policymakers as well. If one considers only pressure politics, one misses the more worrisome side of business influence—namely, the private sector's capacity to make decisions that affect large numbers of people and the private sector's lack of accountability. Technically, such decisions are private policies; they are made by private actors such as corporate chief executive officers, vice presidents, and board members. As a practical matter, however, such private decisions are sanctioned and legitimated by the government—for example, by court decisions upholding private property rights. Charles Lindblom has argued that

Table 1-2 The Policymaking Spectrum: The Scope of Conflict

Narrow	Moderate	Broad
Private decision making (corporate, governance, capitalism)	Representative democracy (candidate elections, conventional lawmaking)	Public decision making (issue elections, aroused public opinion)

business enjoys a "privileged position" in American politics.[27] The government, for better or for worse, has delegated to the private sector primary responsibility for mobilizing and organizing society's economic resources. It might be said that decisions by "private governments" are often as far-reaching as decisions by the government itself.

Large corporations, the private governments under consideration here, have distinctive decision-making processes. The focal point for corporate decision making is the board of directors, which consists of top company executives and prominent business leaders from other companies. At some companies, workers have a representative on the board; at many others, however, labor is not directly represented. According to close observers, corporate boards are dominated by top corporate executives. Even if outsiders constitute a majority of the board members, the strategic decisions are made by insiders and then ratified by the rest of the board.[28] This phenomenon has been referred to as "managerial capitalism."[29]

Most large corporations are free to make policy as they wish, with a minimum of government control. If a steel company decides to shut down a factory and lay off two thousand workers, it is free to do so. In most states, companies are not even required to give their workers advance notice if they make such a decision. Corporations are also free to set prices as they see fit. A privately owned monopoly, such as an investor-owned public utility, is not free to set prices. Under an arrangement that dates back to the early twentieth century, private monopolies, such as public utilities, must accept fairly close government regulation, including price controls, in return for their monopoly status. But public utilities are exceptional. In general, government control is weak and corporate exercise of discretion is pervasive.

Corporate executives argue, with some justification, that they are accountable to the public through the workings of the market. If companies are mismanaged, or their prices are too high, or their products are inferior, consumers "vote with their pocketbooks" and spend their money elsewhere. But markets do not function that perfectly. Information about companies, their products, and their finances is costly to obtain and not easily understood. Consumers are handicapped by inadequate information. Moreover, markets fail to take into account the social costs of "externalities," such as air pollution. Where externalities are substantial, market prices grossly understate the underlying costs of producing services. Finally, government subsidies disguise the real costs of producing some goods and services. It is difficult to know, therefore, whether oil companies are operating efficiently, considering the generous subsidies they receive from the federal government. Indeed, some industries, such as defense and aerospace, receive such huge subsidies that it is difficult to evaluate them at all.

Many companies, especially publicly held companies whose stock is traded in the various stock markets, are accountable to their stockholders, on whom they depend for capital. As a group, stockholders are becoming more aware and more astute. Mobilized by citizen activists, such as Ralph Nader, and by "corporate raiders," stockholders have put pressure on corporate managers and corporate boards to eliminate certain investments, award higher dividends, and change other practices. For the most part, however, stockholders routinely accept the policies of corporate managers. They also typically rubber-stamp the slate of corporate directors proposed by management. If stockholders are relatively weak, workers are even weaker. Although workers can bargain through their unions over wages, benefits, and working conditions, they have virtually nothing to say about the decisions that affect the company's future and theirs. Private corporations are profoundly undemocratic in their governing arrangements. By accepting private ownership of corporate enterprises, the United States government precluded economic democracy and allowed corporate oligarchies to develop. As Robert Dahl observed, "a system of government [that] Americans view as intolerable in governing the state has come to be accepted as desirable in governing economic enterprises."[30]

Public Decision Making

If private decision making epitomizes one end of the policymaking spectrum—a narrow scope of conflict, limited accountability, and government deference to corporations—public decision making epitomizes the other end—a broad scope of conflict, high accountability, and government deference to the public at large. Some decisions are made in "the court of public opinion." When public officials sense that an issue is too controversial to be handled through normal channels, public opinion comes into play and the views of public officials recede into the background. In E. E. Schattschneider's words, the "scope of conflict" expands.[31]

Public opinion is like a slumbering giant, which, when aroused, becomes intimidating. The effects on public policy may thus be considerable. Public opinion has been credited with ending the war in Vietnam, sustaining the environmental movement, promoting tax relief, halting the spread of nuclear power plants, cracking down on drunk driving, and forcing Presidents Lyndon Johnson and Richard Nixon from office. Conversely, positive public opinion helped President Clinton remain in office despite his impeachment and trial in the U.S. Congress during the scandal over his affair with a White House intern. Public opinion also has jeopardized civil rights and civil liberties, encouraging local governments to "exclude" poor people from the suburbs and to undermine efforts to achieve meaningful school desegregation. Public opinion is the stuff of which dreams and nightmares are made.

Public decision making means, for the most part, that public officials defer to public opinion when an issue is highly salient and controversial. But the people also make policy more directly from time to time, at least at the state and local levels. They do so through mechanisms, including the initiative and the referendum, popularized by the Progressives early in the twentieth century. A referendum is the practice by which a measure that has been passed by or proposed by a legislature is placed on a ballot for voter approval or disapproval. An initiative is the procedure by which a measure proposed by citizens becomes law if approved by a majority of voters or by the legislature. To get an initiative on the ballot, a significant number of state residents— usually 5 percent to 10 percent of those voting in the last statewide election— must sign petitions.

Forty-nine state constitutions authorize referenda, and twenty-four state constitutions authorize initiatives.[32] Referenda outnumber initiatives by approximately four to one, but initiatives carry more weight because they enable citizens to adopt policies opposed by elected officials. Initiatives and referenda have been used sporadically since the early twentieth century, but they became popular during the 1970s, as citizens, disenchanted with government, attempted to participate more directly in the policymaking process. In 1998, 235 propositions appeared on a ballot.[33]

Public decision making, whether through initiatives and referenda or through government deference to public opinion polls, is more controversial than it might seem. Many politicians believe that they were elected to make these decisions and that ordinary citizens lack the knowledge to make public policy directly. Politicians also worry about the growing influence of the mass media, which contribute so significantly to the formation of public opinion. If public opinion mirrors the views of journalistic elites, it simply magnifies media influence—a far cry from what the Progressives had in mind.[34]

Politics and Policy

Politics varies from one issue to another because politics reflects issue characteristics such as visibility and complexity. Differences in politics in turn result in different policies and outcomes. To understand such variations, it is useful to think of six policy domains in which political struggles take place. These domains are encompassed by representative democracies, but they also reflect the highly elastic nature of American democracy. They run the gamut from highly private to highly public decision making.

Following are brief descriptions of the six policy domains that can be used as a framework for analyzing the policy process:

1. Boardroom politics: decision making by business elites and profession-als, but with important public consequences
2. Bureaucratic politics: rule making and adjudication by bureaucrats, with input from clients and professionals
3. Cloakroom politics: policymaking by legislators, constrained by various constituencies
4. Chief executive politics: a policy process dominated by presidents, gov-ernors, mayors, and their advisers
5. Courtroom politics: the issuance of court orders, in response to inter-est groups and aggrieved individuals
6. Living room politics: the galvanization of public opinion, usually through the mass media

Each of these domains implies a different arena of combat, a different set of participants, and different rules of conduct. Each also implies a different set of outcomes, ranging from stagnation to incrementalism to innovation, and from limited responsiveness to symbolic responsiveness to policy re-sponsiveness. In short, different institutions yield different sets of policy consequences.

The six policy domains serve as convenient bridges between issue charac-teristics and policy consequences. Each policy domain can be related to both issue characteristics and policy outcomes (Table 1-3). The effects of issue characteristics such as salience, conflict, complexity, and costs on policymak-ing and the implications of various policy processes for change, responsive-ness, and other outcomes—that is, the policy consequences—will be exam-ined. The changes that occur in issue characteristics over time and the consequences of such changes will be highlighted.

The reason for integrating process and substance is the close relationship that exists between the kind of issue under consideration and the policy process. Consider the following propositions:

• Issues that concern large numbers of people are likely to stimulate intense public debate and draw more participants into the policy process than is-sues that concern only a small segment of the public.
• Complex policies and those that call for major changes in public or bu-reaucratic behavior are much more difficult to implement than policies that can be routinely carried out through established organizational networks.

Table 1-3 Domains of the Policy Process

Domain	Principal actors	Common issue characteristics	Common policy outcomes
Boardroom politics	business elites professionals	low salience high complexity hidden costs	stagnation limited responsiveness
Bureaucratic politics	bureaucrats professionals clients	low to moderate salience low to moderate conflict disputed costs	incrementalism limited responsiveness
Cloakroom politics	legislators interest groups executive officals	moderate to high salience moderate to high conflict disputed costs	incrementalism symbolic responsiveness gridlock policy responsiveness
Chief executive politics	chief executives top advisers	high salience high conflict disputed costs	crisis management symbolic responsiveness
Courtroom politics	judges interest groups aggrieved individuals	high conflict manifest costs moderate to high salience	innovation policy responsiveness (to minorities)
Living room politics	mass media public opinion	high salience high conflict manifest costs	electoral change policy responsiveness innovation

- Issues involving hidden costs are handled by the private sector, whereas issues involving disputed costs or manifest costs require some governmental response.

Another reason for linking politics and policy is that substantive results flow from different policymaking processes. Consider, for example, the following:

- Decisions made within the private sector and ratified by government agencies legitimate self-regulation, impose hidden costs on consumers, and preempt meaningful reform.
- Decisions made by low-level or middle-level bureaucrats tend to reflect professional norms, organizational imperatives, and standard operating procedures. Incrementalism, policymaking that changes things only marginally, is the most likely result.

- Decisions made by politicians against a backdrop of public arousal occasionally provide opportunities for policy innovation. Highly conflictive issues that do not quite reach the crisis point often result in gridlock or stalemate, however.
- Politicians frequently make only symbolic responses to aroused citizens, or they may address the problems of only a few individuals, instead of taking broad policy action.
- Decisions made by judges may differ significantly from decisions made by other public officials, in that no effort need be made to dilute or disguise policy change. The Constitution, job security, and strong professional values protect judges from politicians, although not from politics. The courts are capable of addressing problems that paralyze other institutions of government.

An approach to the study of policymaking that highlights different policy domains has several advantages. First, the policy process is dynamic but disorderly. Issues move from one arena to another over time, but they do not follow the same sequence. This observation is fundamentally different from a leading point of view in the policy literature that assumes that issues proceed in a rather orderly fashion from the agenda-setting stage to the policy formulation stage to the policy adoption stage, and so on. Second, institutional settings matter, and they matter in somewhat predictable ways. For example, different branches of government and different levels of government present their own special opportunities and pitfalls. Successful political strategists are attentive to both. Third, our examination of the policy domains will demonstrate that the nontraditional areas of policymaking deserve attention, for without them the picture is incomplete. The discussions of boardroom politics and living room politics will shed light on actors outside government, including business people, journalists, and citizens.

Overall, we will establish that issue characteristics constrain policymakers in significant ways, that there is no single policy process but rather there are several, that controversies shift from one arena to another over time, and that politics is a significant determinant of policy outcomes. This conception of politics involves not only the familiar institutions of government but also business elites, interest groups, the mass media, and public opinion.

Notes

1. E. E. Schattschneider, *The Semi-Sovereign People* (New York: Holt, Rinehart and Winston, 1960).
2. *The Book of the States, 1996–97* (Lexington, Ky.: Council of States Governments, 1997), 105–106.
3. Theodore Lowi, "American Business, Public Policy, Case Studies, and Political Theory," *World Politics* 16 (July 1964): 677–715.

4. See http://www.ncsl.org, accessed September 20, 2000.

5. Richard Neustadt, *Presidential Power* (New York: John Wiley, 1976), 78.

6. Peter Goudinoff and Sheila Tobias, "Arizona Airhead," *New Republic,* October 26, 1987, 15–16.

7. Kenneth T. Walsh, "Clinton's Campaign to End-run Congress. He's Making Policy Changes by Executive Orders," *U.S. News & World Report,* June 26, 2000, 26.

8. Samuel Kernell, *Going Public: New Strategies of Presidential Leadership* (Washington, D.C.: CQ Press, 1986).

9. Coleman Ransone Jr., *Governing the American States* (Westport, Conn.: Greenwood Press, 1978), 96.

10. Richard Nathan, *The Administrative Presidency* (New York: John Wiley, 1983).

11. U.S. Census Bureau, "Public Employment Payroll Data, 1998," *Census of Governments,* online at http://www.census.gov/govs/www/apes.html, July 23, 2000.

12. Tinsley Yarbrough, *Judge Frank Johnson and Human Rights in Alabama* (University: University of Alabama Press, 1981).

13. J. Anthony Lukas, *Common Ground* (New York: Knopf, 1985).

14. *Gideon v. Wainwright,* 372 U.S. 335 (1963); *Miranda v. Arizona,* 384 U.S. 436 (1966).

15. *Johnson v. Santa Clara County,* 107 Sup. Ct. 1442 (1987).

16. For this and other examples, see Michael W. McConnell, "Let the States Do It, Not Washington," *Wall Street Journal,* March 29, 1999, A27.

17. Robert Pear, "State Courts Surpass U.S. Bench in Cases on Rights of Individuals," *New York Times,* May 4, 1986, 1.

18. Richard Neely, *How Courts Govern America* (New Haven, Conn.: Yale University Press, 1981), 7.

19. See David Walker, *The Rebirth of Federalism,* 2d ed. (Chatham, N.J.: Chatham House, 2000), 236.

20. Randall Ripley and Grace Franklin, *Bureaucracy and Policy Implementation* (Homewood, Ill.: Dorsey Press, 1982), 62; Paul Peterson et al., *When Federalism Works* (Washington, D.C.: Brookings Institution, 1986), 218.

21. For more on subgovernments, see Randall Ripley and Grace Franklin, *Congress, the Bureaucracy, and Public Policy,* 3d ed. (Homewood, Ill.: Dorsey Press, 1984).

22. Influence, Inc., *Lobbyists' Spending in Washington: Summary,* 1999 ed., online at http://www.opensecrets.org/pubs/lobby98/index.htm, July 25, 2000.

23. "FEC Releases Information on PAC Activity for 1997–98," U.S. Federal Elections Commission press release, June 8, 1999, online at http://www.fec/gov/press/pacye98.htm, July 25, 2000.

24. See William T. Gormley Jr., "Interest Group Interventions in the Administrative Process," in *The Interest Group Connection,* ed. by Paul S. Herrnson, Ronald G. Shaiko, and Clyde Wilcox (Chatham, N.J.: Chatham House, 1998), 213–223.

25. Cassandra Tate, "Letter from 'The Atomic Capital of the Nation,'" *Columbia Journalism Review* (May–June 1982): 31–35.

26. Pamela Zekman and Zay Smith, *The Mirage* (New York: Random House, 1979).

27. Charles Lindblom, *Politics and Markets* (New York: Basic Books, 1977), 170–188.

28. Lewis Solomon, "Restructuring the Corporate Board of Directors: Fond Hope—Faint Promise?" *Michigan Law Review* 76 (March 1978): 581–610; Victor Brudney, "The Independent Director—Heavenly City or Potemkin Village?" *Harvard Law Review* 95 (January 1982): 597–659.

29. Alfred Chandler Jr., *The Visible Hand: The Managerial Revolution in American Business* (Cambridge: Harvard University Press, 1977), 1–12.

30. Robert Dahl, *A Preface to Economic Democracy* (Berkeley: University of California Press, 1985), 162.

31. Schattschneider, *The Semi-Sovereign People,* 2–3

32. Initiative and Referendum Institute (I&R Institute), "I&R Factsheet," online at http://www.iandrinstitute.org/factsheets/fs1.htm, May 18, 2000.

33. James K. Glassman, "Making Law at the Ballot Box," *Washington Post,* November 3, 1998, A17.

34. See for example, David S. Broder, *Democracy Derailed: Initiative Campaigns and the Power of Money* (New York: Harcourt, 2000), and Elisabeth S. Gerber, *The Populist Paradox: Interest Group Influence and the Promise of Direct Legislation* (Princeton, N.J.: Princeton University Press, 1999).

Chapter 2 **Political Culture, the Economy, and Public Policy**

American political institutions function as parts of the larger national cultural and socioeconomic system. The actions of political institutions and, therefore, the nature of public policy are greatly influenced by these cultural and economic forces, unique to the United States. The country, as a part of the global environment, is also affected by developments in other parts of the world. But the political agenda of U.S. policymakers is not the same as that of leaders in other industrial nations, and it is fundamentally different from those of less-developed, socialist, or formerly socialist countries. The United States has the world's most powerful economy, which is greatly influenced by the actions of privately owned corporations. Government ownership of major industries is an important item of political debate in many countries around the world, but it is not even under consideration in the United States. Public discussions of nutrition and health in the United States often focus on whether Americans eat too much of the wrong kinds of foods and are thus becoming obese; in many other parts of the world discussions of nutrition and health are about how to provide citizens with enough food to keep them alive.

In this chapter we outline some of the underlying features and tendencies of the American cultural and economic environment. Before examining the specific arenas in which public policy is formulated and implemented, we should consider the broader context within which political institutions and actors function.

A Durable Political Culture

Political culture can be defined as the attitudes and beliefs of citizens about how political institutions and processes ought to work, about fellow citizens and their place in the political process, and about the proper rules of the political game.[1] Several enduring values of the American political culture have shaped public policy from the beginning of the Republic. Individualism, the right of people to pursue their self-interest and to be responsible for their own well-being, is a fundamental American cultural value. Personal freedom, which is closely linked to individualism, has meant the right to pursue self-improvement and protection from government interference. Along with individualism, the sanctity of contracts and the right to acquire and own property contribute to the free market ideology that dominates the political and economic systems in the United States.[2]

Americans also believe in democracy—the right of every citizen to participate in the political process. Support is widespread for equal treatment under the law, political equality, and equality of opportunity. In addition to these core political values, cultural values, including religion and the centrality of the nuclear family, have significant political implications. It must be noted, however, that in many ways the United States does not live up to its political ideals, that it is a society with racist and sexist elements. As recently as 1950, black Americans did not have equal access to public schools or the voting booth. Even today, although the government has for years expressed its commitment to breaking down racial barriers, there are relatively few truly integrated communities. Women did not have the right to vote in elections until the beginning of the twentieth century, and they still earn considerably less money than men.

Conflicts and tensions between values and beliefs have frequently been the source of political struggle and debate in the United States. For example, southerners and midwesterners, who rallied around Andrew Jackson, triumphed over the eastern aristocratic cliques that controlled American government in the late eighteenth and early nineteenth centuries by appealing to the public's belief in individualism, pragmatism, and equality of opportunity. Franklin Roosevelt's New Deal, which substantially expanded government management of the economy and publicly funded social welfare programs, represented a victory for democratic egalitarian values over uncompromising individualism and capitalism. Ronald Reagan's policies of the 1980s represented a swing back toward individualism, capitalism, and traditional family values. Bill Clinton's reelection in 1996 marked the end of the Reagan era and ushered in a new era of pragmatism, defined by conservative economic policy (free markets) and progressive social values (equality of opportunity). The dynamism of America's political culture stems in part from the inherent tensions between cherished, yet competing, cultural values. Political struggles that aim to change an existing balance between these values can have dramatic effects on the nature of public policy.

The Market Paradigm and Procedural Democracy

A towering presence in the American political culture is, and always has been, a world view that regards the so-called "free market" as the best allocator of society's goods and services. This viewpoint holds that government's role is primarily one of protecting certain economic, social, and political norms, or rules of conduct, such as competitive markets, private property, and representative government. This world view dominated the thinking of nearly all the Framers of the Constitution.

What is a free market? Or what is the market mechanism for allocating goods in a society? It is a system that relies on voluntary exchanges between autonomous individuals to allocate goods and services in an efficient manner. Efficiency can be defined as the maximum output technology can produce with the minimum use of resources. In free markets producers compete with one another to satisfy consumer demand for goods and services. Consumers are assumed to be willing to give up a certain amount of what they have, usually in the form of money, for various quantities of other goods and services—what economists call a demand function. When voluntary exchanges occur between producers and consumers, both parties are viewed as better off. A producer has given away something (a chair, for example) for something (say, $100) he or she values more. The consumer has given away something, the $100, for something he or she values more, the chair. As long as no coercion is involved, there is no reason to believe that these exchanges are not mutually beneficial.

In such a system those who provide the goods and services on the terms most consumers find attractive should naturally be involved in the most exchanges, whereas those who offer goods on unattractive terms should be involved in the least. Over time, the inefficient producers will fall out of the market. The efficiency of the system, the highest output at the lowest cost, is guaranteed by competition. Furthermore, many people benefit because their preferences ultimately determine what kinds of goods and services are provided and they buy them at the lowest possible cost.

This formulation was fully worked out in the eighteenth century and is usually credited to Adam Smith, who described his theory in his seminal work, *The Wealth of Nations*.[3] The free market formulation was enormously influential because it provided the justification for laissez-faire capitalism and representative democracy, advocates of which were fighting to free societies from the remnants of feudalism and curtail the privileges of the aristocracy. The free market paradigm forms the basis of the individualist ethic so central to American life. The logic of the free market is compelling: give people a chance to produce what they can and those who produce what is most wanted will obtain the greatest rewards. It is both democratic and meritocratic. This seems like a very desirable combination.

Before going further, however, we must carefully examine the free market paradigm. First, it is a theoretical construct, not an empirical reality. Often, a vast difference exists between actual markets and the free market ideal. Like any theoretical construct, it is based on many assumptions. One such assumption is that individuals and businesses behave on the basis of the rational pursuit of self-interest. Rationality requires knowledge; therefore, to work properly, a market must include consumers who have "perfect knowledge" of what the market has to offer. That is, people must be aware of the alternatives to make rational choices about exchanges into which to enter. Otherwise, inefficient producers might be rewarded, and various other market distortions could occur.

Other necessary conditions are open entry into a market and fair competition among producers. If potential producers are excluded from offering their products to consumers, then innovation becomes less likely and efficiency is jeopardized. Similarly, if certain companies are able to engage in unfair behavior—terrorize competitors, produce at a loss for a long period of time, misrepresent their products to consumers—the free market dynamic is upset, and both production efficiency and consumer utility are compromised. The nature of a free market is quite specific, and actual markets are easily distorted. A contemporary example of alleged market distortion is the controversy over Microsoft's dominant position in the computer operating system and software market.

Another essential point about the free market paradigm is that it does not prescribe outcomes. One cannot predict the mix of goods and services that will be available in a society using such a model. One can only assume that people know what they want and attempt to establish rules and procedures that will give society as many of the desired goods and services as is possible within the limits imposed by resources, technology, and individual productive capacity. If markets are free and open and people know what is available, goods and services should be allocated in a way that creates the greatest happiness for the greatest number. The desired outcome, happiness, or what economists call "utility," is defined by the rules and procedures through which it is realized.

Under the free market paradigm, individual freedom is defined as the opportunity that each person has to produce valued commodities and trade them to others for items of value. Giving every individual an equal opportunity to engage in such exchanges is recognized as being necessary if markets are to work properly. Clearly, equality of opportunity was not a reality when the Constitution was first designed, but the free market paradigm convinced many political philosophers and politicians of the validity of the idea of equality of opportunity. If markets were to operate optimally, entry into them had to be free and open; if societies were to be properly ordered, opportunities had to be open to all. When Thomas Jefferson wrote in the Declaration of Independence that "all men are created equal," he meant that all men, except slaves and the indentured, should be free to compete in society for the benefits that were available.

The basic point is that the free market paradigm dominates far more than the discipline of economics and the business sector of American society; it dominates the political and legal spheres as well. American democracy is procedural—it is defined by rules according to which political leaders are chosen by citizens in elections.[4] Its bedrock values—equality of opportunity, freedom of expression, the right to vote, the sanctity of property—spring directly from the free market paradigm. The Constitution elevates these procedural values above all others. Its logic is that justice is defined by procedural guarantees and that maintaining the integrity of procedures is the main task of government. Thus governments have an important but limited role to play in society. Other principal components of the Constitution—separation of powers, checks and balances, and federalism—were designed to limit governmental activity and are best understood as attempts to protect markets from majority power and minority privilege.[5]

Procedural democracy is complex, amoral, antitraditional, and vague about certain questions, such as what happens when property rights conflict with other rights. Therefore, it should not be surprising that procedural democracy is not always implemented perfectly. Equality of opportunity, in particular, has been extremely difficult to realize because capitalist societies have allowed accumulated wealth, and the advantages that go with it, to be passed from one generation to the next. Cultural biases also have been stubbornly persistent in the United States. Nevertheless, the commitment of political elites and citizens to the values of procedural democracy has led to a gradual recognition that obvious contradictions to ideals such as equality of opportunity have to be confronted and resolved. Still, the ultimate goals are procedural. American democracy does not stand for equality of condition, only equality of opportunity; it is decidedly inegalitarian in this sense.

Participatory Democracy

Representative/procedural democracy does not place a great deal of value on direct citizen involvement in the making of policy decisions. For many democratic theorists this is a critical shortcoming. Jean-Jacques Rousseau, one of Adam Smith's contemporaries and acquaintances, said about representative government in England: "The people of England regards itself as free, but is grossly mistaken; it is free only during the election of members of parliament. As soon as they are elected, slavery overtakes it, and it is nothing."[6] He prescribed a much more classical form of democracy, in which citizens would make societal laws directly, submerging their self-interest in pursuit of the collective interest or "general will." Participatory democracy is an alternative to procedural democracy.

Interest in participatory forms of democracy is very much alive among contemporary democratic theorists.[7] For example, Jane Mansbridge has written about what she calls "unitary" democracy, which envisions a common good that is separate and distinct from the outcome of the struggle between competitive interests in a political community.[8] Advocates of unitary democracy contend that community forums in which citizens meet face-to-face (possibly mediated by computer monitors and broadband cables) and work toward consensual solutions to their common problems are both feasible and highly desirable. In such settings issues can be framed in such a way as not to be easily divisible into "we" versus "they" dichotomies, and citizens learn how to work toward commonly desired ends.

A classic example of unitary democracy at work is a town meeting in which a question such as whether to invest in a new water purification facility is discussed. The issue affects nearly everyone in more or less the same way; advocates on both sides debate the issue face-to-face; most participants are looking for a consensual solution; and preferences are registered publicly without behind-the-scenes maneuvering. This form of democracy is still practiced in rural New England and holds considerable appeal for many Americans.

Participatory forms of democracy emphasize the importance of direct citizen involvement in the policymaking process. Such direct involvement, although without face-to-face debate, is present when citizens vote for initiatives and referenda in state and local elections. This form of public decision making is examined at length in Chapter 8. Although the idea of participatory democracy is very much a part of American culture, albeit in a somewhat abstract and mythical form, political reality is typically dominated by citizens voting for representatives in periodic elections, by the pursuit of private interests and affiliations with narrow interest groups, and by legal/adversarial processes and procedures.

Assessing Contemporary Political Culture

Debate about contemporary political culture usually centers on issues such as multiculturalism and diversity, political correctness, distrust of politics and politicians, and the status of so-called "traditional values." All these issues partake of the core American political values—individualism, freedom, private property, democracy, and equality—discussed above. For example, those most in favor of making sure people from different backgrounds are treated fairly place primary importance on equality; their opponents commonly worry about the government providing entitlements for certain groups, which would violate their sense of individualism and fairness. What seems clear is that contemporary political culture is highly textured; many different combinations of values can be found among Americans. Despite this diversity, conflicts among core values remain at the center of most political debate and disagreement in the United States.

During the second half of the twentieth century in the United States, major changes in politics and policy were somewhat easier to identify than changes in political culture and values. In politics and policy the principal eras were the conservative 1950s, symbolized by President Dwight D. Eisenhower, which gave way to the liberal 1960s and 1970s, a return to conservatism in the 1980s, and then to moderation and pragmatism by the mid-1990s. Seminal events were the elections of John F. Kennedy and Lyndon Johnson in the 1960s, then of Ronald Reagan and George Bush in the 1980s, and finally the reelection of Bill Clinton in 1996. The liberal social programs of Kennedy's New Frontier and Johnson's Great Society dominated the political agenda in the 1960s and 1970s, augmented by the environmental movement (also liberal) in the 1970s. The Reagan era shifted the locus of political discussion to more conservative issues such as tax cuts, reduced federal spending, privatization, and antiabortion legislation. Clinton's reelection seemed to confirm public support for moderate-to-conservative fiscal policy (deficit reduction) and moderate-to-liberal social policy (increased support for education, Social Security, Medicare, and environmental protection). The cultural changes that took place over those fifty years did not exactly mirror the political eras just described; they were more subtle and complex.

The central political development in the second half of the twentieth century was Democratic liberalism of the 1960s. Modern American liberalism is closely associated with the Democratic Party. Liberalism and the Democrats rose to power in the 1930s through New Deal legislation that expanded government involvement in social welfare and the economy. Uniting workers, intellectuals, southerners, and various ethnic minorities, the Democrats implemented unprecedented social welfare programs and policies. The most conspicuous and enduring law, the Social Security Act, guarantees financial assistance to the elderly, the poor, and the disabled. During the 1960s and early 1970s large Democratic majorities in Congress worked cooperatively with Lyndon Johnson, and combatively with Richard Nixon, to design new government programs in housing, education, welfare, health, employment, civil rights, and environmental regulation. This second wave of Democratic liberalism seemed to set a political course for the rest of the century.

Even most conservatives would agree that the Reagan era was largely a reaction to the Great Society programs. They would argue that the American people tried liberalism in the 1960s and 1970s but found it wanting. During the 1980s Americans sought to establish a new equilibrium among leading political values, an equilibrium that was more traditional and conservative than that prevailing in the late 1960s and the 1970s. Criticisms of the second-wave liberal Democratic policies were voiced by politicians, researchers, and citizens from the beginning, and they eventually grew stronger. Academic studies of social welfare, civil rights, and regulatory programs revealed many serious flaws of theory, design, and execution. Politicians and intellectuals also questioned the morality of liberalism, especially as it applied to abortion, school prayer, sex education, criminal justice, and the threat of communism. By the 1980s, few politicians willingly identified themselves as liberals. Instead, they called themselves moderates, pragmatists, progressives, or neoliberals.

Although political leaders no longer labeled themselves liberal, Americans continued to support most liberal programs in the 1980s and 1990s. Public support for Social Security has been strong for a long time. In a 1979 poll, for example, nine Americans in ten could cite at least one advantage of the program.[9] Despite years of chronic federal deficits of $200 billion or more, 90 percent of the public thought that either too little or about the right amount of money was being spent on Social Security from 1985 to 1996.[10] A new wrinkle in public attitudes about Social Security is that by

2000 a majority of the public favored the idea of allowing people to invest a portion of their Social Security payroll taxes in a personal retirement account, although this approach held little favor with those over sixty-five.[11] In 1990 a majority of Americans (56 percent) favored a national health insurance system; and even though support for national health insurance declined after 1994, the portion of the public that thought the government was spending too little to protect the nation's health rose from roughly 60 percent in the mid-1980s to 70 percent in the mid-1990s.[12] Of course, one should be cautious about interpreting these poll results as meaning that the public supports bigger government. Since the 1950s, public opinion polls consistently have found that Americans like government benefits but do not like to pay for them. For example, in the summer of 1990, 60 percent thought spending for domestic programs should increase, but 79 percent opposed raising federal income taxes.[13]

One clear change in public attitude that did occur between 1965 and 1975, and remains important today, is the decline in public trust in government institutions and public officials. Although the decline was steepest in the post-Watergate period, thus seemingly disadvantaging Republicans, its continuation is probably more detrimental to Democrats, since they are the ones who believe in active government. Ronald Reagan certainly tapped into this mistrust in his successful presidential campaigns. The percentage of Americans who believe that the government will do "what is right" (always, or most of the time) slid from 80 percent to about 30 percent between 1964 and 1980. It did rise a bit (to around 42 percent) by 1986–1988 but then fell again to just over 30 percent in the 1990s.[14] A similar trend has occurred for all major institutions, public and private. That is, high levels of trust or confidence through the mid-1960s have been replaced by substantially lower levels of trust since then. In government, Congress and the presidency inspired lower levels of confidence in the 1980s and 1990s (20 percent or less having "a great deal of confidence" in them) than the Supreme Court and the military.[15] This lack of trust and confidence in government also reveals itself in low voter turnout rates. In the 1960s, 60 percent or more of those eligible voted in presidential elections, and close to 50 percent voted in off-year congressional elections. Since then turnout in presidential elections has never exceeded 55 percent, dipping to an all-time low of 49 percent in 1996; turnout in off-year congressional elections has failed to reach 40 percent since 1970.[16] Even in states like Minnesota, with election-day registration, voter turnout seldom exceeds 60 percent.

Some critics of modern liberalism argue that it is not the public's distaste for government spending that undermines liberal programs; rather, the public has become disillusioned with the social and moral values spawned by liberalism. If this argument is correct, it should be reflected in surveys about attitudes on abortion, school prayer, gun control, the death penalty, and racial integration. In fact, liberal attitudes have survived or prospered in most of these areas. For example, public support for maintaining legal abortions "under some circumstances" or "under any circumstances" has been above 75 percent since 1975; in the 1990s it was above 80 percent.[17] Similarly, support for gun control (registration requirements for handgun owners) has generally been around 75 percent since the late 1950s; although it did dip to below 70 percent in 1980, it rose to above 80 percent in the 1990s.[18] Americans overwhelmingly believe that black and white Americans should attend the same schools and be permitted to live in the same neighborhoods. Since the 1980s, more than 90 percent of Americans have supported integrated schools.[19] By 1996, 87 percent of white Americans did not think "Whites should be able to prevent Blacks from living in their neighborhoods"; in 1972, only 61 percent of whites held this view.[20]

There are several issues about which the American public has moved away from liberal positions in the second half of the century. One is crime and criminals; the portion of the public endorsing the death penalty rose from around 50 percent in the late 1950s to more than 80 percent in 1994, but declined to 66 percent in 2000.[21] More than 70 percent of the public thought the emphasis of prisons should be rehabilitation of criminals in the 1970s; by the mid-1990s less than 20 percent believed this, and most believed the main purpose of prisons was to keep criminals out of society.[22] Although expressing strong support for integration, white Americans have shown increased levels of opposition over the last thirty years to government interventions such as school busing or affirmative action to assist minorities. By the mid-1990s, most Americans (60 percent) believed that minorities should help themselves, rather than being helped by government (through spending and other means); indeed, most black Americans held this view.[23] Moreover, the public remains committed to certain traditional ideas. Despite the rulings of the Supreme Court, 74 percent of citizens polled in 2000 support prayer in public schools—a level that has declined only slightly (from around 80 percent) over several decades.[24] Although the proportion of the public that views religion as "very important" in their lives remained below the 70 percent level of the mid-1960s, it rose from 52 percent in 1978 to 55 percent in 1989 to 62 percent in 2000.[25]

Detailed studies of American values reveal some generational differences on issues of political culture that are closely tied to life experiences and economic conditions. Americans born after World War II are more likely to exhibit what have been labeled "postmaterialist" values. They are more apt than their elders to believe that giving people a say in government decisions, protecting freedom of speech, and improving the environment are more important than curbing inflation, fighting crime, and expanding the economy.[26] These values, linked to the baby-boom generation, appeared to be somewhat less popular among American young adults in the late 1980s, who showed a great interest in pursuing lucrative careers in business, than they were among youth of that age in the 1970s. However, responses in 1996 to a battery of questions about whether the government should spend more or less on Social Security, health, education, schools, welfare, environment, and government-guaranteed jobs showed voters under thirty to be more liberal than other age cohorts in every area except health and Social Security.[27] This finding is not surprising in that Social Security and Medicare are very salient for older voters, and younger voters are typically more liberal in their political views than middle-age and older voters. However, it also suggests that the baby boomers, now well into middle age, have become somewhat more concerned about the economy (they are still noticeably more liberal than the elder generation), and the younger generation has not eschewed postmaterialist values, although these values are perhaps not as prominent as they were twenty-five years ago.

Americans' responses to direct questions about their ideological leanings reveal a very small conservative shift over the last three decades. Those who regard themselves as liberal (from slightly to extremely) declined from 26 percent in 1972 to 23 percent in 1988, rising slightly to 25 percent by 1996. Conservative self-identification (again, from slightly to extremely) rose from 37 percent in 1972 to 46 percent in 1988, and stood at 45 percent in 1996. To return to the question of liberalism among young adults, in the 1980s those age eighteen to twenty-nine were less inclined to describe themselves as liberals (30 percent) than the same age cohort in 1972 (39 percent) or 1996 (34 percent). The most significant pattern is that most Americans place themselves near the center of the ideological spectrum. In 1972, 72 percent of those surveyed saw themselves as moderates or slight liberals or conservatives; the percentage in these categories changed very little during the 1980s and 1990s.[28] As many public opinion specialists have pointed out, it is not at all clear that respondents have the same understanding of what the terms *liberal* and *conservative* mean when they answer questions about their ideological orientation, thus reinforcing the point that the principal finding is one of ideological moderation on the part of the American public.

Changes have occurred in the percentage of Americans calling themselves Republicans, Democrats, and independents over the last fifty years. In the 1950s and 1960s, 45–50 percent of voters were affiliated with the Democratic Party, and 25–30 percent with the Republican Party, leaving 30 percent or less as independents. In the 1970s Republican affiliation dipped below 25 percent, Democratic affiliation also declined to around 40 percent, and independents increased to just below 40 percent. During the 1980s and 1990s identification with the Democratic Party has ranged from a high of 45 percent in 1982 to a low of 34 percent in 1994; Republican identification was only 23 percent in 1980, but rose during this period, reaching a high point of 31 percent in 1994.[29] The major patterns, therefore, are the decline, of roughly 10 percent, in the portion of the electorate that identifies with the Democratic Party; the increase in the number of independents, which is especially evident among younger voters; and the rebound (of roughly 10 percent) the Republican Party made from its nadir in the 1970s.

Evidence reviewed above suggests that there was some movement in a conservative direction during the 1980s, but there was no massive or unambiguous change in cultural and political values during that decade. The "new conservatism," to the extent that it existed at all as a cultural phenomenon, appeared to consist largely of a resurgence of traditional American values, such as individualism, capitalism, distrust of government, and respect for law and order. The rapid cultural changes of the opposite sort—humanism, postmaterialism, permissiveness—that dominated the 1960s and 1970s have receded, but many liberal values, such as equal opportunity and concern for the environment, enjoy vast popularity.[30] By the end of the century, the bulk of the electorate defied simple classification—as liberal or conservative, for example. Nevertheless, a political typology of Americans developed by the Pew Research Center for the People and the Press based on three dimensions—party affiliation/leaning, political attitudes and values, political attentiveness and propensity to vote—provides a useful summary of the many textures of American political culture; see Table 2-1.[31]

A Powerful Economy

Over the past fifty years the American economy has dominated the world's commerce. The U.S. economy, like most others in the world, was still sputtering from the Great Depression as the country entered World War II. But following the war, the economy experienced twenty to twenty-five years of unprecedented growth. During the 1970s and 1980s the economy experienced a variety of painful problems, but in the 1990s it rebounded and the country enjoyed record growth and prosperity again.

The central economic objectives of U.S. policymakers are quite clear and have remained fairly constant for decades: to promote sustained economic growth without price inflation, to maintain low levels of unemployment and poverty, and to attempt to ensure a high standard of living for American citizens. When unemployment and inflation rise, people suffer and the cost of government also goes up. But keeping unemployment and inflation low is very difficult. Since 1950, the United States has experienced seven recessions—periods when the economy failed to expand during a year, which resulted in high levels of unemployment.

The task of managing the American economy today is very challenging. Whether and how government should intervene in the economy has always been a matter of great controversy in American politics—a central dividing line between liberals and conservatives, Democrats and Republicans. Moreover, the economic realities since 1970 have shattered many of the old

Table 2-1 A Political Typology of Americans

Mostly Republican		Mostly independent		Mostly Democratic	
Description	Percentage of pop.	Description	Percentage of pop.	Description	Percentage of pop.
Staunch conservatives predominantly white, male, and older; extremely satisfied financially, well educated; pro-business, pro-military, anti-environmental, distrustful of government; pro-life, antigay and anti-social welfare; little concern for the poor, unsupportive of the women's movement	10	*New prosperity independents* affluent, well educated, young, less religious; pro-business, pro-environment, and pro-choice; somewhat critical of government; sympathetic toward immigrants, but not as understanding toward black Americans and the poor	10	*Liberal Democrats* most highly educated group, least religious; critical of big business; pro-choice and support civil rights, gay rights, and the environment; most sympathetic toward the poor, African Americans, and immigrants	9
Populist Republicans religious, xenophobic, and pro-life; less educated, heavily female; negative attitudes toward gays and elected officials; sympathetic toward the poor	9	*The disaffecteds* very unsatisfied financially, less educated; anti-immigrant and intolerant of homosexuality; distrustful of government, politicians, and business corporations	9	*New Democrats* middle-income, reasonably well educated; favorable view of government, pro-business, yet think government regulation is necessary; concerned about environmental issues, pro-Clinton; accepting of gays, somewhat less sympathetic toward the poor, black Americans, and immigrants	9
Moderate Republicans white, relatively well educated and very satisfied financially, largest percentage of Catholics; strong environmentalists, pro-business, pro-military, and pro-government; moderate on social issues; little compassion for poor	11	*Bystanders* young, less educated, not very religious; work in manufacturing, construction, and restaurant or retail industries; somewhat sympathetic toward the poor; uninterested in what goes on in politics, rarely vote or are not eligible to do so (noncitizens)	11	*Socially conservative Democrats* older, slightly less educated, satisfied financially, highly religious; positive attitude toward military, think big business has too much power and money, pro–United States, yet disenchanted with government; less tolerant of immigrants and gays	13
				Partisan poor very low incomes, not very well educated, two-thirds female, very religious, largest group of African Americans; xenophobic and anti–big business, pro–labor union; critical of politicians, believe government should do even more for the poor	9

Source: The PEW Research Center for the People and the Press, "Retro-Politics; The Political Typology: Version 3.0," November 11, 1999, online at http://http://www.people-press.org/typo99sec1./html and sec9.html, January 2001.

assumptions, increased the stakes of the game considerably, and multiplied the number and difficulty of choices policymakers face.

Government's Role in a Strong Economy: 1950s and 1960s

Government economic policymaking was easier, and in some ways less critical, when the U.S. economy was expanding at a stable rate during the 1950s and 1960s. Consider the following indicators:

- The economy grew at a healthy rate of over 4 percent annually, and per capita income increased by 2.5 percent per year.
- Productivity growth—the measure of output per person per hour worked—was also impressive; the average annual increase was more than 3 percent.
- Unemployment averaged about 4 percent, and annual inflation rates were seldom more than 2 percent.
- The cost of borrowing money, although gradually rising from a 2 percent interest rate in 1950, did not exceed 4 percent until 1965.
- The economy was running smoothly with slightly less than 60 percent of the adult population in the labor force—more than 85 percent of the men and 37 percent of the women.[32]

Government's role in the economy was fairly uncomplicated, by contemporary standards. When the economy slumped, the government enlarged the supply of money for investors and increased government spending to stimulate growth. Major recessions and accompanying unemployment were thus mitigated or avoided altogether. When a recession hit in 1957–1958, unemployment rose to a postwar high of nearly 7 percent; the federal government increased spending beyond revenues, resulting in a deficit of $13 billion at the end of 1958, also a postwar high. The unemployment rate dropped to 5.5 percent by the following year.

The main purpose of macroeconomic policy—increasing or decreasing the money supply (monetary policy) and the extent of deficit spending (fiscal policy)—was to maintain high levels of employment by stimulating demand for goods and services. With the economic depression of the 1930s and 1940s not far behind them, policymakers were preoccupied with the problem of unemployment. Joblessness was perceived as a problem that applied mainly to male "breadwinners" and was closely related to the condition of manufacturing firms, which employed one-third of the workforce (compared with about one-seventh in today's economy).

The absence of strong competition for consumer markets by other nations was another fact of economic life in the 1950s and 1960s, when practically all products sold in the United States were manufactured domestically. U.S. exports accounted for one-fourth of all world exports and far exceeded imports.[33]

The American standard of living was the highest of any nation. In 1960 the nation's per capita gross national product (GNP), the monetary value of all goods and services produced in a year, was roughly twice that of Western Europe and six times that of Japan.[34] The United States provided a model of economic strength and prosperity that the entire noncommunist world sought to emulate.

The 1950s and 1960s were not free of economic problems. Poverty was quite severe. For more than twenty years after World War II, roughly one American in five lived in poverty by U.S. government standards. In 1960, for example, 40 million Americans—22 percent of the population—were poor. In the 1970s the poverty rate was reduced to about half of the 1960 level.[35] Furthermore, the average American's standard of living was much lower in the 1950s and 1960s than in the 1980s and the present. Taking inflation into account, per capita income was roughly half the level achieved in the 1980s, and 40 percent of the present level.

By the 1960s various sectors of society, especially blue-collar workers, the elderly, and the middle class, began to demand a larger slice of the economic pie. The federal government initiated policies aimed at improving the economic well-being of these and other segments of society. The domestic portion of the federal budget burgeoned as programs for the elderly, the poor, the unemployed, students, veterans, military retirees, and many other groups were either created or enlarged. At the same time, billions of dollars were being spent to fight a war in Vietnam.

Expanding Government's Role

The late 1960s and early 1970s represent a watershed in American policy-making, for hundreds of new spending and regulatory programs were established in that period. It was taken for granted that the economy would grow and that sufficient revenues would be produced to sustain these new government endeavors. Policymakers were not spending money lavishly; indeed, many of the new programs had meager budgets. But the political climate in Washington accepted, and in many ways encouraged, the practice of defusing conflicts by creating programs or regulations to satisfy interest groups and voters. The substantial reduction in poverty during the late 1960s and 1970s can be attributed in large part to federal income transfer programs, particularly Social Security.[36]

This flurry of policy initiatives expanded government spending quite significantly. In 1965 federal spending was just under $120 billion—roughly double the 1952 level. Over the next twenty-one years, the federal budget doubled every six to eight years—in 1972, 1978, and 1986. As a percentage of GNP, federal spending rose from 14 percent in 1950 to 18 percent in 1960, to 20 percent in 1970, to 22 percent in 1980, and to 23.5 percent in 1985. Stimulated by the explosion of federal grant-in-aid programs, state and local government spending also shot up—from $52 billion in 1960 to $369 billion in 1980, to $908 billion in 1990. Government was spending more and relying more heavily on individuals to pay for it. Taxpayers began to feel the pinch. Personal income taxes and Social Security payroll taxes accounted for 60 percent of federal revenue in 1968, 70 percent in 1980, and 78 percent in 1990.

The growth in the Social Security program provides an excellent example of how spending can increase dramatically over time as policymakers adjust programs even in seemingly small ways. During the 1960s and 1970s the basic program for the elderly, known as Old Age, Survivors and Disability Insurance (OASDI), was amended several times. More people were made eligible; benefits were increased; a cost-of-living adjustment was added to offset the erosion in income caused by inflation; and other income security programs, including Supplemental Security Income (SSI), were created for disadvantaged groups. At the time, these actions were not regarded as radical policy decisions. They were far less controversial than the creation of the Community Action Program, the passage of several civil rights acts, or the enactment of medical insurance programs for the poor (Medicaid) and elderly (Medicare, which became part of Social Security). The cumulative effect of these "modest" adjustments in Social Security became clear later on. The federal government allocated $17.5 billion to Social Security programs in 1965; by 1975 outlays for Social Security and Medicare had increased to nearly $78 billion. Social Security and Medicare expenditures had jumped to $150 billion by 1980 and were just under $350 billion in 1990.

Changing Political-Economic Problems: 1970s and 1980s

Mounting public sector spending was only one dimension of the rapidly changing American economy in the 1970s and 1980s. More Americans were working than ever before. The labor force expanded from 70 million in 1960 to 107 million in 1980 to nearly 126 million in 1990; and women's participation in the labor force increased dramatically, from 38 percent in 1960 to 52 percent by 1980 to 58 percent by 1990. The economy shifted away from the manufacturing of steel, automobiles, and heavy equipment and toward services, such as insurance, banking, and information. Between 1960 and 1990 employment in manufacturing remained fairly stable (17 million in 1960, rising to 20 million by 1980, then falling to 19 million in 1990), but service sector employment jumped to 28 million in 1990 from 7 million in 1960.

Economic troubles emerged during the 1970s, and continued through the 1980s, as revealed by the following indicators:

- Economic growth slowed to an annual rate of 3 percent; per capita income growth slowed to an average rate of 2.1 percent.
- Annual productivity increases fell to just over 1.5 percent.

- Unemployment averaged 6.7 percent, and inflation averaged 6.3 percent—both well above the levels from 1950 to 1969.
- Interest rates were more than twice as high as in the 1950s and 1960s.
- Imports exceeded exports in seventeen of the twenty years.
- Economic growth and productivity in some Western European countries and Japan were higher than in the United States.
- The standard of living in several Western European countries edged ahead of the United States for the first time in thirty years.[37]

Various sectors of the economy reacted to the unfavorable economic developments of the 1970s by seeking to protect their vital interests. An ever-expanding number of interest groups pressed lawmakers for more government subsidies or protective regulations. By acceding to the demands of various interest groups, national policymakers shielded society from the negative effects of a sputtering, treadmill economy but avoided confronting the real problems. Americans were running faster—more people working, more money in circulation, higher interest rates—but the economy was going nowhere. The Federal Reserve Board expanded the nation's money supply twice as fast in the 1970s as it had in the 1960s. Government spending consistently exceeded revenues, and the budget deficits mounted. The administrations of Richard Nixon, Gerald Ford, and Jimmy Carter adopted various government policies aimed at curbing spiraling inflation, including outright controls on wages and prices.

By the late 1970s the unprecedented combination of high unemployment, rising prices, and mounting interest rates brought economic hardship to millions of Americans and gave rise to a new economic term—*stagflation*. Inflation became the most dreaded malady in this economy of sorrows, and for good reason. Prices increased by an average of 7.4 percent per year in the 1970s compared with only 2.4 percent per year during the 1960s. Americans shifted their concern from unemployment to inflation and its effect on their standard of living. Everyone wanted to be protected from the negative effects of inflation: unions bargained for inflation-adjusted wages; senior citizens demanded cost-of-living increases in Social Security programs; management passed price increases along to consumers; and landlords raised rents to offset rising utility bills.

Conditions were ripe for change as the 1980 presidential election approached. The extent of the nation's economic deterioration was clear: inflation surpassed 13 percent; interest rates exceeded 15 percent; productivity was declining; and 7 percent of the labor force was jobless. In this economic climate, any president would have been hard pressed to achieve reelection. Ronald Reagan and the Republicans proposed tax and expenditure reductions that the American middle class found understandable and appealing, and President Jimmy Carter was defeated easily.

Ironically, several of the building blocks in the Reagan administration's economic and government reform program had already been put in place during the last two years of the Carter administration. The Federal Reserve Board, under Chairman Paul Volcker, instituted a stricter monetary policy to choke off inflation. The Carter administration began to loosen government regulations in various sectors of the economy and shift spending priorities toward a larger defense budget, freezes or cuts in domestic programs, and a balanced federal budget. These moderate policies reflected a consensus among national policymakers that a new economic order was needed.

There can be no doubt, however, that Reagan's election and the adoption of his economic policies by Congress in 1981 brought about major changes in American politics and the American economy. These policies and their consequences dominated the nation's economic policy agenda in the 1980s. The twin towers of Reagan's economic strategy were the Economic Recovery Tax Act, which slashed personal income taxes by one-quarter over three years, and the Omnibus Budget and Reconciliation Act, which increased defense spending and cut social spending in areas such as government jobs and training, education, and programs for the poor.[38]

This economic strategy was nothing less than audacious. Senate Republican leader Howard Baker called it a "river boat gamble." During the presidential primaries, rival candidate George Bush called it "voodoo economics." Reagan claimed that cutting taxes and domestic spending would invigorate the economy sufficiently to bring in the revenues needed for the continuation of other government programs and for the expansion in military spending.

These predictions were wrong. The economy plunged into the deepest recession in forty years; unemployment exceeded 10 percent in 1982, and the federal deficit increased from $60 billion in 1981 to over $200 billion two years later. Annual deficits averaged almost $185 billion for the remainder of the decade. These large deficits caused the national debt to triple during the 1980s, and interest payments on the debt soared. By 1984, they reached $110 billion, or about 18 percent of all federal spending, climbing to $170 billion by 1989.

One positive result of the painful recession of 1981–1983 was that the inflation genie was put back into the bottle. Inflation fell from double digits in 1979–1981 to 6 percent in 1982 and averaged about 4 percent per year for the rest of the decade. By the end of 1983 an economic recovery was under way—productivity improved substantially (from 1984 to 1987) and unemployment fell steadily through the remainder of the decade. The American economy of the mid-to-late 1980s looked reasonably healthy, but by 1990 another recession had set in. Furthermore, large federal deficits continued into the 1990s, imposing a tremendous long-term burden on American citizens and policymakers.

Other problems, less obvious than the deficits, also lurked in the economy of the 1980s. By 1985, as a result of the recession of 1982, the poverty rate had risen to 15 percent (from 11 percent in 1979), which meant that there were 35 million poor Americans. In the remainder of the decade the poverty rate gradually declined, dipping just below 13 percent in 1989. But the gap between rich and poor widened during the 1980s, as the more affluent households (top 20 percent) enjoyed a substantial increase in their share of personal income, whereas the shares of all others remained about the same or declined.[39] Wealth disparities also increased in the 1980s and were especially pronounced along racial lines; the median accumulation of property and other assets by white families in 1988 was more than $43,000, whereas the comparable figures for blacks and Hispanics were $4,200 and $5,500, respectively.[40]

Another problem was high real interest rates (the difference between nominal interest rates and the rate of inflation) due, to some extent, to the deficits. When individuals and corporations wanted to borrow money, they had to pay more for it in part because they were competing with the federal government, which was borrowing billions of dollars to pay for its activities. From 1981 to 1984, real interest rates in the United States were very high (more than 8 percent); by the middle of the decade they declined to around 5 percent, but this level was still substantially higher than real interest rates in the 1960s (2.75 percent) and comparable rates in many other countries. From 1984 to 1990 the economy grew at a healthy rate (just under 4 percent annually), however, government borrowing continued to limit the Federal Reserve Board's flexibility in adjusting interest rates.

High real interest rates in the United States in the 1980s increased worldwide demand for the dollar and the value of the dollar relative to most other currencies. This led to high annual trade deficits, which averaged more than $110 billion per year between 1984 and 1990. Thus at the end of the 1980s, the U.S. economy was no longer the unchallenged economic powerhouse of the industrial world. Many industrial nations and several less-developed nations had become important economic competitors. For example, in 1986, Japanese companies sold products worth more than $85 billion in the United States, whereas U.S. sales to Japan totaled only $27 billion.[41] The diminished autonomy of the American economy revealed more clearly than ever the intimate connection between government policy and economic performance. What American policymakers decided about trade and tax matters had a direct bearing on the ability of U.S. corporations to compete in the world market against countries and corporations that were governed by different rules.

The debt of less-developed countries added another dimension to U.S. economic difficulties. During the 1970s American banks lent a great deal of money at interest rates ranging from 15 percent to 20 percent to many African and South American countries, whose main form of collateral was raw materials—in most cases, crude oil. At that time oil prices were high and had been projected to stay that way. But when the Organization of Petroleum Exporting Countries (OPEC) lost its control over crude oil supplies in the 1980s, oil prices fell precipitously, putting debtor nations in a terrible position. Many of them could not even pay the interest on their loans, let alone the principal. Brazil and Mexico, for example, owed more than $100 billion each to foreign creditors by 1988, and many debt-dependent countries were spending more than 50 percent of their income from exports on debt repayment. Major U.S. banks had outstanding loans to developing countries of more than $43 billion in 1989 and looked to the government for help in finding a solution to this problem.

The Rising Tide of the 1990s

Much as the economic recovery of the mid-to-late 1980s followed the recession of 1981–1982, the economic boom of the 1990s followed the recession of 1990–1991. In both cases a significant number of jobs were lost. In the 1981–1982 recession it was mainly well-paid, blue-collar jobs that were lost, hundreds of thousands of them. According to one estimate, between 1979 and 1989, 4.1 million manufacturing jobs were lost permanently.[42] Blue-collar workers were hurt again by the recession of 1990–1991, but in this recession a new twist was added: large numbers of white-collar, salaried employees lost their jobs. Between 1991 and 1993 roughly 9 million people lost jobs that they never regained.[43] Furthermore, large-scale job loss continued well after the recession had ended, as the "downsizing" movement swept the corporate world.[44] By 1995 almost every Fortune 500 company, America's largest corporations, had either gone through a downsizing, or had plans to undertake one. As a result, job insecurity was widespread among American workers, which no doubt affected their propensity to demand higher wages when the economy improved. Real wages for industrial workers declined for most of the decade, not catching up to the level of the 1980s until 1998.

To be sure, millions of new jobs have been created from 1992 to the present. And, even though many of these new jobs are temporary and do not carry employee benefits, there is no doubt that the economy as a whole has been strong since the 1990–1991 recession. This is, perhaps, best illustrated by the fact that the unemployment rate reached a thirty-year low of 4 percent during the year 2000. To review the indicators we have used to assess previous periods: during the 1990s, the economy grew at a 3.1 percent annual rate, slightly above the 1970–1989 rate; per capita income increased by 2.7 percent annually, exceeding the increases of the 1950s and 1960s; productivity increases averaged 2.1 percent, midway between the 1950–1969 average and the 1970–1989 average; the average unemployment rate for the decade of 5.8 percent was well above the 4 percent level of the 1950s and

1960s, but the decade ended with the unemployment rate at 4.2 percent and heading downward; interest rates declined about 2 percent from the average levels of the 1970s and 1980s but remained well above the rates of the 1950s and 1960s; the trade deficits fell markedly in the early portion of the decade, only to rise to record levels by the end of the decade; economic growth in the United States exceeded that of Europe and Japan by some margin.[45]

The most remarkable and salutary political/economic development of the decade was the elimination of federal deficits. Many factors contributed to this development, most notably a strong economy accompanied by a booming stock market, but policy decisions at the national level also played an important role. President Clinton made deficit reduction a priority in 1993 with his first budget proposal to Congress, which passed the Senate by a single vote (Vice President Gore's). After winning a showdown with the new Republican Congress over the budget in 1995 (and winning reelection in 1996), he followed up with a historic tax and budget agreement with the Republican Congress in 1997. The basic course followed by Clinton and Congress was to restrain federal spending by sticking to the rules first laid out in budget legislation in 1990, which set caps on discretionary spending and subjected entitlement spending to a pay-as-you-go discipline that prohibited new spending programs or tax cuts unless they were offset by cuts in other programs or new taxes. Spending on defense actually declined in the 1990s, as did overall federal spending as a percentage of the gross domestic product (GDP). The Federal Reserve kept inflation in check and real interest rates low, especially from 1992 to 1995, and in 1998 the federal government saw its first surplus in twenty-nine years.[46] The stock market reacted very positively to this development; thus government surpluses should be appreciated as both a cause and a symptom of economic strength.

The vitality of the economy of the 1990s appears to be the result of the confluence of several favorable internal factors: a post-recession recovery, corporate downsizing that encouraged high stock values amidst job insecurity, large supplies of funds for investment from the retirement accounts of the baby-boom generation and other sources, reduced government spending and borrowing, low inflation, and stable currency values. The main problem with this economy is the inequity with which the benefits were distributed. This is manifested not only in the concentration of income and wealth among the very rich but also in the great disparity in wages and earnings between highly skilled, well-educated workers and those who lack education and skills. Workers in the latter category saw their real wages decline steadily in the 1980s and 1990s.[47] In addition, the poverty rate was stubbornly persistent during the 1980s and 1990s, hovering in the range of 13 to 15 percent, and higher than it was in the 1970s. Income and wealth is distributed more unequally in the United States than in any country in western Europe; clearly, the distribution of economic benefits is, at least potentially, a matter of government policy.[48]

Another very important set of economic developments in the 1990s was the finalization of key international trade agreements, which marked the era of so-called "globalization." Despite their differences, President Clinton and Congress were able to agree on the need to implement the North American Free Trade Agreement (NAFTA) and a new General Agreement on Tariffs and Trade (GATT), which created the World Trade Organization (WTO), in 1994. Both of these were designed to remove national barriers to trade, and ultimately to promote economic growth. In 2000 Clinton and Congress reached another agreement to permanently lift all trade restrictions against China.[49] The WTO included 128 nations as original signatories, and it features a codified system, using international panels, for resolving trade disputes.[50] The WTO, along with the International Monetary Fund (IMF) and the World Bank, form a powerful international triad that aims to promote economic growth and development through the expansion of free markets. These organizations have many critics in the United States and abroad who believe that their actions and policies often work to the disadvantage of poor countries and ignore human rights and environmental issues.[51] Such criticism voiced in several visible protests around the world, along with strong world economic growth, led to a consensus among the United States and Europe in the fall of 2000 to forgive billions of dollars of debt to developing nations in Africa and Latin America in order to give them a better chance of fighting poverty and disease.[52]

A Comparative Perspective

The relationship between cultural values, economic conditions, and public policy is apparent when we compare the United States with other nations of the world. Western industrial nations have quite different governmental operations and public philosophies that reflect diverse cultural and economic experiences. Consider the difference between the United States and western Europe one hundred years ago. In Europe desirable land had long been held by the wealthiest segments of society, economic mobility was minimal, and a large industrial working class had formed. In the United States the government was practically giving away large tracts of land in the West, frontiers remained to be settled, and large fortunes were being made and lost quickly. An industrial working class, composed mostly of European immigrants, was beginning to form, but most parts of the country remained primarily agrarian. American economic development was greatly influenced by the existence of a large property-owning segment of the population and an expanding middle class. These factors help account for some of the distinctive aspects of American politics and the American economy today: its large, fairly autonomous private sector, its relatively modest government

Table 2-2 Government Outlays and Revenues in Selected Countries

Country	Government outlays as percentage of GDP (1998)	Transfer payments as percentage of GDP (1995)[a]	Tax and other revenues as percentage of GDP (1998)
Canada	43	15	44
France	52	26	50
Germany	47	21	46
Italy	49	20	46
Japan	37	14	31
Sweden	57	26	59
United Kingdom	40	16	40
United States	31	13	31

Sources: United Nations, *National Accounts Statistics: Main Aggregates and Detailed Tables, 1995* (New York: United Nations, 1999), parts 1 and 2; Organisation for Economic Cooperation and Development, *OECD Economic Outlook* (Paris: OECD, 1999), 220–221.

[a] Includes Social Security, social assistance grants, and other social insurance benefits.

social welfare spending, and the widespread acceptance of the values of individualism and capitalism.

The social welfare state came relatively late to the United States. Programs to aid sick or injured workers, the elderly and disabled, the unemployed, and new parents were established in western Europe several decades before they appeared in this country.[53] Nearly all western European countries have universal income support programs for the poor and unemployed and national health insurance systems; these have never taken hold in the United States. Although American social welfare spending expanded significantly in the late 1960s and 1970s, other Western democratic governments are considerably more generous in providing housing assistance, unemployment benefits, vacation and maternity leaves, and income security for the elderly.[54] The data presented in Table 2-2 demonstrate that the U.S. government taxes its citizens less and spends less money on social welfare purposes—in the form of transfer payments—than most other industrial nations. Because the private sector/free market ethic continues to dominate the political culture and economy of the United States, American policymakers face choices very different from those in other countries.

Although it is smaller than that of other industrial nations, the public sector in the United States influences nearly every aspect of the nation's social and economic life. Especially influential is the large body of federal, state, and local regulatory law that governs public and private behavior. Federal regulations burgeoned from the 1960s until the election of Ronald Reagan. Between 1960 and 1980, the number of federal regulatory agencies doubled, from twenty-eight to fifty-six; their work force grew by 90,000; and their budgets increased threefold. The *Federal Register*, which is a compilation of all government regulations, grew from about 15,000 pages in 1946 to 87,000 pages in 1980. Reagan administration efforts at deregulation reduced the regulatory state somewhat, highlighted by budget and staff cuts in federal agencies, and symbolized by a reduction in the number of pages in the *Federal Register* to just over 50,000.[55] Perhaps more important, many industries were deregulated, including trucking, banking, broadcasting, and airlines, but in many areas regulatory responsibilities were simply shifted from the government to private companies or to states and localities. During the Bush and Clinton administrations numerous regulatory laws were strengthened, particularly in the areas of civil rights, air pollution, and rights of the disabled. At present, the federal regulatory state is alive and well, with more than 130,000 employees and $16 billion to spend each year.[56]

In the 1960s and 1970s, the regulatory presence in most states increased in ways that mirrored the changes at the federal level. Spheres long regulated by the state and federal governments, such as transportation, food and drug quality, agriculture, occupational licensing, and banking, were joined by consumer product safety, air and water pollution, workplace health and safety, automobile safety, and civil rights. But, as noted above, the Reagan administration's efforts at deregulation often increased, rather than decreased, the regulatory duties of state governments. Furthermore, budgetary pressures at the national level between 1985 and 1995 produced a certain proclivity on the part of Congress to impose direct or indirect regulatory mandates on the states. In 1995, however, Congress made it more difficult for the federal government to impose mandates on the states by enacting the Unfunded Mandates Reform Act.[57]

The sharing of policy responsibilities among different levels of government is characteristic of the American political system. States and localities dominate many important policy areas and share others with the federal government. Subnational governmental power is based on a tradition of local self-determination that is older than the country itself, protected by the Constitution, and sustained by individualistic cultural values. American state and local governments are stronger and more autonomous than their counterparts in most other countries, but it would be a mistake to believe that only in the United States are power and authority vested in subnational governments. Canadian provincial governments have considerable constitutional authority, which gives them a good measure of autonomy from the national government and superiority over the city governments. Many other countries, such as Britain and Sweden, have unitary, rather than federal, systems, and even though there are no local chief executives (governors or mayors) local governments are important political institutions. For example, some large cities have taxing power, and in nearly all countries central government leaders know that they must obtain the support of networks of local public officials to finance and implement education, health, housing, and welfare programs. If one compares state and local government spending as a percentage of total government spending, the countries with federal systems, Canada (56 percent), the United States (46 percent), and Germany (39 percent), rank ahead of the unitary states, Japan (32 percent), United Kingdom (25 percent), Italy (23 percent), and France (19 percent).[58]

Relationships between national and subnational governments undergo change. The independence of state governments from the federal government, which existed in nineteenth-century America, was significantly altered by the New Deal of the 1930s. The liberal Democratic programs of the Great Society in the 1960s and 1970s imposed a host of new national objectives on states and localities. With these sweeping programs, the federal government asserted itself as the leading actor in the intergovernmental system. Grant-in-aid programs and regulatory mandates gave the federal government leverage to alter traditional state and local services and to convince states and localities that they should provide many new ones.

The trend toward greater federal control of policymaking and implementation abated during the 1980s. This change came about in part because of a nearly universal recognition that narrow-purpose federal grants led to fragmented and inefficient government services. Too many programs were attempting to treat related problems without any effective means of coordination. Republican presidents Nixon and Reagan called for a "new federalism," in which states and localities would have more authority and responsibility. Many overlapping, but separately operating, federal aid programs were consolidated into block grant packages, and the responsibility for making policy and program design decisions devolved to the state level. This trend continued in the 1990s under the Bush and Clinton administrations. It is evident that over the last thirty years state governments have grown in stature within the federal system. States have demonstrated their willingness and ability to raise money for public services, and state governments have become more innovative in policymaking and in reforms aimed at improving management.[59]

Summary

The purpose of this brief review has been to show how two broad forces in American society—political culture and the economy—influence politics, government, and public policy. Political culture determines what people expect of government and what role citizens and politicians play in politics. Economic well-being has been the most consistently important issue in American polities, and economic performance is both a cause and an effect of government policy. Political beliefs and expectations and the economy change over time, and these changes are reflected in the policy agenda of government.

Politics in the twenty-first century is markedly different from politics in earlier epochs in American history, and different politics means different policies. Most notably, the politics of deficits have been replaced by the politics of surpluses. Interestingly, however, the positions of major players are not that different. Republicans still favor across-the-board tax cuts and increased spending on national defense; Democrats are wary of tax cuts and want to spend more on domestic programs, especially Social Security and Medicare. Nevertheless, macroeconomic policymaking continues to be complicated. If the government tries to control inflation by employing strict monetary policies, for example, that move hurts the export market. Certain sectors of the economy, such as agriculture, feel the effects quickly and forcefully. If the government tries to alleviate the trade deficit by taxing or limiting foreign imports, American consumers pay higher prices for many products. If the government commits large sums of money to national defense or runs large deficits, less money is available for housing, education, medical care, and public works programs.

Americans have seen different priorities come and go. During the New Deal period federal government spending was seen as the key to prosperity; the private sector reemerged during Dwight Eisenhower's administration. The government came back with more spending and regulation in the late 1960s and 1970s, then drew back from regulation in the 1980s. In the 1990s despite intense partisan bickering, Democrats and Republicans (the Clinton administration and Congress) were able to agree on key economic policies, including limiting federal government spending, pursuing free trade agreements, and keeping Alan Greenspan in charge of the Federal Reserve. From the standpoint of the economy, these proved to be very important areas of agreement, indeed.

The American government's response to the challenges of the present and the future will be shaped by cultural and economic developments and by the actions of policymaking institutions. Understanding the peculiarities of and the distinctions among the different domains of politics is central to the study of American public policy. These domains and their policymaking processes are the subject of Chapters 3 through 8.

Notes

1. See Lewis Lipsitz, *American Democracy* (New York: St. Martin's, 1986), 31.
2. For a more detailed discussion of American political values and beliefs, see Linda J. Medcalf and Kenneth M. Dolbeare, *Neopolitics: American Political Ideas in the 1980s* (New York: Random House, 1985).
3. Adam Smith, *The Wealth of Nations* (New York: Random House, Modern Library, 1937).
4. The concept of procedural democracy is discussed at length in Ira Katznelson and Mark Kesselman, *The Politics of Power,* 2d ed. (New York: Harcourt Brace Jovanovich, 1979).
5. See Alexander Hamilton, John Jay, and James Madison, *The Federalist Papers* (Cambridge, Mass.: Belknap Press, 1966), no. 10.
6. Jean-Jacques Rousseau, *The Social Contract and Discourses,* trans. G. D. H. Cole (New York: E. P. Dutton, 1950), bk. 3, p. 94.

7. See Benjamin R. Barber, *Strong Democracy: Participatory Politics for a New Age* (Berkeley: University of California Press, 1984); Philip Green, *Retrieving Democracy* (Totowa, N.J.: Rowman and Allanheld, 1985); more recently, Benjamin R. Barber, *A Passion for Democracy* (Princeton: Princeton University Press, 1998); and Benjamin R. Barber, *A Place for Us* (New York: Hill and Wang, 1998).

8. Jane J. Mansbridge, *Beyond Adversary Democracy* (Chicago: University of Chicago Press, 1983).

9. See Paul Light, *Still Artful Work: The Politics of Social Security Reform,* 2d ed. (New York: McGraw-Hill, 1995), 56.

10. General Social Surveys, as reported in Barbara A. Bardes and Robert W. Oldendick, *Public Opinion: Measuring the American Mind* (Belmont, Calif.: Wadsworth, 2000), 124. Two major university-based survey research organizations collect data on the political attitudes and behaviors of Americans: the Survey Research Center (SRC) at the University of Michigan, which conducts the American National Election Studies before and after all national elections, and the National Opinion Research Center at the University of Chicago, which conducts the General Social Surveys. The first American Election Study covered the 1948 presidential election; subsequent studies have covered all presidential elections since then and all congressional elections since 1958. The first General Social Survey was conducted in 1972, and more than twenty have been completed since. These two sources are used by many academic social scientists to track trends in political attitudes and behavior.

11. Gallup Organization, "Gallup Poll Topics: A–Z, Social Security and Medicare," August 11–12, 2000, online at http://www.gallup.com/poll/indicators/indsocialsecurity.asp, October 2000.

12. *The Public Perspective 2,* March–April 1991, 7; General Social Surveys and American National Election Studies, as reported in Bardes and Oldendick, *Public Opinion,* 129.

13. *The Public Perspective 1,* July–August 1990, 82.

14. American National Election Studies, as reported in Bardes and Oldendick, *Public Opinion,* 112.

15. General Social Surveys, as reported in Bardes and Oldendick, *Public Opinion,* 110–111. If the responses "a great deal" and "quite a lot" to the "confidence in institutions" question are combined, the levels of trust go up roughly 10 percent for Congress, 15 percent for the Supreme Court, 20 percent for the military, and nearly 30 percent for the presidency; thus using this method for grouping responses, the presidency is ranked closer to the Supreme Court than to Congress. See Gallup Organization, "Gallup Poll Topics: A–Z, Confidence in Institutions," June 22–25, 2000, online at http://www.gallup.com/poll/indicators/indconfidence.asp, September 2000.

16. Federal Election Commission, "About Elections and Voting," online at http://www.fec.gov/elections.html, September 2000.

17. Gallup Organization, "Gallup Poll Topics: A–Z, Abortion Issues," March 30–April 2, 2000, http://www.gallup.com.indicators/indabortion.asp, September 2000.

18. See Bardes and Oldendick, *Public Opinion,* 187.

19. General Social Surveys, as reported in Bardes and Oldendick, *Public Opinion,* 147.

20. Ibid., 152.
21. Gallup Organization, "Gallup Poll Topics: A–Z, Death Penalty," August 29–September 5, 2000, online at http://www.gallup.com/poll/indicators/inddeath_pen.asp, September 2000.
22. See Bardes and Oldendick, *Public Opinion,* 175. Data derived from *The Public Perspective 8,* June–July 1997, 20.
23. American National Election Studies, as reported in Bardes and Oldendick, *Public Opinion,* 158–159.
24. Gallup Organization, "Gallup Poll Topics: A–Z, Education," September 11–13, 2000, online at http://www.gallup.com/poll/indicators/indeducation.asp, September 2000; *Gallup Report,* no. 177 (April–May 1980): 11; *Gallup Report,* no. 217 (October 1983): 18; American National Election Study, summer 1989.
25. Gallup Organization, "Gallup Poll Topics: A–Z, Religion," August 24–27, 2000, online at http://www.gallup.com/indicators/indreligion.asp, September 2000.
26. Ronald Inglehart, "Post-Materialism in an Environment of Insecurity," *American Political Science Review* 75 (December 1981): 880–900.
27. 1996 American National Election Study and 1996 General Social Survey, as reported in Bardes and Oldendick, *Public Opinion,* 139; see also Susan A. MacManus, *Young v. Old* (Boulder, Colo.: Westview, 1996).
28. American National Election Studies, as reported in Bardes and Oldendick, *Public Opinion,* 101, 103. It should be noted that depending on how the question is worded, different polling organizations come up with slightly different results regarding American ideological distribution. Overall, the results of Gallup polls, the General Social Surveys, and the American National Election Studies are quite similar.
29. Ibid., 104, 106. The Gallup Organization shows a somewhat more pronounced increase in the number of independents. Their figures for the 1990s show Republican affiliation running from 29 to 33 percent, Democratic affiliation from 31 to 35 percent, and independents from 32 to 39 percent. See Gallup Organization, "Independents Rank as Largest U.S. Political Group," April 9, 1999, online at http://www.gallup.com/poll/releases/pr990409c.asp, September 2000.
30. For a thorough discussion, see Howard Gold, *Hollow Mandates: American Public Opinion and the Conservative Shift* (Boulder, Colo.: Westview, 1992).
31. The political attitudes and values covered in the Pew surveys that informed the typology included environmentalism, religion and morality, social tolerance, social justice, business sentiment, financial security, antigovernment sentiment, and patriotism/militarism. For details see the Pew Research Center for the People and the Press, "Retro-Politics; The Political Typology: Version 3.0," November 11, 1999, online at http://www.people-press.org/typo99sec1.htm, and http://www.people-press.org/typo99sec9.htm, October 2000.
32. Unless otherwise indicated, the statistics provided in this section were taken from tables in the appendixes to the *Economic Report of the President,* prepared annually by the Council of Economic Advisers. See *Economic Report of the President,* 1986, and *Economic Report of the President,* 2000 (Washington, D.C.: Government Printing Office, 1986 and 2000).
33. "The Reindustrialization of America," *Business Week,* special issue, June 30, 1980, 6–7.

34. GNP was the measure of national economic output commonly used in the United States in the 1960s. It differs from gross domestic product (GDP) in that GNP includes the profits and income of American corporations and individuals that are operating abroad but does not count the profits and income of foreigners or foreign-owned corporations operating in the United States. GDP includes the latter but does not include the former. Since the mid-1980s GDP has become the accepted measure of national economic output. Robert B. Reich, in *The Next American Frontier* (New York: Penguin Books, 1983), 285n., cites Organization for Economic Cooperation and Development (OECD) data on this point.

35. See Harrell R. Rodgers Jr., *The Cost of Human Neglect* (Armonk, N.Y.: M. E. Sharpe, 1982), 18.

36. See Lawrence E. Lynn Jr., "A Decade of Policy Developments in the Income Maintenance System," in *A Decade of Federal Antipoverty Programs,* ed. Robert H. Haveman (New York: Academic Press, 1977), 88–95.

37. Reich, *The Next American Frontier,* 285.

38. See Gregory B. Mills, "The Budget: A Failure of Discipline," in *The Reagan Record,* ed. John L. Palmer and Isabel V. Sawhill (Cambridge, Mass.: Ballinger, 1984), 111–114.

39. Frank Ackerman et al., eds., *The Political Economy of Inequality* (Washington D.C.: Island Press, 2000), 2.

40. See Robert Pear, "Rich Got Richer in 80s; Others Held Even," *New York Times,* January 11, 1991, A1.

41. *New York Times,* January 17, 1988, E4.

42. Carl E. Van Horn, *No One Left Behind,* Report of the Twentieth Century Fund Task Force on Retraining America's Workforce (New York: Twentieth Century Fund Press, 1996), 64.

43. Ibid., 62.

44. William Lazonick and Mary O'Sullivan, "Maximising Shareholder Value: A New Ideology for Corporate Governance," *Economy and Society,* forthcoming.

45. Organization for Economic Cooperation and Development, *OECD Economic Outlook* (Paris, France: OECD, 1999), 66:195.

46. See Richard W. Stevenson, "Roots of Prosperity Reach Past Clinton Years," *New York Times,* October 9, 2000, A16.

47. Ackerman et al., *The Political Economy of Inequality,* 206.

48. Ibid., 7, 36.

49. See, David E. Sanger, "Senate Votes to Lift Curbs on U.S. Trade with Beijing; Strong Bipartisan Support," *New York Times,* September 20, 2000, A1.

50. Frederic S. Pearson and Simon Payaslian, *International Political Economy* (New York: McGraw-Hill, 1999), 185.

51. Roger Cohen, "Growing Up and Getting Practical Since Seattle," *New York Times,* September 24, 2000, sec. 4, p. 1.

52. Joseph Kahn, Wealthy Nations Propose Doubling Poor's Debt Relief, *New York Times,* September 17, 2000, A1; Joseph Kahn, "Congressional Leadership Agrees to Debt Relief for Poor Nations," *New York Times,* October 18, 2000, A1.

53. Rodgers, *The Cost of Human Neglect,* 104–107.

54. Ibid., 57, 103–125; and Ira C. Magaziner and Robert B. Reich, *Minding America's Business* (New York: Harcourt Brace Jovanovich, 1982), 11–27.

55. Norman J. Ornstein, Thomas E. Mann, and Michael J. Malbin, *Vital Statistics on Congress,* 1989–1990 (Washington, D.C.: CQ Press, 1990), 160; see also Cornelius Kerwin, *Rulemaking,* 2d ed. (Washington D.C.: CQ Press, 1999).

56. Edward Sidlow and Beth Henschen, *America at Odds,* 2d ed. (Belmont, Calif.: Wadsworth, 2000), 447–448.

57. See Paul Posner, *The Politics of Unfunded Mandates* (Washington D.C.: Georgetown University Press, 1998).

58. Sidlow and Henschen, *America at Odds,* 504.

59. Barry Rabe, "Power to the States: The Promise and Pitfalls of Decentralization," in *Environmental Policy in the 1990s,* ed. Norman J. Vig and Michael E. Kraft, 4th ed. (Washington D.C.: CQ Press, 2000), 32–54.

Chapter 3 **Boardroom Politics**

Social scientist Harold Lasswell once defined politics as "who gets what, when, how."[1] By that definition, many private sector decisions are as political as those made by government officials. When an automobile company shuts down an assembly plant, the consequences for workers, their families, and the local community can be devastating. When a paper mill discharges poisonous chemicals into the atmosphere or a nearby stream, the consequences for public health may be severe. When a hospital decides to invest in expensive lifesaving equipment, such as emergency helicopters, it may save many lives but may also raise hospital prices. When a business chooses to donate 5 percent of its pretax profits to charity, numerous nonprofit organizations may benefit, but the government may collect less tax money. In each of these cases, private organizations decide who gets what, when, and how.

To describe private decision making that has public consequences, the metaphor "boardroom politics" will be used. At the core of boardroom politics are decisions made by private organizations, usually corporations, over which the government has limited control. Some of these decisions are literally made in corporate boardrooms; others are made at lower levels by corporate managers, subject to constraints imposed by a board of directors. The private sector is not monolithic in its structure, norms, or purposes. There are important differences between publicly held and privately held companies, nonprofit and for-profit organizations, big corporations and small businesses, monopolies and competitive entities. Despite these differences, one statement is true of private corporations: they have an enormous impact on the daily lives of all Americans. Charles Lindblom wrote that the role of the private sector is vital not just in the United States but in all market-oriented societies. "Corporate executives in all private enterprise systems . . . decide a nation's industrial technology, the pattern of work organization, location of industry, market structure, resource allocation, and, of course, executive compensation and status."[2]

The role of the private sector is especially significant in the United States. We can conclude from Table 2-2 that by the late 1990s the private sector accounted for about 69 percent of the gross domestic product in the United States, whereas in the United Kingdom the figure was 60 percent, in France it was 48 percent, and in Sweden it was 43 percent. The overwhelming majority of Americans, approximately 84 percent, are employed by the private sector; in the United Kingdom, roughly 80 percent of all workers are privately employed; in France, 76 percent; and in Sweden, 69 percent.[3] In the United States most vital industries are controlled primarily or exclusively by the

57

private sector. These include railroads, airlines, electric companies, telecommunications firms, oil producers, automobile manufacturers, and mail delivery companies. In Western Europe more of these industries are controlled by government, but the trend is toward greater privatization. In Great Britain, for example, publicly owned utilities, energy, and transportation firms were transferred to private ownership in the late 1980s and early 1990s.[4]

During the 1980s and 1990s the private sector in the United States also grew as a result of privatization and deregulation. Privatization, the transfer of service delivery functions from the public sector to the private sector, spread rapidly at the state and local levels in the 1980s. A 1987 survey revealed that 99 percent of cities with populations over 5,000 and counties with populations over 25,000 contracted out for services; at this same time, approximately 35 percent of U.S. cities contracted with private companies for refuse collection.[5] Contracting for social services, usually with nonprofit organizations, also became widespread in the 1980s. By the mid-1980s almost half of the states contracted for mental health services; in some states 90 percent of mental health funds were being spent this way.[6] Other social services are also provided through contracts, including employment services, child abuse centers, nursing homes, day care centers, drug abuse clinics, and halfway houses for parolees. A 1992 study of more than 1,500 local governments found that, on average, 24 percent of the communities contracted out public works and transportation services (mainly with for-profit firms), and 28 percent contracted out health and human services (mainly with nonprofit companies).[7] By the mid-1990s Indianapolis had adopted a system whereby all municipal programs and services were open to bids from private companies except police, fire, and zoning operations.[8] By 1997 seven states (California, Colorado, Florida, Iowa, Maryland, Michigan, and New Jersey) had privatized more than one hundred programs and services.[9] Privatization has advanced more slowly at the federal level, despite support from the Reagan and Bush administrations, and to a lesser degree, the Clinton administration.

Deregulation, the relaxation of government standards and requirements, has proceeded steadily at the federal level since about 1980. Beginning with the Carter administration, Congress took steps to deregulate the airline, trucking, and financial industries, and the price of oil and natural gas. In the process, the Civil Aeronautics Board (CAB) and the Interstate Commerce Commission (ICC) were abolished, barriers to entry into the trucking industry were reduced, and much greater freedom was given to financial institutions to engage in a variety of lending and investment activities. In the 1980s the Federal Communications Commission (FCC) relaxed government regulation of the broadcasting industry by eliminating limits on commercial time and by issuing licenses for longer periods of time. The FCC's role in regulating AT&T was first reduced in the early 1980s, as a result of an antitrust settlement that permitted AT&T to compete with IBM and other computer companies in the lucrative data-processing market. The telecommunications industry changed rapidly in the late 1980s and 1990s, and new legislation in 1996 further deregulated the industry, allowing AT&T, cable providers, and local and regional telephone companies ("Baby Bells") to compete in an open and expanded market.[10] (The FCC has retained an important role in reviewing mergers and acquisitions within the telecommunications industry to ensure that they serve "the public interest.")

More broadly, led by the Reagan and Bush administrations but continued in a very significant way during the Clinton administration, the federal government has stepped away from intrusive regulation of most areas of the private sector. In some cases, especially during Republican administrations, federal agencies have been discouraged from issuing new, restrictive rules and regulations, but mostly the change has been accomplished through the adoption and implementation of deregulatory legislation. In addition, the government has been reluctant to interject itself into important new industries, such as the Internet. The federal government has also prohibited state governments from taxing the Internet, at least for the moment. As a result of these trends, the power of the private sector in American politics has grown. The American public seems to have mixed feelings about the private sector, particularly large corporations. In a recent poll, roughly two-thirds of the public gave businesses credit for the prosperity of the 1990s, but over 70 percent thought corporations had too much power over too many aspects of American life. Although 68 percent of the public thought big companies made good products, over 70 percent thought corporate executives were paid too much and that corporations had too much political influence.[11]

Corporate Concerns

An agenda, whether corporate or governmental, consists of items or issues thought to warrant serious attention. The building blocks of corporate agendas differ from those of government agendas. The question that faces a private corporation is not whether to make changes in health policy or energy policy or transportation policy, but whether to focus most of its efforts on finance, management, or public relations. Within these broad categories, further choices must be made: whether to concentrate on diversification, modernization, product quality, expansion, or labor relations in order to achieve profit objectives; or to concentrate on advertising, customer relations, community relations, or government affairs. Although the typical business carries on all these activities at once, the emphasis given to one area or another varies considerably.

The Bottom Line

Corporate priorities can be inferred from a variety of sources, including corporate behavior, but when executives speak for themselves they invariably say something about the proverbial "bottom line." As the editors of *Fortune* magazine discovered in their 1986 survey of 500 chief executive officers, the top priority for business leaders was improving profits or earnings.[12] The importance placed on profits is hardly surprising, since most companies cannot survive without them; thus profitability can be seen as an overriding objective for most corporate executives. But, as illustrated in Box 3-1, executives take many factors into account when they evaluate corporate success.

The fact that corporate executives view profits as a necessary condition for success does not make their decisions easy. They must make complicated choices about how to juggle priorities in order to achieve their profit objectives. Corporate agendas are not limited to a single issue, any more than legislative, judicial, or executive agendas are. It should come as no surprise, then, that the priorities established by some corporations do not adequately anticipate all the difficulties they face down the road.

Consider the case of U.S. Steel, now known as USX. During the 1950s and 1960s, steel executives concentrated on profit margins and labor relations. Instead of opting for modern techniques, such as continuous casting and basic oxygen furnaces, U.S. Steel retained open-hearth furnaces and traditional production methods that were becoming obsolete. The Japanese, setting long-term goals, made the most of new technologies. U.S. Steel's ability to compete with Japan and other nations decreased to such an extent that company executives decided to concentrate more on oil and gas production (merging with Marathon Oil) than on steel manufacturing. Seventy-three percent of the company's revenues came from steel in 1978, but that figure dropped to 33 percent in 1985, and then to 25 percent by 1999.[13] U.S. Steel, once the mightiest steel company in the world and a symbol of American know-how, is now only half-heartedly committed to the steel business.

Some companies neglect certain issues because they are preoccupied with other matters; other companies neglect issues because they doubt their importance or see no advantage in dealing with them. For example, from the 1960s to the 1980s it was common for companies to neglect the mental and physical health of their employees because they did not take seriously the connection between employee health and productivity. By the 1990s the awareness of this connection had increased significantly, largely because more commercial mental and physical health services sought to sell it, and more companies were listening. As union membership declined, from approximately 19 million in 1977 to about 16.5 million in 1999, the ability of organized labor to sensitize companies to employee concerns also diminished.[14] Some companies neglect the effect their activities have on the environment, despite laws aimed at regulating it, because they do not wish to incur cleanup costs. As punishment they may pay a fine, but only if the government discovers the violation and vigorously enforces the law.

The mass media occasionally bring neglected issues to the public's attention because layoffs, environmental degradation, and threats to worker safety make good stories. For example, it was media attention that forced corporate

Box 3-1 ***Fortune's* Eight Key Attributes of Reputation and America's Most Admired Companies**

Attributes

Innovativeness
Quality of management
Employed talent
Financial soundness
Use of corporate assets
Long-term investment value
Social responsibility
Quality of products/services

Top Ten Companies

1. General Electric
2. Microsoft
3. Dell Computer
4. Cisco Systems
5. Wal-Mart Stores
6. Southwest Airlines
7. Berkshire Hathaway
8. Intel
9. Home Depot
10. Lucent Technologies

Source: Fortune, February 21, 2000, 108–110. Credit *Fortune* © Time Inc.

officials, and members of Congress, to confront the problems of Firestone tires in Ford Explorers in the summer of 2000. But the media have shown less interest in exposing the potential shortcomings of their own industry. Consider the question of cross-media ownership, the joint ownership of a newspaper and a broadcasting station in the same community. A recent study found that in covering the 1996 Telecommunications Act, newspapers around the country varied in the approach they took to one aspect of the legislation: a provision to loosen restrictions on television ownership. Newspapers owned by companies that stood to gain from this provision reported much less critically on it than those who had no self-interest at stake.[15] Clearly, some issues will remain buried if companies find it convenient to ignore them.

Agenda Determination

Corporate executives are the principal determiners of corporate agendas. As long as the company prospers, corporate managers are free to chart a course for the future. When earnings decline or a crisis erupts, board members intervene in an effort to get the company back on track. Board meetings can provide opportunities for members to establish new priorities, but this is often difficult, in part because top corporate executives usually sit on the board. A board meeting typically is the final step in a long, protracted process, however. Like a congressional debate, a board meeting is the culmination of a long series of discussions, of maneuvers and counter-maneuvers, bargains, and power plays. The meeting may be only a formality because the "decision" has been made. When the board of the Chrysler Corporation met in the spring of 1991, the company was in the midst of an eighteen-month sales slump and desperately in need of a new loan from a group of thirty-eight banks from which it regularly borrowed. In order to convince the banks that the corporation was serious about reducing costs, the board voted to cut the dividend paid to investors in half (saving $33 million per quarter). Some weeks later the banks extended Chrysler a new $1.7 billion line of credit.[16]

Prior to important board meetings, managers may attempt to mobilize support to stave off a policy change or a coup d'état. An embattled Steve Jobs, then the chairman of Apple Computer, threw a dinner party in the spring of 1985, with an influential board member as the guest of honor. Jobs, whose position was in jeopardy, hoped to persuade the board member to rally to his cause. When the board member merely picked at his whole wheat pizza, Jobs began to see the handwriting on the wall. Of course his dismissal from Apple was by no means Jobs's corporate swan song. After some false starts, he scored several successes with computer animated films and then enjoyed the ultimate vindication of being rehired as Apple's chief executive officer (CEO) in 1997. Since he took over, Apple has realized increased revenues, a larger market share, and higher stock values.[17]

Corporate agendas are also influenced by the policies, schemes, and strategies of company rivals. In the early 1980s Ford Motor Company decided to offer a five-year/50,000-mile warranty, and Chrysler had to swallow its pride or up the ante. Chrysler opted for one-upmanship, offering a seven-year/70,000-mile warranty. A similar episode occurred in the summer of 2000 when Ford announced plans to improve the fuel economy of its sport utility vehicles (SUVs) over the next five years. Within one week General Motors (GM) announced that it would do the same, only better. GM's vice chairman said "G.M. will be the leader [in fuel economy] in five years, and in 15 years for that matter."[18] When one company hits upon a successful marketing strategy its competitors must react, thus putting marketing high on their agenda.

Corporations have also thrown each other into a tizzy by staging takeover attempts. If unwelcome, they are referred to as "hostile" takeovers. In the 1980s Ted Turner proposed to take over CBS, forcing a transformation in the network's agenda. For weeks CBS was preoccupied with preventing the takeover. CBS eventually succeeded but later found it necessary to undertake a major management shake-up and massive layoffs. Many at CBS, particularly in the news division, never recovered from the shock of this shake-up. In the 1990s hostile takeovers began to become less frequent and salient in the corporate world, but mergers and acquisitions were on the agenda of numerous major corporations. Chrysler became Daimler/Chrysler, Exxon and Mobil merged, AT&T bought major cable companies such as Tele-Communications and Media One, Time Warner bought Turner Broadcasting, Citibank became Citigroup, Lockheed joined with Martin Marietta to become the largest defense contractor, to list just a few of the prominent mergers.

Corporate agendas also may be shaped by government officials. President Lyndon Johnson issued Executive Order 11246 in 1965, placing affirmative action on the agendas of businesses throughout the nation. Johnson's order prohibited discrimination by government contractors and established a compliance office to ensure cooperation. Because most sizable companies do some business with the government, Johnson's executive order guaranteed that affirmative action would receive serious attention in corporate boardrooms across the land. By offering lucrative contracts to companies willing to design and develop new weapons systems, the Defense Department also has been successful in shaping corporate agendas and in influencing university agendas. Corporate scientists and academics throughout the United States are engaged in research on space, defense, agriculture, energy, and environmental projects funded by the federal government. The Justice Department's enforcement of antitrust law can become a dominant factor in corporate agendas, as Microsoft learned when the Justice Department sought to break it up in 1998.

Ordinary citizens can play a significant part in helping to set corporate agendas. By mobilizing activist shareholders, concerned citizens have attempted to shape corporate agendas through proxy resolutions that address important social issues—civil rights, corporate responsibility, apartheid in South Africa, and more recently the selling of certain kinds of apparel on college campuses.[19] One highly publicized effort in the 1970s was Campaign GM, organized by Ralph Nader (the Green Party presidential candidate in 2000). With the support of the Securities and Exchange Commission (SEC), Campaign GM placed two proposals before the General Motors board: to increase the size of the board and to create a shareholders committee. The hope was that these reforms would increase consumer influence at GM. Neither proposal was adopted; indeed, no public interest proxy proposal opposed by management has ever passed. Nevertheless, in several instances, corporate managers have made modest concessions in return for an agreement by shareholder activists to withdraw their proxy resolutions. More generally, the boards of major corporations are very concerned about their company's public image and discuss it frequently in meetings.

The Public-Private Spectrum

Thus far corporations have been considered as a class. There are, however, differences among corporations, and these differences, apparent in policymaking,

Table 3-1 The Public-Private Spectrum: Degree of Government Influence

Very low	Fairly low	Fairly high	Very high
Privately held firms and foundations (for example, Cargill, Inc., the Ford Foundation)	Publicly held firms: competitive firms and oligopolies (the funeral industry, the auto industry)	Publicly held firms: monopolies (investor–owned public utilities)	Government corporations (for example, TVA, U.S. Postal Service, municipal utilities)

are also apparent in agenda setting. Some businesses "affected with a public interest" are more vulnerable to public pressure than most;[20] other businesses, whose stock is not publicly traded, are less vulnerable than most. In between are those corporations with which the public is most familiar—corporations whose stock is traded but are free to set prices as they please (see Table 3-1).

Public utilities, at one end of the spectrum, are businesses affected with a public interest. These are usually what some economists call "natural monopolies"—an industry where services can be supplied most efficiently by a single company. It is generally accepted that the rates natural monopolies charge for their services should be set by government officials in order to keep prices at a reasonable level. A classic example of a natural monopoly is a regional electric utility company; in many parts of the country the rates such companies charge customers are determined by state public utility commissions. The agendas of public utilities are subject to control by government officials because government regulators have considerable influence over their revenues, allowable costs, and profit margins. Regulators decide whether to grant a utility company's rate hike request in full or in part. A "stingy" public utility commission, in effect, places revenue requirement issues on a company's agenda; a "generous" commission enables a utility company to concentrate on other issues, such as expansion or diversification.

New ideas (like deregulation) and technologies have complicated the realm of so-called monopolies, however. By the late 1970s, Congress decided there was enough competition in the energy industry and that natural gas companies should operate with less price regulation. In the telecommunications industry, Congress first decided (in 1982) that long-distance telephone services should no longer be monopolized by AT&T; then, in 1996, it passed legislation aimed at breaking up regional monopolies that provided local telephone services. Cable television was treated like a public utility, with city councils setting rates, until 1984, when Congress decided that cable television companies should be allowed to set their own rates. Presently, AT&T, cable companies, regional Bells, and even Internet service providers are competing for customers and services. Twenty-four states have relaxed government controls over electricity markets, and Congress is considering legislation to deregulate electrical utilities nationwide.[21]

At the other end of the public-private spectrum are privately held companies, whose stock is not traded publicly but is held by family members or employees. These companies have considerable discretion in what they do and when they do it. In contrast to other companies, privately held companies need not hold an annual public meeting and need not submit extensive financial data to the SEC. Of course, most of these companies are quite small (fewer than twenty-five employees), but privately held companies employ a substantial portion of the workforce (roughly one-half) in the United States.

Foundations, which exist to dispense money to favored causes, constitute a small subset of private organizations that have extraordinary flexibility in setting their agendas. Although bequests sometimes impose constraints, foundations are usually free to set priorities and to change direction rapidly. The Ford Foundation, for example, announced in 1966 a major effort to promote equal opportunity for African Americans in politics, education, employment, and housing. Over the next two decades, Ford supported civil rights litigation through grants to the Lawyers' Committee for Civil Rights under Law, the NAACP Legal Defense Fund, and other groups. Many foundations, including the Andrew W. Mellon Foundation, have played an important role in setting priorities for colleges and universities through their grant programs that support students and faculty. As a result of the huge amount of wealth created in the 1990s, many companies and individuals have set up new foundations to direct their charitable giving. New nonprofit foundations have also emerged from the conversion of nonprofit health care organizations, such as hospitals, into for-profit firms.

Many citizen groups owe their origins to seed money from foundations. In 1983 political scientist Jack Walker noted that 39 percent of citizen groups formed during the postwar era received foundation grants at the time of founding.[22] Without the timely support of leading foundations, many civil rights groups and environmental groups probably would not exist; others would have vanished by now. Many think tanks also depend upon foundation support. Conservative think tanks such as the American Enterprise Institute, the Heritage Foundation, and the Reason Foundation helped to place deregulation, privatization, and a variety of other conservative causes on the government's agenda in the 1970s and 1980s. Through grants to nonprofit organizations, foundations also have transformed the agendas of city councils, state legislatures, and Congress, as nonprofit groups have promoted long-neglected political causes, from civil rights to homelessness.

Corporate Governance

Boardroom politics is more hierarchical than cloakroom politics, more competitive than bureaucratic politics, and more volatile than courtroom politics. It is less visible than chief executive politics and living room politics but more pervasive than both. The scope of conflict—or the extent of public involvement—is relatively narrow, not because the stakes are low, but because many of the issues are regarded as being outside the government's jurisdiction and away from the public eye. As Donald Regan, the White House chief of staff in the Reagan administration, once put it, "Businessmen, for the most part, are not used to the glare of publicity."[23] In fact, there is an important gap between the importance of boardroom politics and the degree of public involvement in it. Although boardroom politics has become more visible and more controversial since the 1960s, it is still largely private.

Who Has the Power?

American corporations wield considerable power and enjoy substantial autonomy. Nevertheless, no corporation is an island. Public utilities operate under constraints imposed by government regulators. Publicly held corporations take the interests and demands of their stockholders into account. All corporations and privately held companies must be sensitive to market forces. During times of upheaval, corporations find themselves responding to social movements, if only to deflect them. During times of crisis, corporations respond to appeals by political leaders that the "national interest" or the "public interest" requires their cooperation. During World War II, for example, corporations stopped producing consumer goods and mobilized to build ships, tanks, and aircraft.

Increasingly, corporations must be sensitive to the wishes and machinations of certain investors, especially institutional investors. Institutional investors include banks, insurance companies, holders of pension funds, colleges and universities, and other entities with substantial stock portfolios. These institutional investors, more aware and active than ever before, wield power by threatening to sell their stock unless corporate policies change. By 1996, institutional investors owned over 47 percent of all stock in American corporations and 57 percent of the stock in the 1,000 largest corporations.[24] In the 1980s corporate raiders, such as Carl Icahn and T. Boone Pickens, were powerful players, frequently creating waves within their target companies and throughout the stock market by letting it be known they intended to take over. Icahn continued to be a force in the 1990s, using his enormous wealth to buy large portions of the stock in companies such as Trans World Airlines and RJR Nabisco to force reforms that would help shareholders against the wishes of management.[25] Presently, corporations pay a great deal of attention to other companies that they might want to acquire, or with which they might want to merge. The globalization of the economy means that many of these companies might be foreign owned and that the policies and actions of other governments must be considered.

Despite pressure from investors and public officials, corporations have considerable autonomy, in large part because they have legal rights that protect them from politicians, bureaucrats, and judges. Government laws and regulations frequently pose obstacles and challenges to corporate officials, but such leaders are usually well equipped (with lawyers, lobbyists, and money) to meet these challenges. Moreover, corporate power can be highly concentrated. A relatively small number of corporations controls a relatively high percentage of many markets. Examples of highly concentrated industries include aircraft production, defense contracting, beer and malt beverages, breakfast cereals, electric bulbs, computer operating systems, and tobacco; many others could be cited.[26] Moreover, power within corporations tends to be concentrated in the hands of a few individuals, including the company's chief executive officer, chief financial officer, president, and board chairman.

The archetype for sociologist Max Weber's hierarchical model of organization was the government bureaucracy, but the modern corporation comes closer to his ideal type than the modern government bureaucracy. As discussed in the following chapter, the bureaucracy's chain of command is blurred by the fact that it has multiple sovereigns (legislators, chief executives, interest groups). In addition, the bureaucracy's political executives must bargain with career executives; they cannot simply issue an order and wait for it to be carried out. Top corporate officials can behave more autocratically if they wish to do so. Private corporations normally operate with a clear chain of command and fixed responsibilities.

Wizards and Whales

There is no such thing as a corporate leader for all seasons because corporations differ in their dependence on sound management, creative experimentation, public favor, and government support. Some corporations require leaders who can play an "insider" game, that is, people who excel at organizational management. Others require leaders who can play an "outsider" game, that is, those who excel at public relations. If demand for a product or service is stable and a company's market share is secure, an insider game may be sufficient. A more volatile situation may require greater reliance on an outsider game.

There are different types of outsider games. In some instances, corporate leaders must win the support of customers; in others, they must curry the favor of investors or government officials. New technology firms, for example, generally need the help of venture capitalists to garner sufficient resources to perfect their product and gain a niche in their market. Established public utilities, in contrast, must be mindful of their image in the regulatory community, for regulators determine what rates they may charge. Television stations, protected to some extent by the First Amendment, are subject to rather light-handed government regulation, but they must constantly be concerned about the popularity of their programming, because advertising revenue is directly dependent on market share or ratings.

Corporate leadership styles are highly diverse. Whitney MacMillan, former chief executive officer and chairman of the board of Cargill, the largest grain company in the world, maintained a very low profile outside the company. He was, by choice, a rather mysterious figure, a sort of Wizard of Oz—one heard about his great deeds and accomplishments but seldom saw the man in the flesh. A twenty-first-century wizard is Jim Clark, who started Silicon Graphics in the 1980s, then Netscape in the 1990s. Most recently he launched into the health care industry with a firm called Healtheon/WebMD. Clark, who was kicked out of his high school in Texas but later managed to earn a Ph.D. in computer science, is a legendary figure in California's Silicon Valley. After Netscape, Clark eschewed day-to-day involvement in the companies he spawned; he became a "concept man." Concept men come up with the ideas; others implement their visions. Although his companies have made billions of dollars, his most absorbing passion seems to be the creation of a sailboat—the largest single-masted one in the world—that he can sail anywhere in the world via computer from his office in San Francisco.[27]

Henry Hillman, reclusive president of his own, privately held company, once explained why he seldom granted interviews: "A whale is harpooned only when it spouts."[28] Of course, other corporate executives spout all the time. In the 1980s Lee Iacocca, Chrysler's chairman, personified the corporate executive as impresario. More visible than any other corporate leader in America, Iacocca routinely took to the airwaves with a direct message: "If you can find a better buy than Chrysler, buy it!" Iacocca's style was bold, direct, forceful, and flamboyant. Ed Woolard, chairman of the board and chief executive officer of the Du Pont Company from 1989 to 1995, was less flamboyant but recognized the need for high visibility and public support in his effort to keep Du Pont profitable. Du Pont, the nation's largest chemical company and one of its largest polluters, is an obvious target of environmentalists. But Woolard, who referred to himself as the company's "chief environmentalist," was able to blunt some of the criticism by making concessions to environmentalists, increasing monitoring at Du Pont facilities, and developing recycling and other technologies that protect the environment.[29] In the 1990s Iacocca's role (as visible corporate leader) was assumed by Michael Eisner, head of the Walt Disney Corporation, who frequently appeared on television to tout the various attractions of his company.

Iacocca and Eisner may represent special cases; most corporate executives prefer to be less visible and resist the cult of personality.[30] For many top executives, public attention is unwelcome because scandals and corporate salaries are the typical lightning rods that attract attention from the press and the public. In addition, the inside and outside games have become increasingly demanding in the era of e-commerce and rapid technological change. Most CEOs have their hands full just trying to stay up with the competition. Furthermore, corporate boards seem less willing to tolerate questionable performance from their top executives. In 2000, CEOs Jill Barad of Mattel,

Douglas Ivester of Coca-Cola, and Dale Morrison of Campbell Soup were all let go after three years or less at the helm because their companies were losing money.[31]

By the late 1990s Microsoft chairman Bill Gates could no longer maintain his preferred low profile. The richest man in the United States, whose company was on trial for antitrust violations, made increasing numbers of public appearances, including testifying before Congress, in an effort to keep his company from being split up by the government. In the end, Gates's foray into the public spotlight did not deter judge Thomas Penfield Jackson from finding against Microsoft and ordering the break-up of the company.[32] In the summer of 2000, Ford chief Jacques Nasser took to the airwaves to deliver his message that throughout the crisis generated by the recall of Bridgestone/Firestone tires (standard equipment on Ford Explorers), Ford's number 1 priority was the "safety and trust" of its customers.

Decision Making

Within corporations many decisions are made by managers, with minimal input from boards of directors; other decisions are made by boards, despite opposition from managers. As a general rule, managers are free to make strategic decisions as long as the bottom line is favorable. When the corporation begins to flounder, board members intervene. In short, corporate boards are most active in times of crisis.

If boards are seldom dominant, they are nevertheless more important than they used to be. Corporate boards were once regarded as little more than rubber stamps; decisions were made by top managers and then were simply ratified by members of the board. The role of the board, it seemed, was to legitimate management decisions and to convince investors that the corporation was in fact being guided, or at least monitored, by a distinguished panel of leading citizens.

Since the early 1980s, this practice has changed, not dramatically perhaps, but noticeably. First, boards are now much more diverse demographically. Women and minorities in growing numbers now sit on boards, which means a greater variety of viewpoints and more lively debates on topics such as affirmative action and the difficulties faced by women in the corporation. A recent census of corporate boards found that women occupy 11 percent of the board seats of Fortune 500 companies, and that 86 percent of the Fortune 500 boards included at least one woman director.[33] A lone African American on a corporate board may not be able to win a showdown vote, but, as most boards prefer to operate by consensus, the first response to a protest by a minority board member is likely to be a search for a compromise.

Second, boards have given greater representation to outsiders—bankers, lawyers, and others who do not work for the company. According to one estimate, by the 1980s about 65 percent of corporate directors were outsiders, meaning that managers occupied fewer seats than before.[34] Although many of these outsiders are handpicked by the managers, the potential for dissent is greater than it used to be. Normally, one or more of these outside directors plays a leadership role on the board. A third trend is to place limits on interlocking directorates in which board members are selected from institutions that have official dealings with the company, such as banks, insurance companies, or law firms. The goal of all these trends is to reduce conflicts of interest and biases that limit the vision and cloud the judgment of corporate boards.

The significance of these trends is that corporate boards, more than ever before, are in a position to voice vigorous dissent, to challenge management decisions, and to identify the corporation's best interest without regard to personal circumstances. These trends increase the potential leverage of boards over managers. Opposition on the board can be dealt with in a variety of ways, however. In March 1991 both Chrysler and Sears voted to reduce the size of their boards—moves that appeared to be motivated by a desire to limit dissent. In the case of Chrysler, one of the seats that was eliminated belonged to United Auto Workers chief Owen Bieber; in the Sears case, reducing the board from fifteen to ten members was seen as a way of making it more difficult for dissident shareholder Robert Monks (a leading shareholder activist) to win election to the board.[35]

Like other institutions important in American politics, corporate boards have found it useful to delegate certain tasks to committees, which then make recommendations to the full board. This practice conserves time and permits some board members to develop enough expertise to challenge managers. Corporate boards have also established audit committees, compensation committees, and nominating committees, which exercise growing influence in decision making.

One way to grasp the role of corporate boards in corporate decision making is to imagine a situation in which the U.S. president's cabinet, selected by the president, is vested with the authority to make policy for the federal government, to fire White House aides, and ultimately to fire the president. Such an arrangement would probably encourage the president and his aides to be more mindful of cabinet opinions. Similarly, corporate boards can influence decisions without having to resort to the ultimate weapon of dismissal.

Strategies and Policies

Although achieving or maintaining profitability and increasing shareholder value are the predominant goals of corporate managers and boards, the strategies and policies for realizing these goals are not always obvious. These strategies and policies include everything from decisions about how much to pay employees to how to comply with government regulations, even whether to merge with another corporation or whether to divest the company of certain divisions.

Adaptability

If corporations are to prosper in a competitive environment, they must be able to adapt to changing circumstances and trends. This is, perhaps, more true today than ever before. The question is not whether corporations are capable of changing but whether they are capable of changing in time. A business tottering on the edge of bankruptcy is desperate enough to try something drastic; a corporation whose strategic decisions will lead to trouble in five to ten years may not yet perceive the need for a new approach.

In the late 1960s and early 1970s the U.S. automakers (Ford, GM, and Chrysler) ignored the handwriting on the wall—the growing popularity of small, economical foreign cars—preferring instead to continue the old, familiar pattern of large cars and large inventories in the United States. Before and after the OPEC oil embargo of 1973–1974 various executives proposed a shift to smaller cars, but Henry Ford II (for one) rejected such suggestions, dismissing small cars as "little shitboxes."[36] Interestingly, Ford did produce a small car for European and other markets, and by the 1980s the Escort was the company's leading seller. The "Big Three" auto companies survived the 1980s (Chrysler needed a government bailout in the late 1970s) by diversifying their products to include several varieties of minivans and light trucks, but they more or less yielded the smaller car market to Honda and Toyota. By the 1990s they were better informed, but not fully reformed, featuring sport utility vehicles that offered room and comfort but not fuel economy.

The basic problem with U.S. auto companies in the 1970s was the unwillingness of top managers to take a long-term perspective. Many other companies suffer from the same affliction. Unable to demonstrate a favorable return on investment in a few years, they routinely reject proposals for risky innovations. Westinghouse, a large company that produced home appliances and other products, was more or less the peer of General Electric (GE) in the 1960s and early 1970s. But Westinghouse was unable to keep up with the changes in the industry—foreign competition, new product lines, and so forth—and suffered severe decline and eventual demise; meanwhile GE continued to be one of America's most successful companies. Indeed, GE has won *Fortune* magazine's "Most Admired Companies" competition for the last three years (see Box 3-1).[37] A big reason for GE's success has been its willingness to unload divisions within the company that were not performing at a high level. CEO Jack Welch followed a strategy by which "businesses" within the company had to be number 1 or 2 in their fields, or they would be sold off. GE eventually got out of several of its previous "core businesses" such as computers, nuclear power, and televisions.[38]

Corporations differ in their inclination and their ability to shift gears quickly. According to economics professors Walter Adams and James Brock, size is a factor—big companies are more conservative and more bureaucratic than small companies.[39] H. Ross Perot, who attempted to change the policies of General Motors from within, remarked that changing GM's corporate culture was like "teaching an elephant to tap dance."[40] Frustrated, Perot resigned from GM's board and turned to other pursuits (such as running for president in 1992 and 1996). Competition is another factor. Public utilities, which until recently faced limited competition for customers, have been notoriously slow to change. Only strong pressure from state public utility commissions in the 1970s persuaded electric utility companies to build fewer plants and redesign their rate structures to promote energy conservation. In contrast, companies that face tough competition, such those in the computer and electronics industries, have to adapt quickly to changing circumstances. Presently Xerox, a firm whose name was synonymous with copying machines in the 1970s and hugely successful at that time, is struggling to survive in a market that features a continuous stream of new products and companies.[41]

Symbols and the Corporate Image

A positive corporate image is a tremendous asset, and a negative image is a major liability. A drug company that symbolizes safety and reliability is likely to prosper; if the same company is suddenly seen as careless or dishonest, its sales plummet. Clever company executives appreciate the close connection between symbols and their company's image. They also recognize that symbols may reinforce or undermine company policy.

A corporate symbol may be a building, a press release, a charitable contribution, a logo, an advertisement, a year-end bonus, or an appointment. When U.S. Steel changed its name to USX, the company was sending an unmistakable message to investors that a new era had begun: a steel company was becoming a diversified conglomerate. When beer manufacturers started running television ads in the late 1990s emphasizing the need for designated drivers, they were trying to avoid the image of a socially irresponsible corporation. Of course, they had the benefit of watching the tobacco companies plumb new depths on the image front. Joe Camel, once viewed as a kind of innocent cartoon figure, had been definitively linked to efforts to sell cigarettes to children, and many states were running powerful antismoking ads on television. Cigarette manufacturers appeared to be in public relations quandary from which there was no escape.

There is no doubt that corporate executives pay attention to symbols. Often, however, they fail to recognize what kind of symbol they are creating, or they have blind spots about the impact of certain symbols on important constituencies. When the management of the Mitsubishi auto assembly plant in Illinois faced a lawsuit filed by female employees alleging sexual harassment in 1994, they probably couldn't have imagined how bad things could get. But within a few years the Equal Employment Opportunity Commission had also filed against them, Jesse Jackson and the National Organization for Women were calling for a boycott of their products, and they had to hire former secretary of labor Lynn Martin, to give some credibility to a review of plant procedures. By 1998, after lurid details of harassment in the plant had been made public by the *Chicago Tribune* and the *New York Times,* the company agreed to pay $34 million in damages to women who had been harassed, and plant production levels were down by 25 percent.[42]

Another negative symbol is the "golden parachute," which became common during the early 1980s when corporate mergers and takeovers swept the country. A golden parachute is a contractual clause that offers top corporate executives a generous severance payment if they are fired as part of a successful takeover. The stated rationale for golden parachutes is that they discourage managerial resistance to hostile takeovers that will ultimately benefit investors. But former labor secretary and Harvard University professor Robert Reich said the golden parachute suggests that "the only way shareholders could trust corporate executives not to feather their nests at the shareholders' expense was to provide them a prefeathered nest at the shareholders' expense."[43] By the 1990s many large companies had responded to the concerns expressed by large shareholders about golden parachutes and other takeover defenses by abolishing them and, at the same time, providing new avenues for shareholder input into company decisions.[44]

Overall, corporate America has an image problem. The salaries of top corporate executives in the 1990s grew at a rate that far exceeded that of workers, or even corporate profits. A 1998 survey of 365 of the largest companies in the United States found that the average annual compensation for CEOs was over $10 million, most if it in stock options.[45] For the average American, compensation at this level is difficult to understand as anything other than a representation of corporate greed and power. Thus it is not surprising that most Americans think big corporations have too much power over too many aspects of American life, including the political system.[46] These negative perceptions are acknowledged within corporate boardrooms, but as long as shareholders are satisfied with a company's performance, there is no real pressure to curb corporate salaries.

Two Views of Profitability

All corporations pursue higher profits, but a recurring question is how to balance short-term costs and long-term benefits. Johnson & Johnson decided to recall Tylenol products after several people died from ingesting poisoned capsules in 1982. The recall and subsequent design and production of tamper-proof packaging was very costly. In the long run, however, the decision enhanced Johnson & Johnson's credibility in a market that depends on consumer confidence, and the company regained its pre-recall market share within a few years. In 1991, when two people died in the state of Washington from Sudafed capsules laced with cyanide, the maker of the product, the Burroughs

Wellcome Company, seemed to take a lesson from Johnson & Johnson because it wasted no time taking Sudafed capsules off the market.

Corporations do not always take enlightened, decisive action in times of emergency, however. In the late 1970s the Firestone Tire and Rubber Company, whose steel-belted radial tires were prone to blow-outs, tread separations, and other dangerous defects, continued to manufacture and sell these tires to unsuspecting customers despite considerable evidence that the tires were hazardous. When pressed by the National Highway Traffic Safety Administration for performance data, Firestone refused and went to court to prevent the agency from releasing to the press the results of a consumer survey. In October 1978, after months of controversy, Firestone agreed to a massive recall. By that time, however, the company's reputation for safety had been badly damaged by hundreds of accidents resulting in at least thirty-four deaths, and the company had a public image of greed and defiance.[47] In the summer of 2000 Firestone once again found itself in the middle of a tire recall controversy that cast doubt on its concern for customer safety (see the next section).

Most people would applaud Johnson & Johnson and condemn Firestone. Confronted by evidence that a product is unsafe, it would seem that a company should act swiftly to withdraw the product or improve it. But the issue is not always so clear-cut. When does a product become unsafe? All automobiles are unsafe to some extent and could be made safer. Should companies make their products as safe as they can be? Should companies make some products safer, others cheaper, so that consumers have a choice? If so, why not allow one company to produce a relatively safe product while another company produces a relatively cheap product? Should consumers be free to place cost above safety? And who should define safety—the companies or the government? At a minimum the public might insist that companies be honest about their products' virtues and vices. But does this require that they go out of their way to reveal flaws and problems? Finally, there are questions about relative risk. Do certain pesticides and preservatives serve a public health function by controlling or eliminating harmful organisms in food, or are their own toxic qualities more of a risk than a benefit to the average consumer?

In the contemporary economy questions of long-term benefits, and profitability, are continually at issue in new and emerging industries such as e-commerce. It seems that most everyone is certain that dot-coms will eventually make money; the question is when and which ones. One of the founding fathers of e-commerce, Jeff Bezos, is confident that his company, Amazon.com, will be the first to return real profits to investors. By 1999 Amazon.com could boast of an impressive customer base of more than 23 million persons and revenues of over $1.5 billion. The problem was that it lost over $700 million for the year. Bezos is predicting that by the end of 2001 his company's revenues will be up to $5 billion, with $1 billion in profit.[48] Meanwhile, e-commerce is spreading like wildfire, with old companies joining new ones in selling their wares over the Internet. The commercial value of Internet activity in 1999 was estimated to be $100 billion, and it is expected to increase more than tenfold by 2003.[49]

After the Board Has Met

After corporate strategies and policies have been established, they must be implemented and their impact must be assessed. In many cases, the impacts reach far beyond the boardroom, affecting many citizens and even entire communities.

Implementation Problems

The implementation of corporate policies is seldom automatic. Just as governments depend on corporate cooperation to implement a policy such as environmental protection, corporations depend on government cooperation to carry out policies such as plant construction. Many businesses have been unable to expand because of antipollution laws that forbid new plants in "nonattainment" areas if a new plant would degrade air quality. Federal agencies such as the Federal Trade Commission have to decide whether they will allow a media giant like Time Warner to purchase America Online (AOL) because of the control the new company might exert over the Internet. For many large corporations and public utilities, implementation of a policy is often the first step in a long chain of problematic events.

The implementation of corporate policies is especially tricky in an intergovernmental setting. In the 1980s many electric utility companies were unable to build nuclear power plants because of government disapproval, either by the Nuclear Regulatory Commission (NRC) or by a state agency. For example, the Pacific Gas and Electric Company (PG&E) needed the approval of the NRC and the California Energy Conservation Commission to build a nuclear plant. Although the approval of the NRC was assured, that of the Energy Conservation Commission was not. Citing a California statute banning new nuclear power plants in the state until a safe means of nuclear waste disposal had been found, the Energy Conservation Commission rejected PG&E's request. The decision was subsequently upheld by the U.S. Supreme Court.[50] Furthermore, the federal government has still not found a solution to the nuclear waste disposal problem.

Implementation is also highly problematic for corporations characterized by a high degree of decentralization, strong professionalism, or both. When a newspaper or magazine owner leans too heavily on a reporter or editor, the journalist may resign rather than submit to censorship. When a hospital administrator instructs doctors to cut costs to improve the hospital's financial picture, doctors may cite the Hippocratic oath—and utter a few other oaths as well—as grounds for refusal. Multinational corporations face special challenges in implementing policies across a far-flung empire. Indeed, this was Union Carbide's defense when it tried to explain a poisonous gas leak that killed an estimated two thousand people in Bhopal, India, in 1984. According to Union Carbide headquarters, its foreign subsidiary failed to conform to company safety policies, with catastrophic results.

Despite these difficulties, there are several reasons why corporate policies are more easily implemented than bureaucratic rules and regulations. First, in the private sector it is easier to fire people who are not performing well than it is in the public sector. Although white-collar corporate employees may take their employers to court if they believe they have been fired without just cause, most of the time corporations can make a convincing case that their actions were not arbitrary, capricious, or reckless. In comparison, government regulations controlling civil service employment include procedures and appeal rights that provide more protection to employees. Second, the private sector has access to considerable financial resources that help to remove obstacles. Corporate lobbyists, or trade association lobbyists representing smaller businesses, intervene directly to prevent government agencies from spoiling the plans of private sector firms. And, of course, corporate and trade association political action committees (PACs) remind politicians that reelection is easier if business interests are on their side. Third, the private sector can use gifted public relations professionals when mass persuasion is necessary. Indeed, many of the leading media experts—the advertising wizards of Madison Avenue and others—are known to politicians, who also make use of their services to win elections. Corporations, like government bureaucracies, face obstacles when they propose controversial policies, but they have more power to remove such obstacles from their path.

In Search of Golden Eggs

To many politicians, corporations are geese that lay golden eggs. This observation is especially true at the state and local levels, where politicians perceive corporations as sources of jobs, taxes, economic development, and prosperity. To persuade corporations to settle within their boundaries, state and local politicians offer special subsidies and tax breaks, and, if these overtures are successful, the politicians can take credit for a coup. The embattled Mitsubishi plant, mentioned previously, has been considered a great prize by political officials in the twin cities of Normal and Bloomington, Illinois, since it opened in 1988. It is Mitsubishi's only plant in the United States, and it employs more than three thousand workers, who make around $24 per hour; an excellent source of employment in central Illinois.[51]

Many communities owe their revitalization to public-spirited corporate leaders. During the 1950s the Mellon family joined forces with the Democratic "machine" to clean up the air in Pittsburgh; in addition, they spearheaded the Pittsburgh renaissance, which included the construction of picturesque skyscrapers and public parks in the city's Golden Triangle. Following a second renaissance in 1988, Rand McNally hailed Pittsburgh as the most livable city in America.[52] In Minneapolis the Downtown Council, a business coalition, supported an extensive downtown revitalization program in the 1950s, including the building of pedestrian skywalks that protect shoppers from Minnesota's harsh winters. Since then, Minneapolis has been praised for its favorable business climate, progressive government, and cultural amenities. In addition, corporations in the Twin Cities (Minneapolis and Saint Paul) have established a tradition of donating generously to local charities. It is no coincidence that many leading corporations are headquartered in Pittsburgh and Minneapolis. In general, local owners demonstrate greater community spirit than absentee owners.

Pioneering corporations offer benefits not just to particular states and communities but to society at large. Consider, for example, the history of Bell Laboratories. Among its many achievements were the development of coaxial cable transmission and microwave radio relay technology, which significantly reduced the cost of long-distance communication. In addition, Bell developed the transistor, which laid the groundwork for portable radios, space flight, and computers. From 1925 to 1975 scientists from Bell Labs acquired an astonishing 18,000 patents.[53] Bell's accomplishments, and those of IBM's Thomas J. Watson Laboratory and Xerox's Palo Alto Research Center (PARC), are the inspiration for Microsoft's new research facility dubbed "Bill Labs."[54]

In recent years, the development of innovative technologies with far-reaching implications has become an almost daily occurrence. Breakthroughs in personal computers, software, the Internet, and electronic transmission (broadband) have not only changed communities (Silicon Valley in California; Redmond, Washington, home of Microsoft; Cambridge, Mass.) but have also brought the world closer together. Still, these new technologies give rise to many questions and concerns. To what extent should the Internet be regulated to prevent fraud? Should e-commerce be subject to taxation? How concerned should we be that most e-commerce is conducted by individuals and families with above-average incomes?[55]

Corporations also demonstrate a sense of social responsibility by donating money to charity, but they differ greatly in their generosity. Many corporations give less than 1 percent of their pretax profits to charity, whereas others give up to 5 percent, which is the maximum tax-deductible contribution allowed by the IRS.[56] Some of the charitable programs set up by corporations have produced compelling results. For example, Merrill Lynch set up a program in 1988 whereby it promised to pay full college expenses for 251 first graders from some of the worst neighborhoods in ten cities around the United States if they graduated from high school in 2000. With the help of the Urban League, over 90 percent of the students included in this program went to college in the fall of 2000.[57] Prominent corporate individuals also give to charitable and humanitarian causes by donating their own money to organizations or by setting up foundations to support worthy causes. Much like the corporate barons of one hundred years ago (Fords, Mellons, Carnegies, and so forth) the new breed of very rich, including Bill Gates, the Hewletts and the Packards of Hewlett-Packard, and many others, are establishing foundations. Much of the foundation money goes to education, but other popular causes include poverty, hunger, affordable housing, and health care.[58] Interestingly, gifts to the arts are not as popular among contemporary philanthropists as gifts to education and helping the poor.

Decisions regarding charitable contributions, although they are significant expenditures, pale in comparison to such big-ticket corporate decisions as those concerning wage settlements, plant modernization, diversification, dividend payouts, and compliance with government regulations. Moreover, these decisions often resemble a zero-sum game in which one party's gain is another's loss. Corporations often must choose between higher profits or higher wages, expansion or environmental protection, higher dividends or a secure future for the company. The natural instinct of all corporations is to pursue higher profits and stock values; today's managers tend to share this goal because much of their compensation is in the form of stocks or stock options. And, increasingly, ordinary employees are also shareholders, as many corporations have extended stock ownership opportunities to employees at all levels. Still, despite the added complication of large-scale employee stock ownership, it is safe to say that the most frequent beneficiaries of corporate decisions are the investors and managers. Employees also benefit, but they are the ones most likely to suffer (wage cuts or lost jobs) in hard times.

Shattered Dreams

Corporate policies can have devastating consequences for workers, taxpayers, and consumers. Unemployment is perhaps the most common negative consequence of corporate policies. For most people unemployment is a bitter pill to swallow. Unemployed workers experience self-doubt, guilt, shame, depression, and despair, which often affect their physical and mental health. Alcoholism, child abuse, spouse abuse, and suicide are occasional side effects. In American society, as in many others, a person's self-image is intimately connected to his or her job. Moreover, unemployment almost always has serious consequences for a family's economic well-being. Even if another member of the household works during the period of unemployment, that one income may not be sufficient, and finding a new job at comparable pay is often difficult.

The effects of unemployment are especially harsh in certain communities and certain segments of society. Small towns, long dependent on a particular industry, may have difficulty coping when a company decides to mothball a plant. Restaurants and shops may close their doors forever, and city services may decline as the city's tax revenue drops. A virtual ghost town may result. Black Americans are disproportionately affected by unemployment, and the black community suffers acutely when unemployment increases. In 1983, at the end of a recession, black teenage unemployment reached nearly 50 percent, an alarmingly high level; even in the booming economy of 1999 the black teenage unemployment rate was nearly 30 percent.[59] These conditions are breeding grounds for crime and drug abuse. A society that tolerates high unemployment pays a high price in many ways.

Unemployment need not be tragic if it is temporary and if it leads to a new, better job. In fact, when workers are laid off from relatively unproductive jobs and find more productive ones, society benefits. Many Western countries have retraining programs that facilitate transition from one job to another by paying for the unemployed, in some cases for as long as two years, to receive training in schools or on the job. In contrast, job-training programs in the United States are severely limited in scope and focus. Most private job training is geared to a particular job rather than to acquisition of a broader set of marketable skills. The U.S. government conducts job-training programs, but they are generally restricted to the unskilled and welfare recipients; there are few programs to retrain people with obsolete skills or those who wish to improve their skills. Moreover, government outlays for job training have not been increasing since the early 1980s. For all these reasons, the consequences of unemployment in the United States are worse than they need be.

Bankruptcy is another possible consequence of corporate policies. From a societal point of view, the occasional bankruptcy is not alarming if it is caused by changing market conditions or technological advances in related industries. But the collapse of a pivotal company can be disturbing, especially if the company is part of a complex web of other companies. Society can ill afford the bankruptcy of major companies in industries that are heavily concentrated or that are central to commerce or national security. Even more disastrous is the collapse of an entire industry. When such catastrophes occur, taxpayers are often asked to mop up the mess. In the 1980s the savings and loan industry collapsed and the federal government had to step in to salvage the situation as best it could. Although this debacle had many causes, including shortsighted government deregulatory policy and a recessionary economy, poor investment choices and extravagant spending by savings and loan executives contributed greatly to the problem.[60] The whole mess ended up costing national taxpayers about $130 billion.[61] This same fiasco forced several state governments to pay millions of dollars to shore up collapsing thrift banks.[62] The cost of a bailout can be very high indeed.

Taxpayers pay in still another way for corporate mistakes. Many industries, especially defense and aerospace, receive large amounts of their revenue from public funds. When these industries are wasteful and inefficient, the costs ultimately are borne by taxpayers. Although the government is partly to blame for awarding these contracts in the first place, or for tolerating cost overruns, corporations bear primary responsibility.

If taxpayers pay for some corporate mistakes, consumers pay for others. There have been numerous instances in which products were sold to millions of consumers and later determined to be unsafe, causing thousands of injuries and hundreds of deaths. To name just a few, the Dalkon Shield, an intrauterine birth control device marketed by the A. H. Robins Company in the early 1970s; Eli Lilly's arthritis drug Oraflex; Ford's Pinto, which had an exploding gas tank; Manville's asbestos; and Dow Corning's silicone breast implants. It is impossible to estimate the costs of these disasters in shattered dreams and shattered lives.

A prolonged spectacle of corporate misdeeds, mistakes, and blame casting took place in the summer of 2000. The main players were Bridgestone/Firestone, Ford, Congress, the National Highway Traffic Safety Administration (NHTSA), and the media. The story first broke in Houston, when a local television station reported on tire safety problems, after which the NHTSA received numerous complaints and opened an investigation. Then, on August 7, 2000, Bridgestone/Firestone announced a recall of 6.5 million tires, most of which were installed on sport utility vehicles, in particular, Ford Explorers. These tires had been shown to be prone to tread separation and blowouts, especially when being driven at high speeds on hot days. At least 101 deaths and more than 400 injuries in the United States were linked to the recalled tires. Of course, Firestone didn't have enough tires on hand to replace all those being recalled, and consumers were told that they would have to wait months to get them. Soon Congress intervened, holding hearings to grill the CEOs of Bridgestone/Firestone (Masatoshi Ono) and Ford (Jacques Nasser) about many aspects of the recall. When did they first discern a pattern involving Explorers and the tires? What had been reported to the NHTSA and when? How safe were the millions of recalled tires still on the road?[63]

With the recall in all the headlines, Nasser moved quickly, appearing on television, first to reassure customers that Ford was committed to their safety and was replacing their tires as quickly as possible, and then to blame Firestone for not being more forthcoming about information linking the tires on Explorers to blowouts and accidents. It seems that Bridgestone had received more than 1,500 legal claims, dating back to 1997, involving the recalled tires. Firestone counterattacked by pointing out that the only way the Explorer had passed rollover tests was by underinflating the tires. Thus Ford had contributed greatly to the problem by designing a vehicle that would either be prone to roll over or would have to run on tires that were not fully inflated, or both. Bridgestone, a Japanese company that bought Firestone in 1988, joined in the finger pointing by suggesting that the bad tires had come from American plants, where equipment did not operate properly. Members of Congress were not amused when they learned that State Farm Insurance had sent the NHTSA a memo in 1998 pointing out the numerous claims it had received involving Firestone tires and Ford Explorers but that the agency had taken no action; indeed, it could not find the memo. They then learned that Ford and Firestone had faced similar patterns of problems in Saudi Arabia and Venezuela, that Ford had even agreed to replace the tires in Saudi Arabia in 1999, but neither company had said anything about all this to the NHTSA.[64] Tire retail businesses around the country began to take down their Firestone signs. As the crisis continued, Bridgestone/Firestone CEO Ono resigned and was replaced by the executive vice president, John Lampe, an American.

Redemption

Corporations do learn from their mistakes. Despite a rather grim future outlook in the early 1980s, U.S. automobile companies did rather well in the 1990s. Many U.S. manufacturing firms whose products are environmentally damaging for reasons ranging from plastic packaging to toxic chemicals have begun to change their processes to make them more environmentally friendly and to develop recycling and waste management programs in order to stave off criticism by citizens and politicians. After observing steep rate hikes and even blackouts in the aftermath of electricity deregulation in states such as Wisconsin and California, other states are taking a more cautious approach to deregulation, with governments and companies working together to ensure that ample capacity is present to meet peak demands without sudden price increases and/or blackouts.[65] The telecommunications industry has multiplied the number of ways we communicate with one another and the commercial and educational value of that communication. Furthermore, the bottom line looks very good; corporate profits overall have increased at record rates throughout the 1990s.[66]

If companies learn from their mistakes, they also learn from the successes of risk-taking pioneers; a "diffusion of innovations" often occurs in the private sector.[67] From some of its early applications, such as editing and production in newsrooms, manufacturing assembly lines, and grocery store checkout lines, computers, particularly personal computers, have transformed the way Americans work and businesses operate. Indeed, the personal computer has penetrated almost all workplaces in the United States; it is hard to believe that there were few personal computers in use twenty years ago. The Internet and biotechnology appear to be the next agents of commercial revolution. Presently, over $100 billion worth of commercial activity is conducted through the Internet, with almost half of this being commerce between businesses.[68] Now that the human genome has been fully decoded by the Celera Corporation, major pharmaceutical companies around the world are exploring the potential applications for treating diseases and other maladies.[69]

During the 1980s and 1990s many U.S. corporations followed exhortations from academics and market analysts to undertake a management approach, commonly attributed to Japanese corporations, that emphasized teamwork between management and labor, inventory control, customer satisfaction, and demonstrable results for investors.[70] So-called "total quality management" (TQM) is widely credited with having turned around many stumbling corporations in the United States. However, as discussed in Chapter 2, the most significant component of this new approach to management was probably the downsizing of corporate workforces in the early 1990s, which affected both blue- and white-collar employees. Although TQM and, more generally, corporate learning have produced positive results for many companies, there is a danger that corporations will respond too quickly to the latest fad. Corporations are probably wise to heed Thomas Peters and Robert Waterman's admonition to stick to their knitting and concentrate on what they do best.[71] Perhaps the best kind of corporate learning is that which recognizes the importance of frequent experimentation. This permits corporations to move in new directions, but one step at a time.

Corporations and smaller businesses have also learned that joint ventures with government (public-private partnerships) can be successful, even profitable. During the 1990s, some of the worst areas of major cities, including Boston, Chicago, Cleveland, New York, Philadelphia, and San Francisco were turned into functioning neighborhoods through the combined efforts of community development corporations, local governments, and private companies. Aided by national legislation such as the Community Reinvestment Act and by a national public/private partnership called the National Community Development Initiative, cities have been able to attract businesses back to depressed neighborhoods, such as the South Bronx, which had been all but abandoned previously. A big part of the community revitalization picture was the willingness of cities and community-based organizations to take on the problems of crime and deteriorating schools. Dealing with these problems was a necessary condition for private sector investment. Another major piece was the emergence of intermediaries, such as the Local Initiatives Support Corporation (LISC) and the Enterprise Foundation, which connected major corporate and foundation capital to local community development corporations and other grassroots groups. Together LISC and Enterprise have channeled $5.5 billion to nearly three thousand community development corporations, which has led to the construction of almost 200,000 housing units and millions of square feet of commercial and industrial space in major cities throughout the country.[72]

Summary

The distinction between public policy and private policy is a cultural artifact. Many Western democracies regard industrial policy as public policy; in the United States, industrial policy is private, with some governmental supervision. Many Western democracies view rail transportation, steel production, electricity, and telecommunications as public enterprises; in the United States, these are, for the most part, private. Some Western democracies rely on the government to employ a substantial number of people and to retrain employees when necessary; in the United States, the private sector provides most of the employment and training.

To use E. E. Schattschneider's terms, we have "privatized" conflict by removing certain issues from public debate.[73] The privatization of conflict limits participation in the policymaking process, but it does not limit policy effects. As a result, there is a mismatch between the importance of many private decisions and the degree of public involvement in them. Most citizens are bystanders and spectators when these critical decisions are made. Although ordinary people are not completely powerless, their ability to affect corporate decisions is quite limited.

The trend in the 1960s and 1970s was toward greater government intervention in the private sector to promote goals such as affirmative action, affordable housing, environmental protection, and consumer protection. In the 1980s and 1990s, however, government intervention, particularly that of the federal government, diminished somewhat as a result of deregulation and privatization. Some see an advantage in these changes because privatizing conflicts reduces the number of issues on which public policymakers must achieve consensus and thus makes governing less difficult. Regardless of how one assesses its merits, the trend toward less government intervention leaves more decisions in the hands of corporate managers and corporate boards.

In making strategic decisions, managers and board members of publicly held corporations are influenced by investors and their perceived interests. But it is often difficult to discern the course of action that will yield maximum benefits for the corporation and its investors. There is the issue of short-term versus long-term profitability, the need to stay on a par with the competition, and the desire to blunt criticisms from consumers and the government. Privately held corporations have greater flexibility in making decisions than government agencies and legislative bodies, but they have similar difficulty in determining what will produce the most favorable bottom line.

Not surprisingly, corporations have made some spectacular mistakes. Employees are the most obvious victims of corporate mistakes; layoffs inflict economic and psychological damage. Moreover, neither the government nor the private sector goes very far to ensure that displaced workers will land on their feet. The U.S. government does little to cushion the blow of unemployment and to prepare workers for new jobs. Consumers also suffer when corporations make mistakes. Despite the work of government agencies such as the Consumer Product Safety Commission, the Food and Drug Administration, the National Highway Traffic Safety Administration, and the Occupational Safety and Health Administration, companies still produce defective automobiles, tires, birth control devices, drugs, toys, and power plants. Finally, taxpayers are harmed by poor corporate judgment. Cost overruns on government contracts and bailouts of failed corporations or industries are the most obvious examples. Companies do learn from their mistakes, but they learn slowly. In the meantime, the nation pays a heavy price for their errors.

Our intention in evaluating boardroom politics is not to be overly harsh. The government bears partial responsibility for many corporate mistakes. In appraising boardroom politics, we must ask not whether it is perfect, but whether it is superior or inferior to other political processes where the scope of conflict is broader. By examining these other political processes in the chapters that follow, we will be able to make useful comparisons.

Notes

1. Harold Lasswell, *Who Gets What, When, How* (Cleveland: Meridian Books, 1958).
2. Charles E. Lindblom, *Politics and Markets* (New York: Basic Books, 1977), 171–172.
3. Harvey Feigenbaum, Jeffrey Henig, and Chris Hamnett, *The Shrinking of the State* (Cambridge: Cambridge University Press, 1999), 13.
4. Ibid., 59–86.
5. E. S. Savas, *Privatization and Public-Private Partnerships* (New York: Chatham House, 2000), 72; E. S. Savas, *Privatization: The Key to Better Government* (Chatham, N.J.: Chatham House, 1987), 131.
6. Mark Schlesinger, Robert A. Dotwart, and Richard T. Pulice, "Competitive Bidding and States' Purchase of Services: The Case of Mental Health Care in Massachusetts," *Journal of Policy Analysis and Management* (winter 1986): 245–259.
7. Savas, *Privatization and Public-Private Partnerships,* 73; data derived from Rowan Miranda and Karlyn Andersen, "Alternative Service Delivery in Local Government, 1982–1992," *Municipal Yearbook 1994* (Washington D.C.: International Management Association, 1994).
8. Jon Jeter, "A Winning Combination in Indianapolis," *Washington Post,* September 21, 1997, A3.
9. Council of State Governments, *Book of the States, 1997–98* (Lexington, Ky.: Council of State Governments, 1998), 32:485.
10. David Masci, "Telecom's Unfinished Business," *CQ Outlook,* March 8, 1999, 8–14.
11. Aaron Bernstein, "Too Much Corporate Power?" *Business Week,* September 11, 2000, 145–150.
12. Maggie McComas, "Atop the Fortune 500: A Survey of C.E.O.s," *Fortune,* April 28, 1986, 26–31. The Fortune 500 is a list compiled annually of the 500 publicly held U.S. industrial companies with the largest sales.
13. John Portz, "Politics, Plant Closings, and Public Policy: The Steel Valley Authority in Pittsburgh" (paper presented at the annual meeting of the Midwest Political Science Association, Chicago, April 9–11, 1987). See also USX Corporation, "Financial Highlights," 1999, online at usx.com/usxfh.htm, September 5, 2000.
14. Yochi J. Dreazen, "Labor Unions Turn to Mergers in Pursuit of Growth," *Wall Street Journal,* September 1, 2000, A2.

15. Martin Gilens and Craig Hertzman, "Corporate Ownership and News Bias: Newspaper Coverage of the 1996 Telecommunications Act," *Journal of Politics* 62 (May 2000): 369–286.
16. Doron P. Levin, "Chrysler Dividend Cut in Half," *New York Times*, March 8, 1991, D1.
17. See Bro Uttal, "Behind the Fall of Steve Jobs," *Fortune*, August 5, 1985, 20–24; and Peter Burrows, "Apple," *Business Week*, July 31, 2000, 102–113.
18. Keith Bradsher, "General Motors Raises the Stakes in Fuel Economy War with Ford," *New York Times*, August 3, 2000, C1.
19. Proxy resolutions are proposals introduced by shareholders and voted on by shareholders. If adopted, they become corporate policy.
20. *Munn v. Illinois,* 94 U.S. 118 (1877).
21. Mary H. Cooper, "Critics Question National Energy Policy," *CQ Outlook,* April 22, 2000, 6–11.
22. Jack Walker, "The Origins and Maintenance of Interest Groups in America," *American Political Science Review* 77 (June 1983): 390–406.
23. Donald Regan, quoted on the *MacNeil/Lehrer News Hour,* April 16, 1987.
24. Robert A. G. Monks, *The Emperor's Nightingale* (Reading, Mass.: Addison-Wesley, 1998), 68.
25. Alex Berenson, "Buccaneer, or the Shareholder's Best Friend?" *New York Times,* September 24, 2000, C1.
26. Arthur O'Sullivan and Steven M. Sheffrin, *Microeconomics,* 2d ed. (Upper Saddle River, N.J.: Prentice-Hall, 2001), 250–251; Robert Sherrill, *Why They Call It Politics,* 5th ed. (San Diego: Harcourt Brace Jovanovich, 1990), 465.
27. Michael Lewis, *The New, New Thing* (New York: W. W. Norton, 2000).
28. Lisa Mesdag, "The 50 Largest Private Industrial Companies," *Fortune,* May 31, 1982, 114.
29. John Holusha, "Ed Woolard Walks Du Pont's Tightrope," *New York Times,* October 14, 1990, sec. 3, p. 1.
30. Steven Prokesch, "Remaking the American CEO," *New York Times,* January 25, 1987, C1.
31. Ram Charan and Geoffrey Colvin, "The Right Fit," *Fortune,* April 17, 2000, 226–236.
32. See Jared Sandberg, "Microsoft's Six Fatal Errors," *Newsweek,* June 19, 2000, 23–28.
33. Catalyst, "Infobrief: Women on Corporate Boards," *The 1998 Catalyst Census of Women Board Directors of the Fortune 500,* 1998, online at http://www.catalyst-women.org/press/infobriefboards.html, September 2000; see also Christine Y. Chen and Jonathan Hickman, "America's 50 Best Companies for Minorities," *Fortune,* July 10, 2000, 190–200.
34. Victor Brudney, "The Independent Director—Heavenly City or Potemkin Village?" *Harvard Law Review* 95 (January 1982): 599.
35. *New York Times,* March 14, 1991, D1.
36. David Halberstam, *The Reckoning* (New York: Morrow, 1986), 462.
37. "America's Most Admired Companies," *Fortune,* February 21, 2000, 175–184.
38. See Monks, *The Emperor's Nightingale,* 96–97.
39. Walter Adams and James Brock, *The Bigness Complex* (New York: Pantheon Books, 1986).

40. Eric Gelman, "GM Boots Perot," *Newsweek*, December 15, 1986, 56–58.
41. Claudia H. Deutsch, "The Fading Copier King," *New York Times*, October 19, 2000, C1.
42. Reed Abelson, "Can Respect Be Mandated? Maybe Not Here," *New York Times*, September 10, 2000, sec. 3, p. 1.
43. Robert Reich, "Enterprise and Double Cross," *Washington Monthly*, January 1987, 17.
44. Leslie Wayne, "Seeking to Stay Out of Proxy Battles," *New York Times*, April 8, 1991, D1.
45. Frank Ackerman et al., eds., *The Political Economy of Inequality* (Washington, D.C.: Island Press, 2000), 64.
46. Michael Arndt, Wendy Zellner, and Peter Coy, "Too Much Corporate Power?" *Business Week*, September 11, 2000, 144–158.
47. Arthur Louis, "Lessons from the Firestone Fracas," *Fortune*, August 28, 1978, 44–48; Stuart Feldstein, "How Not to React to a Safety Controversy," *Business Week*, November 6, 1978, 65.
48. Mark Leibovich, "Child Prodigy, Online Pioneer," *Washington Post*, September 3, 2000, A1; "Can Amazon Make It?" *Business Week*, July 10, 2000, 38–43.
49. Kathy Koch, "Riding the Internet Express," *CQ Outlook*, March 11, 2000, 9.
50. *Pacific Gas & Electric Co. v. State Energy Resources Conservation and Development Commission*, 461 U.S. 190 (1983).
51. Abelson, "Can Respect Be Mandated?," sec. 3, p. 14.
52. Two of the authors of this volume, who grew up in Pittsburgh, heartily agree. The third agrees with Frank Lloyd Wright, who, when asked what should be done about Pittsburgh, thought for a moment and replied, "Abandon it!"
53. John Brooks, *Telephone* (New York: Harper and Row, 1976), 12–16. Dale Russakoff, "A High-Tech, High-Stakes Race Begins," *Washington Post*, national weekly edition, June 15, 1987, 10.
54. Randall E. Stross, "Mr. Gates Builds His Brain Trust," *Fortune*, December 8, 1997, online at http://www.fortune.com/fortune/1997/971208/mic.html, September 14, 2000.
55. Adriel Bettelheim, "Policing the Internet Boom," *CQ Outlook*, February 20, 1999, 8–14.
56. William Ouchi, *The M-Form Society* (Reading, Mass.: Addison-Wesley, 1984), 16–31, 192–193.
57. Kate Zernike, "Pupils Prosper from an Investment," *New York Times*, August 2, 2000, A11.
58. Reed Abelson, "New Philanthropists Put Donations to Work," *New York Times*, July 6, 2000, C1.
59. *Economic Report of the President* (Washington, D.C.: Government Printing Office, 2000), 355, table B-41.
60. Mark C. Rom, *Public Spirit in the Thrift Tragedy* (Pittsburgh: University of Pittsburgh Press, 1996).
61. U.S. House of Representatives, Committee on Banking and Financial Services, *Hearing on the Thrift Depositor Protection Oversight Board Abolishment Act*, September 9, 1997, online at http:// commdocs.house.gov/committees/bank/hba43661.000/hba43661_0.htm, August 24, 2000.

62. Saundra Saperstein, "The S&L Crisis Is Over, but It Won't Go Away," *Washington Post,* national weekly edition, September 2, 1985, 33–34.
63. Keith Bradsher and Matthew L. Wald, "More Indications of Hazards of Tires Were Long Known," *New York Times,* September 7, 2000, A1; Matthew L. Wald, "Rancor Grows between Ford and Firestone," *New York Times,* September 13, 2000, C1; Keith Bradsher, "More Deaths Are Attributed to Faulty Firestone Tires," *New York Times,* September 20, 2000, C2; Matthew L. Wald, "In Testimony Firestone Puts Onus on Ford," *New York Times,* September 22, 2000, C1.
64. Alec Klein and Sandra Sugawara, "A Hard Lesson in Corporate Diplomacy," *Washington Post,* August 23, 2000, A1; Keith Bradsher, "Federal Officials Say They Will Toughen Standards for Tires," *New York Times,* August 17, 2000, C1; Keith Bradsher, "Documents Portray Tire Debacle As a Story of Lost Opportunities," *New York Times,* September 11, 2000, A1.
65. Neela Banerjee, "A Dwindling Faith in Deregulation," *New York Times,* September 15, 2000, C1.
66. *Economic Report of the President,* 2000, 409, table B-88.
67. Jack Walker, "The Diffusion of Innovations in the American States," *American Political Science Review* 63 (September 1969): 880–889.
68. Kathy Koch, "Riding the Internet Express," *CQ Outlook,* March 11, 2000, 9.
69. "Money and Medicine," *CQ Outlook,* September 25, 1999, 19.
70. See Andrea Gabor, *The Man Who Discovered Quality* (New York: Random House, 1990).
71. Thomas Peters and Robert Waterman, *In Search of Excellence* (New York: Warner Books, 1982), 292–305.
72. See Paul S. Grogan and Tony Proscio, *Comeback Cities* (Boulder, Colo.: Westview, 2000).
73. E. E. Schattschneider, *The Semi-Sovereign People* (New York: Holt, Rinehart and Winston, 1960), 1–19.

Chapter 4 **Bureaucratic Politics**

The federal government employs 2.8 million civilians. State and local governments account for roughly 17 million additional public employees.[1] Congress, the presidency, and the courts, with their supporting coterie of staff, advisers, and patronage appointees, make up about 2 percent of the federal total, and their institutional counterparts at the state and local levels claim a similarly small share of their public work forces. Most government employees work in executive branch agencies administering programs or providing services to citizens; these workers are referred to as bureaucrats. The American bureaucracy, or the "administrative state," is often said to constitute a fourth branch of government.[2]

These bureaucrats work in the Internal Revenue Service (IRS) office in Philadelphia sorting tax returns, entering information into computers, and shipping computer tapes to the IRS Center in West Virginia. They work for the Nuclear Regulatory Commission (NRC) as field investigators reviewing plant construction plans with engineers from the Texas Power and Light Company and negotiating agreements on contested issues having to do with power plant construction standards. They are highway patrol officers enforcing speed limit laws.

Sometimes bureaucrats have to make controversial decisions. In 1990, for example, bureaucrats in the Wisconsin Department of Health and Social Services had to decide how to implement a controversial "Learnfare" program aimed at keeping the children of welfare recipients in school. Their decisions determined which welfare recipients would have their Aid to Families with Dependent Children (AFDC) benefits reduced because a child played hookey from school. In some instances, this meant a substantial reduction in benefits.

Central to the political world of bureaucratic agencies are the statutes authorizing their existence and specifying their structure, activities, and budgets. Also central are the relevant legislative committees and citizens whose lives are affected by the particular bureaucracy. Many agencies carry out policies based on broad, vague statutes. The Federal Communications Act of 1934, for example, instructed the Federal Communications Commission to regulate the broadcasting industry in accordance with "the public interest, convenience, and necessity." The Wagner Act of 1935 created the National Labor Relations Board (NLRB) and instructed it to control "unfair labor practices."[3] Even more detailed statutes, such as environmental or social service laws, give agencies significant discretion in determining how a

Table 4-1 Outlays and Employees of Federal Departments and Selected Agencies, 1999

Agency	Outlays (in millions)	Full-time employees
Agriculture	$62,834	95,500
Commerce	5,036	47,300
Defense	261,380	681,000
Education	32,436	4,500
Energy	16,048	15,900
Health and Human Services	359,701	58,900
Social Security Administration	419,788	63,000
Housing and Urban Development	32,734	10,000
Interior	7,815	67,000
Justice	18,317	121,300
Labor	32,461	16,300
State	6,456	29,400
Transportation	41,829	63,700
Treasury	386,698	143,700
Veterans Affairs	43,168	205,500
Small Business Administration	57	4,700
Environmental Protection Agency	6,750	18,100
NASA	13,664	18,500

Source: Adapted from the Office of Management and Budget, The Budget of the United States, FY 2001 (Washington D.C.: Government Printing Office, 2000), 69, 258.

policy will be implemented. After all, legislators cannot anticipate all the contingencies of policy implementation, and in many cases they do not even know what they want out of policies. This discretionary power is a vital component of bureaucratic politics.

The size, structure, and resources of an agency are also essential to its identity. Large staffs and budgets generally carry a certain measure of power and influence and consume the time of the legislatures that debate how agencies should be organized, to whom they should report, and how much money they should receive. The range of variation in staffing and resources is enormous (see Table 4-1). Figure 4-1 shows the organizational structure of a typical bureaucratic agency.

Contrary to popular belief, bureaucrats do not try to be obstructionist or unpleasant. Indeed, they are very attentive to the concerns and preferences of certain individuals and groups—the occupational or categorical groups they serve, the industries they regulate, and the ideological groups with whom they share an affinity; these private sector groups are often referred to as an agency's "clientele." Bureaucrats are particularly attentive to legislative committees and high-ranking executive branch officials. For example, political scientist Steven Balla found that the Health Care Financing Administration (HCFA) responded more quickly to inquiries from members of Congress than to inquiries from private citizens.[4] HCFA also designated higher-level officials to respond to congressional inquiries.[5] Having and maintaining sup-

Figure 4-1 The Department of Health and Human Services

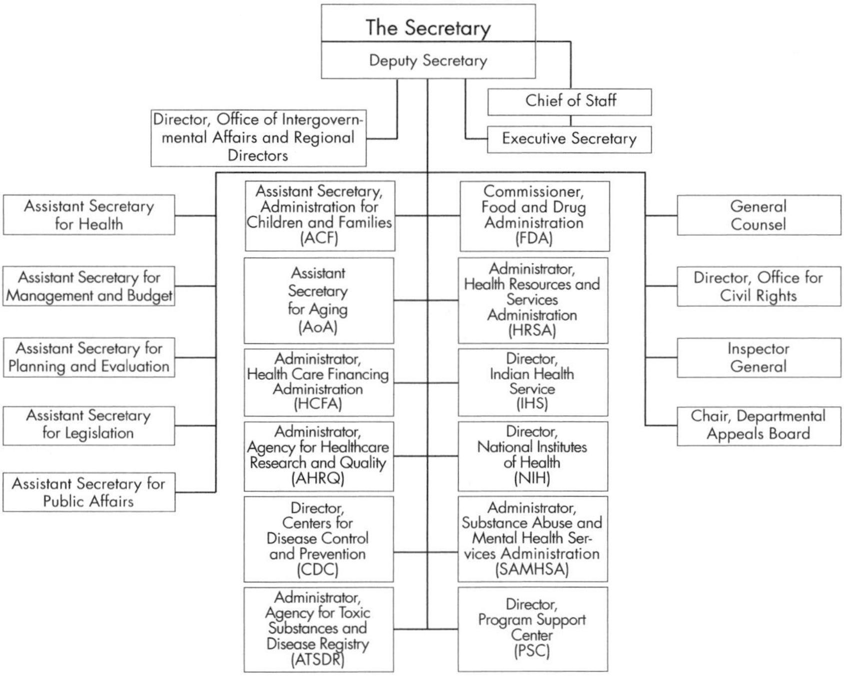

```
                          ┌─────────────────────────┐
                          │     The Secretary        │
                          ├─────────────────────────┤
                          │    Deputy Secretary      │
                          └─────────────────────────┘
                                      │        ┌──────────────────────┐
                                      │        │   Chief of Staff     │
  ┌─────────────────────────┐        │        ├──────────────────────┤
  │ Director, Office of      │        │        │ Executive Secretary  │
  │ Intergovern- mental      │        │        └──────────────────────┘
  │ Affairs and Regional     │        │
  │ Directors                │        │
  └─────────────────────────┘        │
```

Assistant Secretary for Health	Assistant Secretary, Administration for Children and Families (ACF)	Commissioner, Food and Drug Administration (FDA)	General Counsel
Assistant Secretary for Management and Budget	Assistant Secretary for Aging (AoA)	Administrator, Health Resources and Services Administration (HRSA)	Director, Office for Civil Rights
Assistant Secretary for Planning and Evaluation	Administrator, Health Care Financing Administration (HCFA)	Director, Indian Health Service (IHS)	Inspector General
Assistant Secretary for Legislation	Administrator, Agency for Healthcare Research and Quality (AHRQ)	Director, National Institutes of Health (NIH)	Chair, Departmental Appeals Board
Assistant Secretary for Public Affairs	Director, Centers for Disease Control and Prevention (CDC)	Administrator, Substance Abuse and Mental Health Services Administration (SAMHSA)	
	Administrator, Agency for Toxic Substances and Disease Registry (ATSDR)	Director, Program Support Center (PSC)	

Source: http://www.hhs.gov/about/orgchart.html.

porting coalitions both within and outside government is often the key to agency strength and survival. To put it more emphatically, bureaucrats want to be liked.

Internal forces are another aspect of bureaucratic politics. Government agencies typically put many knowledgeable and well-trained individuals to work on highly complex problems; these individuals soon acquire additional expertise and develop preferred ways of dealing with such problems. Expert knowledge and standard operating procedures simplify daily decisions and help to protect an agency from outside criticism. In addition, skillful leadership within the bureaucracy is necessary because an agency's success depends in part on its positive relationships with other government elites.

Civil Servants at Work

What is it that bureaucrats do? How much discretion do they enjoy? To whom are they accountable? To answer these questions, we must first discuss the functions that bureaucracies and the civil servants who work for them are expected to perform.

Executing Tasks

American bureaucracies have two major functions—regulation and service delivery—and the issues of bureaucratic politics fall into these categories. Virtually every administrative agency was created either to regulate private sector industries or to provide services to citizens, including the monthly cash payments made by the Social Security Administration (SSA) and unemployment insurance programs. Many large agencies or departments perform both functions. The distinction between the two is obvious when we contrast, for example, the regulation of food and drug quality with the provision of food stamps or medical care. But it is also obvious that all government service delivery and cash transfer programs must have regulatory components that identify eligible recipients, outline procedures, and prohibit certain actions. The distinction between regulatory and service delivery policy is not hard and fast.

Regulatory policy occupies an important place in American history. Federal laws passed in the late nineteenth century to regulate railroad pricing and corporate mergers were a central part of the Populist/Progressive reaction to the arbitrary practices of big business. These precedent-setting government interventions into the private sector were quite controversial. The present scope of government regulation is enormous, encompassing such areas of private sector activity as advertising, agriculture, air and water pollution, aviation safety, banking, consumer products, corporate mergers, food and drug quality, hospitals and medical practice, nuclear energy, radio and television, transportation, and utility pricing. And regulation is still a controversial enterprise. Regulatory statutes provide aggrieved parties with the right to appeal agency decisions, which means that many of these issues are resolved through formal judicial procedures either within the agency or in the court system. Therefore, two characteristics of regulatory issues are their focus on the actions of private industry and their highly legalistic nature.

Service delivery issues typically involve categorical groups of citizens and public sector organizations—veterans and the Department of Veterans Affairs, welfare recipients and state departments of social services, state and local governments and the Department of Housing and Urban Development. The issues are usually distributive or redistributive in nature. Should education grants received by welfare recipients be counted as income when determining future benefits? Should local in-kind contributions be counted as meeting matching-funds requirements in federal urban development programs? How should garbage pickups be scheduled in different city neighborhoods? The appeals of agency decisions on such matters are likely to be directed at legislators or chief executives, not the courts. Service delivery issues can be contrasted with regulatory issues in that they are confined largely to the public sector and are usually resolved through political rather than legal channels.

Because regulatory policy is aimed at private sector organizations such as businesses and unions, regulatory issues often reflect the concerns of these groups. Bankers are usually the first to react to Federal Home Loan Bank Board rules; and the same is true of radio and television stations and Federal Communications Commission decisions, meat packers and drug companies and decisions of the Food and Drug Administration (FDA), and unions and regulations of the NLRB. The rules promulgated by regulatory agencies and the adjudicative decisions they make also stimulate questions and criticisms from many quarters, however. Citizen groups, legislative committees, other agencies, the media, and ordinary citizens all contribute to the ongoing chorus of commentary about regulatory actions or the need for them. Regulatory issues spring largely from this commentary.

Most service delivery issues originate in much the same way. Services are delivered, and various individuals and groups react. The commentary and subsequent bureaucratic response to it lead to the definition of problems for which solutions must be sought. Like regulatory policy, government-sponsored social service programs in the United States had a slow, halting start, but they are now extensive.[6] The government provides a vast array of cash and in-kind assistance programs to the poor, the elderly, the unemployed, the disabled, the handicapped, veterans, farmers, migrant workers, and many other categories of needy individuals. In 1995 the federal government spent approximately $900 billion on social welfare programs as well as approximately $400 billion in "tax expenditures" on social welfare, such as tax credits or deductions for health and pension benefits.[7] Governments at all levels also supply traditional public services such as highway construction and maintenance, water and sewers, electrical power, police and fire protection, and parks and recreational facilities. The programs through which all these services are provided are subject to varying degrees of scrutiny, as are the agencies that administer them; and issues arise among those who are watching and those who are receiving.

Shaping Agendas

Administrative agencies have an almost instinctive reaction when issues are raised about their performance, and that is to try to define them in non-threatening ways and to process complaints through established channels. If welfare rights advocates are complaining about bureaucratic insensitivity, contradictory and self-defeating regulations, and meager social welfare budgets, the likely response by federal or state agencies will be to define the issues in very specific terms. Should case loads be decreased by a certain percentage? Should day care allowances be increased to $75 from $50 per week? In the regulatory realm, complaints about testing requirements for chemical pesticides, for example, would be whittled down to very specific questions about the number and kinds of tests that have to be completed, the time allowed for test results to be released, and the physical and procedural safeguards that should accompany the use of the chemicals. These are the kinds of questions and issues bureaucratic agencies can deal with effectively. Broad questions about fairness, equity, sensitivity, and the like are usually matters of statutory law and, therefore, have to be decided by legislative and executive authorities.

Bureaucrats normally play what Laurence Lynn calls "the low game." This means that deep within the bureaucracy, issues are narrowly framed and focused. In Lynn's words, "Low games involve the fine-resolution, small-motor processes of government and reflect the concerns of those with operating responsibilities."[8] Thus within the federal Administration for Children and Families the question is not whether to require welfare recipients to work (a high-game decision already made by Congress and the president) but rather how to induce state governments to provide the supportive services needed to make "workfare" work.

Despite the operational specificity of bureaucratic agendas, they are by no means unaffected by the "high games" of politicians. Bureaucratic agendas reflect and change with the politics of the administration. We can take as an example the Civil Rights Division of the Justice Department. During the Carter administration the Justice Department actively pursued affirmative action by arguing on behalf of numerical hiring goals for blacks, women, and Hispanics in cases involving public agencies, most notably police and fire departments, that were being sued for discrimination. Its position on affirmative action changed dramatically under the Reagan administration. The Justice Department began entering employment discrimination cases on the other side, arguing against numerical hiring systems that earlier federal efforts had established. In cities like Detroit, Indianapolis, and New Orleans the department challenged affirmative action plans for police and fire departments that local officials had finally accepted after years of resistance and many rounds of negotiation with federal officials.[9] In contrast, the Clinton administration made a stronger effort to enforce civil rights laws through the Justice Department and the Equal Employment Opportunity Commission (EEOC). For example, the EEOC substantially reduced its backlog of private sector complaints in 1999. More broadly, President Clinton expressed strong support for the concept of affirmative action despite U.S. Supreme Court decisions to the contrary.[10]

The argument put forth here is that the agenda of bureaucratic politics is determined by the interaction of the major "process streams"—problem identification, the formation of policy proposals, and politics—that run through government.[11] Problems are being identified all the time by individuals and groups affected by bureaucratic actions, by legislators, by the media, by agency personnel, and by other levels of government. Problems for which politically and bureaucratically acceptable solutions are available receive attention, and the rest are ignored. Agendas change when these major process streams, particularly the political ones, change. Long lists of identified problems and potential solutions for them are continually circulating around legislative, bureaucratic, and academic communities; those that dominate the agendas of bureaucracies at any given time tend to fit best with the prevailing political climate.[12] Because the chief executive is the most powerful agenda setter, an agency like the Office of Management and Budget, which performs the central clearinghouse and oversight functions for the president, plays a major role in determining what does or does not fit with the administration's politics. Internal bureaucratic forces, such as standard procedures, expertise, and control of information, can offer considerable resistance to changing political winds, but they cannot shield an agency's agenda from the effects of political forces generated at the top.

The Cross-Pressured Bureaucracy

It is now widely recognized that bureaucrats live in a highly political world. Politics and administration are inextricably intertwined. In administering programs and enforcing regulations, bureaucrats are making public policy. Even low-game decisions are laden with policy content. Recognizing this, politicians, interest groups, and judges have stepped up their efforts to control the bureaucracy. As a result, the bureaucracy is more cross-pressured than ever before.[13] Power struggles abound, and the bureaucracy's power resources, so impressive during the days of Lyndon Johnson's Great Society, now seem finite and stretched.

Power

Power in the world of bureaucratic politics comes in a variety of forms. Career bureaucrats, especially professionals and administrators, have power because of what they know and what they do. Their expertise is based in part on access to and control over specialized information that their organizational superiors may not be able to process on their own.[14] Engineers for the Army Corps of Engineers or the National Aeronautics and Space Administration, for example, help to shape the practices and policies of those agencies with their specialized training and knowledge. The same is true, but to a lesser extent, of program analysts and managers in agencies such as the Department of Labor or the Department of Health and Human Services (HHS). Clearly, the rarer the expertise, the greater the power that goes with it.[15]

In addition to power based on expertise there is power conferred by authority. The political executives who are placed at the tops of bureaucratic hierarchies have a certain amount of formal authority to impose their will on an agency or a department. Independent regulatory commissioners have the authority, as specified by Congress, to promulgate rules and adjudicate cases involving the industry practices they regulate. Secretaries of state, attorneys general, and local fire chiefs have a great deal of formal authority over the procedures and policies of their organizations. This power is not always as straightforward as it might first appear, however. There are many areas of overlapping jurisdiction and numerous conflicting claims to authority within the administrative state. This is especially true in the intergovernmental arena, where local, state, and federal agencies frequently compete for power over policy.

A third kind of bureaucratic power comes from outside political alliances, affiliations, and connections. Strong agencies usually have strong constituencies, the client groups they serve or other groups that identify with the agency. Reciprocal relationships between bureaucratic organizations and outside interest groups, in which the groups try to protect the agency from hostile citizens or elected officials in exchange for favorable policies, are common at all levels of government. Notable examples include veterans' groups and the Department of Veterans Affairs and farmers' organizations and the U.S. Department of Agriculture (USDA). How a policy option affects client groups is a very important consideration in agency policymaking, a consideration that can both guide and constrain action. Courting interest groups is not as easy as it once was, however; the number of groups an agency must be concerned about has proliferated, and they often strongly disagree about policy.[16] For example, the Environmental Protection Agency (EPA) tries to keep environmental groups satisfied without alienating business groups.

Power Struggles

Policymaking is a continuous enterprise in most bureaucracies. Line bureaucrats (those in direct contact with clients and problems), investigators, and policy analysts supply a steady stream of policy ideas to legislative staffs for drafting into agency regulations or statutory language. These policy proposals move up through the organizational hierarchy, and high-level officials either accept them or reject them.[17] Top administrators play a pivotal role in the bureaucratic policymaking process because they stand between agency personnel and the central administration and have alliances on both sides. They try to satisfy politicians and career staff by making sure the careerists see some of their ideas put into practice while preventing conflicts with the chief executive's preferences. Central administrative units—budget and policy offices—are now used by nearly all chief executives to review agency regulations and legislative proposals before they go to the legislature, as a further check on policy entrepreneurs or renegades within the bureaucracy.

The most common form of power struggle within an agency occurs between the careerists, who have standard routines, turf, and interests to preserve and protect, and agency heads, who seek to promote partisan or ideological agendas. Normally, outright conflict is avoided through "mutual accommodation."[18] Agency heads often have considerable substantive knowledge of the policy issues they confront and experience with the organization they direct, and they try, for the most part, not to threaten bureaucratic values. On the other side, careerists are accustomed to seeing leaders come and go—the median term of office for presidential appointees is approximately two years[19]—and are willing to make certain concessions to appease the leadership of the moment.

When internal bargaining and accommodation procedures break down, which occurs most often when a markedly new policy direction is being imposed from above, bureaucratic conflict ensues. This situation is generally unpleasant; conflicts attract outsiders—interest groups, the media, legislators, and chief executives—and their entry fundamentally changes a bureaucratic political struggle. The power of these outsiders usually overwhelms the bureaucratic combatants and shifts the dispute into the larger political arena. Such a development represents a failure of administrative politics. In this larger arena almost anything can happen; indeed, it is likely that unusual actions will take place: firings, resignations, or dramatic policy changes or reversals. Shifting policy disagreements to this level is very risky, yet it is sometimes seen as necessary by threatened bureaucratic actors.

A typical scenario of bureaucratic conflict occurs when careerists work through interest groups, legislative committees, or the courts to bring to light unwelcome actions or policies of agency heads. A well-publicized example is the controversy over the EPA during Ronald Reagan's first term. Reagan appointed Anne Gorsuch (later Burford) to head the agency, and she and her top staff, who had little knowledge of or experience with agency procedures or practices, began making major changes, such as new regulations and personnel and budget alterations. Before long, congressional committees, at the prodding of environmental groups and veteran agency employees, began looking into EPA activities. They discovered what appeared to be overt attempts to circumvent environmental statutes.[20] Several resignations resulted, including Burford's, and the president replaced the agency's leadership with a group of experienced EPA administrators headed by William Ruckelshaus.

Conflicts also arise between political executives and their superiors, including the president. In 1996, for example, President Clinton upset several top officials at the Department of Health and Human Services when he signed a welfare reform law eliminating welfare as an entitlement for the poor. Although Secretary Donna Shalala, who urged the president to veto the law, stayed on, several top HHS officials resigned in protest, including Assistant

Secretary Mary Jo Bane, Assistant Secretary Peter Edelman, and Deputy Assistant Secretary Wendell Primus.[21] These resignations highlighted policy differences within the Clinton administration.

The normal state of a bureaucratic agency is low-visibility politics, unchallenged authority over a certain policy and program domain, and support from outside groups and legislative committees. Under these circumstances, internal administrative norms, tempered by statutes and the policy preferences of agency heads, determine policy. Bureaucratic conflict disrupts normal procedures and relationships. When an agency's authority to make certain decisions is challenged, control can be lost to outside institutions—the legislature, the chief executive, or the courts. This situation is obviously one that agencies try to avoid.

Leadership

Leadership in bureaucratic politics consists of strategies and tactics for gaining and maintaining a powerful and autonomous role for bureaucratic actors in the policy process. Bureaucratic officials exercise influence over a certain realm of policy in large part because they are able to use organizational tools to mask the extent of their power. Plainly, certain administrative officials are more successful in this endeavor than others. Robert Moses, who planned and saw through to completion much of New York City's present infrastructure of highways, bridges, tunnels, and parks, was a strong leader. Another was Admiral Hyman Rickover, who, despite the misgivings of most other navy leaders, led the navy into the nuclear era by showing that nuclear reactors could be designed to run submarines. J. Edgar Hoover, who shaped the Federal Bureau of Investigation (FBI) to his own specifications and became powerful enough to challenge presidents, was a leader of almost mythic strength.[22] Analyses of the careers of these and other bureaucratic leaders suggest that leadership in the administrative state has three basic determinants: motivation, context, and personal ability.

Anthony Downs describes five bureaucratic types based on differences in motivation. There are climbers, who are interested only in power, money, and prestige; conservers, who seek "convenience and security" above all else; zealots, who vigorously promote certain ideas and policies and seek power to advance these ideas; advocates, who promote somewhat broader organizational interests and policies and seek power as a way of advancing or elevating their organizational functions; and statesmen, who promote the public interest, and seek power to steer government in a direction that is advantageous to the society as a whole.[23]

The kind of bureaucratic leadership that emerges depends on the political context an agency faces. Young agencies, for example, usually need advocates, and maybe a few zealots, to establish a reputation and power base in policymaking circles. Sargent Shriver's vigorous promotion of the Peace

Corps in the early 1960s is cited as a classic example of effective advocacy on behalf of a fledgling agency. Admiral Rickover was essentially a nuclear power zealot, and he fought to establish his own organizational domain within the navy's Bureau of Ships to get his projects under way. There is no guarantee, however, that zealots will promote the best interests of their organization. If a gap exists between organizational goals and a zealot's world view, "sabotage" is a distinct possibility.[24]

Advocates, but also conservers, can be effective defenders of agencies during periods of budget stringency, a time when more statesmanlike behavior might result in dramatic agency losses. Zealots come to the fore when functional crises hit—when dams break, power plants fail, satellites explode, or reserve stockpiles overflow—because such circumstances put a premium on ideas and people who are sure of their ideas. Robert Moses, Admiral Rickover, and J. Edgar Hoover were always sure of their ideas, and they rose to prominence during crises—the Great Depression, World War II, and the cold war. In quieter times their aggressive brand of leadership may be both less necessary and less acceptable. Indeed, a study of effective leaders who promoted "public school choice" in Minnesota found that they were much better adjusted and much more humane in exercising power than Moses, Rickover, and Hoover.[25]

Many effective bureaucratic leaders are entrepreneurs who extend their organizational domain and become more powerful. Moses used his base as president of the Long Island State Park Commission and chairman of the New York State Council of Parks during the early 1920s to become the head of more than ten city, state, and metropolitan commissions and authorities at the peak of his career in the late 1950s.[26] Entrepreneurs like Moses exhibit the characteristics of advocates and climbers; they aggressively promote their organization and themselves. Bureaucratic imperialism is not always possible or even desirable, however. When the climate of opinion, elite and public, regarding an agency is unfavorable, bureaucratic leaders often try to consolidate rather than extend their authority.[27] At times, bureaucratic leaders even ask that their agency's jurisdiction be narrowed. For example, the head of the Bureau of Indian Affairs (BIA) recently asked Congress to transfer responsibility for recognizing Native American tribes to another agency. Facing a surge of applications by groups hoping to cash in on the benefits offered by tribal casinos, the BIA leader concluded that this task was distracting his agency from other more important assignments.[28]

The need for statesmanlike leadership is most evident in mature administrative organizations and during times of national crisis, when it is important to offset the myopic inclinations of advocates and conservers. Hoover was discredited in part because his zealous leadership was no longer appropriate in a mature and established FBI. One of the most serious problems in the administrative state is not having a leadership that is flexible enough to adapt to changing political environments, and one of the major impediments to flexible leadership is that the most consistently rewarded bureaucratic motives—those of advocates, zealots, and conservers—are not particularly conducive to flexible leadership.

Effective administrative leadership also requires individual ability. Studies of bureaucratic organizations have identified a consistent set of attributes, behavioral patterns, and outlooks associated with successful leaders. Leadership in administrative politics demands intelligence, especially the ability to acquire substantive knowledge and to use organizational processes; the will to achieve or succeed; highly developed interpersonal skills; the willingness and ability to listen and learn from others; and the inclination to enjoy organizational and political work and the exercise of power.[29] Leaders are quick to identify the wielders of power and know how to deal with them in various situations. They are capable of thinking creatively, of solving difficult problems, and of resolving internal conflicts. They appreciate the normative and symbolic aspects of their decisions and actions and take seriously their role as teachers and promoters of esprit de corps. They must also know how to make effective use of the media when circumstances require it or when opportunities present themselves.

Although personal ability is sometimes enhanced by charisma, the two are not synonymous. For example, the head of the Forest Service during the Clinton administration, Mike Dombeck, proved remarkably adept as a bureaucratic leader despite a tendency to speak in a monotone and an image of being a bit of a "square." Ultimately, those traits proved less important than an enormous reservoir of patience, a good sense of humor, and a strong commitment to wilderness preservation. During his tenure at the Forest Service, Dombeck declared a moratorium on the construction of new logging roads in isolated parts of our national forests. He also sharply adjusted employee incentives, rewarding watershed improvement and wildlife protection instead of timber cuts. Even critics concede that Dombeck had a profound effect on his agency's priorities and practices.[30]

Like most analysts, we have stressed the role of high-profile political executives as bureaucratic leaders. But civil servants also provide leadership on numerous occasions. Consider, for example, the role of David Edie, a civil servant with the Wisconsin Department of Health and Social Services. Edie, the department's child care coordinator, became concerned that the department's rules and regulations were limiting the number of licensed family day care homes by imposing substantial economic costs on tiny, fragile business enterprises. Over a period of three years, he spearheaded a departmental effort to craft a new set of rules that would be more acceptable to providers and that would be easier for the department to enforce. The result was a substantial improvement over the status quo.[31] Without Edie's initiative and perseverance, Wisconsin's day care rules would probably have remained untouched. It is important to add, however, that Edie's effort ultimately succeeded because he won the tacit support of political executives within his agency and key members of the Wisconsin state legislature.

How Bureaucracies Decide

The literature on political and organizational decision making is emphatic about the tendency of public bureaucracies to make only marginal changes in existing policies in any given round of decision making, a practice known as incrementalism.[32] Administrative decision makers rarely consider problems in their entirety. They restrict themselves to a specialized slice of the problem, react to feedback about the success or failure of current policy by considering a limited number of alternative approaches, and choose options that seem to satisfy all or most of the major interests in their political environment.[33] Past policy decisions serve as the highly valued base for subsequent decisions precisely because of their political character—they represent the best compromise decision makers could devise in the past, and, in the absence of overwhelming evidence to the contrary, there is no reason to believe that the problems or the attendant politics have changed enough to require a radically new approach.

Incremental decision making is in many ways a result of bureaucratic inertia, the adherence to standard operating procedures or professional norms, and internal support for long-standing policies, which has a powerful conservative effect on administrative decisions.[34] The specialized knowledge and information that exists in the middle and lower levels of the bureaucracy are often effectively used to protect internal interests. From his study of information transmission in the military, Morton Halperin identified eleven different ways information can be packaged to influence decisions.[35] The following are some of them: report only those facts that support the stand you are taking; structure the reporting so that senior participants will see what you want them to see and not other information; request a study from those who will give you the desired conclusions; advise other participants on what to say; direct the facts toward a desired conclusion if necessary and if you can get away with it.[36] In his study of police and other "street level" bureaucratic behavior, Michael Lipsky notes that police often exaggerate the danger connected with their jobs to reduce the likelihood that superiors will impose sanctions on those who take certain "threat reducing" actions—in other words, tough treatment of suspected criminals.[37]

The link between bureaucratic politics and incrementalism does not entirely eliminate the importance of rational or analytic factors in bureaucratic decision making. The so-called rational model of decision making would have administrators look at problems comprehensively and employ certain analytic techniques to evaluate policy options with precision. Rational decision making can be distinguished from incremental/political decision making in that a wider range of alternatives for achieving policy objectives can be considered (nonincremental options are not ruled out automatically) and because decision makers search for solutions that provide the most benefits at the lowest cost rather than for solutions that satisfy as many interests as possible.[38] Rational decision makers use techniques like cost-benefit analysis in identifying the best solutions to policy problems. Increasingly, they also use performance measurement to evaluate programs already in place and the organizations responsible for them.[39]

The Army Corps of Engineers was probably the first government agency to make consistent use of cost-benefit analysis in determining the best water projects to undertake and in justifying the projects to Congress. For example, a proposal to build a dam on a particular river to create a lake would be evaluated by listing all the costs and benefits of the project and then attaching dollar values to them. The costs would include items such as the value of the land that would be flooded, the cost of relocating families whose homes would be destroyed, the value of lost recreational opportunities, and the cost of construction. The benefits would include new hydroelectric power, irrigation water for farmers, new recreational opportunities, and reduced damage from floods.[40]

Market prices are commonly used in assigning dollar amounts to costs and benefits. Where no market values apply, as with questions regarding the preservation of natural habitats or the psychological and social turmoil associated with destroying communities, imagination and creativity must be put to use. The basic rule is that projects whose benefits are larger than their costs should be pursued, and future costs and benefits have to be discounted to their present value to make this determination. When there are many potential projects from which to choose and there is a limited amount of money that can be spent, as is the case in any real-world setting, the projects offering the largest net benefits, often expressed by benefit-to-cost ratios, are preferred.[41] As this brief discussion of cost-benefit analysis illustrates, the technique provides decision makers with fairly clear-cut choices. But many assumptions—that market prices accurately reflect the social value of different outcomes, for example—and a good deal of guesswork, especially in projecting future costs and benefits, go into the final calculations.

Although related to cost-benefit analysis, performance measurement differs from it in its focus on whether existing programs or strategies are working as intended. In the past, performance measurement efforts within government were fairly crude, focusing on agency "outputs" such as the number of inspections conducted, the number of checks written, or the number of penalties imposed. The Government Performance and Results Act (GPRA) of 1993 changed all that by requiring federal agencies to shift their attention to "outcomes" or results such as improvements in air quality, workplace safety, or public health. As of March 2000, federal agencies were required to prepare annual strategic plans and annual performance plans, to compare stated goals with actual results. The General Accounting Office and key members of Congress have expressed "disappointment" at "uneven" progress toward implementing GPRA.[42] But some agencies, such as the Department of Transportation and the Department of Veterans Affairs, have drawn praise from outside investigators.

One problem with rational approaches to decision making is that most administrators find them difficult to use because of the cognitive demands they impose, such as evaluating long lists of alternatives and sorting through highly technical analyses, and because of the economic pressure caused by the amount of staff time needed to complete all the analytic chores. In the case of performance measurement, administrators must wrestle with a more specific dilemma: they have more control over agency outputs but the connection to outcomes may be weak; outcomes matter more but they depend on many factors beyond the control of agency officials. If agency officials truly measure outcomes, they may be unfairly blamed for statistics that reflect the vicissitudes of economic activity, the weather, and other forces well outside their jurisdiction. Not surprisingly, many administrators have viewed performance measurement requirements with nervousness and suspicion.[43]

Overall, the influence that analytic procedures have on administrative decisions varies according to the nature of the problem and the dispositions of decision makers. Highly technical matters invite analytic solutions, but most of the questions administrators confront are too political to be answered wholly by analysis. Richard Zerbe puts it nicely when he argues that "the role of benefit-cost analysis is to provide information relevant to the decision, not to provide the decision."[44] The same is true of performance measurement. If the numbers reveal that a particular strategy isn't working, they do not necessarily indicate whether the solution is to spend more, spend less, fine-tune the strategy, or abandon it altogether. Among bureaucratic officials there are many who dislike and distrust analysis, but a growing number are comfortable with it.[45] Many see mastery of policy planning and analytic activities as a path to greater power and influence in decision-making circles because analysis has become an accepted part of the process by which most organizational decisions are made. Unless the interests associated with policy decisions have numbers to back up their views, they operate at a disadvantage.

Rules and Regulations

Bureaucratic policies come in many different forms. First, there are written rules and regulations that have wide applicability and carry the force of law. Second, there are adjudicatory decisions that settle, through quasi-judicial procedures, disputes between antagonistic parties, usually an agency and a business accused of violating an administrative rule or regulation. Third, there are guidelines, policy statements, and advisory opinions that convey to interested parties an agency's thinking or intentions about various matters but do not have the full legal force of formal rules and regulations. Fourth, there are informal means of settling disputes that do not entail full adjudication. Finally, there are the actions that line bureaucrats take that define the meaning of regulatory or service-delivery policy in practice.

Administrative agencies have developed a mountain of rules and regulations that specify the meaning of legislative statutes. These are published in the *Federal Register* and the *Code of Federal Regulations* and in comparable documents in the states and localities. The adoption of such rules and regulations at the federal level takes place in accordance with procedures spelled out in the Administrative Procedure Act of 1946 (APA); similar statutes exist in most states. When an agency wants to develop rules to enforce provisions of statutes, which Congress has authorized agencies to do, the APA requires that (1) a public notice be entered in the *Federal Register* specifying the time, place, and nature of the rule-making proceedings; (2) interested parties be given the opportunity to submit written, and in some cases oral, arguments and facts relevant to the rule; and (3) the statutory basis and purpose of the rule be indicated. After rules are promulgated, thirty days' notice is required before they take effect.[46] These procedures, known as informal rule-making, are designed to give everyone a chance to participate in this essentially legislative activity.

The APA rule-making procedures can be much more formal and cumbersome when a statute requires rule making "on the record after a formal hearing." Under such circumstances agencies must conduct proceedings that resemble trials; witnesses present testimony and submit data or other evidence, there are opportunities for cross-examination of witnesses, and interested parties are prohibited from contacting agency officials during the proceedings. After the hearings, time is set aside for further evidence to be submitted, and agency officials must go over the entire record and carefully document their reasons for issuing a rule. Such hearings often last for weeks or even months. Although agencies are seldom enthusiastic about this degree of formality, they may use this procedure even when they are not required by statute to do so as a means to blunt criticism of the rules and to bolster their position with the courts, which see adherence to formal procedures as one of the justifications for allowing agencies to exercise rule-making power. Reliance on rules and formal rule-making procedures by agencies increased during the late twentieth century.

Administrative adjudication has a narrower focus than rule making. When there is a disagreement between a company and a union about labor standards, or between the Social Security Administration and a recipient about eligibility for certain benefits, or between a utility company and the NRC about a plant safety issue, a settlement can be reached through adjudication. The procedures are similar to those in a court of law—formal notifications to appear are given to all parties, public records are kept, only certain kinds of evidence are admissible, and each party gets a chance to cross-examine adverse witnesses.[47]

To conduct these proceedings, the bureaucracy employs specially trained personnel, called administrative law judges, who bring with them impartiality and legal and substantive knowledge.[48] The judges interpret administrative law as it applies to the particular case and either issue "orders" (in other words, make a decision) or submit recommendations for a decision to commissioners or chief administrators. In many instances, adjudicated cases are appealed to federal courts. Adjudicated decisions provide a clear indication of agency policies with regard to the specific issues raised in particular cases, but, unlike rules and regulations, they do not establish policy that can be applied with confidence to similar cases.

Bureaucratic agencies also make policy statements and issue advisory opinions (courts refrain from issuing them), but these pronouncements, usually made informally, are not as authoritative as rules and regulations. Statements and advisory opinions enable an agency to tell individuals or companies how it intends to react to certain actions or conditions, or what that agency's operating policy is, with the understanding that such statements do not bind the agency and are subject to full review by the courts, which regard such guidelines as less deserving of deference than formal rules or adjudicatory decisions. An example of a policy statement is a 1990 Internal Revenue Service announcement that cash rebates for energy-saving equipment shall be considered taxable.[49] Businesses of all sorts seek advisory opinions from agencies like the Federal Trade Commission (FTC), the Securities and Exchange Commission, the Labor Department, and the EPA on matters ranging from whether certain employees are subject to provisions of the Fair Labor Standards Act to whether certain air pollution devices will satisfy Clean Air Act requirements.

Advisory opinions often are issued to head off litigation. In fact, most of the disputes about policy enforcement that could lead to litigation or to formal adjudication are resolved through informal agreements between agency personnel and the other parties involved. For example, the Labor Department and a company agree that an outside arbiter should meet with company employees to discuss their grievances, or a utility company promises the NRC that it will make certain changes in plant safety procedures. These informal agreements are another attempt to cope with reality because agencies cannot possibly use formal adjudication to resolve all the disagreements they encounter about matters of fact and policy application.

The day-to-day actions taken by bureaucratic officials in their efforts to administer statutory law represent a final large piece of the policy picture. As incredible as it may seem, despite the thousands and thousands of pages of administrative rules and regulations, many real-life situations are still ambiguous, and on-the-spot bureaucratic discretion is needed. Street-level bureaucrats, such as police officers and welfare case workers, are continually faced with the need to make judgments in ambiguous situations—when to make arrests for certain crimes, when to waive certain evidentiary requirements for benefits or special assistance.[50] Although the use of such discretion may seem inevitable, many argue that the police and others who engage in selective enforcement should establish more rules and follow them in more situations.[51] Policy that is determined through direct action or informal agreement tends to be unsystematic and inconsistent; but there are limits to what can be specified and, in certain circumstances, there are advantages to be gained for the agency and its clients from acting informally.

Symbolism

At first glance bureaucratic politics would not seem to provide fertile ground for symbolism. After all, it is the bureaucracy that has to translate the often ambiguous and symbolic statutes enacted by legislatures into concrete rules and activities. Bureaucrats cannot fudge the details; they have to make decisions about who gets what, where, and how. When an individual is granted public assistance or a firm is fined for polluting a river, that means the administrative state has acted in a tangible, substantive manner. Rules, regulations, and adjudicative decisions allocate benefits, specify administrative procedures, and prescribe certain public sector or private sector behaviors; none of these would seem to be a symbolic exercise. Furthermore, most administrative officials do not conceive of their activity as symbolic. They see themselves as executing the will of the legislature—defining problems, designing solutions, and evaluating the effectiveness of past actions.

Several scholars who have written about bureaucracy have emphasized its symbolic aspects, however. At one extreme, some argue that the administrative state exists largely to carry out symbolic functions.[52] Regulatory policy is said to provide reassurance to the citizens that certain decisions (concerning transportation and utility pricing, for example) are being made with regard for their interests, even though the results of the decisions may not benefit them. Regulatory policy also serves notice to the regulated industries that punitive steps may be taken if they engage in excessively selfish behavior, even though such steps are rarely taken. The administrative policies of social welfare agencies are designed to indicate to the lower classes that they are not entitled to government assistance, even though many of them are, while suggesting to the middle class that assistance is available to anyone who really needs it, even though it is not, and finally to reassure the upper classes that traditional values of individualism and self-reliance are not being abandoned.[53] The thrust of such arguments is that administrative policies, either purposefully or unwittingly, are designed not to solve problems, but to appease or legitimate certain interests and to provide an institutional forum in which recognized interests can compete for influence over policy.

One can find symbolism in other administrative behaviors. Federal and state commissions may hold hearings to obtain citizen input or to grant agenda status to issues raised by grassroots groups but then continue to formulate policies in accordance with bureaucratic or industry preferences, thereby revealing the symbolic nature of their public actions.[54] Highway patrol officers send a symbolic message when they allow motorists to exceed the speed limit by ten miles per hour. Social workers also send symbolic messages if they keep welfare clients waiting in their outer office for long periods of time. Whether bureaucratic officials recognize it in their actions or not, symbolism is an unavoidable aspect of policy implementation and enforcement.

Change

Bureaucracies depend on continuity. Most agencies prefer to build up a solid base of effective policies and then work carefully and patiently to extend that base as they confront new problems. This way of working is the incrementalism described in the previous section. Administrative agencies are capable of change and innovation, however; this observation applies not only to young agencies, where one might expect some novelty, but also to older, established agencies. Politics, not incrementalism, is the constant in bureaucratic life. When political developments convince bureaucratic leaders that change and innovation are necessary, they can bring them about.

During the 1970s significant changes took place in administrative policies, especially in the area of regulation. These changes can be traced to the growing consumer and environmental movements that brought together previously unorganized interests to exert pressure at all levels of government.[55] Regulatory agencies and policies, which were notorious for favoring the industries being regulated, were a primary target of consumer and environmental groups. Over time these reformers were able to achieve an impressive number of victories over the regulatory dragons. Ralph Nader's breakthroughs on automobile safety regulations helped to pave the way for many other reform efforts.[56] State public utility commissions all over the country began eliminating reduced rates for high-volume industrial users after citizen groups armed with the analyses of economists argued convincingly that such pricing schemes discouraged conservation, caused unnecessary strain on generating facilities, and penalized homeowners and the poor. The solutions they proposed—peak-load and marginal cost pricing and lifeline rates— were widely adopted.[57] New leadership and supportive political environments also led to the reinvigoration of the FTC as a protector of consumers in the early 1970s and even to a major change to a more environmentally sensitive philosophy within the Army Corps of Engineers.[58] New forces were pushing their way into the political environments of government agencies and were stimulating policy change.

The bureaucracy changed far less in the 1980s, especially at the federal level. Because he viewed the federal bureaucracy as a threat to a market economy, President Reagan sought to tame it rather than to utilize it.[59] But Reagan's policies contributed in interesting ways to a revival of bureaucratic reform initiatives in the 1990s. By stimulating enormous budget deficits, Reagan made it difficult for politicians to endorse new spending programs or increases in the size of the federal bureaucracy. By lambasting the bureaucracy relentlessly, Reagan helped to ensure that the bureaucracy would be an issue in future presidential campaigns. These and other developments, such as the growing professionalism of state bureaucracies, encouraged a new wave of reforms in the 1990s. President Clinton and Vice President Gore vowed to create a leaner, more efficient federal bureaucracy. Under the banner of "reinventing government," they championed numerous reforms, including quicker procurement processes, a sharp reduction in the size of the federal bureaucracy, and greater emphasis on customer service.[60] Both the Clinton administration and Congress supported devolution initiatives that granted greater discretion to state governments and that substituted intergovernmental "partnerships" for direct mandates.[61] Both the federal government and many state governments enacted performance measurement legislation that required bureaucracies to measure the results of their activities.[62] If the reforms of the 1970s reflected interest group politics, the reforms of the 1990s exemplified managerial politics. Politicians at all levels of government promoted a more efficient, more effective bureaucracy through management reform. By the end of the decade the federal bureaucracy was 17 percent smaller, state bureaucracies enjoyed greater discretion and respect, and greater attention was being paid to what bureaucracies achieve rather than how they achieve it.

Change and innovation are sometimes short-lived. The recent history of the FTC is instructive. As was mentioned, the FTC was an important part of the proconsumer shift in federal policy during the 1970s. With a supportive Senate Commerce Committee headed by Warren Magnuson, D-Wash., in the early 1970s, new personnel, strong statutory backing, and, after Carter's election, Michael Pertschuk, a forceful consumer advocate, as its chairman, the FTC set out to make capitalism fair and safe for the American people. Between 1976 and 1980 it took on the American Bar Association, the insurance industry, the sponsors of children's advertising on television, used-car dealers, and funeral home directors, but it lost as many of these battles as it won. Congress voided many of the FTC's major rulings and imposed a host of restrictions on it beginning in 1977. Sentiment in the House and Senate Commerce Committees had shifted noticeably back to industry, and the FTC fought an uphill battle for change until Pertschuk was replaced by James Miller, a Reagan conservative, who opposed many antitrust regulations and who curbed the FTC's enforcement activities.[63] Under Janet Steiger, President Bush's choice as chairperson, the FTC pursued a more moderate course. Christine Varney and Robert Pitofsky, chairs of the FTC during the Clinton administration, also embraced moderation. For example, in fighting to protect the privacy of Internet users, they supported self-regulation rather than a more classic regulatory strategy.

Winners and Losers

It is commonly alleged that regulatory policies primarily benefit the regulated industries and that social service policies primarily benefit the bureaucrats who administer them. These rather cynical observations can serve as a useful starting point for a discussion of who benefits from administrative politics.

In the regulatory realm the so-called capture theory is often put forward.[64] The basic argument is that over time, regulated industries come to dominate regulatory agencies. This capture takes place because the fervor for reform, usually stimulated by callous industry behavior, results in the creation of a regulatory entity. It quickly becomes apparent, however, that the expertise, interest, and dependable political support the regulatory agency needs to sustain itself reside mainly in the regulated industry. As time passes, a symbiotic relationship—the movement of personnel back and forth and shared interest in each other's priorities and policies—develops between the two, and the capture process is well under way. This analysis has been applied fairly convincingly to the Interstate Commerce Commission (ICC) and the railroads, the Federal Power Commission (FPC) and the natural gas industry, the Civil Aeronautics Board and the airlines, and several other pairs.[65] According to economist George Stigler, industries come to see regulation as a benefit, mainly because most forms of regulation restrict entry into regulated markets, thereby reducing competition.[66]

There is no doubt that the capture concept is apt for many different regulatory situations past and present, but it is also true that not all regulatory agencies are captured, that captured agencies do not necessarily stay captured, and that some regulatory legislation is intended to promote and protect industry. There are also important differences in regulatory realms that need to be taken into account. The capture theory was typically applied to regulatory agencies that focused on a single industry or on a limited number of companies and to situations in which regulatory objectives were primarily economic. Many current regulatory agencies oversee more than one industry and have social objectives, such as environmental protection, health and safety in the workplace, and civil rights. The multifaceted political environments these agencies face make any simple influence model implausible. One would expect these agencies to pursue various objectives—serving the public, accommodating industry, ensuring their own survival—with the emphasis given to each changing over time in accordance with external and internal pressures. As law professor Jonathan Macey has noted, "[t]he interest group that is regulated by a single regulatory agency will be able to influence that agency to a far greater extent than the interest groups that must share their agency with a variety of other interest groups."[67]

Gormley's differentiation of regulatory policies according to complexity and conflict provides a useful framework for sorting out expectations about beneficiaries.[68] Regulations that are not terribly complex, such as seatbelt rules, procedures to cut off service by public utilities for nonpayment of bills, or smoking bans in public facilities, give various groups some say in policy because unusual expertise is not required to exert influence. If citizen advocacy groups are active and skillful, there is a good chance that the public will benefit from the policies or at least that some conception of the public interest will be considered in policymaking. If public advocacy groups are not present, self-interested groups will dominate. When policies are technically complex (for example, the use of genetically altered material, securities fraud, or banking regulations), a proxy advocate is usually needed to secure policies beneficial to the public. In such cases the specialized expertise and political muscle needed for an effective challenge to objectionable industry behavior may not be available except in a government agency.

The argument linking bureaucrats and social service policies is similar in some ways to capture theory. Concern about poverty in the 1960s brought into being some hastily designed programs that were not nearly strong enough to solve the problem, but they did create a certain number of jobs for those interested in administering social services. Some alleged that black community organizers were the primary beneficiaries of many War on Poverty programs because community groups were enlisted to implement programs, and known minority leaders were hired to administer them. The actual subsidies and services provided by the programs were said to be too meager or too difficult to obtain for the truly needy to benefit, and unnecessary or even harmful for many of those who did receive them.[69]

The systematic research that has been done on social service programs does not completely refute the arguments just presented, but it suggests that they are simplistic and misleading. Food stamps have helped to reduce malnutrition among America's poor; Medicaid has allowed many poor people to receive medical treatment previously unavailable to them; job-training programs have helped people find jobs; and Head Start and Upward Bound have enabled many minority students to complete high school and college.[70] It is also true, however, that Medicaid has resulted in expensive and in some cases unnecessary treatment, that some of those who benefited most from job-training programs were not especially disadvantaged, and that the largest welfare programs—Temporary Assistance to Needy Families, food stamps, Medicaid, and housing subsidies—do not always encourage self-sufficiency or reward industry and entrepreneurship. A more accurate appraisal of the beneficiaries of social service programs, therefore, would be that recipients of services as well as bureaucrats benefit from the programs, but there is clearly a need for ongoing programmatic reform.

Distinctions among service delivery programs should also be noted. The War on Poverty programs are often referred to as "social welfare" programs. As the term suggests, these programs aim to improve the lives and aspirations of poor and disadvantaged citizens. But many American social service programs are not aimed at the poor; they have a middle-class clientele. Veterans' benefits and farm subsidies are prime examples, as are Social Security and Medicare. Another category of service programs—highways, mass transportation, water and sewer construction projects—benefits the public as a whole, as well as contractors and their employees. Overall, more money is spent on these nontargeted, middle-class programs than on programs designed to help the poor. In fiscal year 1996 means-tested human services programs, such as Medicaid, Food Stamps, Supplemental Security Income, and public housing, amounted to $261.3 billion.[71] Although a substantial amount of money, this represented only 16.8 percent of the federal budget.[72]

The Quest for Results

We begin this examination of policy consequences with brief descriptions of two programs and then discuss how they illustrate the challenges of converting laws into desired results. Our first example comes from a high-profile social program—Medicare—administered by the federal Department of Health and Human Services. Our second example is a much less visible program that requires all major federal agencies to measure progress toward specified goals and to report that progress to Congress.

Medicare Managed Care

The Medicare program, created in 1965 as part of Lyndon Johnson's Great Society, provides health care benefits to senior citizens and the disabled. For years, Medicare recipients relied exclusively on fee-for-service arrangements to secure medical care from hospitals and physicians.[73] Under fee-for-service, health care consumers purchase medical services from a hospital or a physician, who later get reimbursed for the costs of those services. Fee-for-service medicine offered Medicare recipients the advantage of high-quality care and flexible choice of providers, but it also contributed significantly to the rising costs of health care. During the 1980s, for example, health care costs rose at rates that substantially exceeded the general inflation rate in the United States.

During the 1970s an alternative to fee-for-service medicine emerged, known as managed care. Under managed care, a health care consumer signs up with a managed care organization such as a health maintenance organization (HMO). The HMO receives a fixed fee from the consumer's employer or (in the case of Medicare) from the federal government. The HMO has incentives to reduce the costs of care, because its fee has already been predetermined, regardless of how expensive the care proves to be. The premise behind managed care is that such a payment and service delivery system can encourage both cost containment and quality improvements. The latter may occur if HMOs successfully promote preventive medicine, which is both less costly and more beneficial than treating serious health problems that might have been averted.

Managed care became extremely popular among corporate purchasers of health care during the 1990s.[74] By 2000 the overwhelming majority of Americans whose employers purchased their health care were enrolled in an HMO or some similar type of managed care organization. In contrast, Medicare enrollments in managed care organizations were quite limited.

In 1997 Congress and President Clinton decided to promote Medicare managed care by establishing a program called the Medicare+Choice program. Under that program, Medicare recipients have the option of enrolling in a managed care plan but are not required to do so. Despite its voluntary character, the Congressional Budget Office projected sharp and sudden increases in Medicare managed care enrollments.[75] Congress entrusted the Health Care Financing Administration (HCFA), within HHS, with the responsibility for implementing Medicare+Choice.

Government Performance and Results Act

Members of Congress and other outside critics have long complained about the performance of the bureaucracy, especially the federal bureaucracy in Washington, D.C. A key complaint has been that the bureaucracy is not held to account for its failures the way a private firm in a competitive market would be. Unlike private firms, government agencies seldom compete directly for customers or higher market shares. A further distinction is that politicians and citizens cannot judge government agencies based on their performance the way that stockholders and consumers can judge the performance of Ford Motor Company, IBM, and CBS.

Lacking direct measures of administrative performance, Congress and other interested parties relied for years on indirect measures, such as the number of clients served, the number of checks issued, the number of plants inspected, and the number of monetary fines issued. Although some of these measures are suggestive, they are what political scientists would call "output" measures rather than authentic "outcome" measures. Ultimately, what we would like to know is not whether agencies engage in a lot of activity but rather whether such activity is effective.

With these considerations in mind, Congress and President Clinton agreed in 1993 to enact a law known as the Government Performance and Results Act, briefly mentioned earlier in the chapter. In an effort to shift the emphasis of congressional and presidential oversight of the bureaucracy from inputs and outputs to results, GPRA required virtually every federal agency to adopt a strategic plan, with objectives and subobjectives clearly specified. Then, over a period of several years, GPRA required each agency to develop an annual performance plan and an annual performance report indicating how close it came to achieving its stated objectives and subobjectives.

Although GPRA is quite clear about the deadlines federal agencies must meet in moving toward strategic planning and performance documents, the law is unclear about two key points. First, the law does not define what constitutes a result or outcome, as opposed to an activity or output. Second, the law does not specify what the consequences will be if an agency's performance is weak in a given year. Will the agency be punished? If so, how? And what about agencies that meet or exceed their goals? Will they be rewarded with more money? More flexibility? A pat on the back?

Implementation

In implementing Medicare+Choice, HCFA faced several major problems, including congressional micromanagement, skeptical senior citizens, and unfavorable economic conditions. In the Balanced Budget Act of 1997, Congress imposed numerous restrictions on the rates HCFA could offer managed care companies to induce them to participate in Medicare+Choice.[76] As the economics of managed care turned sour in the late 1990s, HCFA was unable to cope with decisions by many managed care organizations to back away from Medicare managed care. Without additional flexibility, HCFA was powerless. The attitudes of senior citizens also posed an obstacle. Long accustomed to fee-for-service medicine and wary of managed care, senior citizens approached Medicare+Choice with caution bordering on skepticism.

In addition to these external problems, HCFA faced some internal problems as well. Created in an era when fee-for-service medicine was the norm, HCFA lacked some of the requisite skills for dealing with the brave new world of managed care. The skills needed to create a viable Medicare managed care option were those best learned in the private sector, where battles for managed care had already been fought and won. Although HCFA would have liked to hire personnel with valuable experience in administering managed care contracts, such persons were in great demand and they required financial compensation far higher than anything HCFA could offer, given federal civil service pay restrictions. There may have been attitudinal problems as well. According to some critics, HCFA was too committed to fee-for-service medicine to be willing to give managed care a fair chance.[77]

In implementing GPRA, federal agencies faced numerous problems. The first of these was that GPRA was designed to serve several purposes at once, including strategic planning by agencies and improved oversight by Congress. Unfortunately, the measures that an agency might develop to guide itself are likely to differ from those an agency must develop to satisfy congressional overseers. If an agency does both, it may find itself awash in paperwork. A second problem is that GPRA required agency officials to develop measures of program results that are extremely difficult to produce. It is much easier to count the number of inspections the Occupational Safety and Health Administration conducts than it is to measure improvements in workplace safety. It is much easier to count the number of fines EPA officials levy than it is to measure improvements in water quality. The task that GPRA assigned to federal agencies was intrinsically difficult. Third, GPRA sought to institutionalize accountability while at the same time insisting that managers focus more on performance measures beyond their control. Managers can influence the number of inspections conducted or the number of monetary fines levied much more than they can influence workplace safety (which also depends on the behavior of employers and workers) or water quality (which depends on economic activity, the weather, and agricultural practices). In effect, GPRA said to federal agency officials: we will hold you more accountable for measures over which you have less control. This combination proved extremely frustrating to many agency officials, which encouraged negative appraisals of GPRA.

Impact

The Medicare+Choice program did not have much of an impact on the percentage of Medicare recipients who enrolled in managed care programs. From 1997 to 2000, the number of Medicare recipients participating in a managed care program increased only slightly, from 16 percent to 18 percent. Participation in Medicare managed care lagged far behind participation in Medicaid managed care, which reached nearly 56 percent in June 1999.[78] One explanation for the difference is that Medicaid managed care benefited from the strong support of state Medicaid agencies, which actively promoted managed care with HCFA's support. Another explanation is that Medicaid recipients do not enjoy the same positive image as Medicare recipients, who consequently wield greater political clout. Confronted by managed care trends that might or might not be in their best interest in the long run, Medicaid recipients could not fight back if they wished to do so. In contrast, Medicare recipients worked aggressively through organizations such as the American Association of Retired Persons (AARP) to promote their perceived interests.

GPRA's impact is more difficult to determine, partly because the final piece of the GPRA puzzle—annual performance reports—did not become operational until March 2000. Beryl Radin, a close student of GPRA and management reform generally, has noted that some positive changes occurred, especially in areas where agency leaders linked GPRA to their own agendas. Overall, though, Radin's assessment was negative: "Viewed as a whole, GPRA has failed to significantly influence substantive policy and budgetary processes."[79] The same pattern prevailed at the state level, where mini-GPRAs sought to institutionalize greater attention to results. In a study of environmental performance measures in four states, William Gormley found isolated examples of performance measure use. In most instances, however, the measures used were output measures, not outcome measures.[80] Thus, at the state level, as at the national level, performance measurement proved extremely difficult to institutionalize.

Learning

When bureaucracies and their overseers make mistakes, a key question is whether they can learn from them and institute appropriate reforms. Reforms may involve new structural arrangements, decision-making processes, or standard operating procedures.

In the wake of critical commentary on HCFA's stewardship of Medicare managed care, HCFA proposed to create a new office of managed care to ensure "one-stop shopping" for managed care organizations that deal with HCFA. The hope was that a single managed care office would make interactions with HCFA less daunting to providers. Interestingly, this reform would undo a 1995 reform and roughly restore the status quo ante. At the same time, Congress considered more substantial reforms, including a massive restructuring that would remove Medicare managed care from HCFA's jurisdiction and transfer responsibility for these functions to a newly created Medicare Benefits Administration within HHS. Such a proposal would alleviate HCFA's often oppressive workload, but it could also create new coordination problems because Medicare managed care and fee-for-service Medicare would be handled by two different agencies.

After receiving negative feedback from Congress on their annual performance plans, several federal agencies made modest changes to meet congressional objections. In a 1999 report the General Accounting Office lauded federal agencies for moderate improvements.[81] But many fundamental problems remain, including a persistent tendency to measure outputs rather than outcomes and insufficient attention to cross-cutting program issues. Another lingering problem is that neither Congress nor the federal bureaucracy seems much inclined to use performance measures to reallocate resources. Until that happens, the promise of GPRA will not have been realized.

Summary

The Constitution has very little to say about the administrative state. The president is given primary authority over the executive branch, and therefore the bureaucracy, but Congress has the power to create, abolish, organize, and reorganize executive agencies. Congress also can specify authority relationships between the administrative entities it creates and the other branches of government. Any bureaucratic agency can be rendered powerless by

Congress, and most of them can be severely crippled, if not paralyzed, by the president or the courts. For bureaucratic agencies, the exercise of power is mostly a matter of having the backing and support of interest groups and other branches of government that have the political influence or constitutional authority they lack.

This support is by no means automatic. Chief executives frequently try to reshape agencies whose policies they oppose. When an attack of this sort occurs, career bureaucrats may fight back by using sympathetic interest groups, the legislature, and the courts to help them protect their domain. If the assault comes from the legislature, a different coalition must be assembled. Agencies can sometimes compete effectively in the high-stakes, high-visibility arenas of politics by playing one branch of government off against another. This skill is part of what has enabled the bureaucracy to become a fourth institutional force in American government.

Clearly more important than their ability to resist incursions from other institutions is the fact that administrative agencies generally remain outside the political limelight. Their influence over policy is greatest when other institutional powers are not watching too closely. Because their policymaking power is derivative, it is always subject to review and alteration: legislatures can abolish agency rules, adjudicative decisions can be overturned by the courts, and administrative regulations can be changed in the offices of chief executives. But these kinds of checks are used sparingly; the normal environment of bureaucratic agencies permits them to exercise considerable power over public policy precisely because the other branches want the bureaucracy to make the tough, unpopular decisions. The bureaucracy is one of the places in government where "the rubber meets the road."

Notes

1. Bureau of the Census, *Statistical Abstract of the United States: 1999,* no. 534 (Washington, D.C.: Government Printing Office, 1999).
2. Emmette S. Redford, *Democracy in the Administrative State* (New York: Oxford University Press, 1969).
3. On the statutory language for these and other independent regulatory commissions, see Marver Bernstein, *Regulating Business by Independent Commission* (Princeton: Princeton University Press, 1955); Theodore Lowi, *The End of Liberalism* (New York: W. W. Norton, 1969); and Benjamin Taylor and Fred Whitney, *Labor Relations Law,* 4th ed. (Englewood Cliffs, N.J.: Prentice-Hall, 1983).
4. Steven Balla, "Political and Organizational Determinants of Bureaucratic Responsiveness," *American Politics Quarterly* 28 (April 2000): 184–185.
5. Ibid., 178–180.
6. See Theda Skocpol, *Protecting Soldiers and Mothers* (Cambridge: Harvard University Press, 1992); Christopher Howard, *The Hidden Welfare State* (Princeton: Princeton University Press, 1997); and Rebecca Blank, *It Takes a Nation* (Princeton: Princeton University Press, 1997).

7. Howard, *The Hidden Welfare State,* 24–27.
8. Lawerence Lynn, *Managing Public Policy* (Boston: Little, Brown, 1987), 64.
9. See Philip Shenon, "U.S. Acts to Stop Quotas in Hiring It Backed in the Past," *New York Times,* April 30, 1985, A1; John Palmer and Isabel Sawhill, eds., *The Reagan Record* (Cambridge, Mass.: Ballinger, 1984), 204–208.
10. Executive Office of the President, Office of Management and Budget, *Budget of the United States Government: Government-Wide Performance Plan* (Washington, D.C.: Government Printing Office, 2000), 140; Phillip Cooper et al., *Public Administration for the Twenty-First Century* (Fort Worth, Tex.: Harcourt Brace, 1998), 276.
11. John Kingdon, *Agendas, Alternatives, and Public Policies* (Boston: Little, Brown, 1984), 92.
12. Ibid., chap. 6.
13. For an extensive discussion of this trend and its implications, see William T. Gormley Jr., *Taming the Bureaucracy: Muscles, Prayers, and Other Strategies* (Princeton: Princeton University Press, 1989).
14. Francis Rourke, *Bureaucracy, Politics, and Public Policy,* 3d ed. (Boston: Little, Brown, 1984), chap. 3.
15. Ibid., chap. 4.
16. See Lance de-Haven Smith and Carl Van Horn, "Subgovernment Conflict in Public Policy," *Policy Studies Journal* 12 (summer 1984): 627–642.
17. See Robert Gilmour, "Policy Formulation in the Executive Branch: Central Legislative Clearance," in *Cases on Public Policy-Making,* ed. James Anderson (New York: Praeger, 1976), 80–96.
18. Charles Lindblom, *The Intelligence of Democracy* (New York: Free Press, 1965).
19. See James Fesler and Donald Kettl, *The Politics of the Administrative Process* (Chatham, Mass.: Chatham House, 1991), 153.
20. See Norman Vig and Michael Kraft, eds., *Environmental Policies in the 1980s* (Washington, D.C.: CQ Press, 1984), chaps. 5, 7, 8, and 17; and Palmer and Sawhill, *The Reagan Record,* 146–151.
21. Anne Marie Cammisa, *From Rhetoric to Reform? Welfare Policy in American Politics* (Boulder, Colo.: Westview, 1998), 131.
22. See Eugene Lewis, *Public Entrepreneurship* (Bloomington: Indiana University Press, 1980).
23. Anthony Downs, *Inside Bureaucracy* (Boston: Little, Brown, 1967), 88–89.
24. John Brehm and Scott Gates, *Working, Shirking, and Sabotage: Bureaucratic Response to a Democratic Public* (Ann Arbor: University of Michigan Press, 1997).
25. Nancy Roberts and Paula King, *Transforming Public Policy: Dynamics of Policy Entrepreneurship and Innovation* (San Francisco: Jossey-Bass, 1996), 151–152.
26. Lewis, *Public Entrepreneurship,* 214–215.
27. Rourke, *Bureaucracy, Politics, and Public Policy,* 118–119.
28. William Claiborne, "Tribes and Tribulations: BIA Seeks to Lose a Duty," *Washington Post,* June 2, 2000, 31.
29. Laurence Lynn, *Managing Public Policy,* 119–125.
30. Daniel Lewis, "The Trailblazer," *New York Times Magazine,* June 13, 1999, 50–53.
31. William T. Gormley Jr., *Family Day Care Regulation in Wisconsin: The Bureaucracy Heals Itself* (Madison: La Follette Institute of Public Affairs, University of Wisconsin, 1990).

32. See Herbert Simon, *Administrative Behavior: A Study of Decision-Making Processes in Administrative Organizations* (New York: Macmillan, 1957); James March and Herbert Simon, *Organizations* (New York: John Wiley, 1964); Richard Cyert and James March, *A Behavioral Theory of the Firm* (Englewood Cliffs, N.J.: Prentice-Hall, 1963); Aaron Wildavsky, *The Politics of the Budgetary Process,* 3d ed. (Boston: Little, Brown, 1979); and Charles Lindblom, "The Science of Muddling Through," *Public Administration Review* 19 (spring 1959): 78–88.

33. Lindblom, "The Science of Muddling Through," 79–88.

34. Rourke, *Bureaucracy, Politics, and Public Policy,* 29–35.

35. Morton Halperin, "Shaping the Flow of Information," in *Bureaucratic Power in National Politics,* 3d ed., ed. Francis Rourke (Boston: Little, Brown, 1978), 102–115.

36. Ibid., 102–110.

37. Michael Lipsky, "Toward a Theory of Street-Level Bureaucracy," in Rourke, *Bureaucratic Power in National Politics,* 135–157.

38. For a modern version of the rational perspective, see Charles Hitch, *Decision-Making for Defense* (Berkeley: University of California Press, 1965); or E. S. Quade, *Analysis for Public Decisions* (New York: Elsevier, 1975).

39. See William Gormley Jr. and David Weimer, *Organizational Report Cards* (Cambridge: Harvard University Press, 1999), 1–19.

40. A more complete discussion of this example can be found in B. Guy Peters, *American Public Policy: Promise and Performance,* 2d ed. (Chatham, N.J.: Chatham House, 1986), 297–309.

41. For an excellent discussion of the principles and techniques of cost-benefit analysis, see Edith Stokey and Richard Zeckhauser, *A Primer for Policy Analysis* (New York: W. W. Norton, 1978), chaps. 9 and 10.

42. U.S. General Accounting Office, *The Government Performance and Results Act: 1997 Governmentwide Implementation Will Be Uneven,* GGD-97-109 (Washington, D.C.: General Accounting Office, 1997); Stephen Barr, "GOP Sees No Results in Results Act," *Washington Post,* June 9, 1998, 4; Stephen Barr, " 'Performance Reports' Faulted," *Washington Post,* May 4, 2000, 23.

43. William Gormley Jr., "Environmental Performance Measures in a Federal System," June 2000, online at http://www.napawash.org (see Center for the Economy and the Environment, Learning from Innovations, Changing the Federal-State Relationship, Gormley paper), November 2000.

44. Richard Zerbe Jr., "Is Cost-Benefit Analysis Legal? Three Rules," *Journal of Policy Analysis and Management* 17 (summer 1998): 421.

45. Lynn, *Managing Public Policy,* 187; Gormley, "Environmental Performance Measures in a Federal System."

46. See Cornelius Kerwin, *Rulemaking,* 2d ed. (Washington, D.C.: CQ Press, 1999).

47. See Kenneth Culp Davis, *Administrative Law of the Seventies,* supplement to Davis's *Administrative Law Treatise* (Rochester, N.Y.: Lawyers Cooperative Publishing, 1976), chap. 8.

48. See A. Lee Fritschler, *Smoking and Politics,* 3d ed. (Englewood Cliffs, N.J.: Prentice-Hall, 1983), 93–98.

49. Thomas Lippman, "Utility Rebates for Energy-Saving Equipment Deemed Taxable," *Washington Post,* November 25, 1990, 3.
50. Lipsky, "Toward a Theory of Street-Level Bureaucracy."
51. See Davis, *Administrative Law of the Seventies,* chap. 4.
52. See Murray Edelman, *The Symbolic Uses of Politics* (Urbana: University of Illinois Press, 1964), chap. 3.
53. See Frances Fox Piven and Richard Cloward, *Regulating the Poor* (New York: Vintage Books, 1971); or Piven and Cloward, *Poor People's Movements* (New York: Vintage Books, 1979).
54. William Gormley Jr., Joan Hoadley, and Charles Williams, "Potential Responsiveness in the Bureaucracy: Views of Public Utility Regulation," *American Political Science Review* 77 (September 1983): 704–717; William Gormley Jr., *The Politics of Public Utility Regulation* (Pittsburgh: University of Pittsburgh Press, 1983), 113–130.
55. See Andrew McFarland, *Public Interest Lobbies* (Washington, D.C.: American Enterprise Institute, 1976); or Jeffrey Berry, *Lobbying for the People* (Princeton: Princeton University Press, 1977).
56. See Mark Nadel, *The Politics of Consumer Protection* (Indianapolis: Bobbs-Merrill, 1971); Kenneth Meier, *Regulation* (New York: St. Martin's, 1985), 96–97.
57. Gormley, *The Politics of Public Utility Regulation;* Douglas Anderson, "State Regulation of Electric Utilities," in *The Politics of Regulation,* ed. James Q. Wilson (New York: Basic Books, 1980), 3–41.
58. On the FTC, see Meier, *Regulation,* 106–113; on the Army Corps of Engineers, see Daniel Mazmanian and Jeanne Nienaber, *Can Organizations Change? Environmental Protection, Citizen Participation, and the Corps of Engineers* (Washington, D.C.: Brookings Institution, 1979).
59. Gormley, *Taming the Bureaucracy,* chap. 6.
60. Donald Kettl, "Building Lasting Reform: Enduring Questions, Missing Answers," in *Inside the Reinvention Machine,* ed. Donald Kettl and John DiIulio Jr. (Washington, D.C.: Brookings Institution, 1995), 9–83.
61. A good example is the National Environmental Performance Partnership System inaugurated by the EPA in 1995. See National Academy of Public Administration, *Resolving the Paradox of Environmental Protection* (Washington, D.C.: National Academy of Public Administration, 1997), 143–169.
62. For an interesting discussion of state-level reforms, see Maria Aristigueta, *Managing for Results in State Government* (Westport, Conn.: Quorum Books, 1999).
63. See Meier, *Regulation,* 106–113; Michael Pertschuk, *Revolt against Regulation* (Berkeley: University of California Press, 1982); B. Dan Wood and Richard Waterman, *Bureaucratic Dynamics: The Role of Bureaucracy in a Democracy* (Boulder, Colo.: Westview, 1994), 43–48.
64. See Bernstein, *Regulating Business by Independent Commission;* Theodore Lowi, *The End of Liberalism,* 2d ed. (New York: W. W. Norton, 1979); Grant McConnell, *Private Power and American Democracy* (New York: Alfred Knopf, 1966); and George Stigler, "The Theory of Economic Regulation," *Bell Journal of Economic and Management Sciences* (spring 1971): 3–21.
65. See Bernstein, *Regulating Business by Independent Commission;* Bradley Behrman, "The Civil Aeronautics Board," in Wilson, *The Politics of Regulation,* 57–120; David Howard Davis, *Energy Politics,* 3d ed. (New York: St. Martin's,

1982), 130–165; and Jonathan Macey, "Organizational Design and Political Control of Administrative Agencies," *Journal of Law, Economics, and Organization* 8 (March 1992): 93–110.

66. Stigler, "The Theory of Economic Regulation."

67. Macey, "Organizational Design and Political Control of Administrative Agencies," 99.

68. Gormley, *The Politics of Public Utility Regulation,* 152–159.

69. For evaluations of American social welfare programs by authors with contrasting ideological perspectives, see Piven and Cloward, *Regulating the Poor;* Charles Murray, *Losing Ground: American Social Policy, 1950–1980* (New York: Basic Books, 1984).

70. See Robert Haveman, ed., *A Decade of Federal Antipoverty Programs* (New York: Academic Press, 1977); John Schwarz, *America's Hidden Success* (New York: W. W. Norton, 1983); Karen Davis and Kathy Schoen, *Health and the War on Poverty* (Washington, D.C.: Brookings Institution, 1978); and Robert Taggart, *A Fisherman's Guide: An Assessment of Training and Remediation Strategies* (Kalamazoo, Mich.: W. E. Upjohn Institute for Employment Research, 1981). For an evaluation of Head Start, see Valerie Lee et al., "Are Head Start Effects Sustained?" *Child Development* 61 (April 1990): 495–507.

71. House Committee on Ways and Means, *1998 Green Book* (Washington, D.C.: Government Printing Office, 1998), 1413.

72. Ibid., 1420.

73. Jonathan Oberlander, "Managed Care and Medicare Reform," *Journal of Health Politics, Policy, and Law* 22 (April 1997): 595–631.

74. George Anders, *Health against Wealth* (Boston: Houghton Mifflin, 1996).

75. Theodore Marmor, *The Politics of Medicare,* 2d ed. (New York: Aldine de Gruyter, 2000).

76. William Scanlon, *Medicare+Choice: Impact of 1997 Balanced Budget Act Payment Reforms on Beneficiaries and Plans,* testimony before the Senate Committee on Finance, 106th Cong., 1st sess. (Washington, D.C.: General Accounting Office, 1999).

77. Stuart Butler, *Reorganizing the Medicare System to Ensure a Better Program for Seniors,* Heritage Foundation Backgrounder, no. 1294 (Washington, D.C.: Heritage Foundation, 1999).

78. "National Summary of Medical Managed Care Programs and Enrollment, June 30, 1999," online at www.hcfa.gov/medicaid/trends 99.htm.December 22, 2000.

79. Beryl Radin, "The Government Performance and Results Act and the Tradition of Federal Management Reform: Square Pegs in Round Holes?" *Journal of Public Administration Research and Theory* 10 (January 2000): 133.

80. Gormley, "Environmental Performance Measures in a Federal System."

81. U.S. General Accounting Office, *Managing for Results: Opportunities for Continued Improvements in Agencies' Performance Plans,* GAO/GGD/AIMD-99-215 (Washington, D.C.: General Accounting Office, 1999), 3.

Chapter 5 **Cloakroom Politics**

Much of American politics and policymaking takes place in the cloakrooms, committee rooms, and chambers of city councils, state legislatures, and the U.S. Congress. Legislative institutions are often perplexing and frustrating to members and ordinary citizens alike. Describing and assessing the way legislatures operate is a little like retelling the story of the blind men who try to say what an elephant is by describing what they can feel. The impression one gets depends on where one is standing.

Legislatures embody many political paradoxes. They are highly democratic, open institutions that are also responsive to narrow, specialized interest groups. Legislatures are powerful actors in the policy process, but they delegate responsibility for many significant decisions to other political institutions. Legislatures are the most responsive political institutions and in some ways the least responsible. To many observers, legislative policymaking is both appealing and appalling.

Compared with other domains of politics, cloakroom politics is perhaps the most visible, open, chaotic, and human. Only chief executives command more public attention; only living room politics is more open to citizen participation. Legislatures embody a fundamental urge in the American experience— to have a place where the conflicts of public life are debated, deliberated, and decided in full view.

Legislatures are a focal point for the inside players. Government administrators, lobbyists, citizen activists, and journalists have easy access to the legislative chambers and committee rooms and offices. Legislators do not dominate the policy process, but they insinuate themselves into all aspects of public policy. They raise important issues, allocate public goods and services, and influence public and private behavior even when they delegate decisions to others.

Although Americans approve of what Alexis de Tocqueville called "the great political agitation of American legislative bodies," citizens often are frustrated by the chaos of legislative life.[1] In the decade of the 1990s, Congress had a public approval rating of roughly 25 percent.[2] Legislatures reflect not only democratic impulses but also the interests of the powerful. Sometimes legislatures courageously tackle the tough issues of the day; at other times they seem to cower before the challenges that face them. Sometimes legislative actions make the situation worse; when legislatures do nothing, things sometimes get better. Legislatures mirror the conflicts that exist in American society. Consensus is achieved slowly, and it can evaporate quickly.

The Crowded Agenda

The scope of cloakroom politics is incredibly broad. It includes economic affairs, environmental protection, defense and foreign policy, and issues of health, education, and welfare. Every year members of legislatures cast hundreds of votes on public laws and resolutions. Countless issues receive attention from committees, subcommittees, and individual members. The scope of cloakroom politics is illustrated by the issues considered during the 106th Congress (1999–2000). The list in Box 5-1 is incomplete, but it conveys the breadth of Congress's responsibilities and public policy interests. As American legislatures go, Congress is not unusual in having a far-reaching policy agenda. State legislatures also have extremely varied agendas. During a recent session the Massachusetts legislature held hearings and passed legislation covering topics as diverse as a patients' bill of rights for patients in health maintenance organizations (HMOs), paid parental leaves for new parents, measures to prevent racial profiling by police, a requirement that insurance companies pay for women's contraceptives, creation of "buffer zones" around abortion clinics, the voiding of a 1963 law that outlawed tattooing in the state, the imposition of further disclosure requirements on cigarette manufacturers, and the working out of a deal to build a new Fenway Park for the Red Sox.[3]

One might at first conclude that legislatures, their committees, and their members consider practically everything imaginable. Open as they are, however, legislatures do not respond to everyone who knocks on their doors. Legislatures are collections of many smaller organizations—the offices of the senators and representatives and legislative committees. Most issues are handled first by subcommittees and committees, especially in Congress, and are given scant attention by legislators other than committee members. Committees and subcommittees have wide latitude to conduct hearings on, investigate, and review legislation within their jurisdictions. With input from party leaders, committees are then able to formulate bills (major and minor) that go to the floor for action by the entire chamber.[4]

Most legislative activity is debate and discussion rather than lawmaking, and legislatures can influence policy without making laws. Legislatures often engage in protracted considerations of issues without making decisions because, unlike other institutions, they are important democratic and political forums—where symbolism can be just as important as substance. A great deal of time and energy is spent raising issues, seeking publicity, educating the public, helping political supporters, and embarrassing opponents.

If a problem is not already on the institution's agenda, it can be difficult to get it there. One scholar noted that the bulk of Congress's time is consumed

Box 5–1 **Some Issues Considered in the**
106th Congress, 1999–2000

Abortion: legislation making it a crime to take a girl across state lines to circumvent parental consent

Agriculture: legislation to lower the premiums farmers pay for crop insurance

Banking: overhaul of regulatory framework for the financial services industry

Commerce: federally subsidized loans for steel, oil, and gas industries

Congress: campaign finance reform

Defense: FY2000 defense authorization bill, proposal to restructure the Energy Department's nuclear weapons program, missile defense plan, test ban treaty

Education: reauthorization of the Elementary and Secondary Education Act (ESEA)

Employment and labor: proposal to increase the minimum wage

Environment: nuclear waste storage, overhaul of Superfund program

Foreign affairs: State Department reauthorization bill, sanctions in Iran and Russia, ground forces in Kosovo, Peace Corps reauthorization

Government operations: the 2000 census, legislation requiring government agencies to detail the cost and benefits of proposed rules

Health: bills to protect patients enrolled in managed care plans, legislation to protect the privacy of medical records, organ procurement rules

Impeachment: of President Clinton

Industry and regulation: deregulation of electric utility industry

Law and judiciary: juvenile justice legislation, extension of independent counsel law, bill to recognize the fetus as distinct from the pregnant woman, victims' rights, assisted suicide

Science: reauthorization of NASA

Social policy: Social Security overhaul, affordable housing for the elderly

Taxes: Republican tax cut bill

Technology and communication: legislation to allow satellite television companies to deliver local broadcast stations, Internet gambling ban

Trade: proposal to lift tariffs on goods made in the Caribbean, Central America, and Africa; China trade

Transportation: reauthorization of Federal Aviation Administration, creation of Federal Motor Carrier Safety Administration

Source: CQ Weekly, November 27, 1999, 2848–2888.

considering matters that recur each year.[5] The struggles to get a vote on the floor of the House or Senate are often intense because the time these institutions can spend in collective deliberation is scarce and there are many claimants to it. It is not unusual for sponsors to have to wait several years after committees have finished work on a bill to get it on the floor. Legislatures frequently must revisit past policy actions or deal with unfinished business from previous Congresses. Many of the issues listed in Box 5-1 are bills that were passed by Congress five, ten, or even forty years ago, but in a different form.

Another large chunk of legislatures' limited time is consumed by crises. A war in the Middle East, a space shuttle disaster, famine in Africa, Americans being held hostage, bank failures, stock manipulation on Wall Street, an oil spill, scandals, and other problems command the immediate attention of elected representatives. In some cases their response is quick legislative action. But in other cases they do a lot of talking about whether and how to respond, while looking to the chief executive for direction. In 1990, when Iraq invaded Kuwait, Congress waited several months before taking votes on resolutions to either give or withhold authorization for the president to use military force against Iraq (they gave him wide authorization). However, in December 1998, when President Clinton ordered air strikes against Iraq just as the House prepared to discuss his impeachment, many Republicans in Congress openly questioned his motives.[6] By 1999 Congress was content to let President Clinton conduct air strikes in Kosovo for nearly three months, but they asserted their "power of the purse" very quickly after the air strikes succeeded in driving the Serbian military out of Kosovo and the issue became who would pay for ground troops in the area.[7]

Many features of cloakroom politics keep the legislature's doors open to a broad range of views; power is dispersed, and there are many ways to gain access to the institution's agenda. Legislatures respond to the concerns of members and of a wide range of outsiders, including presidents and governors, executive agencies, interest groups, and individual citizens, but the response is not always the same in kind or degree. In general the attention of a single representative may be easily gained, but not that of an institution.

Members

The issue agendas of individual legislators are strongly influenced by the concerns of citizens and organizations from their districts. Dealing with constituency problems consumes much of the time of members and their personal staffs. Representatives use their influence to speed up approval of grants for sewer projects, obtain funds for the building of research laboratories, obtain tax breaks for a new sports arena, or fight for more financial aid for students. Collectively, the concerns of constituents play a strong part in shaping the policy activity of legislatures. According to Alan Rosenthal, by the late 1990s, "anywhere from one-third to two-thirds [of state legislators] would now cite constituency service as an important, or even *the* most important, part of the job of being a legislator."[8] The impulse to consider one's constituency helps to shape many aspects of legislative behavior, from staff organization to floor voting.

When legislators run for reelection every two, four, or six years, they must account, however loosely, for their action or inaction on important matters. Voters, interest groups, and journalists, who shape evaluations of legislators, like to ask, "What have you done for us lately?" Despite the fact that nine members of Congress in ten who seek reelection win their contests, most "run scared" even in districts that appear safe for the incumbents. Indeed, one reason so many seats are safe is that members work so hard at reelection.[9] The uncanny ability of Democratic incumbents to secure reelection in the 1970s and 1980s led President Bush in 1991 to endorse a constitutional amendment to limit the number of terms members of Congress can serve. Support for this amendment became part of the Republicans' Contract with America, and the GOP scored a huge victory in the 1994 congressional elections, gaining majorities in both houses of Congress. The 1994 elections were notable in that thirty-four House Democratic incumbents (15 percent of those running) were defeated, and the Republicans won virtually all the open races (those that did not have an incumbent running).[10] This result was widely viewed as a rejection of the Democratically controlled 103d Congress and the policies, in particular health care reform, of President Clinton. However, in the congressional elections of 1996, 1998, and 2000, high rates of incumbent reelection prevailed, and the Republican interest in term limits waned.

Some legislators develop reputations as "policy entrepreneurs" because they exhibit a keen interest in advancing a cause, an idea, or a new program. That interest, combined with ambition, makes them very influential. As they seek legislative accomplishments or perhaps higher office, they push new items onto committee or subcommittee agendas. They respond quickly to national and international events and mass media reports. Policy entrepreneurs do not necessarily want to expand government spending programs. For example, Sen. Rick Santorum, R-Pa., who led the charge for reductions in federal spending in the 1990s, is no less an entrepreneur than Sen. Edward Kennedy, D-Mass., a longtime advocate of expanded education, child care, and public health insurance programs.

Legislators also use their committee and subcommittee positions to focus attention on scandals or government mismanagement and fraud. Investigations throw light on the members as well as the issues. A congressional probe was launched in early 1999 after newspaper reports of an alleged spy ring created by the Chinese government to obtain military and other technology secrets from the Los Alamos National Laboratories captured national attention. A bipartisan House investigative committee, headed by Christopher

Cox, R-Calif., issued a report in May 1999, which largely confirmed the newspaper allegations. The report also contained numerous recommendations for improving security at Los Alamos and other nuclear facilities run by the Energy Department. The most significant of the recommendations called for the establishment of a separate National Nuclear Security Administration (NNSA) within the Energy Department. This step was opposed by Energy secretary Bill Richardson, who saw it as a dangerous congressional encroachment into his department's jurisdiction, but the new agency was established when President Clinton signed the FY 2000 defense authorization bill. Richardson responded by asking Clinton to let him (Richardson) take on the duties of heading the NNSA, but upon hearing about this maneuver angry House Republicans fought back by creating a special panel to oversee nuclear security within the Energy Department and threatening, among other things, to cut Richardson's travel budget.[11]

Richardson's position that he, not Congress, should be in charge of nuclear security was greatly undermined when two computer hard drives containing nuclear weapons data turned up missing in a Los Alamos secure laboratory in June 2000. Richardson's critics on Capitol Hill didn't hold back. Sen. Jon Kyl, R-Ariz., said: "You could not blame someone who was in charge and doing his best to cooperate. But it's hard to give any slack to someone who said, 'Don't interfere in my domain—this is my deal, I'm going to take care of it, and I'm going to assume full responsibility for whatever occurs.' It's like the candidate who campaigns on some grand reform theme, and then you find out he himself is guilty of the same thing. He's dead." Even some Democrats joined in the criticism. At a Senate Intelligence Committee hearing, Robert Byrd, D-W.Va., told Richardson point blank: "[Y]ou will never again receive the support of the Senate of the United States for any office to which you might be appointed. It's gone. You've squandered your treasure, and I'm sorry."[12] At this point Richardson was pledging his full support for the newly appointed head of the NNSA, former Air Force general John A. Gordon. Similar dramas, although not necessarily of the same level of visibility, occur dozens of times each year and help to set Congress's agenda while enabling members to increase their visibility back home.

The agendas of legislators are shaped by many factors; constituency pressures are always important, but pressures from outside groups also figure prominently. Executive branch agencies and interest groups generally focus their concerns on the committees and subcommittees that develop the policies and programs that affect them most directly. Indeed, many of the issues considered by legislative committees originate in administrative agencies. Outside interest groups influence legislators because these groups supply the milk and honey of politics—money and grateful voters. Running for office costs a great deal of money; Senate campaigns run to millions of dollars. The quest for campaign funds compels legislators at least to listen to the concerns of their contributors. Organizations with money employ several methods to get the attention of subcommittees and committees. They hire lobbyists to monitor legislation, meet with members and staff, and invite legislators to speak at group meetings. Organizations that cannot deliver money or votes have a much tougher time gaining attention.[13] Although committee chairs and other influential committee members exercise a great deal of independent power, they are usually responsive to concerns expressed by the executive branch and prominent interest groups.

The Institution

Issues that dominate the attention of the entire legislature are broad societal concerns and issues advanced by presidents, governors, or legislative leaders. An especially good example was air pollution legislation in 1990. In that year, both President Bush and Senate majority leader George Mitchell announced that new clean air legislation was their top legislative priority. Congress had tried unsuccessfully over a thirteen-year period to revise the Clean Air Act, but with both Mitchell and Bush pushing for action Republicans and Democrats were able to agree on compromise legislation. Despite considerable opposition from both affected industries and environmental groups, the 1990 revision of the Clean Air Act passed both houses of Congress and was signed by the president.[14]

Under certain circumstances the mere mention of a policy initiative by the president or a governor can stimulate legislative activity and may yield new laws. Just after taking office in 1991, Governor Lowell Weicker of Connecticut threw the legislature, and most of the citizens, into a flurry of debate by proposing a new set of tax laws that included the state's first-ever income tax. For a state that had long prided itself on not having an income tax, these proposals were political dynamite. Instantly, the Weicker tax proposals leaped to the top of the Connecticut legislature's agenda.

Legislatures listen to outsiders, especially chief executives, but the partisan and entrepreneurial instincts of members and committees also bring new ideas to the agenda that chief executives would prefer to ignore. During the last two years of the Reagan administration (1986–1988) Congress made sweeping changes in national immigration policy, passed a massive highway building and rehabilitation program, revised the Clean Water Act, and imposed economic sanctions on the South African government. None of these policies was promoted by President Reagan; some he actively opposed, but the Democratic majorities in both houses, with help from numerous Republicans, enacted them anyway.

The most dramatic example of partisan agenda-setting occurred during the 104th Congress when Speaker of the House Newt Gingrich attempted to steer the Republican Contract with America through the legislative process. The Contract covered a variety of topics including anticrime legislation, welfare reform, middle-class tax relief, increased penalties for child pornography, legal reform, so-called "unfunded mandates" the federal government placed on states, term limits for members of Congress, and the line-item veto for presidents. Gingrich and his leadership team revamped the committee system, appointed party loyalists to head all the major committees, and succeeded in getting the House to pass most of the legislative vehicles (ten bills and three resolutions) that embodied the Contract with America. Very little in the Contract with America, other than the line-item veto, was favored by President Clinton, but it definitely dominated the congressional agenda in 1995. Although many of the bills became law (legal reforms, penalties for child pornography, paperwork reductions, limits on unfunded mandates, the line-item veto), most were either rebuffed by presidential vetoes or delayed and reformulated in the Senate.[15]

The intense partisanship exhibited in the 104th Congress, the single most important institutional development of the last fifteen years, was not entirely new. Depending upon one's viewpoint, it began with the Supreme Court nomination of Robert Bork in 1986, which was torpedoed by congressional Democrats and liberal interest groups, or the ouster of House Speaker Jim Wright, engineered by Newt Gingrich; but setting aside the question of who started it, partisan warfare was evident in Congress throughout the 1990s. The most notable effect of this on the agenda-setting process was that during the bulk of the Clinton administration (1994–2000) congressional leaders went to great lengths within and outside their chambers to reject the president's legislative agenda as articulated in the annual State of the Union addresses or other speeches. However, Republicans frequently found themselves trumped by the president (through use of the veto or appeals to the public) on high-profile issues such as tax cuts, spending on education, Social Security, and prescription drugs for senior citizens. Thus, despite their efforts, congressional leaders were not able to ignore the president's agenda.

Legislative leaders occasionally can turn the spotlight on policy issues even when they do not percolate up from committee and subcommittee power centers. For example, in 1986, after two well-known athletes—a college basketball star and a professional football player—died of cocaine overdoses, Congress wasted little time in passing new antidrug legislation, which appropriated nearly $2 billion for drug prevention programs even though such legislation was not being pushed by traditional sources of policy proposals—committees, executive agencies, major interest groups. Spurred on by President Reagan (with his wife, Nancy), who made a televised appeal for a "national crusade" against drugs, Congress reacted to what opinion polls showed to be increasing public anxiety about drug abuse among young people, especially the use of crack cocaine. The *New York Times* reported: "Antidrug bills that have lingered in committees for months or years are now passing out 'in minutes.' . . . Cost doesn't seem to be an object now."[16]

A similar situation occurred in the spring of 1991, when members of Congress could not wait to pass legislation granting new or expanded benefits to past and future veterans of military conflicts despite the looming presence of the largest budget deficit in history. They began by passing a long-delayed bill to provide compensation to Vietnam War veterans suffering from the effects of exposure to the herbicide Agent Orange. They went on to pass new educational, small business, home loan, and medical care benefits for participants in the Persian Gulf War.[17]

Legislative staff members are another fertile source of policy proposals. Congress employs an army of professional analysts, lawyers, and political advisers—a personal and committee staff numbering more than 17,000. Another 10,000 work for support agencies, including the Congressional Research Service (CRS), the General Accounting Office (GAO), the Congressional Budget Office (CBO), and the Government Printing Office (GPO).[18] These agencies provide general and specific research assistance to legislative members and committees, conduct studies either on their own initiative or in response to requests by members or committees, and review and investigate the actions of executive agencies. State legislatures used to rely almost entirely on centralized staffs (offices of legislative councils and reference bureaus) that served entire chambers, but they have now "congressionalized" by greatly increasing the number of staff personnel and assigning them to work for committees, legislative parties, and individual members. Nationally there are about 27,000 full-time state legislative staffers.[19]

Entrepreneurial Politics

Although legislatures can engage in policy debates and focus public attention on social and economic problems, it is much harder for them to take decisive action. When legislators want to make policy, they must deal, bargain, and compromise in order to develop the several majorities required to enact legislation. This majority-building enterprise is difficult and complicated, in large part because cloakroom politics is molded by the complex contemporary political and economic environment. Legislatures do not function in hermetically sealed chambers; deliberation and debate within them reflect societal differences about public problems and solutions.

Suppose someone asked for an explanation of why a landmark minimum wage law was passed in 1996 but not in 1986 or 1992. We might begin by outlining the basic features of the political landscape in 1995–1996. Both houses of Congress were controlled by Republicans, and a Democrat was in the White House. Public opinion polls were revealing widespread support (80 percent) for an increase in the minimum wage, which stood at its lowest level in forty years in terms of purchasing power. Furthermore, polls were showing growing displeasure with hard-line Republican leadership of

Congress, which was blocking floor votes on the minimum wage bill. President Clinton's popularity, in contrast, was on the rise, and the 1996 election loomed on the horizon. With 10 million workers standing to benefit directly, Republicans in the Northeast and Midwest broke with their leadership and helped pushed the legislation through.

Painting minimum wage politics in such broad brush strokes, however, conceals important nuances. Policy entrepreneur Sen. Edward Kennedy first recognized the opportunity the legislation represented for Democrats, and he teamed up with minority leader Tom Daschle, D-S.D., to use Senate rules to disrupt the scheduled flow of legislation by proposing to add the minimum wage bill to every piece of legislation the Senate considered in the spring and summer of 1996. Disarray in the Senate carried the threat of reflecting badly on Majority Leader Robert Dole, who was also a presidential candidate. Making the best of a bad situation, Republicans entered into serious discussions with Democrats and attached a host of tax provisions favorable to small business and families to the minimum wage bill, thus satisfying the demands of dozens of legislators and interest groups. After passage the president staged a gaudy signing celebration on the White House lawn designed to emphasize the close relationship between Democrats and American workers. Even Clinton's arch rival, Newt Gingrich, conceded: "I would say to my friends, the Democratic Party, you won a great victory. Some of us swallowed more than we wanted to, but it was clearly the American people's will."[20]

Similar politics molds hundreds of bills that do not make headlines. In the cloakrooms of every capitol, politics is characterized by fragmented power, bargaining and compromise, deadlines, and legislative and executive leadership.

Fragmented Power

No one controls or commands legislatures. At times it seems that there are 535 leaders on Capitol Hill and no followers. House and Senate elected leaders retain their positions only as long as the members support them. Unlike bureaucracies, where there is a hierarchy of authority, legislatures are collections of independent contractors. Environmental Protection Agency regulations governing auto emission standards are issued by the administrator, who may seek advice from staff, industry, and the public, but the final decision on many matters rests with the administrator. When Congress writes laws governing air pollution, 535 members may have some say in the outcome.

Legislatures are not without organization. Committees and subcommittees are the heart and soul of legislative policymaking. Writing about Congress in 1885, political scientist (later president) Woodrow Wilson referred to its committees as "little legislatures."[21] What Wilson observed then is no less true today. Committees are powerful vehicles for policy deliberation and

---

Box 5–2 **Subcommittees of Two
Congressional Committees**

Senate Finance Committee

Health Care
International Trade
Long-term Growth and Debt Reduction
Social Security and Family Policy
Taxation and IRS Oversight

House Transportation and Infrastructure Committee

Aviation
Coast Guard and Marine Transportation
Economic Development, Public Buildings, Hazardous Materials,
   and Pipeline Transportation
Ground Transportation
Oversight, Investigations and Emergency Management
Water Resources and Environment

Source: CQ Weekly, March 13, 1999, 630–662.

---

action. In fact, a legislature's ability to shape public policy is vastly expanded by the division of labor and development of expertise made possible by the committee and subcommittee system.

Congress is divided into hundreds of little legislatures. The Republican takeover of the House in 1994 did have the effect of substantially reducing the number of committees and subcommittees; in 1990 there were 22 major committees and 138 subcommittees in the House, whereas in 1999–2000 the House had 19 major committees and 85 subcommittees. In the 106th Senate there were 17 committees and 69 subcommittees. Because subcommittees are chaired by members of the majority party, about 40 percent of the Republicans in the House chaired a subcommittee, and almost every majority party senator chaired one subcommittee and many chaired two.[22] The subcommittees of the Senate Finance Committee and the House Transportation and Infrastructure Committee are listed in Box 5-2.

In fact, power is so widely dispersed in legislatures that the mass media and the public have trouble keeping track of the star players in each legislative ball game. Even powerful groups, such as the House Ways and Means Committee, which handles such matters as taxation, trade policy, Social Security, and health programs, are practically invisible to the public. Most committees and subcommittees are even more obscure. Few people outside

Washington, D.C., know that the House Appropriations Subcommittee on Labor, Health and Human Services and Education appropriates roughly one-third of all federal spending, excluding Social Security and interest payments on the national debt. Fewer still have heard of the Subcommittees on Aviation and Ground Transportation (of the Transportation and Infrastructure Committee)—the two largest subcommittees in the House—let alone have the foggiest idea about what they do.

The policy issues handled by each subcommittee give rise to "issue networks" that include members of Congress and their staffs, executive agencies, interest groups, journalists, and academics.[23] Many important policy decisions that go unnoticed by the public are made within this subcommittee-centered power structure. The fragmented system satisfies legislators because it permits more of them to exercise power. Interest groups are pleased because they gain access to the process and attention to their concerns. If the fishing industry is feeling threatened by environmental regulations, industry representatives know that they can go to the Subcommittee on Fisheries Conservation, Wildlife and Oceans (of the House Resources Committee) and the Subcommittee on Fisheries, Wildlife and Drinking Water (of the Senate Environment and Public Works Committee), where they will have an opportunity to press their case in a public forum. Executive agencies also recognize some benefit from the convenience and familiarity of dealing with a limited number of legislators who are knowledgeable about a particular agency's programs and policies.

Committees and subcommittees also create power bases for promoting innovative policies. In the 1970s and 1980s the chairman of the House Energy and Commerce Committee, John D. Dingell, D-Mich., and the chairman of the Health and Environment Subcommittee, Henry A. Waxman, D-Calif., used the Energy and Commerce Committee as their platform for launching investigations and formulating sweeping changes in health policy, environmental protection, and telecommunications. Although frequently at odds, especially over environmental policy matters such as auto emission standards and acid rain, both Dingell (representing Detroit's auto interests) and Waxman were very effective issue entrepreneurs, compiling impressive records of legislative accomplishments. In the 1990s, the chairman of the Senate Health, Education, Labor and Pensions Committee, James M. Jeffords, a moderate Republican from Vermont, parlayed his ability to communicate with Democrats and groups typically affiliated with Democrats (teachers unions) to craft many successful policy innovations. One example was legislation to consolidate virtually all federal job-training programs (Workforce Investment Act, PL 105-220), which was enacted by the 105th Congress in 1998.

Bargaining and Compromise

Because power is widely dispersed, bargaining and compromise are central to legislative politics. Fragmentation enhances the power of members

and subcommittee leaders, but it makes reaching consensus more difficult; a few determined individuals can stall the process. Legislatures may
fail to make progress on important policy issues for months or even years.
At times, the legislative process moves at a snail's pace. Yet when agreement is reached and the deals are struck, legislatures can move with blind-
ing speed.[24]

A majority of legislators must support a bill repeatedly before it reaches a
chief executive's desk for signature. Majorities must be obtained in subcommittees and committees, and in the entire House and Senate. If there are
disagreements between the House and Senate—and there usually are—a
temporary conference committee is appointed to iron out the differences
and then seek yet another majority in each chamber.

Deference to the legislative handiwork of committees can simplify the
majority-building process. Until the late 1960s, members approved most of
the committee proposals that came to the floor, making few or no amendments. By the mid-1970s, however, floor debates had changed dramatically;
members insisted on introducing large numbers of amendments after committee bills reached the floor. In the Senate the loose rules governing floor
debates gave (and still give) the new breed of policy-active senators ample
opportunity to amend legislation and engage in a variety of delaying tactics
on the floor.[25] By the mid-1980s, floor amending activity had produced so
much frustration in the House that the Democratic leadership, working
through the Rules Committee, took action to place significant new restrictions on the making of floor amendments.[26]

House Republicans, who had often felt silenced by Rules Committee
restrictions of Democratic leaders, promised to open the floor to amendments if they gained power over the chamber. However, after the Republicans took control of the House in 1994, the leadership quickly learned the
advantages of using restrictive rules and have made frequent use of them
ever since. Moreover, House Republican leaders have also frequently
ignored or bypassed committees in order to advance the versions of legislation they preferred.[27] For example, Newt Gingrich used "task forces" to
expedite passage of the Contract with America.[28]

Although members of Congress often take cues from party leaders and
the president, majorities assembled to pass one law may not stick together
for the next battle. As new issues arise, majorities must be put together at
all stages of the legislative process, often one vote at a time. Building coalitions is painstaking work that involves difficult negotiations. David Stockman, President Reagan's first budget director, called the task of pulling
coalitions together in Congress the "politics of giving."

> An actual majority for any specific bill had to be reconstructed from scratch
> every time. It had to be cobbled out of the patchwork of raw, parochial deals
> that set off a political billiard game of counter-reactions and corresponding

demands. The last ten or twenty percent of the votes needed for a majority in both houses had to be bought, period.[29]

If presidents, governors, and some party leaders prefer "wholesale" politics—sweeping, popular ideas—most legislators prefer "retail" politics—rewards for their district or state. A House leadership aide put it simply: "No matter how members ask the question it always comes down to one issue—how will it affect me?"[30] Crafting laws requires many different types of agreements. Deals may involve one member agreeing to vote yes on a bill with the understanding that the favor will be returned when that member has a bill that needs support. Or legislation may be modified to include a higher appropriation, lower taxes, or favorable treatment for an industry in a member's district as the price for a positive vote.

German chancellor Otto von Bismarck once remarked, "Politics is like sausage. Neither should be viewed in the making." Nevertheless, the American political process is open to many observers and some of them regard the horse trading, compromise, and vote swapping that characterize the legislative politics as distinctly unsavory. But the nature of representative democratic institutions makes it unlikely, and even undesirable, that they would operate without these kinds of transactions taking place. To fashion laws in an open democratic institution, a broad consensus must be achieved and sustained. "Good" policy benefits, or at least does not harm, the people and interests represented by elected officials.

Deadlines

This underlying dynamic helps explain why the members of legislatures often procrastinate until the last possible moment before reaching a decision. Just before adjournment or an election, legislatures often rush through hundreds of bills, or combine a large number of bills into "omnibus" legislation. For example, the 105th Congress waited until September/October of 1998 (just before adjourning for midterm elections) to pass most of the important bills—defense authorization, higher education reauthorization, an overhaul of public housing programs, a moratorium on taxing the Internet, funding for the International Monetary Fund (IMF), and an omnibus spending bill—that it would successfully enact into law.

The omnibus spending bill contained almost four thousand pages of text, which few if any members had time to read before voting, and included a vast range of spending and nonspending measures that had been bogged down throughout the session. Many objected to this blatant example of last-minute policymaking. One of the principal architects of the legislation, House Appropriations Committee Chairman Robert Livingston, said about the slap-dash manner in which the final bill was assembled: "I am not going to defend the process. I hate the process." Sen. Robert Byrd remarked:

"Now someone said . . . that making legislation is like making sausage. Don't kid yourself. I have made sausage, and I can tell you that what we did this year is significantly more sloppy."[31] After the 1998 elections, the 105th House reassembled for one more legislative act: it voted articles of impeachment against President Clinton on December 19, 1998.

Why does a legislature facing a deadline act like a football team executing a two-minute drill—quickly and efficiently moving the ball down the field for a touchdown, when at first they seemed unable to move it two feet? Why does a legislature not always act as if the deadline is fast approaching? Action is postponed primarily because everyone waits until the end to get the best deal. Knowing that decisions on major legislative initiatives and tax and spending bills may not be made until the eleventh hour encourages everyone to hold off their commitments.

Legislators also delay action in the hope that unfavorable political conditions will improve. Perhaps public opposition to a controversial policy will soften; maybe the governor will take a different position; perhaps the next election will bring more like-minded individuals to the legislature. Without deadlines, legislatures find it difficult to make decisions. The end of a fiscal year, the expiration of a law's authorization, an impending election, or adjournment forces legislatures to act, whether they are ready or not.

Leadership

Fragmented power and the need for compromise increase the importance of leadership in putting things together. Legislative leaders assemble coalitions and set priorities for the institution.[32] But leaders derive their power from the members and often must defer to their wishes to keep their support. The positions that legislative leaders take on policy issues are heavily influenced by the views of other legislators in their party.

According to Randall Ripley, a perceptive student of American politics, congressional leaders perform five policy-related tasks:

1. They help determine who sits on and chairs the most powerful committees.
2. They help decide when and in what form legislative business will come to the floor of the House and Senate.
3. They help organize votes on the floor of the House and Senate by contacting—whipping—members to attend and vote.
4. They communicate leadership preferences and collect information on member needs and preferences.
5. They serve as focal points for contact with the White House, the leaders of the other chamber, and the press.[33]

A leader's most important power is the ability to persuade his or her colleagues to follow. Majority and minority leaders generally exercise more influence on procedural matters—when a bill is considered or how an issue is framed for a vote—than they do on the substance of legislation, its policy objectives and strategies.[34] Leaders often package issues so that fellow party members can cast votes that help them satisfy their constituents or interest groups. When Robert Dole, R-Kan., was Senate majority leader in 1985, he arranged for Republican senators seeking reelection to introduce budget amendments restoring proposed cuts in popular programs in their states. Senators from urban states called for increases in urban development grants and mass transit aid. Senators from tobacco-growing states asked for decreases in the cigarette tax. Senators from agricultural states demanded higher price supports, and so on. The value of such techniques has been magnified by television coverage of House and Senate proceedings.

Members are most likely to play follow-the-leader when it advances their electoral goals. But members have a compelling excuse for ignoring a leader's requests: "I can't vote with you because it could cost me reelection." Even the leaders themselves sometimes resort to this defense. House majority leader Jim Wright, D-Texas, opposed his party's tax reform bill in 1986 because it was not sufficiently generous to the Texas oil and gas industry. Wright did not suffer for his defection; he was elected Speaker of the House a few months later.

Congressional leaders are the essential glue for holding coalitions together, but until the late 1980s they did not show much inclination to advance their own legislative agendas. By 1987, Democrats in the House were sufficiently frustrated by six years of Ronald Reagan's presidency to want stronger congressional leadership. And Jim Wright was eager to lead. Using a three-pronged strategy that included generous provision of services to members to aid in coalition building, the structuring of choices to serve the policy ends of the House leadership, and the expansion of leadership organizations and circles to include as many members as possible (the strategy of inclusion), Wright, Majority Leader Tom Foley, and Whip Tony Coelho were able to establish an agenda (clean water legislation, aid for the homeless, a trade bill, catastrophic health insurance, welfare reform, and tax increases) and move it through the chamber.[35] This example was followed in the 101st Congress (1989–1990), when Senate majority leader George Mitchell employed many of the same strategies to achieve similar ends. Perhaps the clearest indication of strong Democratic congressional leadership in the 101st Congress was the ability of Senator Mitchell and then-Speaker Foley to confront President Bush on the budget and get him not only to agree to new taxes (reversing his "no new taxes" campaign pledge) but also to accept a tax package that the Democrats developed.[36]

The most audacious attempt at legislative governance under divided government in the twentieth century was Newt Gingrich's leadership of the 104th Congress. Gingrich not only hand-picked the committee chairmen, he also appointed a series of task forces to oversee the work of committees in order to make sure the legislation they reported conformed to the letter and spirit of the Contract with America. If, despite all this, committees reported legislation at odds with the wishes of the leadership, Gingrich and his leadership team (including Majority Leader Dick Armey, R-Texas, and Whip Tom DeLay, R-Texas) would simply make changes in the bills before they reached the floor. As promised by Gingrich, nearly the entire Contract had passed the House during the first 100 days of the 104th Congress. Furthermore, Senate Republicans under Robert Dole's leadership also felt some compunction to advance the Contract, but, despite Dole's efforts, much of the legislation passed by the House did not make it through the Senate. The main goal of this exercise was to challenge President Clinton for national leadership after the 1994 elections. By the end of the 104th Congress, it seemed pretty clear that this experiment in party-based legislative governance was not working. This was confirmed in the way that speaks the loudest on Capitol Hill—the Republicans lost three House seats in the 1996 elections. House Republican rule changes since 1996 have restored much of the power over policy formulation to committees.[37]

From the 1960s through the 1980s, as state legislatures developed from amateurish assemblies into modern, professionally staffed institutions, legislative leaders were generally more influential than congressional leaders of that same era. Well-known leaders of the time included Jesse Unruh of California, Vern Riffe of Ohio, William Bulger of Massachusetts, John Martin of Maine, and Willie Brown of California. These and other presiding officers in state legislatures were able to appoint the members and chairs of standing committees, decide which committee would consider legislation, determine when bills would be "posted" for a vote, and closely monitor and manage deliberations on the floor of the chamber. They also promoted substantive programs and persuaded standing committees to implement them. But even during this period, the exercise of policymaking power in state legislatures was far from centralized. Alan Rosenthal, a leading authority on state legislatures, wrote: "Aggressive policy leadership is probably the exception rather than the rule."[38]

In the 1990s Rosenthal observed a decline in the power of state legislative leaders. This decline appears to have been the result of more partisan politics, which augmented the strength and importance of party caucuses; and term limits, which brought in more rebellious newcomers, who are not content to have the legislatures governed by entrenched leaders.[39] As was the case at the national level, 1994 was something of a watershed year. Republicans went from controlling roughly one-third of the state legislative chambers before that election to controlling one-half after it, and the term limit movement was enjoying great success around the country.[40] According to Rosenthal, legislatures in states with term limits are losing their ability to control their own affairs. In addition to having weak internal leadership, they have been beset by all sorts of restrictions and requirements by the public, speaking through ballot initiatives. These include rules by which legislation will be considered, the timing of legislative sessions, and the salaries and working conditions of legislators.[41]

Ironically, legislatures are probably more readily and effectively led by chief executives than by internal leaders. Presidents and governors can go directly to interest groups and to the public upon whom legislators depend for support. They have the wherewithal not only to set the legislative agendas but also to formulate policies and then push them through to final adoption. "Whatever the precise sources of policy formulation," Rosenthal observed, "the processes by which proposals make the agenda, receive serious consideration, and get adopted may depend considerably on executive leadership."[42] Although divided government very significantly diminishes the possibilities for legislative leadership by chief executives, presidents and governors have political powers that are unavailable to members of Congress and state legislatures (see Chapter 6). Chief among them is the ability to be heard above the clamor of voices. As Rep. David Obey, D-Wis., said, "The President has the only megaphone in Washington."[43]

Rites of Passage

The characteristics of cloakroom politics profoundly influence what legislatures do. What does this mixture of individual needs, fragmented power, compromise, and leadership produce in the way of public policies?

Symbols over Substance

Symbol often triumphs over substance in cloakroom politics. Much legislative activity involves talk, not action. Hearings are held, bills are introduced, speeches are delivered, but no legislation passes. Significant policy results are often hard to achieve because they may require legislatures to wield the coercive power of government (to regulate public or private behavior, or to impose taxes), and unpopular action of this type can cost members their jobs. A popular alternative to decisive action is symbolic policy. A small explosion of symbolic policymaking occurred in the spring of 2000, after presidential candidate George W. Bush made an appearance at Bob Jones University during the primary campaign (against John McCain) in South Carolina. In addition to such notorious practices as banning interracial dating, the university was known for a statement its founder once made describing Catholicism as a "cult." After the primary, which Bush won, effectively ending the McCain challenge, Cardinal John

O'Connor of New York wrote candidate Bush a letter scolding him for not speaking out about this and other issues when he visited the university. O'Connor's letter, and resolutions introduced in the House and Senate by Democrats Joseph D. Crowley of New York City and Robert G. Torricelli of New Jersey inviting Congress to condemn "the discriminatory practices prevalent at Bob Jones University," helped to focus congressional Republican attention on a potential electoral problem. Senate majority leader Trent Lott, R-Miss., and Speaker of the House J. Dennis Hastert, R-Ill., quickly blocked consideration of the Democratic resolutions, but they did allow their respective chambers to vote on and approve resolutions awarding the Congressional Medal of Honor to Cardinal O'Connor, praising the past and present contributions of Catholic schools, and opposing efforts to expel the Vatican from the United Nations.[44]

As the example above illustrates, laws that are primarily symbolic are often passed to reassure politically aroused groups.[45] Without offering tangible benefits, the legislature addresses the concerns of aggrieved parties with policy pronouncements that mollify them. Disadvantaged groups, such as the unemployed and the poor, seldom have sufficient political clout to hold elected officials accountable.[46]

A variation on the symbolic policy theme is the tendency of legislatures to adopt policies that are long on goals but short on the means for carrying them out. Such policies may strike only a glancing blow at the problem. The gulf between rhetoric and reality is frequently exposed by the difference between the authorizing language and the actual appropriations bills. Authorizations set out the objectives and strategies for ameliorating a problem; appropriations bills supply money for programs and benefits to people. The Head Start Program, which provides preschool education and other support to low-income children, is a rarity among domestic social service programs in that it is popular among both Democrats and Republicans. In 1990 the reauthorization of Head Start received a good deal of attention, and ambitious funding levels were prescribed in the new legislation ($2.4 billion in FY 1991, rising to $7.7 billion in FY 1994). The actual FY 1991 appropriation for Head Start was only $1.95 billion; by FY 1999 it had increased to $4.66 billion but remained well below the level authorized for FY 1994.[47]

Actions taken for largely symbolic reasons may still have important consequences. Early public concern over the degradation of the environment was met with the National Environmental Policy Act of 1970, which announced the government's intention to protect the environment but did not specify many enforcement mechanisms. Among its seemingly innocuous provisions was a requirement that federal agencies prepare environmental impact statements for federally funded projects. Working through the courts, environmental activists have used this requirement on numerous occasions to block projects whose effects are perceived as detrimental to the environment.

Incremental Change

The drawn-out policy process and fragmented power often yield only minor policy changes. When legislatures finally act, problems typically are addressed in small, manageable steps—modest departures from past practice. The stabilizing forces holding back substantial change are very powerful indeed. Agendas are crowded with proposals; only a few receive serious attention. Legislators opposing change have abundant opportunities to veto or water down proposals.

Policy issues are rarely considered comprehensively. Legislatures slice up broad policy areas into many parts so that a large number of members serving on committees and subcommittees can participate. Rather than structure a government-wide policy on health care, for example, Congress divides health-related issues into discrete programs such as Medicare and Medicaid. Fear of the unknown also inhibits rapid and radical change. In contrast to business leaders, many of whom are risk takers, legislators tend to be risk avoiders. When they vote for a law, they want to be certain that it will not make things worse. Under these circumstances they choose to tinker with solutions, through trial and error, rather than to embrace innovative approaches that have the potential of disastrous consequences. Reconsiderations are practically guaranteed; most laws have a three- to five-year life span, so a legislature can look at the issue again and make changes.

Future policy directions often are molded by past decisions. Legislators find that the compromises reached by their predecessors serve as useful guides. Because lawmakers want to avoid controversy and conflict during a drawn-out process, they find it politically feasible and prudent to seek modest changes in current policy. Opposition is less likely when changes in the status quo are minor and nonthreatening to other vested interests.

Congressional policymaking with regard to the annual budget demonstrates incrementalism at work. Congress usually makes minor adjustments from year to year. Major departures, such as the substantial increase in defense spending during the 1980s, are rare; they take place only if accompanied by strong presidential leadership. The budget under consideration usually equals last year's budget, plus or minus a small percentage.[48] Indeed, during most of the 1990s, budget legislation more or less guaranteed incremental results because annual spending caps were imposed on most key areas of the budget, such as defense and domestic discretionary programs. Battles occur over what seem like inches of territory to the outside observer. Will spending increase by 2 percent or 3 percent? Will formulas governing grant-in-aid programs benefit smaller or larger cities? Should the federal gasoline tax rise or fall by five cents? The competition is fierce, but the public rarely understands what, if anything, is at stake. To insiders, these battles are important because they are, quite literally, the principal policy issues before the legislature.

Pork-Barrel Policies

Legislators want to deliver benefits, sometimes known as pork-barrel programs, to people, businesses, and communities in their states and districts. The desire to parcel out "particularized benefits" produces what are called distributive policies.[49] Members of Congress are not the only ones who want to participate in the politics of giving and credit claiming; ample supplies of pork are available to many state legislators. Each year the New York legislature provides funding for hundreds of "member items." In 1995 roughly $150 million was allocated for these items; this averaged out to about $700,000 for each member to spend on local projects. Until recently Florida allocated generous amounts for each member's local pork projects, which were referred to as "turkeys." Media attention to this practice led to reforms that have greatly limited the number of "turkeys."[50]

Pork-barrel politics is perhaps most evident in the contemporary Congress when highway and mass transit bills are being formulated. The acknowledged king of pork in the House is the chairman of the committee (Transportation and Infrastructure) that develops such legislation, Bud Shuster, R-Pa. Shuster rules the largest committee in the House and employs a system of "earmarks" to make sure members of his committee and others can have local projects included in the highway and mass transit bills. Shuster's rule of thumb is that roughly 5 percent of the funding authorized in these bills should be devoted to "earmarks"; the 1998 highway bill authorized $218 billion in federal spending for a six-year period. Despite the anti-pork reform rhetoric of the Republican House leadership, Shuster has not only survived, he has flourished. His committee, all seventy-five Republicans and Democrats, will vote as a bloc to protect his and its power. Shuster defends his earmarking system with vigor: "Are there bad projects? Certainly there are some bad projects. But 99 percent of the 5 percent are good projects. And if a member doesn't know what is good for his district, he isn't going to be a member for very long."[51]

Organized interests typically benefit the most from this system of handing out government largesse. The economically disadvantaged and politically unorganized usually lose when their interests conflict with those of more powerful groups. For example, in the spring of 2000 a trade bill that was originally designed to bolster the economies of two of the poorest areas in the world—the Caribbean Basin and Africa—was loaded up with special provisions to benefit U.S. corporations on its way to passage. The core of the legislation was an agreement by the United States to relax quotas and tariffs on textiles imported from the Caribbean and Africa so that countries in these regions could build up their textile industries. But the price of passage was special protection for several clothing and agricultural firms. As the trade package progressed, liberal senators Dianne Feinstein, D-Calif., and Russell Feingold, D-Wis., proposed that African countries be allowed to produce their own versions of AIDS-fighting drugs, rather than having to pay the high prices charged by the U.S. companies holding the patents for these drugs. This proposal was rejected.[52]

Innovation

Occasionally, public policy undergoes radical change. Landmark laws may increase government involvement in matters previously left to the private sector, such as health insurance for the elderly and poor (Medicare and Medicaid). The Social Security Act of 1935, which guaranteed government support for senior citizens; the Civil Rights Act of 1964, which forbade discrimination against minorities and other groups; the Reagan tax and spending cuts enacted in 1981; and welfare reform in 1996 represent fundamental innovations in public policy.

Certain conditions foster innovation by legislatures. According to political scientist Charles O. Jones, significant policy shifts may occur when a well-organized and vocal group of citizens unites and demands government action, or when policymakers achieve a temporary consensus on unprecedented proposals.[53] Strong political leadership, often from the president or governor, and economic and political conditions that make the need for change apparent are also powerful agents of policy innovation. President Lyndon Johnson was able to turn his strong electoral showing in 1964 into a mandate for liberal change, and he then drew on his experience as a legislative leader to push Congress to enact his Great Society programs. Sen. Edmund Muskie, D-Maine, who chaired the Senate Committee on Environment and Public Works, took advantage of growing bipartisan consensus on the need to protect the environment in the early 1970s and promoted passage of the Clean Air Act of 1970 and a number of other environmental laws that Presidents Nixon and Ford signed into law. Bipartisan consensus and presidential support enabled Congress to pass landmark welfare reform in 1996.[54] Overriding concern about crime, especially murder, prompted the Maryland and California legislatures to pass ground-breaking hand-gun control legislation in 1988–1989.

Events, political conditions, and the state of the economy all affect the degree of innovation. As a general rule, when budget deficits are high, opportunities for new and innovative spending programs are severely restricted, but other innovations, such as deregulation and privatization of public services, become more likely. Conversely, when revenues exceed projected expenditures, new programs may be born. President Johnson's Great Society programs came about in an era of surplus; and when state governments realized a revenue bonanza in the late 1980s, major reforms in education and economic development strategies were quickly initiated. Similar conditions in the late 1990s led to another round of innovation in the states. Republican control of Congress, a strong economy, and favorable trade conditions led to the passage of the Freedom to Farm Act of 1996, which called for the dismantling of the system of direct federal payments to farmers that was put in place during the 1930s.

Significant policy breakthroughs inevitably create problems, but once new government initiatives are established, the fundamental questions are discussed less frequently. Instead legislators try to fix and refine—to "rationalize" breakthrough policies. Political scientist Lawrence Brown makes a useful distinction: breakthrough policies are normally highly partisan, ideological, contentious, and visible; rationalizing policies are less partisan and contentious and concern relatively fewer citizens or interest groups. Debates about how to rationalize breakthrough policies generally revolve around proposed incremental changes that reflect perceptions of what has worked and what has not, rather than ideological preferences.[55] Still, some breakthrough policies never seem to take hold.

The history of federal programs dealing with unemployment provides examples of breakthrough policies that became accepted and some that did not.[56] During President Franklin Roosevelt's administration, a major breakthrough in unemployment policy occurred when the government provided assistance to the jobless through unemployment insurance and job creation programs. Since then, the unemployment insurance program has been modified dozens of times—increasing or decreasing benefit payments, expanding categories of program recipients—but it has never been seriously threatened with elimination. It is the largest and most durable government program for helping the unemployed; annual expenditures for this program averaged $8.6 billion in the 1970s, $16.6 billion in the 1980s, and $22.4 billion in the 1990s.[57]

In contrast, federal job creation programs have been alternately embraced and rejected by U.S. politicians over the years. The depression-era public works programs vanished during World War II when unemployment declined. During the 1970s, federal job programs employed as many as 700,000 people at an annual cost of $3 billion, but they were completely eliminated as a result of the Reagan budget-cutting initiative in 1981. In recent years public employment has been off the national agenda completely, except in the context of welfare reform.

Gridlock

When legislatures deal with extremely controversial policies, the policy process sometimes gets stuck in a gridlock of opposing viewpoints and power plays. Rep. David E. Price, D-N.C., has observed: "Congress is often difficult to mobilize, particularly on high-conflict issues of broad scope."[58]

Legislatures have ground to a halt over civil rights policy, aid to education, environmental policy, and other issues in the past, but the longrunning "battle of the budget" in the 1980s and 1990s deadlocked Congress repeatedly, thus severely curtailing its ability to act. Congressional budget scholar Allen Schick's observation of the early 1980s remains apt today: "Congress now has difficulty legislating because the role demanded of it by economic conditions is not congruent with the type of legislation encouraged by its organizations and behavior."[59]

The twenty-year battle of the budget began with President Reagan's breakthrough budget policies of 1981 (tax and domestic spending cuts with increased defense spending). After Reagan's success in 1981, Democrats, who controlled the House, resisted further cuts in domestic programs during Reagan's first term. The inevitable result was ballooning deficits ($200 billion by 1985). The deficit deadlock stemmed not so much from disagreements over whether the problem was serious, as from a core partisan difference over which course of action to pursue. Most Democrats favored tax increases and lower defense spending. Most Republicans preferred no tax increases and less domestic spending. No matter which party prevailed, meaningful deficit reduction required one or more unpleasant policy actions—hiking taxes or slashing popular programs.

While Congress groped for answers, the debt and deficit problem worsened, and the options became fewer and more painful. By the end of 1985 the public debt had risen above $1.8 trillion—more than double what it was at the beginning of 1981; by 1990 it had grown to over $3 trillion. This spectacular growth in the nation's debt brought about an even more spectacular growth in interest payments to service the debt—from $53 billion in 1980 to approximately $130 billion in 1985 to $180 billion in 1990.[60]

The gridlock was first addressed legislatively in 1985 when Congress passed the Gramm-Rudman-Hollings (GRH) Deficit Reduction Act—named after its sponsors, Sen. Phil Gramm, R-Texas; Sen. Warren Rudman, R-N.H.; and Sen. Ernest Hollings, D-S.C. The act mandated reductions in federal deficit spending that would achieve a balanced budget by fiscal year 1991. Unlike previous budget-balancing resolutions, it empowered the president to make automatic, across-the-board spending cuts should Congress fail to reach specified reductions by the beginning of each fiscal year. Social Security benefits, existing contracts for defense and other projects, programs for poor people, and interest on the national debt were excluded. House Budget Committee counsel Wendell Belew said, "It's a kind of mutual assured destruction theory of fiscal policy. What they're doing is creating a kind of artificial crisis . . . an action-forcing mechanism."[61] However, little action occurred in GRH's early years (1985–1990) as deficit reduction targets were met by resorting to one-time gimmicks, accounting tricks, and sales of government assets.

But the finessing came to an end in 1990 when the deficit reached $220 billion and the FY 1991 GRH target was $64 billion—no amount of blue smoke and mirrors could bridge this gap. Congress and President Bush locked horns over the budget but eventually reached an agreement: Bush would raise taxes, breaking his "no new taxes" campaign pledge, and a new set of budget rules and procedures would be put in place.[62] The budget agreement did away with deficit targets for entitlement programs in favor of a "pay-as-you-go" system of budgeting (all new spending provisions must be offset by cuts in other programs or by revenue increases), and it imposed caps on discretionary spending.

During the Clinton administration the battle continued. Clinton was able to persuade Congress to pass tax increases during his first year, but in 1995 he was confronted by the new Republican congressional majority and their plan for balancing the budget. The Republican plan called for reduced spending on domestic programs, tight controls on spending in entitlement programs, and tax cuts. Clinton vetoed it. The Republicans retaliated by withholding funding for government operations, thus shutting down the federal government. The Republican gamble didn't work; the public sided with the president, and he was reelected the following year.

In 1997 Clinton and the Republicans in Congress did agree to a new budget plan that involved tax cuts for Republicans, spending increases for the president, the retention of spending caps, and the promise of a balanced budget by 2002. But the economy leaped ahead of legislators, and the FY 1998 federal budget showed a surplus for the first time since 1969.[63] Was the battle of the budget finally over?

Not by a long shot. The new battle of the budget focuses on what to do with projected surpluses, rather than how to reduce deficits. The positions are familiar: Republicans want to cut taxes and spend more on the military; Democrats want to "fix" Social Security and add benefits, such as prescription drug payments, to Medicare. Both parties give lip service to reducing the debt, but this does not appear to be the top priority of either. Clinton vetoed tax cut measures passed by Republicans in 1999 and 2000, and by the fall of 2000 budget discipline collapsed as both sides agreed to let discretionary spending exceed the levels prescribed in the 1997 agreement.[64] Thus, despite some apparent breakthrough agreements on the budget, policy gridlock continued through the 2000 presidential election because the parties (one in control of the White House, the other in control of Congress) disagreed fundamentally on what actions should be taken.

Shaky Ground Rules, Unreliable Watchdogs

Legislative lawmaking is often a blunt instrument for addressing public problems. The precision with which courts and the executive branch can sometimes perform is rarely evident. Broad, vague, and sometimes contradictory policies are a direct by-product of the need to reconcile competing claims and preferences. Consequently, many public laws contain ambiguous statements that a majority of the legislature can endorse. The task of translating aspirations into programs and services is delegated to government administrators, other levels of government, courts, private businesses, and citizens. Indeed, the more controversial the policy, the more likely that legislatures will ask others to make the tough choices.[65]

When legislators delegate hard decisions to others, they can garner political rewards while shifting the wrath of aggrieved parties elsewhere. Delegating authority also gives legislators leeway to blame federal agencies or other levels of government for failing to fulfill legislative intent and to take credit for correcting faults by conducting oversight hearings and investigations, and by undertaking constituent casework.[66]

The most common form of policy delegation occurs when Congress or a state legislature defines a problem in legislation and then mandates federal or state agencies to solve it. Recognizing and defining a problem are important, but the task of deciding precisely how to cope with it is likely to be much more difficult. Consider the problem of hazardous waste management. State legislatures around the country have required the construction of safe facilities for the storage and disposal of dangerous wastes generated by chemical and other industrial plants. The choice of where to locate these facilities is up to state environmental protection agencies or special commissions, and their siting decisions have frequently outraged citizens, leading to threats of civil disobedience, violence, and lawsuits, and in some cases, to passage of legislation to block implementation of the decisions.[67]

Legislators also impose difficult policy tasks on individuals and businesses. Laws like the Americans with Disabilities Act (ADA) impose potentially expensive demands on private organizations, which must then decide whether to follow the letter and spirit of the law or to evade it. Responsibility for enforcing immigration laws rests with private employers, who must verify an individual's citizenship or permit to work in the United States. Failure to do so can result in a substantial fine. Often the courts must rule on whether congressional intent has been followed by private firms.

Congress frequently hands complicated problems to state and local governments, and state legislatures pass tough issues on to local governments. Legislatures also mandate changes in policies and programs at other levels of government, without providing adequate resources, and then hold them accountable, which is particularly irksome for those on the receiving end. Congress has ordered state and local governments to upgrade the education of young children, reform their welfare systems, enhance air and water quality, and improve highway safety, but many state and local officials believe that the funds appropriated for these purposes are insufficient to permit the realization of policy goals and expectations. This problem of "unfunded mandates" was addressed, to some extent, by a law passed in 1995. It allows members of Congress to object (raise a point of order) if proposed legislation imposes unfunded requirements on states, and it requires the federal government to provide reports on the cost of federal legislation to state and local governments and private firms.[68]

The nature of cloakroom politics influences not only the shape of laws and policy objectives but also the results. Even when legislatures delegate authority, they establish the ground rules for who gets what, when, and how from government. Legislatures are often the final arbiters of how much government spends on important societal goals and how money will be raised to pay for those commitments. Few individuals, institutions, and organizations are untouched by legislative action or inaction.

Policy Implementation

Laws are seldom written with potential implementation problems in mind. Because it is so difficult to reconcile competing interests, legislators expect administrative agencies and others to figure out how to put laws into effect. Furthermore, ambitious legislative goals are often regarded as an effective method for stimulating change. The authors of the Clean Air Acts of 1970, 1977, and 1990 insisted on including tough air quality standards in the legislation, even though it was obvious to most of those involved that the standards would not be met.[69] They reasoned that setting high standards would force the automobile industry to work harder to reduce pollution. In fact, the method worked; the deterioration of air quality decreased, and there have been some significant improvements.[70]

Nevertheless, a disregard for potential implementation difficulties can reduce the likelihood of achieving positive results. Public laws are sometimes endorsed without legislators ever carefully defining the problems the laws are supposed to address. Policy entrepreneurs who perceive a need for government programs may not be sure how to translate their aspirations into workable laws. The know-how to "solve" problems like minority youth unemployment or drug use may not yet be available, but legislators seize opportunities to advance innovative policies concerning these issues when they arise.

Legislators tend to be concerned about the distribution of program benefits provided by law and about the efficient application of administrative regulations. Generally, they assume that programs or policies will be helpful to people if implemented properly—even though this view may be highly inaccurate. For example, a member of the House Education and the Workforce Committee may believe that spending more money on education, for computers and the hiring of additional teachers, is an end in itself. The committee member's basic goal is to get more resources out to teachers and schoolchildren, not to determine the ultimate results of education programs, because such results will not show up for years and will be difficult to gauge definitively.

This perspective on policy impacts not only influences lawmaking; it also has consequences for the distribution of benefits in society.

Government benefits come in many different forms: tax breaks for companies; grants to fund social service programs or to build bridges; regulations that protect domestic industries from foreign competition; and income-support payments for the unemployed, poor, and retired. Underlying all tax and expenditure decisions, regulations, and policies is the struggle over who benefits and who does not. In general, legislative policy tends to favor the haves over the have-nots, the organized over the unorganized, and the middle class over the lower class because the poor and unorganized have great difficulty making a case for themselves to legislators, who view most decisions through electoral lenses.

When government programs try to serve poor Americans exclusively, they often have difficulty surviving. From the Resettlement Program of the 1930s, which aimed to increase black land ownership in the South, to the public service employment programs of the 1970s, which provided jobs for the long-term unemployed and the poor, to welfare (formerly known as Aid to Families with Dependent Children, or AFDC, and now called Temporary Assistance for Needy Families, or TANF), programs that help only the poor have been vulnerable to attack. Charges of mismanagement or corruption make headlines and lead legislators to withdraw support. Effective lawmaking depends upon finding the delicate balance of benefits that holds the majority together long enough for passage, and can maintain majority support when negative claims about program implementation are aired.

Ignoring implementation issues when laws are crafted may erode respect for government. To get laws enacted, legislators (and chief executives) may exaggerate not only the problem but also the potential effectiveness of the remedy under consideration. Then, if the problem fails to go away, the public and many legislators may falsely conclude that it cannot be remedied with government programs or that the policy approach was misguided. Repeated rounds of hyperbole and rising expectations followed by disappointment and condemnation undermine public support for governmental solutions.

Policy Impacts

Sometimes laws are written so as to have clear and immediate impacts. This usually occurs after several earlier legislative attempts to solve a problem have failed, and the problem and a solution become well defined. The Voting Rights Act of 1965 is a good example. Previous civil rights laws (1957, 1960, 1964) had attempted to solve the problem of low black voter registration in counties in the Deep South by encouraging citizens who had been intimidated or otherwise discouraged by local registration officials to go to federal courts with their grievances. This approach resulted in only marginal increases in black voter registration, and by 1965 Congress was ready for more decisive action. This time it simply declared that federal officials would be sent to any county where black registration was below 50 percent of the black population to make sure black citizens could register without interference. Black voter registration in the seven states of the Deep South covered by the law increased by more than 1 million between 1964 and 1972, an increase to 57 percent from 29 percent of eligible black voters. Effective implementation of the law depended on federal officials and the courts, but congressional initiative was critical to making progress.[71]

Still, legislatures are probably more notable for their delays or failures to act than for their willingness to grapple with difficult problems. And legislative inaction can have serious consequences. The problems created by harmful chemicals in the nation's water supply and by worldwide air pollution can be traced to careless and unregulated industry practices. Strong federal regulations were not legislated until the 1970s, and decades of neglect meant slow progress in improving environmental quality. The failure of state legislatures to take strong action against drunk drivers until the mid-1980s probably resulted in thousands of unnecessary deaths. Congress's inability to curtail the federal deficit during the 1980s and much of the 1990s imposed a heavy burden of debt on future generations of Americans.

Oversight and Learning

As elected representatives grope for solutions to difficult problems, such as cleaning up toxic waste dumps, or ameliorating poverty, or curbing the AIDS epidemic, they often approve politically appealing but poorly designed policies. Legislators typically do not concern themselves with the details of program administration unless bureaucrats and private citizens run into trouble and people start complaining. But political institutions can and do learn from experience. Feeble and misguided attempts can be reshaped through trial and error. After several attempts, Congress successfully revised and strengthened education programs for disadvantaged youngsters in the 1970s and 1980s. It took more than a decade, but by the mid-1980s, compensatory education programs could be shown to have narrowed the gap in test scores between disadvantaged and non-disadvantaged students. However, progress halted in the 1990s, and Congress had to again consider ways to make compensatory education programs more effective.[72]

Legislators form their impressions of program performance from what they hear from constituents and interest groups, from reports in the news media, from testimony at hearings, and from evaluations conducted by government agencies and others. Over time, members acquire pictures of success or failure that become the basis for intervening in program administration and for major legislative reforms.[73]

Objective evaluations of how programs work are difficult to achieve and expensive to conduct, and their results are sometimes distrusted or ignored by legislators.[74] Many systematic studies do not yield unequivocal answers because it may not be possible to establish cause-and-effect relationships for government programs or policies. Suppose, for example, that we needed to determine whether the multibillion dollar food stamp program improves the nutrition and health of the eligible population. We would have to monitor the health and eating habits of people before and after they received aid, track similar groups of people who did not receive it, and compare the results. Most likely, large numbers of the people we tried to track would drop out of our study before it was completed, and this would give rise to questions about the validity of our findings. Furthermore, such attrition would be only one of many problems that make definitive policy impact studies difficult (see Chapter 10). Nevertheless, when evaluations provide clear evidence that a program works or does not work, they can be quite persuasive. For example, despite repeated attempts, the Reagan administration could not persuade Congress to eliminate education and training programs for the disadvantaged that are run by the Job Corps because strong evidence, gathered through numerous systematic evaluations, indicated that the program worked.

Since the 1970s, Congress has paid a good deal of attention to oversight for many reasons. First, limited resources due to chronic deficits (until recently) have severely constricted the possibilities for creating new programs, and committees and subcommittees have therefore devoted more of their attention to overseeing the programs that are in place. Second, public displeasure at government performance, especially revelations of fraud, waste, and abuse, has motivated congressional interest. Third, partisan conflict and competition between presidents and congressional majorities have raised the stakes in oversight. Fourth, the staff resources—personal, committee, GAO, and CRS—available to members for oversight activities increased greatly during the 1970s–1990s; they were cut back a bit in 1995.[75] The GAO alone produces more than 1,000 reports annually (most of which are responses to congressional requests for information), and its representatives testify at more than 200 hearings per year.[76] Thus Congress today has both the capability and the incentive to conduct more oversight.[77]

Increased interest in oversight does not necessarily translate into systematic, comprehensive, or even rational oversight activity.[78] Indeed, like most other congressional activities, oversight has a decidedly partisan flavor to it. In the 1980s congressional Democrats often suspected that the Reagan and Bush administrations were not implementing programs in good faith and conducted oversight hearings to show this. They also used oversight hearings to defend programs the White House had targeted for cuts or elimination. In the 1990s the Republicans turned the tables and used the oversight function to bash agencies for adhering to Clinton White House directives in carrying out certain laws, rather than following the wishes of Congress.[79] As we have seen in the area of budgetary policymaking, partisan gridlock has characterized much of the effort to employ oversight in the improvement of programs, particularly with regard to environmental laws and educational programs.

In making up their minds about programs, many legislators use whatever information they can get. The problem is that unsystematic and anecdotal information is often more available and influential than careful, systematic evaluations. Impressions about policy success or failure enter the policy process through many channels. Senior citizens write members of Congress to complain about exorbitant fees for routine visits to the doctor, or CBS's *60 Minutes* exposes fraud in contracts for highway construction, or the *Washington Post* reports alarming increases in airline safety violations. In the late 1980s a legislative staffer in Arizona described the impact of a carefully selected presentation.[80] During a hearing on licensing procedures for beauticians, a woman with bright orange (originally brown) hair appeared at a hearing to complain about the incompetence of unlicensed practitioners. Her vivid portrayal persuaded lawmakers to strengthen state requirements and monitoring efforts. Such evidence may be inconclusive or unrepresentative, but it exerts a powerful influence on a legislator's judgments about government programs.

Legislative oversight of public policies can be harmful, especially if the legislators reach inaccurate conclusions. The resulting criticism heaped on administrators can be demoralizing, and more important, reacting to the criticism may distract public officials from essential tasks. Since members of Congress and of state legislatures engage in oversight activities with an eye to possible electoral payoffs, it should come as no surprise that such activities are greeted by experienced administrators with a mixture of alarm and cynicism.

When the policy process is competitive and diverse points of view are fully expressed, legislatures are best able to learn from their mistakes. For example, careful scrutiny of environmental laws has been ensured by continuing public health fears and the high degree of controversy surrounding proposed solutions. The Superfund Toxic Waste Cleanup Law, which was first passed in late 1980, turned out to be anything but super during its early years of implementation. Congress, during intense oversight efforts focused on toxic dumps in their districts, discovered from the EPA that only about 30 of the nation's 950 toxic waste dumps had been cleaned up. This discovery led to the passage of a much stronger cleanup law in 1986.

There is an interesting paradox in legislative politics and policy. Widespread consensus is usually required to implement innovative policies, but some amount of disagreement and conflict is necessary to refine them. Too much consensus in the policy environment either supports the status quo—however effective or ineffective it may be—or fosters large, experimental policy initiatives that have little chance of achieving success.[81] Severe conflict and disagreement, however, may deadlock efforts to revise policy. Thus institutional learning is most likely when parties and interest groups not only advance diverse policy remedies for the problems of program implementation but also approach the oversight process with a willingness to compromise.

Summary

No major government activity can be undertaken without the consent of legislatures, whether federal or state. No money can be borrowed or spent and no taxes can be levied unless the elected representatives willingly consent to the request of the president or a governor. No executive agency or top administrator can function for long without legislative support. The ground rules for the distribution of public goods, services, and regulations are established by legislatures, which may attempt to influence program implementation at any time.

Congress and the state legislatures are responsive to the changing mood of public opinion and to the views expressed by constituents, interest groups, and chief executives. But the desire of legislators to serve the public and curry favor with potential voters and supporters creates problems. Legislative institutions are subject to fads and whims and tend to respond to the loudest, most persistent demands. Legislators can be manipulated by outsiders who can stir up public support for a position or raise campaign contributions. Groups that are already powerful tend to get what they want, or at least avoid harmful legislative action.

The desire to be responsive and democratic also shapes the organization and practices of American legislatures. The dispersal of power across committees and subcommittees creates opportunities for legislators to influence public policy and gain the gratitude of potential supporters who will help to keep them in office. But because they are fragmented and operate by consensus and compromise, legislatures find it difficult to speak with a clear and consistent voice when making public policy. The need to accommodate diverse political interests often produces confusing public policies or no policy at all. Legislatures sometimes are unable to look ahead or to address controversial issues decisively.

Legislative indecision reflects not only uncertainty about how to ameliorate public problems, but also deep partisan cleavages. If public demand for action is strong and clear enough, legislatures have little trouble moving swiftly to clean up the environment, crack down on drug dealers, or raise the legal drinking age. But in recent years, conflict between presidents and Congresses has led to stalemate and gridlock in many areas of policy. Indeed, Congress has even tried to set the nation's agenda and wrest policy leadership from presidents of the opposite party, but this is an unusual posture for American legislatures to assume. The greatest strength of legislatures lies in acting as a forum where state and national controversies are debated in public. Legislatures are at their best when they educate the public, provide an outlet for the expression of diverse viewpoints, and forge consensus on new directions for public policy.

Notes

1. As quoted by Charles O. Jones in *The United States Congress: People, Place, and Policy* (Homewood, Ill.: Dorsey Press, 1982), 13; Alexis de Tocqueville, *Democracy in America* (New York: McGraw-Hill: 1981), 141.
2. The Gallup Organization, "Gallup Poll Topics: A–Z; Confidence in Institutions," June 22–25, 2000, online at http://www.gallup.com/poll/indicators/indconfidence.asp, September 2000.
3. Daniel Barbarisi, "Lesser-known Bills Finally Get Attention," *Boston Globe*, July 30, 2000, A1.
4. Richard L. Hall, *Participation in Congress* (New Haven, Conn.: Yale University Press, 1996).
5. Jack L. Walker, "Setting the Agenda in the U.S. Senate: A Theory of Problem Selection," *British Journal of Political Science* 7 (1977): 423–445.
6. Miles A. Pomper, Chuck McCutcheon, and Pat Towell, "GOP Leaders Refuse to Close Ranks with Clinton on Bombing Iraq," *CQ Weekly*, December 22, 1998, 3359–3361.
7. Miles A. Pomper and Vanita Gowda, "Congress Weighs Next Kosovo Move with a Tight Hold on Purse Strings," *CQ Weekly*, June 12, 1999, 1389–1391.
8. Alan Rosenthal, *The Decline of Representative Democracy* (Washington D.C.: CQ Press, 1998), 16; see also Richard C. Elling, "The Utility of State Legislative Casework as a Means of Oversight," in *Legislative Studies Quarterly* 4 (August 1979): 353–379.
9. Thomas Mann, *Unsafe at Any Margin* (Washington, D.C.: American Enterprise Institute, 1978).
10. See Gary C. Jacobson, *The Politics of Congressional Elections,* 4th ed. (New York: Longman, 1997).
11. *CQ Weekly,* November 27, 1999, 2865–2866.
12. Chuck McCutcheon, "Hill Takes a Hands-On Approach to Tightening Nuclear Security," *CQ Weekly*, July 1, 2000, 1619–1620.
13. On the relationship between congressional committees and campaign contributions, see Richard L. Hall and Frank W. Wayman, "Buying Time: Moneyed Interests and the Mobilization of Bias in Congressional Committees," *American Political Science Review* 84 (September 1990): 797–820.
14. See Richard E. Cohen, *Washington at Work: Back Rooms and Clean Air* (New York: Macmillan, 1992).
15. John Healey, "Clinton Success Rate Declined to a Record Low in 1995," *Congressional Quarterly Weekly Report,* January 27, 1996, 193–198.
16. Joel Brinkley, "Competing—or the Last Word on Drug Abuse," *New York Times,* August 7, 1986, A10.
17. Robert Pear, "Congress Pushes to Pass Benefits for Gulf Veterans," *New York Times,* February 19, 1991, A12.

18. Anthony Quain et al., eds., *The Political Reference Almanac,* 1999–2000 ed. (Arlington, Va.: Keynote Publishing, 1999); David R. Tarr and Ann O'Connor, eds., *Congress A to Z,* 3d ed. (Washington D.C.: CQ Press, 1999).

19. National Conference of State Legislatures, "Size of State Legislative Staffs: 1979, 1988, and 1996," June 1996, online at http://www.ncsl.org./programs/legman/about/stfl.htm, August 16, 2000.

20. Alison J. Rubin, "Congress Clears Wage Increase with Tax Breaks for Business," *Congressional Quarterly Weekly Report,* August 3, 1996, 2175–2177; *Congressional Quarterly Weekly Report,* November 2, 1996, 3150.

21. Woodrow Wilson, *Congressional Government* (New York: Meridian Books, 1956).

22. See "Special Report: CQ's Complete Committee Guide," *CQ Weekly,* March 13, 1999, 630–663.

23. Hugh Heclo, "Issue Networks and the Executive Establishment," in *The New American Political System,* ed. Anthony King (Washington D.C.: American Enterprise Institute, 1978), chap. 3.

24. John F. Hoadley, "Easy Riders: Gramm-Rudman-Hollings and the Legislative Fast Track," *PS,* winter 1986, 30–36.

25. See Barbara Sinclair, *The Transformation of the Senate* (Baltimore: Johns Hopkins University Press, 1989), 111–138.

26. See Steven S. Smith, *Call to Order: Floor Politics in the House and Senate* (Washington, D.C.: Brookings Institution, 1990).

27. Barbara Sinclair, *Unorthodox Lawmaking* (Washington D.C.: CQ Press, 1997).

28. See Roger Davidson and Walter Oleszek, *Congress and Its Members,* 6th ed. (Washington D.C.: CQ Press, 1998), 218.

29. David Stockman, *The Triumph of Politics* (New York: Harper and Row, 1986), 250–251.

30. Interview by authors, Washington, D.C., December 10, 1984.

31. Andrew Taylor, "Congress Wraps Up and Heads Home on a Trail of Broken Budget Caps," *CQ Weekly,* October 24, 1998, 2885–2889.

32. Legislative leaders in this sense are individuals elected by their respective party memberships. In Congress the leadership is the Speaker of the House, the majority and minority leaders, assistant leaders (sometimes called party whips), and the party caucus officers in the House and Senate.

33. Randall B. Ripley, *Congress and the Policy Process,* 4th ed. (New York: W. W. Norton, 1998), 210–212.

34. Barbara Sinclair, *Majority Party Leadership in the U.S. House* (Baltimore: Johns Hopkins University Press, 1983); and Randall B. Ripley, *Majority Party Leadership in Congress* (Boston: Little, Brown, 1969).

35. See Barbara Sinclair, "House Majority Party Leadership in the Late 1980s," in *Congress Reconsidered,* 4th ed., ed. Lawrence C. Dodd and Bruce I. Oppenheimer (Washington, D.C.: CQ Press, 1989), 307–329; and John Barry, *Ambition and Power* (New York: Penguin Books, 1989).

36. See Donald C. Baumer, "Senate Democratic Leadership in the 101st Congress," in *The Atomistic Congress: An Interpretation of Congressional Change,* ed. Ronald M. Peters and Allen D. Hertzke (Armonk, N.Y.: M. E. Sharpe, 1991).

37. Sinclair, *Unorthodox Lawmaking;* and James G. Gimpel, *Fulfilling the Contract* (Boston: Allyn and Bacon, 1996).

38. Alan Rosenthal, *Legislative Life* (New York: Harper and Row, 1981), 167–168.
39. Rosenthal, *The Decline of Representative Democracy.*
40. Alan Rosenthal, "The Legislature: Unraveling of Institutional Fabric," in *The State of the States,* ed. Carl E. Van Horn (Washington D.C.: CQ Press, 1996).
41. Rosenthal, *The Decline of Representative Democracy,* 72–80.
42. Rosenthal, *Legislative Life,* 266.
43. Interview by authors, Washington, D.C., May 29, 1985.
44. Peter Wallsten and Karen Foerstel, "Republicans Scramble to Shore Up Pivotal Support among Catholics," *CQ Weekly,* March 4, 2000, 459–462.
45. Murray Edelman, *The Symbolic Uses of Politics* (Urbana: University of Illinois Press, 1964).
46. Randall B. Ripley and Grace Franklin, *Congress, the Bureaucracy, and Public Policy,* 5th ed. (Pacific Grove, Calif.: Brooks/Cole, 1991); see also Frances Fox Piven and Richard A. Cloward, *Poor People's Movements* (New York: Vintage Books, 1979).
47. See *Congressional Quarterly Weekly Report,* November 3, 1990, 3702; also see Department of Health and Human Services, Administration for Children and Families, "Fact Sheet, Head Start," June 2000, online at http://www.acf.dhhs.gov/programs/opa/facts/headst.htm, August 8, 2000.
48. Aaron Wildavsky, *The Politics of the Budgetary Process,* 3d ed. (Boston: Little, Brown, 1979).
49. David Mayhew, *Congress: The Electoral Connection* (New Haven, Conn.: Yale University Press, 1974); and Theodore Lowi, *The End of Liberalism,* 2d ed. (New York: W. W. Norton, 1979).
50. Rosenthal, *The Decline of Representative Government,* 316–317.
51. Jeff Plungis, "The Driving Force of Bud Shuster," *CQ Weekly,* August 7, 1999, 914–919.
52. Lori Nitschke, "Third World Trade Bill Likely to Have Limited Impact," *CQ Weekly,* May 6, 2000, 1020–1027.
53. Charles O. Jones, "Speculative Augmentation in Federal Air Pollution Policy-Making," *Journal of Politics* 36 (May 1974): 438–464.
54. See Anne Marie Cammisa, *From Rhetoric to Reform: Welfare Policy in American Politics* (Boulder, Colo.: Westview, 1998).
55. Lawrence Brown, *New Policies, New Politics: Government's Response to Government's Growth* (Washington, D.C.: Brookings Institution, 1983).
56. See Donald C. Baumer and Carl E. Van Horn, *The Politics of Unemployment* (Washington, D.C.: CQ Press, 1985).
57. Figures derived from *Economic Report of the President* (Washington D.C.: Government Printing Office, 2000), 357, table B-43.
58. David E. Price, "Congressional Committees in the Policy Process," in *Congress Reconsidered,* 3d ed., ed. Lawrence C. Dodd and Bruce I. Oppenheimer (Washington, D.C.: CQ Press, 1985), 211–222.
59. Allen Schick, "The Distributive Congress," in *Making Economic Policy in Congress,* ed. Allen Schick (Washington, D.C.: American Enterprise Institute, 1983), 258.
60. *Economic Report of the President,* 2000, 397–399, tables B-76, B-77, and B-78.
61. Jonathan Rauch and Richard E. Cohen, "Budget Frustration Boiling Over," *National Journal,* October 12, 1985, 2138.
62. See Donald F. Kettl, *Deficit Politics* (New York: Macmillan, 1992), 95–105.

63. Daniel J. Parks, "A Legacy of Budget Surpluses and Thriving Markets," *CQ Weekly,* February 5, 2000, 228–233.

64. Daniel J. Parks, "Prompt and Parsimonious," *CQ Weekly,* April 8, 2000, 822–824; Steven A. Holmes, "Congress Poised for Big Increase in U.S. Spending," *New York Times,* September 10, 2000, A1.

65. Lowi, *The End of Liberalism.*

66. Morris Fiorina, *Congress: Keystone of the Washington Establishment* (New Haven, Conn.: Yale University Press, 1977), chaps. 7 and 8.

67. Barry Rabe, *Beyond NIMBY: Hazardous Waste Siting in Canada and the U.S.* (Washington D.C.: Brookings Institution, 1994).

68. Daniel Hosansky, "GOP Confounds Expectations, Expands Federal Authority," *Congressional Quarterly Weekly Report,* November 2, 1996, 3117–3122.

69. Charles O. Jones, *Clean Air: The Policies and Politics of Pollution Control* (Pittsburgh: University of Pittsburgh Press, 1975).

70. Norman J. Vig and Michael E. Kraft, *Environmental Policy in the 1990s* (Washington D.C.: CQ Press, 1997), 20.

71. Charles S. Bullock III and Charles V. Lamb, *Implementation of Civil Rights Policy* (Monterey, Calif.: Brooks/Cole, 1984), 20–54.

72. Michael Kirst and Richard Jung, "The Utility of a Longitudinal Approach in Assessing Implementation: A Thirteen-Year View of Title I, ESEA," in *Studying Implementation,* ed. Walter Williams (Chatham, N.J.: Chatham House, 1982), 119–148; David Nather, "Dozens of Amendments Make for Slow Progress on Senate's ESEA Bill," *CQ Weekly,* May 6, 2000, 1046–1048.

73. Baumer and Van Horn, *The Politics of Unemployment,* 53.

74. See Beryl A. Radin, *Beyond Machiavelli: Policy Analysis Comes of Age* (Washington D.C.: Georgetown University Press, 2000), 39.

75. Davidson and Oleszek, *Congress and Its Members,* 7th ed. (Washington D.C.: CQ Press, 2000), 328.

76. U.S. General Accounting Office, "GAO at a Glance," 1999, online at http://www.gao.gov, August 18, 2000; see also Frederick Mosher, *The General Accounting Office* (Boulder, Colo.: Westview, 1979), 178.

77. See Joel D. Aberbach, *Keeping a Watchful Eye* (Washington, D.C.: Brookings Institution, 1990).

78. See Mathew McCubbins and Thomas Schwartz, "Congressional Oversight Overlooked: Police Patrols versus Fire Alarms," *American Journal of Political Science* 28 (February 1984): 180–202.

79. Michael Wiessman, "Hearings Loss: Oversight in the Republican Congress," *The American Prospect,* November/December 1998, 50–55.

80. Telephone interview by authors, June 1, 1987.

81. See Jones, *Clean Air,* and Jones, "Speculative Augmentation."

Chapter 6 **Chief Executive Politics**

Americans have always preferred politics with a personal touch, making heroes and villains out of public figures and evaluating politicians on the basis of human qualities such as integrity, leadership ability, and physical attractiveness. It is rare for the American public to be mobilized by ideological debate or to be interested for very long in institutional deliberations and actions. Political interest typically focuses on individuals, and in most cases this means chief executives—presidents, governors, and mayors. Chief executives are the most visible, and in many ways the most important, actors in American government.

The prominence of chief executives in American politics today is commonly attributed to the media. The modern media, especially television, find that covering powerful individuals in government is much more appealing and manageable than following developments in legislative, judicial, or bureaucratic institutions. The visibility of chief executives contributes to the public perception that politics and government are principally about what they do.

But media attention is only part of the reason that American politics centers on chief executives. The system of governance set up by the federal and state constitutions also helps to explain the phenomenon. The United States is notable in the world for the number of independent, elected chief executives in government. Presidents have a nearly exclusive claim to a national electoral constituency, and unlike the prime ministers in parliamentary governments, they are independent of the national legislature. Governors and "strong" mayors have a somewhat less distinctive electoral position, but they are also independent of the legislatures in their jurisdictions and the national government.[1] Politics centered on the chief executive is not simply a cultural oddity encouraged by media that seek above all else to sell more cornflakes; rather, it reflects in many ways the intentions of writers of the national and state constitutions.

The term *chief executive politics,* as used here, does not encompass the full range of policymaking activity of American chief executives; it includes only those aspects that are most exclusively attributable to these public officials. In this chapter we explore the more visible and important positions taken, decisions made, and policies whose enactment is secured by chief executives— the public record by which they are judged. These records have two main components: decisions made by chief executives during crises and policy initiatives or innovations sponsored by chief executives. Chief executives are also involved in a great many routine policy actions, most of which are covered in Chapter 4.[2]

Rulers of the Agenda

Chief executives dominate the agenda-setting process in the United States. More often than not they are able to transform policy ideas from items of discussion among a few to items of discussion among the many. Because they have the public's attention, they force other politicians to pay attention to the matters they think are important. This gives them a tremendous advantage over any rivals in defining the issues for the public and, ultimately, for other politicians. In short, chief executives typically set the terms of debate about political issues at the national, state, and local levels. This is not to say that chief executives are always, or even usually, successful in securing enactment of the policies they prefer. Indeed, it must be understood that chief executives are more impressive in the issue creation and agenda-setting process than in policy formulation and adoption.[3]

Modern presidents are expected to be opinion leaders. Their unique relationship with the national electorate gives them a certain flexibility in choosing issues and policies that other national policymakers do not have. Woodrow Wilson championed the League of Nations, Franklin D. Roosevelt pushed the New Deal, Lyndon B. Johnson began the Great Society, Richard M. Nixon made a breakthrough with China, Ronald Reagan launched an antigovernment crusade, George Bush forged a new relationship with the Soviet Union, Bill Clinton tackled the federal deficit and balanced the budget, and George W. Bush promoted tax cuts. Chief executive politics encompasses the entire spectrum of policy types, including distributive, redistributive, regulatory, social and moral, intergovernmental, intragovernmental, economic, foreign, defense, and national security.

Chief executives dominate certain issue domains more than others. At the national level, presidents traditionally have dictated American foreign and military policy. This power has enabled them to shape public opinion about America's proper role in the world; indeed, recent presidents have regarded the international scene as a vast set of "opportunities" for improving their popularity at home, especially around election time. Nixon was an adept exploiter of these international opportunities, presenting the SALT I agreement and Henry Kissinger's pledge that "peace was at hand" in Vietnam as he faced reelection in 1972, and taking trips to the Middle East and the Soviet Union as the Watergate scandal heated up.[4] Civil war in Kosovo and Bosnia awarded Clinton the opportunity to position himself as a concerned protector of victimized peoples.

International crises and foreign and military policy adventures also have caused big problems for presidents. Since the Vietnam War, negative responses by the national media, Congress, and the public have become a more common reaction to statements presidents have made and actions they have taken in the international arena. Jimmy Carter's and Ronald Reagan's presidencies were damaged by festering foreign policy problems (the Carter administration's handling of the hostage crisis in Iran and the Soviet invasion of Afghanistan, and the Reagan administration's trading of arms for hostages with Iran and support of Nicaraguan contras). George Bush's management of the war in the Persian Gulf created opportunities to demonstrate his leadership in wartime but also tested his skill in bringing stability to the troubled Middle East. Bill Clinton also tried to bring peace and stability to the Middle East, but he could not convince Israeli and Palestinian leaders of the need to resolve their differences. International affairs continue to offer opportunities for presidents to mold public opinion, but there are limits to the public's inclination to believe what presidents say about the world and America's place in it.

Within their respective jurisdictions most governors and many mayors take the lead on issues and policies. As is true of presidents, the combination of the media attention and their formal powers makes them substantially more visible and influential than other state and local politicians. The public and other policymakers look to them for new ideas and new proposals, and they have a flexibility in articulating policy concerns and proposing remedies that elected officials with narrower constituencies do not share. Governor Tommy Thompson of Wisconsin focused his administration's efforts on implementing a radically different welfare program based upon work requirements, strict eligibility limits, and increased ancillary services to smooth the transition from welfare to work. Governor Pete Wilson succeeded in reducing the size of California's state government in addition to scaling back social services and policies such as affirmative action. Mayor Rudolph Giuliani attempted sweeping changes to New York City's homeless shelter programs and police force. Indianapolis's mayor Steven Goldsmith was a staunch advocate of privatizing city services.

Issue Choice and Definition

Although chief executives have a good deal of freedom to choose their issues, there are limits to this freedom. Occasionally, an issue in the form of a crisis is thrust upon the chief executive. Iraq's invasion of Kuwait in 1990 was a crisis that demanded an immediate, and then prolonged, presidential response. Stability in the Middle East and the world's oil supply were threatened and a policy needed to be formulated at once. Serbian escalations of the civil war in Bosnia and demands from European allies provoked President Clinton to take action and deploy peace-keeping troops. The Supreme Court's decision in *Webster v. Reproductive Health Services* (1989) placed immediate demands on governors to reassess their positions on the state role in regulating abortions. The enactment of welfare reform in 1996, known as the Personal Responsibility and Work Opportunity Reconciliation Act, devolved control over welfare programs to states and forced governors to reconsider their role in implementing welfare programs.

Not all crises are as compelling as the examples just cited, but chief executives have considerable latitude in labeling an event a crisis or a noncrisis. Reagan often portrayed the presence of the Sandinista government in Nicaragua as a national security crisis to persuade Congress to aid the contras. Many regard the destruction of the rain forests in South America and the increase in world temperatures as a crisis demanding immediate and forceful responses from the president, but neither George Bush nor Bill Clinton applied the crisis label to this problem. During his presidential campaign and first years in office, Clinton continually made reference to the health care crisis in the United States in order to focus national attention on this problem. In part, crises exist in the eyes of the beholders, and presidents are able to open or close those eyes.

In Table 6-1 we show some of the relationships between issues, stages in the agenda-setting process, and chief executive discretion or range of choice. Crisis situations tend to involve problems that are very difficult for chief executives to ignore, but they usually give chief executives a good deal of flexibility in defining the problem for other policymakers and the public and in choosing a response. For issues that chief executives choose to promote, what happens at the different agenda-setting stages follows the opposite pattern. Chief executives have wide choice in the selection of problems to address and they have a strong position from which to define these problems; but their ability to craft innovative responses is limited because they must take into account the preferences of the many other actors in the policymaking process, most of whom defer to chief executives during crises.

Available evidence suggests that governors and mayors may have somewhat less discretion than presidents in choosing issues to emphasize. For these politicians there are certain perennial issues, reflecting the basic services that state and local governments provide—education, streets and highways, law enforcement and prisons, and social services—and these issues are nearly always addressed by leading candidates and officeholders.[5] There are exceptions to this pattern; for example, natural disasters, such as hurricanes or floods, or man-made crises, such as terrorism or increasing gun violence, demand responses from local or state chief executives.

In the 1980s, taxes frequently dominated all other issues at the state level, sometimes to the point of ensuring the end of the political careers of incumbents who raised taxes and giving other candidates no real choice about how to position themselves.[6] Caught between the constitutional requirement to balance budgets and the cutback of federal grants to states, many governors

Table 6-1 Issues, Agendas, and Chief Executive Discretion

	Problem/issue	Agenda stage	
		Problem definition	Specification of policy alternatives
Crisis Situation	Civil war in Kosovo	Serbian aggression American humanitarian responsibility	Military action
	Inmates riot at state prison	Prisoners take hostages and threaten lives Prison conditions cause violent responses Lax security creates crisis	Address prisoners' demands Negotiation Use of force
Level of chief executive discretion	Low	Moderate	Moderate/high
Noncrisis Situation	Health care	Millions uninsured Rising health care costs Quality of care concerns	National insurance plan Regulation of insurance companies Regulation of HMOs
	Education reform	Declining literacy in society Low pay for teachers Teacher union resistance to innovation	Improve educational facilities Adopt performance-based pay system Increase teacher salaries across the board
Level of chief executive discretion	Moderate/high	Moderate	Moderate/low

were forced to raise taxes—an action that ended many political careers. In the 1990 election, for example, six of twenty-eight governors who stood for reelection were defeated. In almost all instances voter anger over tax increases brought about incumbent defeats. And several governors chose not to seek reelection, in part because they had backed tax increases to balance state budgets.[7]

In the late 1990s, this situation became even more complex for state and local leaders. Low unemployment and increased revenues from income taxes created surpluses in most states and many cities. In the early years of the twenty-first century, the question of how to distribute this newfound fiscal bounty is often at the forefront of political conflict, as it was in the 2000 presidential election. To further complicate matters, increasing devolution of social program responsibilities from the federal government to states and localities forces state and local officials to increase their funding for these programs. In these instances, anticipated surpluses may vanish rapidly.

Decisions made in Washington command the attention of many state and local officials because intergovernmental grants-in-aid represent about 15 percent of state and local revenue.[8] Domestic spending cuts begun during the first Reagan term and continued during the Bush presidency forced many states to assess their budget priorities and decide whether and how to replace lost federal funds. The "devolution revolution" that began in the Reagan years has continued unabated into the new millennium, requiring states to juggle increased fiscal responsibilities while fulfilling federal requirements for program performance.[9] In short, the leading issues for states and localities often are "givens" that represent long-standing or pressing problems.

Presidents and other chief executives are rarely, if ever, whimsical or free-wheeling in their choices about what issues to emphasize; too much is at stake for decisions to be made haphazardly. Presidential scholar Paul Light stated, "All presidential decisions are purposive. Presidents select issues on the basis of their goals."[10] He listed the principal goals as reelection, historical achievement, and good policy.[11]

Most chief executives want to be reelected and therefore choose issues they think will help them garner votes. In general, they believe their positions on issues matter—indeed, that their own success or failure can hinge on issue stances and policy pledges.[12] This belief does not mean that chief executives are always aggressive in taking positions on a wide range of issues. It means that most perceive a need to address some important issues and to act in a way consistent with what they have said, even if vigorous follow-up is lacking. With all the media hype and money that go into contemporary campaigns, chief executives with reelection in mind are likely to be listening to their political advisers, media consultants, and public opinion pollsters as much as to their policy specialists. President Clinton prepared for his reelection campaign by "going to the people." Through focus groups and public opinion polls, Clinton sought to determine the concerns of the average American and to discover effective language to communicate with potential voters.

Policy agendas are often formed around issues that are evocative and remedies that are thought to be popular, rather than being based on a serious effort to diagnose what is wrong and to find viable solutions. For example, in the 1980s and 1990s most governors and presidents took strong stands in favor of tougher criminal penalties for drug use, including the death penalty for so-called drug kingpins. In taking on drug users and drug pushers, chief executives were clearly addressing a popular cause with a popular remedy that never had much of a chance of actually ameliorating the problem.

In recent years many governors and mayors have announced their support for requiring students to wear uniforms in public schools, arguing that it would encourage greater discipline in schools and promote less competition, harassment, and violence among children. This would seem to be an example of chief executives promoting an appealing remedy and being able to say that they had addressed an issue of concern to most Americans but not really dealing with the deeper problems of American society and schools.

Not all chief executives are concerned with reelection. In fact, some of them—presidents in their second term, governors who have reached the legal limit of their tenure in office, or others who decide they do not wish to run again—do not have to think about it at all. For most presidents, governors, and mayors, an election is a means to some larger and more substantive end, such as initiating good public policies, not an end in itself. Chief executives want to leave a favorable historical legacy, and most of them recognize that sponsoring noteworthy and effective public policies is the best way to achieve this goal. The goals of historical recognition and good policies typically blend into one effort. Fortunate chief executives have knowledgeable advisers with ideas that are worthy of consideration. Chief executives who succeed in getting these ideas translated into policy are recognized and remembered.

President Clinton found himself in a somewhat unusual and awkward situation after his election to his second (and last) term. With the stain of scandal surrounding him, he had to work hard throughout his last four years in office to promote his policy initiatives and tout his accomplishments in order to divert public and media attention away from the scandals and to shape a positive historical legacy.

Sometimes chief executives use their positions to promote particular ideologies, and ideological expression cannot be neatly subsumed under the categories of reelection, historical recognition, or good public policy. Chief executives emphasize certain issues that have strong ideological content, even though some of them are not particularly popular, as part of a larger effort to build, maintain, or repudiate a dominant ideological coalition. Lyndon Johnson, who had not been a strong supporter of civil rights policies, became in the mid-1960s a champion of programs for poor and minority citizens in an effort to defend and expand the liberal Democratic ideology (and political coalition) that his predecessor, John F. Kennedy, had begun to build. Reagan led an effort to destroy this coalition and replace it with one built around conservative causes. He attacked all of the most ideologically loaded policy legacies of the Kennedy/Johnson era, such as public school busing, affirmative action, social welfare programs, reduced military spending, prohibitions on school prayer, and intrusive regulations.[13] President Clinton championed the idea of a "New Democrat" in order to reposition the Democratic Party in the mainstream of American politics. Clinton eschewed the liberal ideologies of the past and incorporated more centrist policies—such as debt reduction and balanced budgets, welfare reform, and anticrime measures, including support for the death penalty.

In every administration there is tension among those who are concerned about issues that contribute to short-term popularity, those who seek to promote ideological principles, and those who are interested in establishing policies of long-term effectiveness. Achieving a balance between these forces is one of the main tasks of chief executives, and some are better at it than others. Franklin Roosevelt offered ideas that brought not only electoral success but also historical recognition for his policy accomplishments and his ideological leadership. No president since has matched this record. Of the two presidents since Roosevelt who have achieved reelection (Reagan and Clinton), Reagan provided ideological leadership but had relatively few policy accomplishments; Clinton oversaw unprecedented economic prosperity and achieved several important policy breakthroughs, but his efforts at centrist leadership seemed to inflame rather than cool partisan differences.

Chief executives, particularly presidents, are rarely at the cutting edge of new issues or policy ideas. In a strict sense, they do not initiate agenda issues or lead the way to innovative approaches to problems. The real initiators are likely to be political activists, interest groups, researchers, or even legislative staffers or bureaucrats.[14] Most new issues and policy ideas have humble beginnings with only a small number of people interested in them. Some of these ideas, however, attract the attention of more visible spokespersons, become widely discussed, and eventually attract coalitions of supporters.[15] At any given time there are streams of acknowledged problems and potential solutions—policy proposals—flowing around and through policymaking institutions.[16] Chief executives and their policy advisers pick out those that fit with their philosophy and direction and promote them. For example, "Megan's Law" originated from a small group of concerned New Jersey parents following the murder of a four-year-old girl by a convicted sex offender. Clinton moved this issue to the national agenda by including it in his anticrime platform. Megan's Law, requiring convicted sex offenders to register with local officials, then became part of federal anticrime legislation in 1996.

Obviously, many considerations figure in choosing issues, among them the political costs associated with certain ideas and the fit between the new idea and the other positions taken by a chief executive.[17] Political parties add another voice to the process of selecting issues. Every four years the parties' platforms give various groups and advocates the opportunity to debate policy ideas, thereby helping chief executives determine those that have broad support.[18] Typically, chief executive policy leadership does not consist of a flash of inspiration and a headlong rush to legislative action; most often it consists of a set of cautious, purposive decisions made by chief executives and their advisers after surveying the ideas and proposals circulating among the politically active and aware.

Chief executives' agendas frequently follow a predictable pattern dictated by their economic and political environments. For example, in times of economic recession, governors and presidents invariably emphasize government support for public works projects and the importance of helping private sector firms expand. When the economy is strong, the attention of chief executives is likely to shift to quality of life issues, such as educational opportunity or environmental protection. Governors and presidents just taking office are likely to promote bolder ideas and plans for "cleaning up" the mess of the previous administration—especially if it was left by a different political party. Chief executives seeking reelection are more likely to cling to mainstream proposals and to highlight recent accomplishments.

Neglected Matters

Compared with other American policymakers, chief executives raise an exceptionally wide variety of issues. As tribunes of the people they are free to discuss just about any policy question they wish. Still, certain kinds of issues are systematically neglected or excluded from their policy agendas; the spectrum of chief executive politics may be wide, but it is far from unlimited. With two major parties each striving to assemble majority coalitions, American politics has an undeniably centrist bias. Like the parties, and usually as leaders of them, chief executives need majorities to support them. Therefore, they aim most of their political pitches at the largest sector of the electorate. Because most Americans belong to the middle class, U.S. politics tends to revolve around issues that most directly affect the middle class. A serious socialist agenda is consequently irrelevant, and few, if any, conservative leaders seriously challenge the New Deal reforms.

A striking example of this tactic was President Clinton's cooptation of portions of the traditional Republican agenda to position himself and the Democratic Party at the center of American politics. For example, strict work requirements for welfare recipients had traditionally been a part of the Republican agenda for welfare reform. Clinton championed an "end to welfare as we know it" by requiring a transition from welfare to work. Although it may be difficult to pin down, a kind of majority consensus defines the acceptable range of political discourse in the United States, and successful chief executives remain within this range.[19]

Generalizations such as the one just offered are deliberately imprecise and can be easily misinterpreted. Our emphasis on middle-class/centrist politics does not mean that minorities and the poor are neglected altogether. The political history of black Americans—neglect by the white majority for many years, followed by selective attention as their political significance was recognized—confirms the basic thrust of the claim about the forces that dominate agendas, but it also demonstrates that the trends can change. Significant events, media attention, and effective advocacy coalitions can turn a neglected issue into a salient issue in a fairly short time. By the same token, an issue may remain submerged indefinitely if no one with political muscle chooses to promote it. This is often the case for issues that concern the poor or disadvantaged in the United States. Groups without money have a hard time getting politicians to pay attention to their concerns. For example, the plight of homeless Americans rarely is addressed in the political arena because homeless people do not vote and do not have the money or resources to organize and influence politicians.

The collapse of the savings and loan industry in the 1980s and the subsequent government-sponsored bailout is perhaps the best illustration of an issue that was long ignored at great cost to the American public. The deregulated savings and loan industry of the 1980s compiled a stunning record of "greed, mismanagement, fraud, and lax government regulation," yet nothing was done to address the problem systematically until Congress passed a savings and loan cleanup law in August of 1989. But by then, the federal government and the public were faced with the biggest bailout in U.S. history. The federal government spent more than $480 billion, including interest, to bail out these failed institutions.[20]

There are no absolutes in the issue creation process. Societies change, sometimes rapidly, and policy ideas that seemed outlandish at one time can become serious agenda items at another. For example, the issue of the digital divide—the disparity between the technological haves and have-nots in the United States—and policies to address the issue, such as Clinton's multi-billion dollar proposal to increase access to computers and the Internet through funding technology infrastructure, did not attract widespread attention until the late 1990s.[21] Economic, technological, and environmental developments are not the only causes of these societal changes; human beings may be the agents of social and political change. Chief executives can and do change the nature of political discourse by daring to explore new directions. Clinton's emphasis on a national health care crisis brought proposals for a national health care program that had not been seriously considered in previous administrations. Although Clinton's plan was ultimately rejected by Congress, some of the principles he fought for, such as managed care, competition, and consumer protection, have subsequently been embraced by many state governments.

The Power to Persuade

The presence or absence of crisis conditions is of overarching significance in explaining the politics associated with chief executive policymaking. During crises normal politics is suspended, and the power to decide comes to rest with chief executives and those they choose to advise them. Policy is determined in a centralized, hierarchical manner. This is one of those matters about which there is nearly universal consensus among legislators and other policymakers. Presidents are expected to lead during times of crisis, and other political elites recognize that presidents need room to maneuver if they are to do this effectively. With this unilateral power goes the responsibility for the decisions that are made. Crises test a chief executive's leadership and decision-making ability in an arena where the stakes are very high.

From the time that Saddam Hussein's armies invaded Kuwait on August 2, 1990, to the cease-fire on February 27, 1991, President George Bush was firmly in charge of U.S. policy and strategic actions. With little or no input from Congress, the president initially ordered the deployment of 240,000 troops to Saudi Arabia. That task completed, he expanded the American commitment by another 200,000. He forged a worldwide coalition against Iraq and committed the United States to spending at least an additional $13 billion on war preparations. Not until five months later, in January 1991, when it was clear that the president was about to end the policy of economic sanctions and embark on a war to rid Kuwait of Iraqi troops, was Congress invited to pass a resolution endorsing the president's actions. Throughout the entire Persian Gulf War, it was clear that Congress was no more than a sideline player.[22]

In noncrisis situations chief executives have to employ different political skills. Their ability to act unilaterally is greatly diminished, and their most important asset becomes the capacity to persuade others that their policy ideas deserve consideration and action. One aspect of this political skill is working with advisers and executive officials to put together an attractive program of policies. The other is selling the program to the legislature or the bureaucracy. In general, the government apparatus is stacked against chief executives who seek to innovate. There are many competing power centers that can frustrate the designs of chief executives if those centers are ignored or dealt with improperly. To be successful in normal politics, chief executives have to demonstrate the ability to be a leader among equals.

The crises in the Persian Gulf in the early 1990s and the subsequent regional conflicts in Kosovo and Bosnia stand in sharp contrast to President Clinton's health care reform effort in 1993. President Clinton made health care reform the top domestic policy objective of his first term. If successful, the reform would have made history by completely restructuring the health care insurance industry and the government's role in it. But Clinton was faced with intense opposition from the insurance industry, which invested millions of dollars in advertising campaigns to convince the American people that government involvement in health care would be a disaster.[23]

Despite the fact that health care was considered a top concern of more than half of the American people in public opinion polls of the early 1990s, most were confused by Clinton's technically laden proposals and easily swayed by the television advertisements.[24] Furthermore, Clinton's handling of the task force on health care was questioned by Republicans on Capitol Hill and ordinary citizens alike. His appointment of his wife, Hillary Clinton, to head the task force was controversial as was the task force's reliance on closed-door meetings. The task force produced a thick document detailing a confusing national health plan that failed to muster the support of Congress and the public. The health care reforms that Clinton was eventually able to achieve were relatively modest changes in existing programs, such as Medicare and Medicaid, and fell far short of his original grand vision.

Tools of the Trade

Richard Neustadt's influential book *Presidential Power* provides a useful framework for understanding how chief executives exercise power.[25] Neustadt points out that executive power in American government is both protected and restricted by the Constitution. Presidents have a great deal of authority over the implementation of laws passed by Congress and over foreign affairs and military matters, but their domestic policymaking authority is limited. Certain presidents, however—Franklin Roosevelt was always uppermost in Neustadt's mind—have exerted tremendous influence over both foreign and domestic policy.

This observation leads to one of Neustadt's major points: executive power is largely potential. Actual power depends on the ability of chief executives to leverage their formal powers and to stretch their influence over as many aspects of government as possible. Success implies that chief executives have convinced other government actors that going along with the plans and policies of the chief executive is in their best interest. Because this kind of governing entails extensive bargaining, Neustadt's primary and best-known conclusion is that presidential power lies mainly in the ability to persuade.

Political scientist Alan Rosenthal elaborates on Neustadt's observation, pointing to the various tools that governors have at their disposal to practice the art of persuasion. They include several important powers, such as the powers of initiation, rejection, provision, publicity, and popularity.[26]

The line-item veto is an especially useful weapon that governors can use in political battles. Whereas the Constitution does not afford the president the authority to strike out individual sections of bills, governors in most states can veto parts of bills that offend them or even revise sentences in legislation to make them more to their liking. If the legislators try to graft unrelated language onto a bill or attempt to insert projects to benefit particular legislative districts, governors can strike whatever they want from the bill without rejecting the entire law. For example, Governor Tommy Thompson of Wisconsin exercised nearly eight hundred partial vetoes between 1987 and 1989, yet the Democratic-controlled legislature could not muster enough votes to override any of them.[27]

This is also an example of the role of the veto in divided government. When the legislature is controlled by one party and the chief executive is from another party, the veto allows the chief executive to have much more control over legislative outcomes than would otherwise be the case. Since it is highly unlikely a president or governor could continually veto whole bills and stay politically popular or viable, the line-item veto becomes a powerful tool. Presidents of both parties have been aware of this for some time and have argued for line-item veto power. Congress granted a form of this power to the president in the Line Item Veto Act passed in 1996, but the veto provisions of this law were soon revoked by the U.S. Supreme Court.[28]

The governorships in most states have evolved in a way that closely parallels the evolution of the presidency; the once largely ceremonial offices are now the engines of state politics. But the formal powers of governors are constrained in many important ways, which makes bargaining skills even more necessary. Governors may face tougher persuasive tasks than presidents because in most states certain cabinet officers are elected by the voters, not appointed by the governor. It is not unusual for these officials to be political rivals or opponents of the governor. In either case, their political independence is a virtual certainty. Big-city mayors face a similar situation in that major bureaucratic officials are either elected by the citizens or selected by boards or commissions; therefore, the mayors may have a difficult time persuading these officials to support their policies. Governors and mayors operate in smaller arenas than presidents, which reduces somewhat the number of powerful political actors with whom they must contend. But they do not have as much formal authority over their executive branches as presidents.[29]

Chief executive power is clearly elastic. Chief executives with similar or identical formal powers exert widely varying degrees of influence within their governments. Part of this variation can be attributed to political or economic factors, such as the presence or absence of crises, which affect the degree of centralized leadership. There can be no doubt, however, that the aspirations and abilities of chief executives also influence how much power they wield. As governors, George W. Bush of Texas, Pete Wilson of California, Mario Cuomo of New York, and Bill Clinton of Arkansas exerted more influence on the national political scene than their recent predecessors, in part because they harbored ambitions to influence national politics and policy. At the national level, President Carter's inability to gain control of the political process during his administration, despite the presence of solid Democratic majorities in both houses of Congress, reveals him to have been considerably less adept at the power game than Lyndon Johnson or Ronald Reagan. President Clinton had difficulty managing Congress during the early years of his first term, even though there was a Democratic majority. After revising his agenda to include more centrist policies and appeals to the American public, however, Clinton succeeded in getting the Republican Congress to pass several of his initiatives.

Comparisons between the most recent presidents and those who served in the 1940s, 1950s, or 1960s should leave the student of contemporary politics somewhat uneasy. Political conditions have changed, and these changes have affected the way chief executives exercise power. Probably the most important changes have been in the number of active participants in the political process and the relationship between politicians and their constituents. Also, except for the Carter administration, all the presidents since 1968 have dealt with Congresses controlled by the opposition party. It remains to be seen whether George W. Bush can effectively use his Republican colleagues in control of Congress to achieve his agenda.

In the days of Franklin Roosevelt and Dwight D. Eisenhower, there were a limited number of truly powerful interest groups, and like-minded groups often worked together so that deals could be struck with the leaders who represented broad segments of society, such as business, labor, and agriculture. Party leaders exercised a great deal of influence over their ranks, which simplified presidential negotiations with Congress. There were some strong and independent executive branch officials and military leaders who had to be taken into account, but as Neustadt has emphasized, one man with sound management ability, good interpersonal skills, a knowledge of politics, and a clear sense of direction could hold the various pieces of government together throughout the bargaining process.

By the 1970s many presidential scholars had begun to doubt whether anyone could do what Roosevelt had done.[30] The increasing number and variety of interest groups, the staunch independence of elected officials, the accompanying erosion of party cohesion, and the persistent institutional conflict and competition seemed to produce an unmanageable pluralism. It was and is unmanageable if the chief executive uses traditional bargaining strategies. Reagan demonstrated that power can be amassed in a significant new way. He did not rely on bargaining with political elites; instead he took his message directly to the people, using his weekly radio broadcasts and speeches on television to persuade them to pressure political officials to endorse his initiatives. The mass media emerged as the most potent weapon in a president's arsenal, and Reagan, the "great communicator," used it to his advantage. In the mass media age it may not matter very much whether political power brokers admire a chief executive's political acumen, as long as they have sufficient respect for, or fear of, the chief executive's ability to arouse the public through direct appeals.[31]

Increased use of direct appeals to the public as a way of enhancing chief executive power is well suited to contemporary political reality, just as bargaining was an appropriate strategy to pursue in the political environment of the 1950s. The independence of other elected officials comes from their certainty that they have established, and can maintain, a favorable image with voters. These relationships hinge more and more on money and the use of advanced communication technology. To the extent that chief executives can break into these relationships, the independence of other political actors is threatened. Legislators pay close attention to constituent opinions, and chief executives who use the media effectively can influence these opinions.[32] When this kind of influence occurs, or when politicians think it is occurring, resistance to a chief executive's policy preferences dissipates, and persuasive power has been exercised.

Clinton's response to proposed Republican tax cuts provides a good example. During the balanced budget deliberations of the mid- and late 1990s, Republicans proposed tax cuts that could be covered only by reducing funding for many social programs, such as Medicare, Medicaid, education, and the environment.[33] Facing opposition from the Republican-controlled Congress, Clinton went directly to the public to preserve the funding levels for these programs. Through his weekly radio address and other media outlets, the president continually repeated his commitment to those programs. By arousing public concern and support, Clinton pressured the Republicans in Congress to forgo the proposed tax cuts and preserve more funding for his priorities.

The ability to persuade is still the major determinant of chief executive power. Political persuasion is a multifaceted enterprise, however; it can be accomplished through traditional political bargaining among self-interested parties, through momentum-building appeals to the public, or by some combination of the two. When opportunities for "going public" are plentiful, as they are in contemporary national politics, one should expect extensive use of this tactic by telegenic politicians.[34] But bargaining and other customary political skills will continue to dominate when direct appeals to voters are difficult, when chief executives lack media appeal, or when there is a manageable number of ranking participants in the policy process. In most circumstances, chief executives must find the right mix of wholesale (public) and retail (private) politics to achieve their objectives.

Leaders and Followers

Most of those who have written on the subject seem to agree that the acquisition of power is the sine qua non of executive leadership.[35] Without power, leadership is virtually impossible. The fragmented nature of American government at all levels makes coherent action difficult; therefore, the essence of chief executive leadership is providing government with a direction or purpose. Implied in this conception of leadership is change. Leaders need to produce tangible results, and typically these take the form of identifiable changes in government organization or policy.[36] Planned changes that are effective and long-lasting and decisive action in crises are the hallmarks of effective leadership.

The essential ingredients of chief executive leadership are both personal and institutional. Judgments about personality or character are highly subjective; therefore, it is difficult to generalize, but personality seems more important than ever in the age of media politics. James David Barber, who has made a career of studying the role of personality in politics, points out that some chief executives derive positive feelings, such as satisfaction, exhilaration, and joy, from their political activity, whereas others experience mostly negative feelings, such as paranoia, resentment, and sadness.[37] Exhibiting some sort of positive disposition is part of effective leadership. Advisers, subordinates, and even rivals and opponents are at their best when they are driven by a forceful and inspiring personality.

The institutional side of executive leadership is concerned with the selection of advisers, analysts, political operatives, public relations specialists, and the others who are part of an administration. Most chief executives are able to surround themselves with a sizable cadre of loyalists, and their success at channeling the energies and skills of these individuals on behalf of their objectives is critical in determining their ultimate effectiveness as political leaders. Once the appointees are in place, the chief executives make the most critical choices: whose advice to take and when. And their range of options is quite large. They can rely on many advisers or a few; they can make frequent or little use of cabinet officials, outside specialists, or members of their personal staff; or they can establish hierarchical, competitive, or collegial relationships among their advisers. There are no proven formulas for success, but the experiences of several presidents provide useful insights into this aspect of chief executive politics.

Having many close and able advisers who represent various perspectives is widely regarded as a prudent practice, although relatively few presidents have followed it. Franklin Roosevelt and John Kennedy usually get the highest marks on this score. Nixon's complete reliance on three or four advisers during his second term is regarded as a reason for his downfall and should serve as a warning to other presidents of the dangers of inaccessibility.[38] Despite the Nixon precedent, concerns about leaks of politically sensitive information to the press and the natural unpleasantness associated with hearing unfavorable reports about their administration limited the openness of the Ford, Carter, Reagan, and Bush presidencies. President Clinton set out to assemble a cabinet that "looked like America" and achieved greater diversity in race and gender than any of his predecessors.[39]

President George Bush, by all accounts, arranged his White House staff hierarchically with Chief of Staff John Sununu at the top. He also placed trusted friends and allies in three important cabinet posts: James Baker as secretary of state, Nicholas Brady as secretary of the treasury, and Richard Cheney as secretary of defense. In contrast to Bush, Clinton's staff was organized in such a way that several senior staffers had access to the president. This often resulted in hours of deliberation, a lack of clear policy aims or proposals, and leaks to the news media.[40]

Governors have needs very different from those of presidents and organize their staffs accordingly. Governors have an average of 56 staff members; governors of small states like Wyoming have only 14 staff members, whereas the governors of New York and Florida have 203 and 264 staff members, respectively.[41] Nearly all governors employ political advisers, legislative liaisons, bureaucratic liaisons, press secretaries or public relations specialists, legal advisers, and budget experts.[42] The use of teams of agency officials and political advisers to develop policy initiatives is common. Most governors regard selling their policy ideas to the legislature as one of their most difficult tasks, a true test of their leadership ability.[43] Mayors also need this kind of assistance. Bureaucratic liaisons, often called chief administrative officers, help mayors handle challenges from independent-minded bureaucratic agencies.[44] Depending on the extent of their appointment power and resources, mayors may also employ political advisers, press secretaries, and budget specialists.

Facts and Politics

Making a distinction between decision making in crisis situations and that in normal, noncrisis situations helps simplify the enormous variation in the way presidents, governors, and mayors go about carrying out their responsibilities. At one end of the spectrum are visible and threatening crises in which the number of participants is small, advice consists mainly of substantive information and analysis, and chief executive decisions are authoritative. At the other end are controversies over domestic initiatives in which the number of active participants is large, political advice and calculations are usually more important than analytical information, and chief executives and legislatures battle with one another over the ultimate outcomes. The power of chief executives is obviously greatest during crises, but some aspects of these situations are dangerous, in that they create political risks, and unpleasant, because difficult choices must be made when many would rather avoid them.

Presidents and governors often try to achieve greater control over policymaking by defining problems in crisis terms and then demanding that legislatures comply with their suggestions. Ronald Reagan declared a "war on drugs" in the early 1980s, and Bill Clinton spoke often of the health care and welfare crises in the 1990s. At the state level, many governors argued that their state's schools were performing so poorly that rapid and substantial change was required to remedy the situation. They called special legislative sessions and introduced far-reaching reforms. By taking this approach, they hoped to put additional pressure on the legislature and on interest groups to act swiftly and in accordance with the governors' objectives.

The chief executive sets the basic outline of policy action in campaign promises and other statements. Translating these ideas into concrete policy proposals is the job of advisers and policy development groups. The personal involvement of chief executives in the formulation process varies with their personalities and abilities. Some try to master most of the details, whereas others content themselves with sketching the big picture; some are rigid and doctrinaire, and others are flexible and accommodating. Reagan, Carter, and Clinton offer illustrative contrasts. Clinton impressed other politicians and his staff members with his intelligence and command of the details of policies and policy options. He involved himself in the development and technical details of virtually every proposal. Carter impressed other politicians with his command of the details of policy options, but he could never chart a clear course with the policies he promoted. Reagan's knowledge of policy was quite general, in some cases mostly anecdotal, but many of his pronouncements inspired successful and significant policy actions that reflected the conservative philosophy he championed.

Once preferred policy approaches have been devised, chief executives and their staffs turn their attention to eliminating the many barriers to enactment. The outcome of this effort is determined largely by their ability to persuade others to follow their lead. If those with a stake in a decision can be herded into a few identifiable groups and agree to be bound by the bargains their leaders strike, policy change is likely. Unless competing interests are brought together, initiatives get shredded in the fragmented governmental machinery.

Chief executives have an array of persuasive devices that can be deployed on behalf of their initiatives—the invocation of party loyalty, direct appeals to the public, the dispensation of special favors, the making of political trades and promises, the real or threatened use of a veto—and these strategies are commonly used in this high-stakes arena of power and politics.

The enactment of the nation's toughest laws governing the purchase and ownership of assault weapons in New Jersey is a case of strong gubernatorial leadership against entrenched opponents. During his campaign for the New Jersey statehouse, Governor Jim Florio announced that if elected he would seek a ban on the sale and ownership of the assault weapons often used by drug dealers in street fighting against police officers. Within a month of his inauguration, he called upon the legislature to pass a tough ban on assault weapons. With the public opinion polls showing overwhelming public support, he pushed for action and lined up backing from gun control and law enforcement organizations.

The National Rifle Association (NRA), sportsmen's organizations, and hunting groups quickly organized to stop or water down the Florio proposal. Knowing that public support would not be forthcoming, they focused their fire on legislators and the governor. Thousands of letters poured into legislators' offices, phone lines were jammed with calls from irate gun owners. Most effective were the weekend visits made by anti–gun control advocates to legislators at their homes and local offices to engage in face-to-face lobbying. A week before the vote, more than five thousand gun enthusiasts rallied in the state capital and cheered as their leaders denounced Governor Florio and warned legislators that they would pay a price at the polls if they supported the ban on assault weapons. On the day of the vote, hundreds of NRA members chanted threatening slogans in the courtyard outside the legislative chambers while their leaders tracked individual legislators and reminded them of the consequences of voting against the NRA.

As the vote neared, the staff in the governor's office became fearful that the NRA tactics were working. Several Democrats were threatening to vote against the governor's plan. Wavering or uncommitted legislators were brought to the "front office" (the governor's office in Trenton) and reminded that they would need the governor's support for future measures. The ban finally passed both senate and assembly, with no votes to spare. Governor Florio had succeeded in the art of persuasion, but not without putting maximum pressure on some of his supporters. As one senior New Jersey legislator described the experience, "I never want to be put through that kind of vote again. I am not cut out for suicide missions."[45]

The Buck Stops Here

Harry Truman, in characterizing his presidency, was fond of saying that "the buck stops here." Indeed, chief executives are involved in a staggering list of issues because the ultimate authority to carry out governmental policy nearly always rests with them. It is helpful to think of this vast range of issues as falling into three categories: (1) international and intergovernmental policies and actions; (2) economic and budgetary policies; and (3) domestic "quality of life" policies.[46]

As the international economy becomes more extensively interwoven, states and cities are having more frequent direct dealings with foreign nations. But foreign policy is still reserved mainly for presidents. Modern presidents usually make foreign policy their highest priority because they have more power to determine policy in this area and they cannot ignore international crises. Economic and budgetary policies come next; presidents recognize that perceptions about the success or failure of their administrations hinge on the state of the economy. Domestic policies tend to come last because breakthroughs in this area are so difficult to achieve.[47]

President Clinton was an exception to this general rule. With the end of the cold war, issues that had demanded primary attention of previous presidents practically disappeared. Clinton focused on domestic policy issues. Unlike George Bush, who was well prepared as a military and foreign policy leader, Clinton's lack of military service as well as draft-dodging allegations made him less qualified to build his presidency on a legacy of military activity in foreign lands. Clinton's experience in state government prepared him to deal with the domestic issues he tackled, such as welfare reform, health care, education reform, balancing the budget, and downsizing the government bureaucracy.

For governors and mayors, budgetary and social policy matters dominate. Budgets are particularly important; they represent the ultimate expression of the chief executive's priorities and are a principal means of exercising control over the legislature, the courts, and the bureaucracy.[48] Budget preparation affords chief executives at the state and local levels the opportunity to assert their preferences on nearly every aspect of policy—from the cost of college tuition to the cost of a bus ride. Budget decisions may be especially difficult for them because, unlike the federal government, they are typically unable to borrow money when revenues fall short of government needs. Instead they must cut programs, raise revenues, or both to get through tough times. Due to shortfalls in projected revenues during 1990, for example, twenty-six states increased revenues and twenty states reduced government spending to avoid year-end deficits.[49] This practice changed with the strong economy of the mid- and late 1990s. Growing state budget surpluses allowed governors to reduce state taxes and fees and increase spending. According to the National Governors' Association, governors cut taxes each year from 1994 to 2000 and implemented modest spending increases—an average of 5.3 percent over the years 1995–2000.[50]

For more than a decade, budget decisions overshadowed all others at the national level as Congress scrambled to cope with huge deficits. Washington insiders spoke of the "budget driving the policy process," by which they meant that substantive policy questions were subordinated to budgetary considerations, such as not exceeding the spending levels specified in budget resolutions when new programs were authorized or, more commonly, when old programs were reauthorized. With the shift from deficit politics of the mid-1990s to surplus politics in 1999–2000, this trend changed somewhat. Social Security became the center of a debate about how to use government surpluses: should they be used to overhaul the Social Security system to ensure its future viability; or should they be used to pay off the national debt or reduce taxes?

Slogans and Symbols

Presidents, governors, and mayors inhabit worlds filled with symbolism. Aside from the many ceremonial functions associated with these offices, symbolic rhetoric is used to build consensus on matters of general principle or for specific policies. For example, President Clinton continually invoked certain themes and slogans in relation to his politics. Education and tax credits were ways to help the middle class, which had been "losing ground," and welfare reform, which emphasized work to "end welfare as we know it" and to "break the cycle of dependency." When the policies of a chief executive are announced, they are often described in highly symbolic terms, typically portraying the chief executive as being above parochial politics and working in the larger interest of the nation, state, or city.

Political scientist Jeff Fishel has studied the relationship between presidential rhetoric and policy actions in great detail and has compiled some interesting data (see Table 6-2).[51] For the most part these data support the conventional wisdom about the inclinations of recent presidents to use rhetoric and action. Kennedy made many promises and followed up on most of them but had some trouble with Congress. Johnson's 1964 campaign was high on rhetoric and very low on specific promises, but he was exceptionally effective in getting what he wanted from Congress. Nixon had trouble with the Democratic-controlled Congresses with which he had to work. Reagan stands out for making only a few specific policy pledges and for neglecting most of them; his overall record with Congress was mediocre, although his success rate in 1981–1982 was quite high. Clinton made a promise to pass significant, ground-breaking legislation within his first hundred days in office but encountered stiff opposition in a Congress controlled by his own party.

Nonrhetorical symbols also contribute to the leadership mystique of chief executives. By jogging and playing golf, Bill Clinton sought to reinforce the image of a vigorous man who is strong enough to handle the job and who shares the average American's love of recreation and sports. By playing jazz saxophone he positioned himself as an admirer of an important component of American culture. Projecting a compelling image can be useful to effective political leadership.

It is not uncommon for political observers to complain that certain chief executive policies are merely symbolic. This charge has often been leveled against policies in such areas as civil rights, welfare, environmental protection, and foreign policy, where rhetoric usually exceeds action by a large margin. The civil rights statutes of 1957 and 1960 and executive orders dating back to 1950 did little to reduce the various forms of discrimination at which they were directed. Eventually, however, they led to stronger and more effective statutes—the Civil Rights Act of 1964 and the Voting Rights Act of 1965 and executive orders in 1965 and 1969—that produced significant changes in black employment and voting.[52] Given the nature of American policymaking, initial steps that are high on symbolism and low on substance are often necessary to pave the way for policies that produce real change.

Table 6-2 Presidential Promises, Action, and Policy

	Kennedy (1960)[a]	Johnson (1964)[a]	Nixon (1968)[a]	Carter (1976)[a]	Reagan (1980)[a]
Number of identifiable campaign promises[b]	133	63	153	186	108
Percentage of campaign promises calling for concrete action[c]	64	60	64	67	36
Percentage of campaign promises for which full or partial executive action was taken[d]	67	63	60	65	43
Percentage of congressional dependent promises for which executive action was taken and which were enacted[e]	53	62	34	41	44

Source: The categories first appeared in Gerald Pomper, Elections in America (New York: Dodd, Mead, 1968); data for Johnson and Nixon compiled by Fred I. Grogan in "Candidates Promises and Performances, 1964–1972" (paper presented at the 1977 meeting of the Midwest Political Science Association); the rest of the data presented by Jeff Fishel in Presidents and Promises (Washington, D.C.: CQ Press, 1985), 33, 39, 42.

[a] Year in which promises were made.
[b] The figures for Johnson and Nixon include some foreign policy promises (14 for Johnson, 36 for Nixon). All the others include domestic policy promises only.
[c] Fishel uses four categories of campaign promises: pledges of continuity, expression of goals and concerns, pledges of action, and detailed pledges. The latter two comprise this category.
[d] Fishel uses seven categories of executive action: proposals that were fully or partially comparable to promises, token action, contradictory action, no action, mixed action, and indeterminate. Categories one and two are collapsed here for these low percentages.
[e] The total from which these percentages were calculated is slightly lower than the number of promises because some promises were not dependent on congressional actions (for example, orders and unclassified promises).

In May 2000, South Carolina legislators finally approved a bill to remove the Confederate flag from the top of the capitol building. This action followed a five-day, 120-mile protest march led by the mayor of Charleston, Joseph P. Riley, to demand action on the issue.[53] The Confederate flag exemplifies how powerful and divisive symbols can be in politics. Heated debate divided the state legislature for days, and the bill was approved by a slim majority.

Symbolism also plays a major role in crisis decision making. The conduct of the Persian Gulf War was, in effect, a series of carefully orchestrated symbols. Before launching a war against Iraq, President Bush visited the troops at Thanksgiving, consulted with world leaders at the White House, and summoned congressional leaders to his office for private briefings. The purpose of all this was to demonstrate that the president was carefully and deliberately weighing the options before risking American lives.

These examples point up how difficult it is to make definitive judgments about symbolism and substance, particularly with regard to the high-visibility policies of chief executive politics. Chief executives sponsor policies for both symbolic and substantive reasons; the balance between the two is probably best judged after the results of such policies have surfaced and been analyzed.

Opportunities for Innovation

The conservative inclinations of American government are likely to be embodied in chief executive policies. Nevertheless, the elective institutions of American government can make innovative decisions, and when they do, it is almost always chief executives who provide the driving force. Presidential scholar James Ceaser pointed out that "presidents have an important role to play in covering the struggle of self-interest [that pervades American politics] with a veneer of poetry and calling at certain moments for sacrifice for the common good."[54]

A crisis creates an opportunity for a chief executive to pursue innovative policies. Wars permit all sorts of unusual measures—industry seizures, rationing, strict wage and price controls, and plans for world government. The Great Depression brought forth the New Deal programs and the beginning of the welfare state. It is difficult to overstate the significance of agencies like the Rural Electrification Administration (REA) or the Tennessee Valley Authority (TVA) for the millions of rural Americans who lived in primitive conditions until the New Deal brought them electrical power, or of minimum wage and labor relations laws for the millions of blue-collar workers of that era. Policies that produce changes of such magnitude have long-standing political force and enshrine the leaders who sponsored them. They also encourage other chief executives to aspire to similar accomplishments.

It would be a mistake, however, to equate crises and innovation in American politics. One of the most significant revelations of a crisis like the depression is that centralized policy action is possible when the president can count on support in Congress. President Johnson supervised a Democratic majority with a broad consensus on the need to alleviate poverty, and they worked together to create innovative policies. But from the 1950s to the 1990s, the presidency was more often than not in the hands of the Republican Party, and Congress was under the control of the Democrats. During most of the 1990s the presidency was held by Clinton, a Democrat, whereas Congress was under the control of the Republicans. Such divided government frequently leads to gridlock or compromise but seldom to rapid policy innovation.

In recent years conditions favoring change in governmental programs have existed more frequently in state capitals as governors and legislatures of the same party have tackled such difficult problems as education and welfare reform, environmental concerns, and economic development. Welfare reform is an especially good example of state leadership eventually pushing the federal government to act. Beginning in the 1950s, federal policymakers bemoaned the dismal performance of welfare programs but failed to effect significant change. Then, in the late 1980s and early 1990s, governors in various states forged a new consensus. Put simply, welfare programs had to be redefined; entitlements that were said to encourage dependency were replaced by welfare-to-work programs, such as Florida's GAIN program, to foster self-sufficiency. A strong emphasis on work activity was implemented through the use of work requirements as a condition for receiving assistance. By the time the federal government enacted its version of welfare reform, many states had already adopted similar programs.

Working majorities in legislatures do not simply appear out of the blue. They come about because popular chief executives make an effort to assemble them. Policies and politics are inseparable. Innovative policies are most often the product of an evolutionary process that includes an awareness among politicians of widespread public concern about certain problems, the selection of popular solutions, and the use of persuasive techniques to build a policy majority among legislators. Chief executives can easily stumble in any of these steps, but they can also succeed; their successes are policies that produce change.

Benefits for Whom?

Chief executives are fond of claiming that their policies benefit all members of society. In a sense this is true. To the extent that macroeconomic policies contribute to overall economic growth, there are widely shared gains. When threats to national security are effectively rebuffed, everyone benefits. When bureaucracies are reorganized to function more efficiently or law enforcement is improved to reduce crime, the whole society is said to be better off. Analysis easily uncovers variations in the benefits different population segments or geographical areas realize from policies, however. And, not surprisingly, these variations have political roots.

Like most elected officials, chief executives pursue policies that benefit their main constituents. This support of constituent interests is not always a matter of narrow partisanship or cynicism about doing what is best for the collectivity. For most chief executives there is a natural merging, over time, of their views about what is best for society and their preference for policies that disproportionately benefit their supporters. New Deal Democrats, for example, tended to view the world as the struggle of workers and other ordi-

nary citizens to use government to curb the abuses of big business. The policies of Franklin Roosevelt and Harry Truman were aimed primarily at helping white male workers, who became the core of the Democratic Party as
the quality of their lives improved during the 1940s and 1950s.

In the early 1960s, John Kennedy presided over an increasingly fragile
Democratic majority coalition that needed the votes not only of blue-collar
whites but also of blacks to control national elections.[55] This need led to the
serious pursuit of civil rights policies and programs to aid the poor, but
always with an eye to not alienating white, middle-class Democrats. Since
the 1960s black Americans have been the most cohesive Democratic voting
bloc.[56] Reagan's antigovernment policies were aimed at pleasing the middle
and upper classes, from which the Republican Party draws its strength.
Bush's program to lower capital gains taxes and to assert a more sensitive
environmental policy was designed to hold on to hard-core Republican supporters and to expand the base to include younger Americans, who tend to
be more concerned about protecting the environment.

Clinton's centrist platform was an attempt to win back many of the conservative Democrats, independents, and moderate Republicans who had
stopped voting for Democratic presidential candidates in the 1980s. His
emphasis on issues such as Medicaid, Medicare, education, and the environment during his 1996 reelection campaign and the beginning of his second
term was an attempt to put these issues on the national agenda and help
Democrats get elected in future congressional elections.

The meshing of chief executive policies and constituent preferences is
never by any means complete. The policy universe is too crowded and
complicated for chief executives always to help their friends and hurt their
enemies. Carter lost the support of organized labor because he did not
push minimum wage and national health insurance legislation hard
enough to suit union leaders.[57] Clinton left many of his most liberal supporters disillusioned because he did not push for policy changes such as
allowing homosexuals to serve in the military and preventing state restrictions on abortion.

It is not uncommon for chief executives to contradict one of their publicly stated positions rather than to pursue policies that displease important
voting blocs. For much of his public career, George Bush supported a
woman's right to choose an abortion, but he shifted positions 180 degrees
in order to fit comfortably on the Republican ticket in 1980. By 1988,
when he sought the presidency on his own, Bush had become an ardent
advocate of restrictions on abortion. Reagan often changed his mind at
politically opportune moments, making adept adjustments in his positions
on Social Security, farm subsidies, public works programs, and import
restrictions. For much of his public career, Clinton supported policies
aligned with liberal ideologies. He shifted his position somewhat in order

to garner enough mainstream support to defeat Bush in the 1992 presidential elections. By 1995 it was often difficult to tell the difference between his policy proposals and those of the Republican Congress. Ironically, political leaders sometimes have to follow changes in the political wind in order to stay in charge.

Promises and Performance

Chief executive policies are born of grand promises and often generate great expectations about societal change. Invariably the results fall short of what was promised, but what is accomplished may be quite significant nonetheless. The true results of chief executive policies are realized over an extended period of time as programs and procedures become institutionalized and policies are modified. Studying the consequences of such policies reveals many examples that confirm the essentially political nature of the implementation process and underscore how difficult it is to make precise judgments about the effects of public policies.

In 1967 Lyndon Johnson came up with an idea for helping the poor with one of their most pressing problems, the lack of decent, affordable housing. The deplorable conditions in many cities had led to rioting, and no one seemed to know how to improve matters. Johnson remembered that the federal government owned land in most cities and could more or less give the land to builders who would construct low-cost housing. With federal help the cities could build "new towns in-town."[58] Johnson brought together the relevant agency heads and a program was launched. Four years later the program had produced almost no new housing in the seven cities chosen to demonstrate its viability. Why?

The problems encountered during the implementation of the new towns program are familiar to experienced observers of public policy: local political opposition; inadequate federal resources, incentives, and guidance; poor communication between federal and local implementers; and a faulty program design.[59] What struck Johnson as a great idea made many community groups irate, left local elected officials cold, and kept bureaucrats confused.

Similar effects occurred in the welfare reforms enacted in 1996. Fueled by the idea that local and state governments are more equipped to determine the needs of the poor population of their state, welfare reform devolved much of the implementation responsibility to states. Five years later most states were still struggling with the implications of reform provisions such as term limits for recipients. Should recipients with families who have emotional problems or addictions be terminated after two to five years on welfare if they have few realistic job prospects? If so, what happens to them after that? Much like Johnson's housing program, welfare reform has been charged with inadequate resources for support services such as childcare, a strange mix of regulation and flexibility, and poor communication between federal and local implementers.

The more general lesson is that pluralism and federalism make chief executive initiatives in domestic policy extremely difficult to implement. Many well-intentioned programs have floundered because of the difficulties associated with getting bureaucratic agencies, elected officials, and citizen groups to cooperate.

Implementation problems are by no means limited to domestic policies; they also occur in foreign policy, even during crises. The most common difficulties are the same as in the domestic area: presidential intentions may be poorly communicated; implementers lack the resources necessary to carry out directives; and implementers sometimes resist doing what they are told.[60] The State Department and the military are notorious for their adherence to standard procedures—perhaps the most common form of bureaucratic resistance to orders from above. At critical times during the Cuban missile crisis of 1962, President Kennedy ordered the navy to move its blockade closer to Cuba and not to act belligerently toward the first few Soviet ships it encountered after the quarantine had been declared. Evidence indicates that the navy did not move its quarantine line as the president ordered, and a long argument ensued between Secretary of Defense Robert McNamara and Admiral George Anderson about how intercepted Soviet ships would be treated. It ended with Anderson waving the *Manual of Navy Regulations* at McNamara and remarking, "Now Mr. Secretary, if you and your Deputy will go back to your offices, the Navy will run the blockade."[61] The navy's reluctance to depart from standard operating procedures in the midst of this type of crisis shows that even when the president is directly involved, and the need for effective action is obvious, implementation is by no means automatic.

The existence of problems should not obscure the fact that some policies are effectively implemented with little apparent difficulty. Social Security, for example, is mainly a matter of eligibility determination and the issuance of checks, and the government seems to be capable of executing these tasks quite well.

The chances of encountering major problems during the implementation of chief executive policies are largely dependent upon (1) the amount of societal or organizational change the policy seeks to generate; (2) the complexity of the implementation process—how many different bureaucratic agencies and elected officials are involved; and (3) the level of consensus among the principal implementation actors about the desirability and feasibility of making planned changes.

Policies that seek to bring about fundamental change are difficult to implement successfully because they call for widespread modification in behavior, and the government usually has only limited resources for encouraging it. The degree of difficulty associated with implementing policies of fundamental change is also affected by the complexity of the implementation process and the level of consensus among the implementers. A major innovation such as tax reform, carried out by a simple organizational network in which those involved understand and support programmatic goals, has a good chance of succeeding. Complex implementation arrangements and competing priorities among implementers are almost certain to distort the original goals of innovative policies such as education or welfare reform.

For policies aimed at producing limited change the expectations are quite different. In general, such policies are likely to be implemented with reasonable effectiveness. They can be derailed by a cumbersome implementation process or fundamental disagreement among implementers, however. Johnson's new towns program was not dramatically new in what it sought to accomplish, but the organizational network required to implement it was complex and clumsy, and the consensus among implementation actors was decidedly narrow. These two factors accounted for the program's minimal success.

Intended and Unintended Consequences

Ambitious and innovative programs often have effects that can be clearly identified only many years after they are implemented. In an interesting and revealing study, political scientist Lester Salamon examined the effects of a New Deal program thirty years after it had been terminated. The Resettlement Program of 1934 authorized the federal government to purchase nearly two million acres of land in two hundred different locations and to supervise specially designed agricultural or industrial communities that would make use of the land.[62] A common way of implementing the agricultural program was for the government to break large plantations up into family-size parcels and sell them under lenient terms to tenant farmers, regardless of their race. Because black land ownership in the South was uncommon, and black poverty was pervasive, this program, although small in scale, represented a "bold experiment in social reform."[63] Not surprisingly, the program had many critics, primarily white southern legislators, and it was killed in 1943, nine years after it began. The fact that it was terminated led to the general view that the program had been a failure. Salamon's analysis of the effects of the program in 1973, however, documented a solid record of land retention by the black families it had assisted. These families had moved out of poverty into the middle class. They now owned cars, television sets, and refrigerators. Their children had obtained white-collar jobs, and as a group they were active in political and community organizations and promoted causes. The effects, which Salamon called "sleepers," took many years to emerge in a discernible form.[64]

Head Start, a product of Johnson's War on Poverty, did not seem an unqualified success in its first major evaluation, which was conducted in 1969, four years after the program's inception; but more recent studies have documented long-term positive effects for the participants, and funding was substantially increased in the 1990s.[65] Much the same pattern of delayed effects has held for other major social welfare programs like job training, food stamps, and Medicaid.[66]

The main problem with sleeper effects is that they do nothing to relieve the pressure chief executives feel to produce visible, short-term results from the policies they sponsor. Because of this, chief executives favor programs that have more immediate payoffs. Policies that cannot survive by demonstrating quick positive results must maintain a certain level of political popularity during the time it takes for definitive effects to emerge.

Chief executive policies often produce unintended results, and these, like latent or sleeper effects, must be considered if the full impact of a policy is to be accurately assessed. The iron curtain was an unanticipated result of Truman's effort, known as the Marshall Plan, to rebuild the economies of Western Europe after World War II. Kennedy's determination to land a man on the moon by 1970 resulted in many technological breakthroughs that have had a tremendous influence on the commercial electronics industry and the way of life in the United States. Acid rain in New England and Canada is widely believed to be caused in part by coal burned in the Midwest, a practice furthered by the Carter administration's energy program, which sought, through subsidies for coal conversion, to reduce the industrial use of crude oil and natural gas. The precarious state of the U.S. airline industry in the early 1990s is due in large part to deregulation initiatives in the late 1970s that were intended to strengthen the industry. It should be clear that chief executives do not always get the results they expect from the policies they sponsor.

Even more basic than the uncertainties introduced by time and unanticipated results is the problem of establishing cause-and-effect relationships between policies and outcomes. This is particularly true of chief executive policies because they are often aimed at making significant changes in society, but such changes almost always have complex causes. The Reagan administration's monetary and fiscal policies—the tax cut and stricter control of the money supply—are frequently credited with reducing inflation during the 1980s. Similarly, Clinton's balanced-budget policies are given credit for reducing, then eliminating, the federal deficit. Clinton also takes credit for the booming economy Americans enjoyed during most of his administration. However, in both cases, factors such as global markets and increasing foreign competition in certain core industries, lower energy costs, and natural economic cycles may have had as much to do with economic outcomes as did government monetary and fiscal policy. Indeed, whenever economic conditions are bad, presidents point to forces beyond their control; when conditions are good, they point to their policies. State reforms of education have been praised, but linking changes in teaching techniques, approaches to discipline, or working conditions in the schools with student aptitude and achievement test scores is a notoriously complex task.[67]

Foreign policies and subsequent developments are also difficult to connect. How much did the allegedly "soft" foreign policy of the Carter administration have to do with the Soviet invasion of Afghanistan? How much did the more belligerent Reagan foreign policy affect the willingness of the Soviet Union to sign meaningful arms control agreements? How much did Clinton's public criticism of North Korea have to do with the subsequent deliberations between North and South Korea? It should be emphasized that politicians show little reluctance to assert that positive cause-and-effect relationships exist between policies they support and favorable outcomes and that the opposite is true of policies they oppose.

Some chief executive policies and results have fairly straightforward relationships. It is possible to determine the amount of money elderly recipients receive from Social Security and then to measure the impact of such payments on poverty, defined as a monetary threshold, among the elderly.[68] Decisions about the size, accessibility, and location of state highways have undeniable effects, such as changes in population, property values, and commercial sales. Precise, carefully defined relationships can be established between certain policies and their effects, but many chief executive policies are so broad that the results and their causes are unclear.

The Management Puzzle

Organizational management and policy administration are core responsibilities of chief executives. But because of the pressures and incentives to take the lead in setting the policy agenda and pushing for the enactment of policies, few chief executives have the time or the inclination to oversee the implementation of the policies they have championed. Therefore, most of the institutional learning that results from the implementation of chief executive policies takes place in bureaucracies or specialized legislative committees. At this point chief executive politics gives way to bureaucratic or legislative politics.

Efforts to reorganize the executive branch are perhaps the most common form of chief executive activity that reflects institutional learning. Bureaucratic resistance to chief executive initiatives has been recognized as a problem at least since the turn of the century. Franklin Roosevelt, Truman, Nixon, Carter, Reagan, and Clinton all sponsored executive branch reorganizations aimed at establishing more rational bureaucratic structures and enhancing central control. The results usually fell short of expectations, mainly because Congress and the interest groups that were tied to the existing subgovernmental networks effectively opposed the changes these presidents sought.[69]

Through the Civil Service Reform Act of 1978, President Carter tried to shake up the bureaucracy, starting with individual employees. The act provided incentives for high-ranking civil servants to take on special tasks at the request of the president or cabinet officer, and it made the hiring, firing, and transfer of civil servants somewhat easier. During his 1992 presidential campaign, Clinton promised to cut his White House staff by 25 percent. He and Vice President Al Gore vowed to reinvent government starting with their own executive branch, and they accomplished their 25 percent goal in the spring of 1993.[70] Clinton and Gore also promised to reinvent government through downsizing the federal bureaucracy so that it works better and costs less. But studies by independent scholars argue that such promises have not been fulfilled. Although there may be only 1.9 million full-time salaried government workers today, the smallest number since the 1960s, reports argue that this number is misleading. In reality, almost 17 million people work for the government, providing goods and services directly or indirectly.[71]

In state government, reorganizations have been common. Since 1965, half of the state governments have undergone comprehensive reorganizations and nearly all states have reorganized at least part of their government operations.[72] Many governors have also pushed for higher standards in the hiring and retention of government employees, the inclusion of more jobs in civil service or merit systems, and the improvement of in-service training. The goals of these reforms are basically the same as those of federal reforms: establishing clear chains of command and making public service delivery more economical and responsive to central control.

Chief executives are not reluctant to get involved with implementation problems if questionable results become public concerns. In fact, chief executives who sponsor policy innovations that are adopted—either their own or those inherited from their immediate predecessor—are likely to assign a high priority to certain matters of program delivery. A common reaction to implementation problems is to propose program reform. Many of the War on Poverty programs were designed to avoid reliance on entrenched federal and state bureaucracies and to restrict state discretion because the policy formulators in the Kennedy and Johnson administrations doubted the commitment of those bureaucratic and political officials to the programs' goals. Not surprisingly, these policies generated their own implementation problems, such as duplication of service, lack of coordination among related programs, and state and local political resistance, which Republican presidents Nixon, Reagan, and Bush used to justify proposals for a "new federalism." The result of new federalism reforms is a modified intergovernmental program delivery system, fewer separate programs, and a larger state role in implementation decisions.

Summary

Chief executive politics commands the attention of almost every American. More than any other politicians, chief executives define and articulate the leading issues of the day and propose policy solutions. Much of what they say and do is covered by the media and becomes the focus of discussion among citizens. Their visibility and their formal powers give chief executives enormous political influence.

Their political strength is clearly evident in their ability to define issues and set agendas. The concerns they choose to address become issues for the entire political community. They can force others to pay attention to their priorities and accept their definitions of issues. Their domination of the political agenda gives them a tremendous advantage in policy development.

Many chief executive proposals fail to gain the approval needed to become policy, which diminishes the political strength of the leaders who offer them. Chief executive power and policy effectiveness, therefore, depend for their success on the ability of the individuals who occupy high office to convince the public and other political elites of the merit of their proposals. When the quality of chief executives' leadership is widely questioned, their political muscles atrophy. The ability of chief executives to overcome the many hurdles that confront them on the path to policy change may justifiably earn them legendary reputations.

All chief executives have long lists of important policy proposals they hope to have enacted. If they are successful, the public has a tangible basis for evaluating chief executive performance. Concrete policy accomplishments are a valuable form of political currency. Established politicians display a strong allegiance to the status quo, but the values of the public are continually changing. Chief executives, taking advantage of their unique relationship with the public, frequently have acted as agents for change in American politics.

All the time and energy chief executives devote to voicing public concerns and securing adoption of new policies naturally limits the attention they can devote to matters of administration and policy implementation. Still, because new policies tend to breed implementation problems, issues of program design and delivery frequently command the interest and concern of chief executives.

When crises occur, nearly every aspect of chief executive politics changes. Media and public attention become a hindrance rather than an asset, and other political actors become much more cooperative and deferential. The power to act usually belongs unambiguously to chief executives, but the repercussions of ill-advised action can be severe. Effective crisis management is how many chief executives build their reputations as effective leaders.

Notes

1. Most governors have formal powers that are similar to those of presidents. They serve four-year terms and can run for reelection at least once. Often they can appoint high-ranking state officials, although some state legislatures share this power and some state officials are elected. Governors have considerable control over the budget process and have a veto over legislative actions, in some cases a line-item veto. Strong mayors are those who have formal powers much like those of presidents and governors. The characteristics of a strong mayoralty are terms longer than two years, the power to appoint heads of executive departments, veto power over city council actions, and a large role in the budget process. Most major cities have a strong mayor-council form of government. For more details, see Thad C. Beyle, "Governors," in *Politics in the American States,* 3d ed., ed. Virginia Gray, Herbert Jacob, and Kenneth Vines (Boston: Little, Brown, 1983), 193–203; Larry Sabato, *Goodbye to Good-Time Charlie,* 2d ed. (Washington, D.C.: CQ Press, 1983); and Robert C. Lineberry and Ira Sharkansky, *Urban Politics and Public Policy,* 3d ed. (New York: Harper and Row, 1978), 161–169.
2. In describing the president's agenda, Paul Light categorizes executive branch proposals in the same way as the Office of Management and Budget, separating those that are in accordance with the president's program and that have been mentioned in a State of the Union address. This scheme is an appropriate way to distinguish the issues and policies that we regard as proper to chief executive politics from those that are more appropriately viewed as part of administrative politics. See Paul C. Light, "Presidents as Domestic Policy Makers," in *Rethinking the Presidency,* ed. Thomas E. Cronin (Boston: Little, Brown, 1982), 351–370.
3. See John Kingdon, *Agendas, Alternatives, and Public Policies* (Boston: Little, Brown, 1984), 26.
4. James K. Oliver, "Presidents as National Security Policy Makers," in Cronin, *Rethinking the Presidency,* 396–397.
5. See Beyle, "Governors," 211.
6. See Sabato, *Goodbye to Good-Time Charlie,* 105–110, 115–116.
7. Dick Kirschten, "Targets of Discontent," *National Journal,* November 10, 1990, 2736–2742.
8. U.S. Census Bureau, "State and Local Government Finances by Level of Government, 1995–96," online at http://www.census.gov/govs/estimate/96stlus.txt, August 11, 2000.
9. Richard P. Nathan and Fred C. Doolittle, *Reagan and the States* (Princeton, N.J.: Princeton University Press, 1987).
10. Light, "Presidents as Domestic Policy Makers," 361.
11. Ibid., 362–364.
12. Jeff Fishel, *Presidents and Promises* (Washington, D.C.: CQ Press, 1985).

13. Stephen Skowronek discusses the intellectual/ideological and practical aspects of several efforts to build and then reform national government in *Building a New American State: The Expansion of National Administrative Capacity, 1877–1920* (New York: Cambridge University Press, 1982).

14. See Thomas Cronin, "On the Separation of Brain and State: Implications for the President," in *Modern Presidents and the Presidency,* ed. Marc Landy (Lexington, Mass.: Lexington Books, 1985), 54.

15. Ibid., 54–58.

16. Kingdon, *Agendas, Alternatives, and Public Policies.*

17. Light, "Presidents as Domestic Policy Makers," 365.

18. Fishel, *Presidents and Promises,* 26.

19. For a discussion of bias in presidential agendas, see ibid., 20–22. For more general treatments of this subject, see E. E. Schattschneider, *The Semi-Sovereign People* (New York: Holt, Rinehart and Winston, 1960; rev. ed., 1975); Peter Bachrach and Morton S. Baratz, *Power and Poverty: Theory and Practice* (New York: Oxford University Press, 1970); and Steven Lukes, *Power* (London: Macmillan, 1974).

20. Robert A. Rosenblatt, "GAO Estimates Final Cost of S&L Bailout at $480.9 Billion," *Los Angeles Times,* July 13, 1996, D12; Kitty Calavita, Henry N. Pontell, and Robert H. Tillman, *Big Money Crime: Fraud and Politics in the Savings and Loan Crisis* (Berkeley: University of California Press, 1997), 1.

21. Ilene Rosenthal, "The Clinton-Gore Digital Divide Proposal," *Technology and Learning,* May 2000, 10–11.

22. Christopher Madison, "Sideline Players," *National Journal,* December 15, 1990, 3024–3026.

23. Margaret Carlson, "Another Dose of Harry and Louise," *Time,* November 24, 1997, 34.

24. Jennie Jacobs Kronenfeld, *The Changing Federal Role in U.S. Health Care Policy* (Westport, Conn.: Greenwood Publishing, Praeger, 1997), 15.

25. Richard E. Neustadt, *Presidential Power: The Politics of Leadership from FDR to Carter* (New York: John Wiley, 1980).

26. Alan Rosenthal, *Governors and Legislatures* (Washington, D.C.: CQ Press, 1990), 35–45.

27. Ibid., 10.

28. Ted Gest, "Vetoed: The Line Item Veto," *U.S. News & World Report,* July 6, 1998, 44; "Line-Item Veto Not an Option," *ABA Journal,* August 1998, 46.

29. See Duane Lockard, *The Politics of State and Local Government,* 3d ed. (New York: Macmillan, 1983), chaps. 7 and 8.

30. See Bert A. Rockman, *The Leadership Question* (New York: Praeger, 1984).

31. This argument is presented more fully by Samuel Kernell in *Going Public* (Washington, D.C.: CQ Press, 1986).

32. Ibid., chap. 6.

33. William J. Clinton, "Remarks at a Democratic National Committee luncheon in New York City," *Weekly Compilation of Presidential Documents,* April 3, 2000, 667–673.

34. Kernell, *Going Public.*

35. See Rockman, *The Leadership Question;* James MacGregor Burns, *Leadership* (New York: Harper and Row, 1978); and Neustadt, *Presidential Power.*

36. Rockman, *The Leadership Question,* chap. 2.
37. See James David Barber, *The Presidential Character,* 2d ed. (Englewood Cliffs, N.J.: Prentice-Hall, 1977).
38. Arthur M. Schlesinger Jr., *The Imperial Presidency* (Boston: Houghton Mifflin, 1973).
39. James P. Pfiffner, *The Strategic Presidency* (Lawrence: University Press of Kansas, 1996), 151–153.
40. Bob Woodward, *Inside the Clinton White House* (New York: Simon and Schuster, 1994).
41. The Council of State Governments, *The Book of the States: 1998–1999* (Lexington, Ky.: Council of State Governments, 1998), 32:20.
42. Coleman B. Ransone Jr., *The American Governorship* (Westport, Conn.: Greenwood Press, 1982), 109–111.
43. Ibid., 114.
44. Lockard, *The Politics of State and Local Government,* 242.
45. Personal interview with author, March 1990.
46. These categories are a slightly modified version of those used by Thomas Cronin in *The State of the Presidency,* 2d ed. (Boston: Little, Brown, 1980), 145–153.
47. Ibid.
48. Thad L. Beyle, "Being Governor," in *The State of the States,* 3d ed., ed. Carl E. Van Horn (Washington, D.C.: CQ Press, 1996).
49. Marcia Howard, *Fiscal Survey of the States, September 1990* (Washington, D.C.: National Governors' Association, 1990).
50. Terrel Halaska, *50 State Reports on 2000 Budgets Released* (Washington, D.C.: National Governors' Association, 2000), online at http://www.nga.org/Releases/PR4January2000finalfiscalsurvey.asp, August 10, 2000.
51. Fishel, *Presidents and Promises,* 30–45.
52. See Harrell H. Hodgers Jr. and Charles S. Bullock III, *Law and Social Change* (New York: McGraw-Hill, 1972), chaps. 2 and 5; and Phyllis Wallace, "A Decade of Policy Developments in Equal Opportunities in Employment and Housing," in *A Decade of Federal Antipoverty Programs,* ed. Robert H. Haveman (New York: Academic Press, 1977).
53. Teresa Malcolm, "South Carolinians Rally to End Flag Debate," *National Catholic Reporter,* April 21, 2000, 8.
54. James C. Ceaser, "The Rhetorical Presidency Revisited," in Landy, *Modern Presidents and the Presidency,* 33.
55. See Frances Fox Piven and Richard A. Cloward, *Regulating the Poor* (New York: Vintage Books, 1971).
56. For specific figures on black voting for Democratic presidential candidates, see Herbert B. Asher, *Presidential Elections and American Politics,* 3d ed. (Homewood, Ill.: Dorsey Press, 1984).
57. See Fishel, *Presidents and Promises,* 93.
58. Martha Derthick, *New Towns In-Town* (Washington, D.C.: Urban Institute Press, 1972).
59. Ibid., 82–102.
60. Morton H. Halperin, "Implementing Presidential Foreign Policy Decisions: Limitations and Resistance," in *Cases in Public Policy Making,* ed. James E. Anderson (New York: Praeger, 1976), 208–236.
61. Graham T. Allison, *Essence of Decision* (Boston: Little, Brown, 1971), 132.

192 **Politics and Public Policy**

62. Lester M. Salamon, "Follow-ups, Letdowns, and Sleepers: The Time Dimension in Policy Evaluation," in *Public Policy Making in a Federal System,* ed. Charles O. Jones and Robert D. Thomas (Beverly Hills, Calif.: Sage, 1976), 257–283.

63. Ibid., 267.

64. Ibid., 263.

65. The original Head Start evaluation was done by Westinghouse Learning Corporation and Ohio University; see *The Impact of Head Start: An Evaluation of the Effects of Head Start on Children's Cognitive and Affective Development,* report to the Office of Economic Opportunity (Washington, D.C.: Government Printing Office, 1969). For subsequent research, see Irving Lazar, *Summary: The Persistence of Preschool Effects* (Ithaca: Community Service Laboratory, New York State College of Human Ecology at Cornell University, 1977). For a bibliographic summary, see Ada Jo Mann, *A Review of Head Start Research since 1969* (Washington, D.C.: George Washington University, 1978). For a recent study, see Steven W. Barnett and Greg Camilli, "Definite Results from Loose Data: A Response to 'Does Head Start Make a Difference?'" (New Brunswick, N.J.: Rutgers University Press, 1996). For numerous recent studies, see U.S. Department of Human Services, Administration for Children and Families, *Annotated Bibliography of Head Start Research: 1985–Present* (Washington, D.C.: Government Printing Office, 2000), online at http://www.acf.dhhs.gov/cgi-bin/hsb2/biblio/index.cgi, June 20, 2000.

66. On the impact of federal job-training programs, see Robert Taggart, *A Fisherman's Guide: An Assessment of Training and Remediation Strategies* (Kalamazoo, Mich.: W. E. Upjohn Institute for Employment Research, 1981). For a summary, see Michael Borus, "Assessing the Impact of Training Programs," in *Employing the Disadvantaged,* ed. Eli Ginzburg (New York: Basic Books, 1980). On the impact of food stamps, see U.S. Senate, Committee on Agriculture, Nutrition, and Forestry, Subcommittee on Nutrition, *Hunger in America: Ten Years Later,* 96th Cong., 1st sess., 1979, S. Rept.; also Congressional Budget Office, *The Food Stamp Program: Income or Food Supplementation?* (Washington, D.C.: Government Printing Office, 1977). On Medicare and Medicaid see Karen Davis and Cathy Schoen, *Health and the War on Poverty: A Ten-Year Appraisal* (Washington, D.C.: Brookings Institution, 1978).

67. See Egon G. Guba, "The Failure of Educational Evaluation," in *Evaluating Action Programs,* ed. Carol H Weiss (Boston: Allyn and Bacon, 1972), 250–266; James S. Coleman, "Problems of Conceptualization and Measurement in Studying Policy Impacts," in *Public Policy Evaluation,* ed. Kenneth M. Dolbeare (Beverly Hills, Calif.: Sage, 1975), 19–40.

68. For an excellent example, see Laurence E. Lynn Jr., "A Decade of Policy Developments in the Income Maintenance System," in Haveman, *A Decade of Federal Antipoverty Programs,* 55–117.

69. For a discussion of presidential reorganization efforts, see Erwin E. Hargrove and Michael Nelson, *Presidents, Politics, and Policy* (New York: Knopf, 1984), 249–265.

70. James P. Pfiffner, *The Strategic Presidency* (Lawrence: University Press of Kansas, 1996), 154.

71. Paul Light, "The True Size of Government," *Government Executive,* January 1999.

72. Beyle, "Being Governor," 38.

Chapter 7 **Courtroom Politics**

It is sometimes said that courts implement policies made by other branches of government. But for many issues—such as abortion, capital punishment, search and seizure, school prayer, and school desegregation—the opposite is true: the courts make policy, and other political institutions respond to their lead. When politicians are silent or ambiguous, judicial action involves more than just policy implementation; in fact, there may be no policy to implement until the courts act. For a wide variety of other issues, such as the environment, welfare, and communications, the courts, although their powers are somewhat circumscribed, have considerable discretion. Judges do more than resolve disputes in accordance with the law. Through their decisions, they create law every bit as much as legislators do.

The policymaking role of U.S. courts arouses considerable controversy because it is unique. In Great Britain, judges are more accurately described as technicians than as policymakers. With a few exceptions, their role is to dot *i*'s and cross *t*'s.[1] U.S. courts are more powerful than other courts in the Western world, and their power is growing. Law professor Donald Horowitz observed, "The courts have tended to move from the byways onto the highways of policymaking."[2] Although from time to time politicians object to the growing power of the courts, the main reason for judicial policymaking is the abdication of responsibility by elected officials.

Many courts make policy, including federal courts and state courts. As the highest federal court, the U.S. Supreme Court is the ultimate arbiter of legal controversies. The Supreme Court's preeminence should not be construed to mean that other courts play a minor role, however. In fact, the Supreme Court decides fewer than a hundred cases each year.[3] In contrast, the other courts combined handle millions of cases annually, and many of these cases have far-reaching policy implications.

Cases and Controversies

The issues confronted by courts are rich and diverse. Many of them, classified as private law, involve disputes between private parties. This category comprises contracts (Is an agreement legally binding?); property (Has property been illegally damaged or confiscated?); and torts (Have people or property been directly harmed?). In public law cases, government officials are parties to a legal dispute. Under this category are questions of constitutional law (Are decisions by government officials constitutional?); statutory law (What is

Figure 7-1 Branches of Law

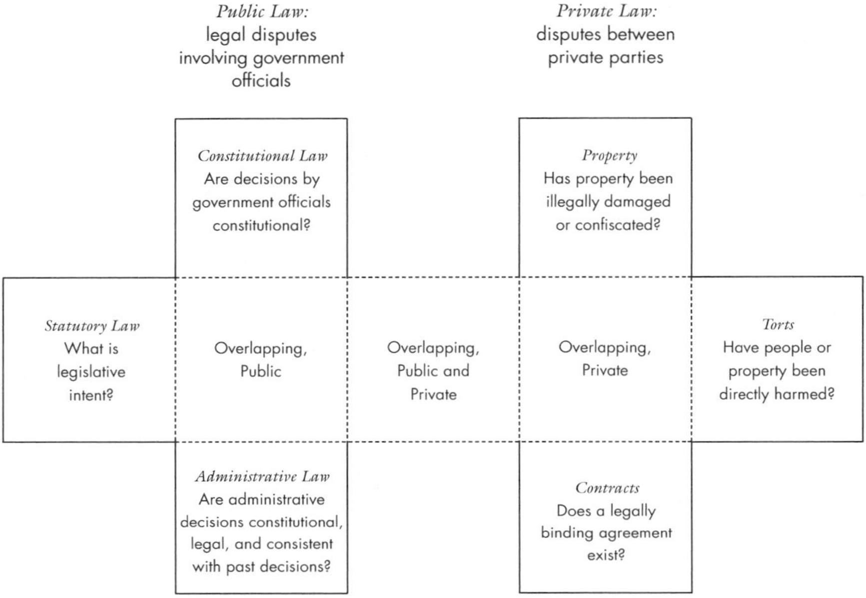

legislative intent?); and administrative law (Are administrative decisions constitutional, legal, and consistent with past decisions?).

These categories overlap in many ways (see Figure 7-1). Antitrust actions by government officials often have public and private components. For example, government officials function as prosecutors in a case, but the charge is that one company has engaged in anticompetitive behavior against another. Torts become public when a private party sues a government official or an agency for malfeasance or nonfeasance. Overlaps within categories are even more common. In many administrative law cases, the key is legislative intent; in many constitutional law cases, the constitutionality of a statute is questioned; in both instances, statutory law is involved.

Because the concern here is public policy, the focus is on public law cases, which have broader implications for society than do private law cases. If one person sues a neighbor over a barking dog, the world does not anxiously await a verdict. If an administrative agency proposes a change in welfare eligibility rules, the verdict may affect many thousands of people. Examples from administrative law and constitutional law are cited to illustrate differences in judicial behavior. Although administrative law occasionally overlaps with constitutional law, each more often overlaps with statutory law. In administrative and constitutional law, questions of statutory interpretation are seldom far from view.

Constitutional Law

Constitutional law raises questions about civil liberties, states' rights, interstate commerce, and other protections guaranteed by the U.S. Constitution or the constitutions of the states. The questions are enormously varied. Under what circumstances is evidence gathered by police admissible in a criminal proceeding? Under what circumstances may state governments provide financial assistance to parochial schools? What conditions may states impose on abortions? Do abortion opponents have a right to protest in close proximity to a health clinic that performs abortions? When must an individual's right to privacy yield to freedom of the press? When must freedom of the press yield to an individual's right to a fair trial? Do grandparents have a right to visit a child when the only living parent objects? May employers specify the sex of applicants in want ads?

As these questions illustrate, constitutional law concerns some of the most vexing dilemmas facing society. These issues of social policy are difficult, not because they are technically complex (although some are), but because they pit one right against another—a woman's freedom of choice versus the rights of an unborn fetus, a criminal's right to a fair trial versus a newspaper's right to freedom of the press, and so forth. Obviously, the stakes are high, and some interests will be adversely affected, whatever the court decides. Constitutional law is characterized by a high degree of conflict, salience, and manifest costs.

Some courts are especially likely to handle constitutional law cases. The U.S. Supreme Court deals almost exclusively with such cases, which explains the tendency among laypersons to equate judicial review with constitutional interpretation. State supreme courts also deal with constitutional issues much of the time. But the overwhelming majority of lower court decisions, at the state and federal levels, do not pertain to constitutional issues. These cases almost always concern private law, statutory law, or administrative law. Some of these cases involve criminal defendants, whereas others involve civil litigation.

Administrative Law

Administrative law cases focus on the behavior of administrative agencies— their interpretation of statutes and their application of administrative rules, regulations, and procedures. Should automobile manufacturers be required to install airbags? Should a dam be built if it poses a threat to an endangered species? When are utility rates unjustly discriminatory? When does a nuclear power plant pose an unacceptable health risk to the public? May a hospital deny service to a poor person without forfeiting federal tax breaks? May an interstate highway be built through a public park? May a newspaper be owned by a television station or a radio station in the same city? What criteria should be applied to the location of a halfway house? These questions require courts to consider whether an administrative agency has acted in accordance with legislative standards and with provisions of the federal Administrative Procedure Act of 1946 or its state-level counterparts. These laws spell out the procedures that agencies must follow in different situations and the criteria for judicial review.

Administrative law cases are enormously complex. Federal courts have evaluated the adequacy of statistical experiments on foam insulation, the health effects of benzene and lead, and the capacity of the auto industry for technological breakthroughs. In passing judgment on public utility commissions, state courts must decide whether depreciation rates have been properly calculated, whether the utility's rate base should include plants under construction, and whether a given rate of return allows the utility to compete for capital. One judge, exasperated by such complexities, decided to narrow the focus of the case to a single issue, rate of return.[4] Otherwise, he argued, the court's task would be hopeless, and the case interminable.

Administrative law cases are decided initially by administrative agencies. If they are appealed, many administrative agency decisions at the federal level may go directly to the circuit courts of appeals, bypassing federal district courts. Some circuit court decisions on administrative law are appealed to the U.S. Supreme Court, but most never go that far. For all intents and purposes, circuit courts are final arbiters of many administrative decisions. Among circuit courts, the District of Columbia Circuit Court of Appeals handles a higher percentage of administrative law cases than do other circuit courts.[5] It has sometimes been called the second most powerful court in the land. On questions of administrative law, it is, in practice, the most powerful. At the state level, administrative law cases are handled by intermediate appeals courts and further appealed to state supreme courts.

Statutory Law

Statutory law requires judges to construe the meaning of legislative language and the nature of legislative intent. Statutory law grew in importance in the late twentieth century as scholars increasingly reached the conclusion that statutes reflected bargains struck by politicians to accommodate private interests. This perspective encouraged closer judicial scrutiny of legislative bargains.[6] Does a law prohibiting racial discrimination in the election of legislative representatives apply to elected judges? When a statute prohibits the "use" of a firearm, does that apply to a situation in which someone trades a machine-gun for cocaine? These are the kinds of issues that statutory law raises.

Statutory interpretation is tricky even if laws contain plain language and judges believe in honoring legislative intent. Should judges focus on the statute itself or its legislative history, including committee reports? Should judges seek to clarify the meaning intended by the law's authors or that understood by a real-world audience? Should they be guided by the meaning borrowed from ordinary usage or that shaped by the purpose of the law? Should they focus on one or two key words or the entire text? Even "textualists," who favor judicial deference to the legislative branch, disagree on how to answer these questions.[7] Other judges, who subscribe to what is sometimes called republicanism, seek to correct defects in the legislative process by promoting fundamental values such as the protection of disadvantaged minorities who are poorly represented in the political branches of the government.[8] Such judges reject what one scholar refers to as an "archaeological" approach to statutory interpretation in favor of a more dynamic approach.[9]

Neglected Issues

Courts seldom address issues in two important policy domains: foreign policy (responses to international crises or the use of armed forces abroad) and macroeconomic policy (taxing and spending decisions). The failure of courts to address these issues is due more to self-restraint than to a lack of plaintiffs. Many taxpayers would love to take Uncle Sam to court, if only they were permitted to do so. Although the courts have lowered barriers to standing — the right to sue — by consumer advocates and environmentalists, they have refused to facilitate taxpayer suits.[10] Taxpayers often wind up in court as defendants, with the Internal Revenue Service or its state counterpart as plaintiff, but they seldom appear as plaintiffs in taxation cases. In 1998 Congress made it easier for taxpayers to obtain an expedited tax court hearing without the need for a lawyer. Congress also shifted the burden of proof in civil disputes over tax bills from taxpayers to the IRS. Nevertheless, taxpayers cannot use the courts to challenge tax legislation that they regard as confiscatory.

On the rare occasions when the courts address questions of macroeconomic policy, they normally defer to elected officials, especially when elected officials are in agreement. When Congress granted President Richard Nixon the authority to impose wage and price controls in 1970, a special federal district court panel upheld the statute as a constitutional delegation of power to the president.[11] Similarly, the U.S. Supreme Court has upheld congressional delegations of authority to the president in foreign affairs.[12] Justice William H. Rehnquist wrote in *Dames & Moore v. Regan* (1981), "Presidential action taken pursuant to specific congressional authorization is supported by strongest presumptions and widest latitude of judicial interpretation, and the burden of persuasion rests heavily upon anyone who might attack it."

In plain English, even the Supreme Court is reluctant to second-guess politicians in foreign policy.

Selection of Cases

Unlike other public policymakers, judges can address only those issues that come before them. Although courts are alike in their inability to initiate cases, they differ in their freedom to ignore them. As a general rule, supreme courts have more discretion than other courts. With the exception of a few cases, which seldom arise, the U.S. Supreme Court may decline to hear appeals from other courts.[13] Although the Constitution assigns "original jurisdiction" over certain cases to the Supreme Court, that is not much of a constraint in practice. For example, the Supreme Court may satisfy its constitutional obligation to act as a trial court for cases involving disputes between states by appointing a special master to gather facts, conduct hearings, and write a report. The Supreme Court need not hold hearings on the report. Federal district courts and circuit courts of appeals are supposed to hear all cases within their jurisdiction that come before them.[14] In recent years, however, circuit courts of appeals, overwhelmed by a steadily growing caseload, have used shortcuts to reduce the time required for individual cases. Such shortcuts include one-word rulings (affirmed or denied) and unpublished decisions, which do not establish precedents.[15]

A similar pattern prevails at the state level, although state supreme courts differ in their discretion. In some states, the supreme court must hear appeals from trial courts; in others, the supreme court is free to choose only "significant" cases if it wishes. The variations can be explained by the existence in some states, but not others, of intermediate appeals courts. In general, supreme courts have more discretion over their caseload in states with such courts. The assumption is that one appeal from a trial court decision should be available to all parties, but that two may be excessive.

Judicial Coalitions

It is sometimes said that the courts are more independent than other institutions of government. This is true in one sense but not another; judges are remarkably independent of politicians, but they are not independent of politics. Indeed, partisan politics is a significant factor in judicial recruitment and judicial behavior. Once appointed to office, federal judges are independent of the politicians who put them on the bench. Although federal judges may be impeached by the House and convicted by the Senate for "high crimes and misdemeanors," this cumbersome machinery has been used successfully only five times in U.S. history. State judges are also independent of politicians, but not always of the electorate. In thirty-six states, judges may be removed from office by the voters through regular elections or through retention elections in which the judge runs unopposed but may be unseated by a vote of no confidence. Unpopular judges are unseated from time to time (Rose Bird, the former chief justice of the California Supreme Court, for example), but the overwhelming majority of judges who must face the voters are reelected. Appointed judges may also be thrown out of office, through a process of impeachment and conviction. Occasionally, judges step down voluntarily rather than face the embarrassment of a public trial. In 1986 Rhode Island chief justice Joseph Bevilacqua resigned after being accused of associating with organized crime figures; in 1993 Rhode Island chief justice Thomas Fay resigned in the wake of charges that he used his office to help a relative and friends.[16] In 2000 the New Hampshire House impeached Chief Justice David Brock for alleged ethical misconduct, but the New Hampshire Senate acquitted him.[17]

Judges are not immune from partisan politics. Most federal judges belong to the party of the president who appointed them, and the same is true of state judges and the governors who appointed them. Furthermore, judges remain remarkably faithful to their party while in office. Although this loyalty may vary from issue to issue, party identification is the single best predictor of judicial voting behavior.

Diffuse Power

Many textbooks on American government portray the court system as a pyramid, with the U.S. Supreme Court at the apex. This image conveys a false impression, implying a hierarchical route that in reality very few cases follow. Most lower court decisions are never reviewed by higher courts. The majority of federal district court decisions are not appealed to the circuit courts; the majority of circuit court decisions are never appealed to the U.S. Supreme Court; and most circuit court decisions appealed to the Supreme Court are not accepted for review. The situation at the state level is much the same.

State supreme court decisions are usually final. Although decisions raising constitutional questions may be appealed to the U.S. Supreme Court, the Court hears no more than fifty such cases in any given year. Even if the Court reverses the state supreme court and returns the case for further proceedings, the state supreme court may reiterate its basic conclusion while modifying some of the specifics. Although state and federal court systems intersect, they are more independent than is commonly supposed (see Figure 7-2).

When a higher court declines to review a lower court decision, that does not necessarily imply approval. Rather, it may mean that although the higher court would have decided the case differently, it cannot say that the lower court made a mistake. It may mean that the higher court is not prepared to address a certain legal issue, or it may mean that the higher court has too many other cases to hear.

Figure 7-2 The Structure of the Judicial System

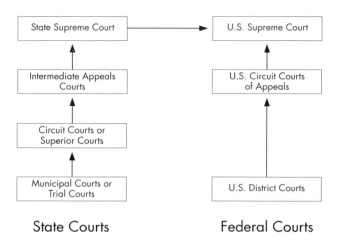

State Courts   Federal Courts

All cases are not created equal, and the more important cases tend to be heard in the higher courts. Nevertheless, many critical decisions have been made by federal district court judges. For example, in the 1970s Judge Arthur Garrity desegregated Boston's public schools and Judge Frank Johnson Jr. reformed Alabama's prisons and mental hospitals. In the 1980s Judge Harold Greene ordered the divestiture of AT&T. In 1999 Judge Thomas Penfield Jackson ruled that Microsoft used a variety of illegal business tactics to monopolize the market for personal computer operating systems and to extend its dominance into the market for Internet browsing software. These cases illustrate the degree to which judicial power is dispersed throughout the United States.

Leadership Styles and Strategies

When a federal district court judge issues a decision, he or she acts alone. Higher courts are characterized by collective decision making. Intermediate appeals court decisions usually are made by three-judge panels, and supreme court decisions are made by all the members. Coalition building is essential in such courts. Before a case is decided and the opinion written, a majority of judges must agree on the outcome and on the reasoning behind it. This consensus requires leadership—a mysterious but not altogether incomprehensible quality.

Within the courts there are three forms of leadership: political, institutional, and intellectual. Political leaders are those who can build coalitions, and the task of political leadership often falls on the shoulders of the judge assigned to write the opinion. To satisfy other members of the court, the opinion writer inserts new phrases and deletes others, with the goal of securing as many votes as possible in support of a coherent opinion. The opinion writer also seeks to discourage dissenting opinions, which convey judicial fragmentation. Centrists or "swing voters" are strategically situated to exercise political leadership because they hold the balance of power, especially when a court is ideologically divided, as was the Burger Court and as is the Rehnquist Court. The late Justice William Brennan exemplified political leadership on the Court. Under chief justices as diverse as Earl Warren and Warren Burger, Brennan parlayed his charm, persuasiveness, and gift for compromise into coalitions supportive of racial equality, gender equality, freedom of expression, welfare rights, and the rights of the accused.[18] On more than one occasion, Brennan tempered his own convictions somewhat in order to extract an elusive majority in support of a key principle. Political scientists Lee Epstein and Jack Knight refer to this as "strategic opinion writing."[19] Despite an increasingly conservative Court, Brennan used his "playmaker" skills to advance a variety of liberal principles. As law professor Kathleen Sullivan remarked upon his death, "he was the most influential Justice of his era."[20]

Institutional leaders are those who defend the courts against various external threats and who attempt to develop the courts as institutions. When Chief Justice Charles Evans Hughes denounced President Franklin Roosevelt's attempt to "pack" the Supreme Court, he was exercising institutional leadership.[21] Chief Justice Warren Burger led the battle to add judges to the federal bench and for more discretion in case selection, which he thought would protect the Supreme Court from "overload." Various state judges also have exercised institutional leadership when they fought to modernize the courts, to reorganize the judiciary, or to reform judicial selection procedures.

Intellectual leaders are those who influence their colleagues—and subsequent generations—through the force of their reasoning and the power of their ideas. Harlan Stone's argument that "discrete and insular minorities" warrant special protection under the Constitution—an argument buried in a footnote in the 1938 case *United States v. Carolene Products*—provided the rationale for broad interpretations of the Fourteenth Amendment by subsequent courts. Hugo Black's strong views on civil liberties provided the intellectual underpinnings for many of the decisions of the Warren Court. Judges on other courts have also exercised intellectual leadership. Judge Harold Leventhal of the District of Columbia Circuit Court of Appeals articulated the "hard look" doctrine of administrative law, which justifies careful judicial scrutiny of the reasoning behind administrative decisions. His colleague, David Bazelon, is credited with (or blamed for) the view that the mentally ill have a right to treatment under the Constitution. The reverberations from these ideas continue.

Although courts are less hierarchical than other government institutions, the chief justice or chief judge has certain powers. The chief justice of the U.S.

Supreme Court presides at Court conferences and is the first to speak. If the chief justice votes with the majority, he (or she) assigns the opinion to a particular justice. Because the reasoning behind a decision matters considerably, chief justices exercise power even when they choose not to write. The chief judges of other federal courts are more constrained. The chief judge of a federal district court assigns cases to other judges, but randomly. The chief judge of a federal circuit court of appeals assigns the opinion when the court sits en banc, or all together, provided he or she is in the majority. Most circuit court of appeals cases are decided by three-judge panels, however, and the cases are assigned randomly.

At the state level, there appears to be considerable variation in the leadership potential of chief judges. In states where supreme court judges are elected, partisan conflict often is intense enough to thwart attempts at leadership. In states where supreme court judges are appointed, the opposite is true.[22] At the local level, chief judges have the authority to assign cases.[23] Because the chief judge of local courts is usually selected by peers, he or she must be careful not to offend sensitive colleagues.

Decision Making

If leadership is a variable that adds an element of surprise to the judicial process—the "wild card" in the judicial deck—there are four more predictable elements of judicial decision making. They are law, evidence, party identification and ideology, and judicial activism.

Law. In resolving constitutional disputes, judges get a good deal of guidance from the constitution itself, whether federal or state. A constitution is not a legal cookbook, but neither is it a Rorschach test. Perhaps it is best to say that a constitution establishes a set of presumptions or burdens of proof. The U.S. Constitution does not define phrases, such as freedom of the press, freedom of speech, or freedom of religion, but these phrases are laden with meaning from years of precedents, prior decisions that command respect. Although precedents are seldom determinative, they serve as guideposts to judges as they wrestle with difficult problems. For example, political scientists Lee Epstein and Jack Knight found that Supreme Court decisions overruling past precedents represent far fewer than 1 percent of all cases available for overruling.[24] In general, courts pay more attention to their own precedents and to those of higher courts than to the precedents of other courts.

Constitutions have less relevance for administrative law because most administrative law cases do not raise constitutional questions. Precedents are scarcer in administrative law; the administrative state is only about sixty-five years old, and higher courts offer less guidance on administrative law than on constitutional law. As judges evaluate administrative law cases, their guides are the federal Administrative Procedures Act (APA) and state administrative procedure acts. If administrative procedures are informal, the courts ask whether the agency acted "arbitrarily and capriciously." If administrative procedures are relatively formal, the courts ask whether the agency's decision is based on "substantial evidence" in the record. The latter is a more exacting form of judicial review. Agencies face a higher burden of proof as formality increases.

Evidence. Whether a case concerns constitutional law or administrative law, courts base their decisions on evidence submitted by litigants. For the most part, evidence consists of historical facts, such as who did what to whom. Courts also look at social facts, the probable consequences of decisions. Courts have been guided by empirical research on the effects of segregation on blacks (*Brown v. Board of Education,* 1954), the effects of teacher experience on pupil performance (*Hobson v. Hansen,* 1967, 1968), and the effects of judicial procedures on the rehabilitation of juvenile offenders (*In re Gault,* 1967). Trial court judges sometimes face a quandary when experts disagree on key points relevant to the case. In one case involving experts who disagreed on whether the drug Benedictin causes human birth defects, the trial court judge dismissed expert testimony based on animal studies and unpublished research. The U.S. Supreme Court, however, overruled that decision, arguing that trial court judges must be "flexible" in their analysis of expert testimony. According to the Supreme Court, it is better to weigh the veracity of disputed evidence through cross-examination and presentation of contrary witnesses than it is to ignore evidence that is not generally accepted.[25]

Some litigants have a distinct advantage in presenting evidence. In particular, the "haves," who tend to be repeat players who know how to use the court system, usually are better at the game than the "have-nots," who tend to be one-shot participants.[26] This gap has narrowed as a result of court decisions granting certain have-nots the right to counsel in criminal cases (*Gideon v. Wainwright,* 1963) and the creation of legal aid societies, which represent the poor in civil cases. Public interest groups draw on their experience and resources in representing the disadvantaged or the public in court. The National Association for the Advancement of Colored People (NAACP) has filed numerous school desegregation suits; and the American Civil Liberties Union (ACLU), many First Amendment suits. Environmentalists have been represented in court by the Natural Resources Defense Council, Environmental Defense, the Sierra Club, and other groups. These public interest groups have won a wide variety of cases securing protection of wilderness areas and wetlands and enforcement of antipollution laws. In some instances the federal government has reimbursed them for the costs of successful lawsuits—a practice known as intervenor funding.

Party identification and ideology. Few judges would cite party identification as a factor in their decisions. Indeed, many judges would take umbrage at the implication that partisanship enters into judicial decision making. Nevertheless, it is well established that Democratic judges and Republican judges decide certain kinds of cases differently. Democratic state supreme court judges are much more liberal in deciding worker's compensation cases than are their Republican counterparts.[27] They are also more supportive of the claims of criminal defendants, the disadvantaged, and individuals alleging deprivations of civil liberties.[28]

This pattern holds at all levels of the federal judiciary: Democratic judges tend to be more liberal and Republican judges more conservative.[29] That is especially true for cases involving the right to privacy, economic regulation, and discrimination against racial minorities.[30] Therefore, it is a matter of some consequence whether a Democrat or a Republican sits in the White House. Federal district court judges appointed by President Ronald Reagan have acquitted criminal defendants only 14 percent of the time; the figure is 52 percent for President Jimmy Carter's appointees.[31]

A president's ideology also matters, especially in the appointment of Supreme Court nominees. Despite Reagan's failure to place staunch conservatives Robert Bork and Douglas Ginsburg on the Supreme Court, he was successful in appointing one staunch conservative—Associate Justice Antonin Scalia—and two moderate conservatives—Associate Justices Sandra Day O'Connor and Anthony Kennedy—to the nation's highest court. He also designated the most conservative member of the Court, William Rehnquist, as chief justice.

In general, President George Bush appointed conservatives and President Bill Clinton appointed liberals to the federal bench, including the Supreme Court. Justice David Souter, appointed by Bush, has been more free-spirited in his voting behavior than expected. But Justice Clarence Thomas, appointed by Bush, has been a reliable conservative, and Justices Ruth Bader Ginsburg and Stephen Breyer, appointed by Clinton, have voted as liberals on most cases.

Judicial activism. Although ideology is an important component of each judge's political philosophy, it is by no means the only element. Felix Frankfurter, who professed to be an unswerving civil libertarian, dissented against Warren Court decisions protecting individuals against the government. Frankfurter believed the courts should defer to other branches of government under most circumstances. Oliver Wendell Holmes took a similar view. As he saw it, judges should uphold laws even though they epitomize economic mistakes or futile experiments.[32] This point of view is sometimes referred to as the doctrine of judicial restraint. Other judges have been much more willing to overturn statutes. William O. Douglas and Hugo Black, staunch civil libertarians, routinely voted to void statutes that diminished First Amendment liberties. Black and Douglas were also judicial activists who believed that the courts should not defer to other branches of government, especially when First

Amendment rights are at stake. In constitutional law a critical question for judges is whether to override the legislative branch; in administrative law, they must decide whether to overrule administrative agencies. During the 1970s the Supreme Court developed a reputation for overturning state and local laws as well as acts of Congress.[33] At the same time, the U.S. Circuit Courts of Appeals took an increasingly "hard look" at administrative agency decisions.[34] Since then, the pendulum has swung back to some degree in the other direction. Swings of the pendulum are seldom equal, however. Although the courts today are perhaps less activist than they were in the 1970s, they are far more activist than at the beginning of the twentieth century. From 1996 through 2000, the Supreme Court invalidated twenty-four acts of Congress, an extraordinary display of judicial activism. According to critics, the Supreme Court inadvertently enhanced its reputation for activism when it prevented a recount from taking place in the Bush-Gore presidential election dispute.[35]

New Wine in Old Bottles

Judges, like other policymakers, are attentive to appearances, but judges are less likely than other public officials to substitute symbolic action for substantive action. Very few court decisions are purely symbolic. Unlike other public officials, judges do not avoid difficult problems or unpopular solutions. Instead, they confront many of society's most vexing problems, and having done so, they then rely on symbols to legitimate their decisions.

Two norms confirm judicial attentiveness to symbols. First, judges seek to avoid public feuding, viewed as unseemly and detrimental to the image of the courts. In contrast, public feuding is a popular legislative sport. Second, judges try to convey the impression of an unbroken line of precedents, dating back to the Founding Fathers, whereas politicians are forever talking about new ideas, new deals, and new American revolutions. Judges care especially about two symbols: unity and continuity.

Unity and Continuity

The school desegregation rulings of the Warren Court demonstrate the commitment to unity. Since the decision in *Brown v. Board of Education* (1954), the Court has struggled to maintain the appearance of unity on this extraordinarily divisive issue. During the Warren years, the justices were remarkably successful. Despite deep divisions, they managed to issue a series of unanimous decisions, which sent an important message to recalcitrant school boards, especially in the South: Desegregation is the law of the land.[36]

School desegregation cases also demonstrate the commitment to continuity. The *Brown* decision reversed *Plessy v. Ferguson* (1896), a ruling that upheld the constitutionality of segregated facilities and services. In reversing *Plessy* as untenable in a modern age, the Court cited a wide variety of precedents that supported a broad interpretation of the Fourteenth Amendment. In subsequent cases the federal courts portrayed court-ordered busing as a logical outgrowth of *Brown* and the Fourteenth Amendment. Then, in the late 1990s, federal courts applied the brakes to busing to achieve racial integration, citing the same constitutional provisions and precedents but interpreting them differently. Politicians serve old wine in new bottles, but judges prefer to serve new wine in old bottles. This modest deception legitimates policymaking by public officials who, according to a narrow reading of the Constitution, are not supposed to be making public policy.

A commitment to unity and continuity was also evident in the controversy over the presidential election contest between Vice President Al Gore and Texas governor George W. Bush. When the seven-member Florida Supreme Court ruled that three counties should be allowed a few more days (but no more) to recount their ballots, it did so unanimously. Despite the unusual circumstance of an extraordinarily close presidential election, the Court portrayed its decision as a routine effort to harmonize conflicting statutory language. History will determine the significance of the Florida Supreme Court's commitment to unity. To achieve unanimity, some justices may have agreed to a deadline so soon that it was impossible for two of the three heavily Democratic counties (Miami-Dade County and Palm Beach County) to recount their ballots. If so, it is possible that the Court's pursuit of unanimity cost Gore the election.

Innovative Decisions

The commitment of courts to continuity may be good for the Republic, but it obscures the extent to which judges are innovators in American politics. It also conveys a false impression that judicial policies differ only incrementally from earlier policies. Although most court decisions, like most decisions of other political institutions, are incremental, a remarkably high percentage of decisions made by the highest courts are innovative, especially when the issues are divisive and the decisions will have far-reaching effects.

It is widely acknowledged that the Warren Court was innovative. Its decisions on school desegregation, criminal justice, school prayer, and other matters transformed the Bill of Rights into a blueprint for economic and political equality. Other Warren Court decisions, on less visible topics, were equally revolutionary. For example, in *New York Times v. Sullivan* (1964) the Warren Court ruled that public figures must demonstrate actual malice to win a libel suit against a newspaper. This decision, which overruled 175 years of settled legal practice, virtually immunized the press against libel suits.[37]

Scholars are beginning to recognize that the Burger Court was also remarkably innovative.[38] In *Furman v. Georgia* (1972) the Burger Court found existing capital punishment statutes unconstitutional, which triggered changes in these statutes throughout the country. In *Roe v. Wade* (1973) the

Burger Court established different ground rules for abortion during the three trimesters of pregnancy and ruled that a woman's right to privacy, although not absolute, is a constitutionally protected right. The Burger Court was also innovative in a wide variety of other areas, such as commercial free speech, sex discrimination, procedural due process, and freedom of the press.

The Rehnquist Court has been innovative in one area in particular—federalism. Despite numerous precedents upholding a broad interpretation of congressional authority under the Commerce Clause of the Constitution, the Rehnquist Court departed from those precedents in some high-profile cases. In *United States v. Lopez* (1995), the Court invalidated a federal statute prohibiting the possession of a firearm within 1,000 feet of a school. Then, in *Printz v. United States* (1997), the Court struck down the Brady Bill, which required state and local officials to check the backgrounds of gun buyers. Subsequently, the Court made it difficult for parties to sue states for violations of trademark and patent rights.[39] In *Miller v. French* (2000), the Court sided with state and local governments against federal judges who issue sweeping orders governing the operation of state and local prisons and jails. In *United States v. Morrison* (2000), the Court overturned a federal law allowing rape victims to sue their attackers in federal court. In these and other cases, the Rehnquist Court strengthened state discretion under the Tenth Amendment at the expense of congressional authority under the Commerce Clause. As Justice Rehnquist put it in *United States v. Morrison,* "The Constitution requires a distinction between what is truly national and what is truly local."

The Rehnquist Court's enthusiasm for federalism left many Court watchers scratching their heads in the wake of the Bush-Gore election dispute. With the entire nation watching, the Supreme Court overturned the judgement of the Florida Supreme Court on three straight occasions. These decisions sealed a Bush victory by preventing a recount advocated by Vice President Al Gore. When the Supreme Court, or any other court, behaves with apparent inconsistency, one needs to take a closer look at the factors highlighted in this chapter: law, evidence, party identification, and ideology. The Court's defenders might argue that an old federal election law required a reversal of the Florida court; the Court's critics might argue that Republican judges betrayed their principles in order to elect a Republican president who would appoint Republican judges to the Court. Whatever one's view of this particular dispute, the overall legacy of the Rehnquist Court has been to encourage greater deference to the states.

State supreme courts have also blazed new trails in public law. The New Jersey Supreme Court outlawed the use of the property tax as the sole basis for local school financing, established a right-to-die procedure for permanently comatose patients, and held hosts liable for drunk-driving accidents if they knowingly served alcohol to an intoxicated person. In *Southern Burlington County NAACP v. Township of Mt. Laurel* (1975), a landmark decision, the New Jersey Supreme Court ruled "exclusionary zoning" unconstitutional.

Some state supreme courts have taken the lead in civil liberties questions. For example, state supreme courts in eighteen states have struck down school funding formulas that relied heavily on local property taxes as discriminatory, despite a U.S. Supreme Court ruling that such formulas are compatible with the U.S. Constitution (*San Antonio Independent School District v. Rodriguez,* 1973).[40] State supreme courts in Alaska, California, Massachusetts, Michigan, New York, and Pennsylvania have gone beyond the U.S. Supreme Court in protecting the rights of criminal defendants.[41]

State supreme courts can go beyond the U.S. Supreme Court because the federal court sets a floor, not a ceiling, on constitutional rights. If state supreme courts find that state constitutions provide stronger protection than the U.S. Constitution, they are free to follow the state constitution, provided their conclusion is based primarily on state law (*Michigan v. Long,* 1983). According to one estimate, from 1970 through 1992 state courts handed down seven hundred decisions extending civil liberties under state constitutional law.[42] State supreme courts in the western part of the United States were especially likely to produce expansive interpretations of civil liberties doctrines.[43]

State court procedures have also shown innovation. For example, state courts have been pioneers in allowing electronic and photographic media coverage of court proceedings, including criminal proceedings.[44] In 2000, forty-seven states allowed some broadcasting coverage of court proceedings.[45] Many observers believe that state courts have managed to promote freedom of the press without inhibiting constitutional rights to a fair trial.[46] Indeed, even the U.S. Supreme Court has conceded that television coverage of a criminal proceeding does not automatically violate a defendant's constitutional right to a fair trial (*Chandler v. Florida,* 1981). After experimenting with cameras in federal district courts and federal circuit courts of appeal, the Judicial Conference of the United States allowed federal appeals courts to decide whether to televise proceedings. As of 2000, however, only two of the nation's thirteen federal circuit courts of appeal have chosen to do so.[47] The U.S. Supreme Court has steadfastly refused to televise its proceedings, despite external pressure to do so. When CNN asked the Supreme Court to televise oral arguments for the historic Bush-Gore election dispute on December 1, 2000, the Court declined to do so. It did, however, subsequently release an audio tape of the oral arguments, in a notable departure from precedent.

Minorities as Beneficiaries

Students who take courses in constitutional law and administrative law must wonder whether they are learning about the same judicial system. Constitutional law students hear the courts described as liberal; administrative law students hear them described as conservative. Constitutional law students are told that the courts are champions of the underprivileged; administrative law students learn that the courts are protectors of special interests. These impressions are not without foundation: constitutional law and administrative law benefit different groups in society.

The argument may be summarized as follows: (1) courts adopt policies favorable to minorities, despite opposition to such policies; (2) in constitutional law, the courts adopt policies that benefit disadvantaged minorities such as blacks, the handicapped, and the mentally ill; and (3) in administrative law, the courts adopt policies that benefit advantaged minorities—for example, utility companies, insurance companies, and transportation companies.

Constitutional Law

Because the U.S. Supreme Court is preeminent in matters of constitutional law, scholars interested in assessing the beneficiaries of constitutional law decisions have focused on this court. Most recent studies of the Court find considerable support for disadvantaged minorities in its decisions.[48] Of the twenty-eight cases in which the Court overturned a congressional statute between 1958 and 1974, twenty-seven upheld minority rights, as guaranteed by the Bill of Rights or the Fourteenth Amendment.[49] The principal beneficiaries in these cases were blacks and other disadvantaged minorities. Political scientists Reginald Sheehan, William Mishler, and Donald Songer have also confirmed the influence of minority groups at the Supreme Court. In a study of Supreme Court decisions from 1953 through 1988, they found that minorities were remarkably successful in comparison to other groups, including some with more financial resources.[50] In fact, as indicated in the net advantage column of Table 7-1, only the federal government and state governments were more successful than minorities during this time period. In contrast, businesses, corporations, and unions were less successful, despite their superior financial resources.

Some scholars assert that these studies give too much weight to the Warren Court (1954–1969), whose strong commitment to civil liberties is universally acknowledged. Political scientist Robert Dahl found that most Supreme Court decisions overturning congressional statutes through 1957 actually harmed minorities.[51] According to Dahl, the Court reinforces majoritarian decisions made by Congress. In 1985 law professor Geoffrey Stone noted that 85 percent of the Court's "noneasy" (not unanimous) civil liberties decisions during the 1983–1984 term were decided against minority rights.[52] In his view, the Burger Court launched a new era of "aggressive majoritarianism." But the Burger Court's reputation as majoritarian in a conservative era can be traced directly to its criminal procedure decisions. In this area the Burger Court was more sensitive to public safety than to minority rights. In *Michigan v. Long* (1983), for example, the Burger Court upheld protective searches of the passenger compartment of a car if police have a reasonable belief that the suspect is dangerous. In *New York v. Quarles* (1984) the Burger Court ruled that the police may postpone the reading of a

Table 7-1 Success Rates of Supreme Court Litigants, 1953–1988 (in percentage)

Type of party[a]	(1) Overall success rate	(2) Success rate as respondent	(3) Appellant's opponents success rate	(4) Net advantage[b]
Poor individual	31.2	38.5	70.5	-32.0
Minorities	55.6	44.3	34.9	9.4
Individual	42.9	35.2	52.6	-17.4
Unions	53.9	39.0	36.4	2.6
Small business	42.7	29.2	46.9	-17.7
Business	44.3	36.0	47.9	-11.9
Corporations	38.6	29.3	48.6	-19.3
Local gov't	45.8	43.1	49.4	-6.3
State gov't	54.1	51.0	39.8	11.2
Federal gov't	67.3	59.1	23.2	35.9

Source: Reginald S. Sheehan, William Mishler, and Donald R. Songer, "Ideology, Status, and the Differential Success of Direct Parties before the Supreme Court," *American Political Science Review* 86 (June 1992): 465.

Note: Because the Supreme Court often reverses decisions from below, litigants who appeal are more likely to win than those who are respondents. Thus the overall success rate may be misleading. To control for this difference, the table reports the success rate of litigants in cases in which they are the respondents as well as that of their opponents in cases where the opponents are respondents. The difference between these two measures is the net advantage of each class of litigant.

[a] In order of increasing status.
[b] Column 2 minus Column 3.

defendant's *Miranda* warnings until they have investigated a potential threat to public safety. The Court also upheld vehicle searches by border patrol officials, provided that circumstances are suspicious and that intrusions on privacy are limited (*United States v. Brignoni-Ponce,* 1975; *United States v. Cortez,* 1981). Despite these decisions, a fair appraisal of the Burger Court's entire record, not just its criminal procedure rulings or the decisions of a single term, must acknowledge a general pattern of support for minority rights.

Even the Rehnquist Court, widely expected to be conservative, has handed down many decisions favoring minorities. It voted to extend the reach of the Voting Rights Act (*City of Pleasant Grove v. United States,* 1987), to allow special job protections for pregnant workers (*California Federal Savings and Loan Assn. v. Guerra,* 1987), and to invalidate a referendum aimed at restricting the rights of gays and lesbians (*Romer v. Evans,* 1996). On affirmative action the Court ruled in *United States v. Paradise* (1987) that a judge may order agencies to use promotion quotas temporarily when there is a history of "egregious" racial bias. In *Johnson v. Santa Clara County* (1987) the Court ruled that employers may give special preferences to women in hiring and promotion decisions even if no prior discrimination existed. In *University of Pennsylvania v. Equal Employment* (1990) the Court held that universities accused of discrimination in tenure decisions must make relevant personnel files available to federal investigators. And in *United States v. Virginia* (1996), the Court held that the Virginia Military Institute must open its doors to women cadets.

To be sure, decisions unfavorable to minorities can also be cited. In *Wards Cove Packing Co. v. Atonio* (1989), the Court made it more difficult for minorities to win employment discrimination cases. In *Miller v. Johnson* (1995) and *Bush v. Vera* (1996) the Court ruled against the creation of congressional districts dominated by a racial minority through racial gerrymandering. In *Richmond v. Croson* (1986), the Court overturned a rigid racial quota in awarding public contracts in Richmond, Virginia. This decision cast a pall over long-standing minority preferences in local government contracts. Specifically, it required "strict scrutiny" of all race-based action by state and local governments. Later, in *Adarand Constructors, Inc. v. Pena* (1995), the Court applied the same "strict scrutiny" doctrine to federal contracts. The Court also distanced itself from strong school desegregation mandates involving school systems in Georgia (*Freeman v. Pitts*, 1992) and Missouri (*Missouri v. Jenkins*, 1995). Clearly, the Rehnquist Court has been less sympathetic to minorities, especially racial minorities, than its predecessors. Even the Rehnquist Court, however, has ruled in favor of minority rights in numerous cases outside the criminal justice area.

Although less is known about other courts, a study of federal district court decisions on education policy confirms a strong tendency for judicial support of disadvantaged minorities. A study of sixty-five education policy decisions between 1970 and 1977, sixty-four of which concerned constitutional issues, found that minority plaintiffs were successful 71 percent of the time.[53] Plaintiffs in these cases included blacks, Hispanics, Native Americans, aliens, women, the handicapped, the poor, the elderly, and nonconformists such as long-haired students. These findings are especially interesting because the authors deliberately excluded school desegregation cases from their sample. Their findings do not simply reiterate the well-known conclusion that school desegregation cases have been decided in favor of minorities.

What accounts for the relatively strong support of courts for disadvantaged minorities in constitutional law cases? In particular, what caused the noticeable shift in the disposition of the courts that began in the mid-1950s? One possibility is that judges are more liberal than they used to be, and this liberalism may be attributed to changes in judicial selection practices at the state and federal levels. Consultation with bar associations prior to appointment to the bench may have encouraged the selection of judges who share the bar's commitment to civil liberties, and the appointment of more women and blacks may have further sensitized courts to minority rights.

Changes outside the courtroom—in the political and legal culture— probably explain more than changes inside the judiciary. The U.S. Constitution and the state constitutions provide a formidable arsenal of legal weapons to minorities who are willing and able to use them. Until the 1950s minorities were aggrieved but not aroused, victimized but not mobilized. Since then, public interest groups have emerged to champion minority rights in the courts and in other forums. These groups—such as the NAACP, the ACLU, and the National Organization for Women (NOW)—have fought successfully to extend the frontiers of the First, Fourth, Fifth, and Fourteenth Amendments. As a result of their efforts, the Constitution has become the functional equivalent of the Statue of Liberty—a beacon to the weak and the oppressed. Whatever the intentions of the Founding Fathers, the language of the Constitution, in its modern interpretation, offers considerable hope to the disadvantaged.

Administrative Law

The most common result of judicial review of administrative agency actions, either at the state or federal level, is for the court to sustain the agency.[54] This result confirms law professor Marc Galanter's argument that repeat players have the advantage in civil litigation.[55] The government is the quintessential repeat player. It has greater expertise, fewer start-up costs, greater bargaining credibility, and a greater stake in shaping the rules of the game than other litigants, especially the one-shot litigant. It is not surprising that the government wins most of its cases.

Nevertheless, a substantial minority of administrative decisions reviewed by the courts are reversed or remanded, which means sent back to the agency for reconsideration. According to a study of state supreme court reviews of administrative agencies' decisions, nearly 44 percent of the court decisions did not fully support the agency.[56] Even the more deferential U.S. Supreme Court reverses 30 percent of federal agency decisions.[57]

The willingness of the U.S. Supreme Court to reverse a federal agency decision depends on many factors, including the ideology of the sitting justices. According to one recent study, the Warren Court and the Burger Court were equally likely to sustain federal agency decisions, but they handled liberal and conservative decisions differently. For example, conservative decisions by social regulatory agencies were sustained 63.4 percent of the time by the Warren Court, 81.7 percent of the time by the Burger Court. As expected, liberal decisions by the same agencies were sustained more often by the Warren Court than by the Burger Court. And liberal justices were more likely to sustain liberal decisions.[58]

Who benefits when the courts reverse the decision of an administrative agency? The answer depends on who the plaintiff is and what issue is under consideration.[59] When the courts reverse a social welfare agency decision, the plaintiff is almost certain to be an individual claimant—a welfare recipient or a disabled worker, for example. Typically, the beneficiaries are members of a disadvantaged minority, and the losers are the citizens, in their role as tax-payers. When the courts reverse a regulatory agency decision, the plaintiff is almost certain to be a business such as an insurance company or a utility company. Normally, the beneficiaries here are members of an advantaged minority, whereas the losers are citizens, in their capacity as consumers.

If this pattern looks fairly symmetrical, it seems less so when one realizes that disappointed individuals are far less likely to challenge an adverse administrative action in court than are disappointed corporations. Only 8 percent of all final Social Security Administration (SSA) decisions go to court, and only one-third of these result in the restoration of benefits for the claimant.[60] In contrast, about 40 percent of state public utility commission decisions in major rate cases are appealed to the courts.[61] The most frequent appellants are business groups, usually utilities, and the most frequent winners, when the public utility commission is overruled, are also business groups, again usually utilities.

These figures highlight an important difference between the "bias" of the judicial system and the "bias" of individual judges. There is no reason to believe that judges are biased in favor of business groups. If they were, one would expect the courts to be noticeably tougher on regulatory agencies, whose decisions are challenged by business groups, than on social welfare agencies, whose decisions are challenged by disadvantaged minorities. This does not appear to be the case.[62] The system is biased, however, in that certain claims are more likely than others to be adjudicated. It is not absolutely clear that business groups use the courts more effectively than other groups, but it is clear that business groups use the courts more often than other groups. For this reason, tough judicial scrutiny of administrative agencies tends to benefit business groups.

The principal exception to these general rules is in the area of environmental policy. Environmental statutes encourage citizen participation in administrative and judicial proceedings, and the courts generally have granted standing to these litigants. Many different environmental groups have taken the government and industry to court. Indeed, the most frequent plaintiffs in federal district court cases concerning environmental disputes are environmental groups.[63] Moreover, in many instances, environmental litigants are well funded, experienced, and persistent.

Who wins environmental cases in court? In one respect, the familiar pattern holds: the government is most likely to win. In another respect, however, a new pattern emerges: when the government loses a case, business groups are not necessarily winners. Rather, environmental groups are as likely to win these disputes as are industry groups.[64] This pattern, well-documented during the 1970s, persisted through the 1980s. Environmental group victories declined in the early 1990s as judges appointed by Presidents Ronald Reagan and George Bush grew more influential, but President Clinton's appointees should prove much more sympathetic to environmental causes.[65] These findings suggest that a well-organized majority can neutralize the advantages of the business community in court, if legislators adopt stringent statutes and if the courts are liberal in giving environmental groups standing to sue in court.

The latter of these conditions was met more often in the 1970s and the 1980s than in the 1990s. In landmark decisions such as *Sierra Club v. Morton*

(1972) and *United States v. SCRAP* (1973), the Supreme Court indicated that environmental groups could secure standing to sue an administrative agency or a private firm in court by demonstrating some injury to their members. Significantly, the Court noted that an economic injury was not necessary and that an aesthetic injury would do. Throughout the 1990s, however, the Supreme Court took a tougher stance on environmental group standing. In *Lujan v. National Wildlife Federation* (1990) and *Lujan v. Defenders of Wildlife* (1992), the Supreme Court refused to grant standing to environmental groups that sought to challenge decisions by the Department of the Interior. In these and other decisions, the Supreme Court stressed the need to demonstrate a specific injury that falls within the zone of interests protected by the relevant statute. For example, it is not enough for an environmental group to assert that some of its members use some portion of a tract of land that has been designated by an agency for uses that some members oppose. Still, the Supreme Court is capable of occasional surprises. In *Friends of the Earth v. Laidlaw Environmental Services* (2000), the Supreme Court granted standing to an environmental group even though evidence submitted in court suggested that the injury to group members was more imagined than real.

Constitutional Law versus Administrative Law

Constitutions in the United States explicitly protect disadvantaged minorities. These minorities are identified with some precision in various constitutional amendments. Administrative procedure acts are more neutral. They seek to protect affected parties from arbitrary and capricious behavior by the bureaucracy, but they do not specify which parties are to receive protection. At the time of passage, the federal APA was expected to benefit business groups in particular, and it often has done precisely that. But the emergence of broad-based public interest groups, which have secured standing, has transformed the APA into an instrument for protecting well-organized groups generally, whether they represent an advantaged minority or the majority of citizens.

Another important difference between constitutional law and administrative law is that the Supreme Court sets more precedents in the former than in the latter. The Court, with limited time, has chosen to focus on constitutional law, which gives a certain coherence to constitutional law. In contrast, administrative law is largely the province of other courts, especially state supreme courts and federal circuit courts of appeals, and they frequently disagree. Moreover, administrative agencies sometimes announce that they will not follow administrative law precedents set by lower courts when they conflict with the directives of the agency head.[66] This remarkable doctrine, which has no legal basis, limits the ability of lower courts to set precedent and makes administrative law less coherent than constitutional law. This practice also illustrates another point: a court decision is only the beginning of a lengthy process with consequences that may be either narrower or broader than anticipated.

The Long Road to Justice

A court order may seem final and definitive, but it is typically the beginning of a complex, convoluted process. The ultimate impact of the court on public policy depends on a host of intermediaries who may not be willing or able to carry out the court's order.

Confusion and Reluctance

Judges depend on other public officials to implement their policies. Implementers include bureaucrats such as regulators, police officers, and social workers; legislative bodies such as Congress, state legislatures, and city councils; quasi-legislative bodies such as school boards and zoning boards; and other judges—lower courts are expected to implement the policies of higher courts. The implementation of judicial policies, like the implementation of other policies, is not without problems, which may include unclear standards, poor communication, inadequate resources, and hostility.[67]

Unclear standards. Judicial policies are sometimes vague, contradictory, or variable. This is particularly true of appellate court opinions, which must accommodate the views and sensibilities of more than one judge. As noted earlier, the judge assigned the task of writing an opinion for an appellate court often finds it necessary to yield to a colleague on an important point. A first draft that is crisp, blunt, and direct may end up as a patchwork of compromises. The Supreme Court's decision in *Swann v. Charlotte-Mecklenburg County Board of Education* (1971) illustrates this phenomenon. Divided but anxious to issue a unanimous opinion on school busing, the Court (1) endorsed busing as a permissible remedy but warned against busing small children; (2) established a presumption against one-race schools but declined to prohibit them; and (3) allowed lower courts to correct for residential segregation patterns but only if caused by school board decisions. Reflecting on *Swann*, a federal judge observed, "There is a lot of conflicting language here. It's almost as if there were two sets of views laid side by side."[68]

An ambiguous opinion is only one of several sources of confusion. Even a clear opinion, decided by a close vote, sends conflicting signals. Astute court watchers know that a 5–4 decision against including evidence in a criminal case may yield to a 5–4 decision the other way in a subsequent case. A flurry of concurring and dissenting opinions attached to Supreme Court decisions also generates confusion. Although such opinions make it easier for judges to write their memoirs, they make it more difficult to implement judicial policies.

Poor communication. People responsible for implementation are sometimes unfamiliar with the specifics of important court decisions—especially street-level bureaucrats, who do not make a habit of reading court opinions over their morning coffee. Following *Miranda v. Arizona* (1966), police officers did not clearly understand what was required of them.[69] After *Mapp v. Ohio* (1961), in which the Court ruled that evidence obtained in violation of the Fourth Amendment could not be used in state trials, police officers could not be absolutely certain under what circumstances evidence was inadmissible in court.[70] Following *Goss v. Lopez* (1975), in which the Court ruled that students who were suspended have the right to due process, schoolteachers had a "muddled" understanding of the procedures to be followed in school discipline cases.[71]

Some blame can be laid on the mass media, which are notoriously negligent in their coverage of court decisions, except that of major U.S. Supreme Court decisions. When the Pennsylvania Supreme Court announced that public utilities are not constitutionally entitled to rates high enough to guarantee their financial viability—a decision hailed by one observer as an "extremely important" victory for ratepayers—the *Pittsburgh Press* covered the news in a brief notice on page fourteen. When a U.S. circuit court of appeals overturned a lower court decision concerning comparable worth, the same newspaper covered the story on page eight, despite the assertion that "the ruling could set standards for similar disputes across the country." Such limited coverage of important court decisions is quite common, and public ignorance of court rulings is, therefore, hardly surprising.

Inadequate resources. Many court orders explicitly or implicitly require the expenditure of additional funds for public purposes. School boards may have to purchase buses, hire drivers, and obtain more insurance if the courts require school busing as an antidote to racial segregation. When the courts require back pay for victims of employment discrimination by the government, agencies must somehow obtain the funds to carry out the order. When the courts require state bureaucracies to upgrade the services to the mentally ill and the mentally retarded, the states need to spend more money on psychiatrists, custodians, and physical facilities.

Lacking the power of the purse, the courts depend on legislative bodies to allocate the funds to implement court orders. But politicians have their own priorities, and minority rights are seldom high on their agendas. When Judge Frank Johnson ordered improvements in the quality of Alabama's prisons, Governor George Wallace accused him of trying to turn the state's prisons into Holiday Inns. Eventually, the Alabama legislature increased appropriations to the state's prisons but not by enough to comply with the judge's directives.

Hostile attitudes. Judges are widely respected in American society, but their views do not automatically command deference. People charged with implementation often question the wisdom of judicial decisions, especially on matters of social policy. Many school board members strongly disapprove of busing; many teachers fervently believe in school prayer. Many police officers object to court decisions that limit their ability to put criminals behind bars. Where such hostility is present, resistance may develop.

If hostility runs deep enough, the implementers may not comply. The members of the Boston School Committee, all of whom were white, refused to draw up a desegregation plan demanded by Judge Arthur Garrity, who then took over the school system. Outright noncompliance is rare, but evasion is not at all uncommon. For example, as a response to tough evidentiary requirements in *Mapp*, some police officers resorted to perjury.[72] The public sometimes refuses to comply by taking evasive action. Many whites responded to court-ordered busing by sending their children to private schools or by moving to the suburbs.

It is clear that the implementation of judicial policies cannot be taken for granted, but we should distinguish between short-term and long-term implementation problems. Short-term problems are often formidable, but they do not necessarily doom judicial policies to failure. Most court orders are eventually implemented, and there are several reasons why this is so.

First, a single case may be ambiguous, but several interrelated cases enable the courts to establish a pattern of decisions that can guide implementers. Blockbuster opinions, such as *Brown, Miranda,* or *Mapp*, usually are followed by a series of interpretive opinions that reduce confusion. This clarification is strongest when the courts are reasonably consistent, as they have been in libel cases. Even when the courts are less consistent, as they have been in criminal cases, additional decisions usually clarify more than they obscure. Precedents are often deflected but seldom overturned. The norm of *stare decisis,* meaning deference to precedent, encourages courts to render reasonably consistent opinions over time, especially in matters of constitutional law, where the brooding presence of the U.S. Supreme Court ensures a modicum of consistency. As Justice O'Connor argued in *Bush v. Vera* (1996), the Supreme Court's legitimacy requires adherence to stare decisis, especially in highly sensitive political cases.[73]

Second, knowledge of court orders travels slowly at first but eventually trickles down to the bureaucrats responsible for day-to-day implementation. Indeed, the mass media deserve some of the credit for this. For example, anyone who has watched a police drama on television knows about *Miranda* rights and their importance. As Justice Rehnquist noted in reaffirming the *Miranda* decision in *Dickerson v. United States* (2000), "Miranda has become embedded in routine police practice to the point where the warnings have become part of our national culture."[74] Ironically, citizens and street-level bureaucrats may have been enlightened about court decisions more by the entertainment programming of television than by the news reports of newspapers.

Third, institutions can deal with resource shortfalls in various ways, if given sufficient time. The deinstitutionalization of mentally ill and retarded residents was a quick way of coping with court requirements for improved care. Administrative reorganization and the hiring of more skilled personnel is another strategy. The Army Corps of Engineers responded to court orders to prepare environmental impact statements by establishing environmental units in their district offices and by hiring personnel with the necessary training.[75]

Fourth, courts can go quite far in requiring spending to remedy a problem. For example, in *Missouri v. Jenkins* (1990) the U.S. Supreme Court upheld a lower court ruling requiring expenditures by the state of Missouri and the Kansas City school district to remedy school segregation. The Court even upheld the lower court's decision to mandate a tax increase, although the Supreme Court stressed that the tax hike must be approved by local authorities. The Supreme Court also stressed in a later version of the same case (*Missouri v. Jenkins,* 1995) that there are constitutional limits to a federal court's ability to order additional spending in the quest for racial desegregation. Thus federal district court judges must tread carefully when they order spending increases.

Finally, attitudes change over time. Police officers may not be enthusiastic about *Miranda* requirements, but they have learned to live with them. School boards may not be happy about racial integration, but they also have adapted. Immediately following an important court ruling, the disappointed parties assume the end of civilization. But when the world does not come to an end, acceptance often follows. Perhaps the most striking illustration of this is the sharp change in the attitudes of whites toward school desegregation. In the late 1950s, 83 percent of southern whites objected to sending their children to a school that was half black; by 1981 only 27 percent objected.[76] According to polls conducted in the 1990s, southern attitudes toward school desegregation no longer differed much from those of other regions. Although southerners prefer other solutions than court-ordered busing, so too do most other Americans.[77] For years, scholars have debated whether "stateways" can change "folkways." Although there are limits to what courts can accomplish, it appears that they have influenced attitudes on some basic issues.

Real Solutions and Solutions as Problems

Many scholars are reluctant to ascribe so much influence to the courts, instead seeing the policy impact of the courts as rather limited.[78] Political science professor Lawrence Baum writes, "In reality, the Court's impact on society is severely constrained by the context in which its policies operate."[79] Similarly, political scientist Gerald Rosenberg argues that the Supreme Court is a "hollow hope" for advocates of social reform.[80] At first glance, this conclusion appears reasonable, given the implementation problems mentioned earlier. But most studies of the policy impacts of court decisions focus exclusively on short-term effects. If we look at long-term effects, we see the power of the courts.

One of the most conspicuous successes of the courts is the effort to promote racial justice. In education, voting rights, employment, and housing, the courts have breathed life into constitutional requirements for due process of law and have helped to ensure equal opportunity for racial minorities, especially blacks. This has not happened overnight. For a full decade after *Brown,* southern schools remained separate and unequal. In the mid-1960s, however, the picture began to change. By the 1972–1973 school year, 91 percent of black students in the South were going to school with whites.[81] Progress in northern schools, although slower, has also been noticeable.[82]

Court decisions on voting rights have produced results more quickly, in part because all three branches of government moved aggressively on this issue. The Voting Rights Act of 1965 was followed one year later by an 8–1 Supreme Court decision affirming the act in full (*South Carolina v. Katzenbach,* 1966). Over the next two years, the Justice Department sent federal examiners to some southern voting districts and appointed poll watchers in others. The effects were dramatic. From 1964 to 1968, black voter registration rates in the South jumped from 38 percent to 62 percent.[83] Increased registration led to higher black voter turnout and to the election of black local officials, which in turn generated increases in public employment and other public services for blacks.[84]

The courts have been less aggressive in promoting equal opportunity in housing, partly because of the tradition of judicial deference to local zoning boards and city councils.[85] Several state supreme courts have invalidated exclusionary zoning practices as violations of state constitutions, however. The desegregation of housing, like the desegregation of the public schools, is likely to proceed slowly. Eventually, the elimination of exclusionary zoning practices should result in some affordable housing for racial minorities even in affluent white suburbs.

Court decisions in administrative law have also had significant impact, especially in communications and environmental policy and in standards for institutional care. For years, station WLBT-TV in Jackson, Mississippi, fanned the flames of racial discontent in its editorials against integration and its acceptance of advertisements paid for by a local racist group. When well-known blacks were featured on network newscasts, the general manager would sometimes show a "Sorry, Cable Trouble" sign until the segment ended. A church-related citizen group, the Office of Communication of the United Church of Christ, opposed in court the renewal of the station's license on the grounds that the station had violated the Federal Communications Commission's (FCC's) fairness doctrine.[86] In two important decisions, *United Church of Christ v. Federal Communications Commission* (1966 and 1969), the U.S. court of appeals, District of Columbia Circuit, agreed with the church and ordered the FCC to grant the license to someone else. The immediate

consequences for Jackson television viewers were that the license was awarded to another company, which promptly hired a black general manager,
assigned a black anchor to read the evening news, and improved the quantity and quality of news and public affairs programming.[87] The long-term consequences were even more significant. Using these cases as precedents, citizen groups intervened in administrative and judicial proceedings on behalf of
television consumers, and in many cases, they secured important concessions.
In addition, these cases helped to establish standing for aggrieved consumers
in other issue areas.

Court decisions on environmental impact statements have also generated
far-reaching changes. The National Environmental Policy Act of 1969
(NEPA) requires administrative agencies to file an environmental impact
statement for "major federal projects with a significant environmental effect,"
and the federal courts interpret the words "major" and "significant" rather
liberally. When in doubt, they require the agency to prepare an environmental impact statement. The repercussions have been widespread. The Army
Corps of Engineers, long known for its "edifice complex," began to look at
nonstructural alternatives to dams and dredging projects.[88] The courts' interpretations of NEPA also sensitized other agencies to environmental impacts.

The consequences of judicial efforts at institutional reform have been
equally profound. In 1973 a federal district court ordered the closing of
Willowbrook, a New York facility for the mentally retarded, where conditions were shown to be unsanitary, unsafe, and inhumane. The immediate
effects of judicial intervention were disappointing. The state's Department
of Mental Health at first refused to yield client records and failed to submit progress reports on time, as required by the court. Between 1976 and
1979, however, the state bureaucracy opened 100 group homes for 1,000
Willowbrook residents. Community placement was achieved without low-
ering property values or destroying neighborhoods. Audits revealed that
group homes were properly administered and, more important, that the
lives of the residents had improved. At first, the group homes resembled
"puppet shows." Choreographed to behave as more intelligent people
would, residents played parts they did not understand. Eventually, the pup-
pets became animated, as they learned how to make decisions concerning
choices of food and clothing.[89] Such choices, which most people take for
granted, marked a major breakthrough and signaled a significant improvement in their quality of life.

These examples demonstrate the capacity of the courts to effect changes
that are in the public interest, especially over time. Many court decisions produce tangible results that benefit disadvantaged minorities or the public. A
problem with court decisions, however, is that they are not easily contained.
They have spillover effects never imagined by judicial decision makers. Many
of these unintended consequences are undesirable. At best, they detract from
judicial policies; at worst, they undermine them.

The *Mapp* decision, extending the exclusionary rule to local police departments, appears to have resulted in greater reliance on plea bargaining in cases where evidence may have been obtained through questionable methods.[90] The *Goss* decision, requiring a hearing before suspension from school, discouraged teachers from disciplining disruptive students.[91] *Gault*, which established formal procedures for trying juveniles accused of a crime, made it difficult for juvenile court judges to counsel and advise informally, as they had done, in cases where no crime had been committed.[92]

The unintended consequences of school desegregation and environmental policy decisions have been especially troublesome. In many cities court-ordered busing prompted whites to abandon inner-city public schools and to place their children in private schools or move to the suburbs. When Judge Garrity took over Boston's public schools in 1974, 61 percent of the pupils were white; when he terminated his involvement in 1985, only 27 percent were white.[93] In those eleven years, numerous white parents, feeling abandoned by the courts, decided to abandon Boston's public schools.

Court decisions on air pollution have also been a mixed blessing. The courts imposed tough standards for the design of new industrial plants, for example, by requiring the "prevention of significant deterioration" in air quality in wilderness areas and polluted cities. In enforcement cases, however, the courts relaxed the standards for existing plants, such as utilities, steel mills, and smelters. In effect, the courts have frozen existing technologies and facilities and discouraged the building of modern plants. According to some observers, this unintended consequence has increased the costs of achieving clean air.[94]

In environmental policy, as in school desegregation, the courts have accomplished what they intended to accomplish. School segregation and air pollution have declined appreciably, and the courts deserve much of the credit. The country paid a high price for these gains, however, probably higher than necessary. Nor is this surprising. Judges are not very good at calculating costs, and they are not particularly inclined to do so. Judges think in terms of rights and duties rather than economic analysis. In contrast to politicians, judges have no need to hide the costs of their actions or to think much about them. There is, in short, an irony here. In courtroom politics, costs are often manifest, but irrelevant. The costs of judicial decisions, although unintended, are not always unforeseen, but judges maintain that they are not responsible for the adverse consequences of their actions.

The Paradoxical Decree

Although they are less sensitive to costs than other public officials, judges are more sensitive than is commonly supposed to the consequences of their actions. Judges recognize the limitations of a single court order and, because they see the potential for implementation problems, judges sometimes are unwilling to entrust the delicate tasks of implementation to the bureaucracy. In certain cases, judges have assumed responsibility for carrying out their own orders, becoming, in effect, managers and administrators.

Nowhere is this more evident than in the behavior of federal district court judges who have coped with institutional reform cases. These judges have not issued orders and hoped for the best. Rather, they have upgraded the court's capacity to receive feedback, to learn from it, and to correct errors. The principal mechanism for this judicial role is the court decree, which judges use to fashion relief in an ad hoc manner and on a continuous basis.[95] The modern decree is a paradox. It is at once extremely specific as to the affected parties and extremely fluid, giving the judge wide latitude. It contains detailed instructions and calls for a continuing dialogue, progress reports, and midcourse corrections. All of these characteristics reduce implementation problems and narrow the gap between intended and actual policy impacts.

One characteristic of the decree is its specificity. When Judge Garrity issued his first order concerning Boston's schools, he specified not only the racial balance to be achieved but also the geographic boundaries of new school districts. Garrity became, in effect, the superintendent of the Boston school system. He assigned pupils, hired staff and administrators, closed or upgraded schools, and acted on spending requests. He justified these controls on the grounds that it was necessary to prevent sabotage by the Boston School Committee, which had openly resisted the court's efforts to desegregate the public schools.

Judges have been equally specific in institutional reform cases. Judge Johnson took over Alabama's prisons and mental health facilities, issuing detailed requirements for nutrition, personal hygiene, recreational opportunities, educational programs, and staffing ratios.[96] Judge Orrin Judd took control of Willowbrook, ordering outdoor exercise for the residents five times a week, a ratio of one attendant for every nine residents, and the repair of all the home's toilets.[97]

A second characteristic of the decree is its continuity. In contrast to the standard pattern, a judge does not simply issue a single decision. The decree is the first step in a long, interactive process. The judge meets frequently with parties to the case and listens to their grievances, receives progress reports, dispenses criticism and praise, and issues new orders. Judge Garrity issued 415 school desegregation orders from 1974 to 1985. Although this probably qualifies him for the *Guinness Book of World Records,* other judges have also issued numerous court orders.

A third characteristic of the decree is its fluidity. In anticipation of unexpected developments, judges retain the option of modifying their initial order. To assist them, they often appoint special masters to advise them or receivers to run the failing program. The use of masters is not new, but it has grown, especially in school desegregation cases. Garrity appointed four masters and two experts; the masters held hearings and proposed a plan, which Garrity modified and incorporated into his second decree.[98]

The selection of a master or a receiver is one of the most important decisions a judge can make in an institutional reform case. When District of Columbia Superior Court judge Steffen Graae interviewed David Gilmore for the job of running the District of Columbia's Housing Authority, he thought that he was "the perfect guy" for the job.[99] He was right. When Gilmore began work in 1995, 20 percent of the District's public housing units were uninhabitable and the Department of Housing and Urban Development assigned the District a grade of 22 on a 100-point scale, well below passing. Five years later, the District received a score of 83 on the same scale. Under Gilmore's stewardship, the quality of public housing units improved sharply, the vacancy rate declined dramatically, and rent collections increased.

In contrast, the persons assigned by federal district court judges to run the city's mental health system and its foster care system were far less successful. Gilmore succeeded because of his valuable experience as a public housing authority manager, his accessibility, his willingness to respond quickly to constituent complaints, and his unwillingness to accept the possibility of failure. It also helped that the District of Columbia Housing Authority, financed entirely by the U.S. Department of Housing and Urban Development (HUD), could be easily separated from the District's troubled political environment. When Judge Graae announced the completion of Gilmore's work at a final hearing in 2000, he broke down and shed tears of gratitude.[100]

Judges are fallible, and their decrees are seldom perfect. Judge Garrity unnecessarily polarized the races by pairing Roxbury, the heart of the black ghetto, with South Boston, the citadel of white resistance to busing. A more judicious solution might have been to pair South Boston with nearby Dorchester or to intersperse South Boston and Roxbury students throughout the city. Judge Johnson undermined his credibility by insisting that all Alabama prison cells be sixty square feet. No Alabama prison cell met this specification, which lent credence to Governor Wallace's charge that Johnson was insensitive to the costs of prison reform. Johnson later modified his order on prison cell size, and other judges have done the same.

The issuance of far-reaching decrees in institutional reform cases abated in the late twentieth century. This was especially noticeable in the area of prison reform. Legal scholars Malcolm Feeley and Edward Rubin attribute this decline to growing conservatism among federal court justices and to the undeniable success of earlier decrees in eliminating some of the most egregious conditions in our nation's prisons.[101] Thanks to these interventions, southern prisons, where numerous violations of inmates' constitutional rights occurred, now more closely resemble prisons elsewhere in the country. For a variety of reasons, Congress and the Supreme Court have tired of such interventions. In 1996 Congress enacted the Prison Litigation Reform Act, which invites state and local officials to file suits demanding an end to continued supervision of state and local prisons by federal district courts.[102] In 2000, in *Miller v. French,* the Supreme Court upheld that statute.

At its best, the modern decree is an error-correction device that works two ways. First, it enables the judge to identify and correct errors made by government officials, who may not share the court's commitment to a particular policy goal. Second, it enables the judge to correct errors made by the court when it goes too far. The judicial decree, therefore, represents a milestone in judicial policymaking. It is the court's way of saying that judicial activism and judicial responsibility go hand in hand. If judges are going to make public policy on controversial issues, they cannot simply render a decision and walk away. Although the decree does not guarantee that the courts will be alert to implementation problems, it does provide ample opportunity for judicial oversight.

Summary

The failures of other branches of government and the litigious character of U.S. society go a long way to explain the courts' prominence in making public policy. Although courts avoid macroeconomic policy and foreign policy disputes, they directly address other issues, which are characterized by a high degree of conflict and manifest costs. Issues addressed by the courts are also marked by a high level of technical complexity, a high level of moral complexity, or both. They are among the most vexing problems society faces.

In reaching decisions on these issues, judges are guided by factors that transcend politics, such as law and evidence. But judicial decision making is also political. Judges are usually affiliated with a political party, and their voting behavior reflects party affiliation. Internal politicking, especially on supreme courts where several judges must agree on the wording of an opinion, gives judges the opportunity for leadership. But coalition building often requires compromise. In the courts, as elsewhere, political leaders sometimes prefer a weak or ambiguous policy to no policy at all. In contrast, intellectual leaders adhere more steadfastly to principle.

Many court decisions are at first diluted by unclear standards, poor communication, inadequate resources, and hostile attitudes. Over time, however, most are successfully implemented and have the impact they were intended to have. Unfortunately, they often have unintended consequences, some of which may be attributed to judicial insensitivity to consequences. But even if judges wish to take consequences into account, they cannot foresee every result.

Courts have changed in many ways. More women and blacks sit on the bench, lending more judicial support to minority rights in constitutional law disputes. More public interest groups litigate in court, which results in occasional triumphs for environmental and consumer interests. Finally, the choice between judicial activism and judicial restraint is resolved more frequently in favor of judicial activism. Despite talk of restraint, the courts are more likely to overturn statutes and administrative agency decisions and more likely to prescribe specific ground rules and remedies than they were a half century ago.

Activism and liberalism are not one and the same. In constitutional law, activism often runs in a liberal direction; in administrative law, activism often runs in a conservative direction. Criminal justice and environmental protection are exceptions to these general rules. In criminal justice, judicial enthusiasm for defendant rights waxes and wanes; in environmental protection, the courts support environmentalists on standards, business groups on enforcement. Whatever the policy tilt of the courts, the fact remains that judges are making policy.

Notes

1. Martin Shapiro, *Courts: A Comparative and Political Analysis* (Chicago: University of Chicago Press, 1981), 105–124; Richard Posner, *The Federal Courts: Crisis and Reform* (Cambridge: Harvard University Press, 1985).
2. Donald Horowitz, *The Courts and Social Policy* (Washington, D.C.: Brookings Institution, 1977), 9.
3. In the 1998–1999 term, the Supreme Court decided only seventy-five cases; in the 1999–2000 term, the Court decided only seventy-three cases.
4. Richard Neely, *How Courts Govern America* (New Haven, Conn.: Yale University Press, 1981), 212.
5. J. Woodford Howard Jr., *Courts of Appeals in the Federal Judicial System: A Study of the 2nd, 5th, and D.C. Circuits* (Princeton: Princeton University Press, 1981), 25–33; Christopher Banks, *Judicial Politics in the D.C. Circuit Court* (Baltimore: Johns Hopkins University Press, 1999), 36.
6. William Popkin, *Statutes in Court* (Durham, N.C.: Duke University Press, 1999, 152).
7. Ibid., 184.
8. Ibid., 189–194.
9. William Eskridge, *Dynamic Statutory Interpretation* (Cambridge: Harvard University Press, 1994), 13.
10. See *United States v. Richardson*, 418 U.S. 166 (1974); *Valley Forge Christian College v. Americans United for Separation of Church and State*, 454 U.S. 464 (1982).
11. *Amalgamated Meat Cutters v. Connally*, 337 F. Supp. 737 (1971).
12. *United States v. Curtiss-Wright Export Corp.*, 299 U.S. 304 (1936); *Dames & Moore v. Regan*, 453 U.S. 654 (1981).
13. By statute, the U.S. Supreme Court is required to hear appeals stemming from decisions by special three-judge federal district courts. Some voting rights cases have traveled to the Supreme Court's docket via that route.
14. Federal judges are not entirely powerless in these matters. District court judges can—and do—encourage parties to settle a case without going to trial. Also,

judges may refuse to hear a case on the grounds that a party lacks standing, that
the issue is not ripe, or for other reasons.

15. William Glaberson, "Caseload Forcing Two-Level System for U.S. Appeals," *New York Times,* March 14, 1999, 1.

16. Pamela Ferdinand, "N.H. Chief Justice Faces Impeachment," *Washington Post,* July 6, 2000, 3.

17. Pamela Ferdinand, "Impeached N.H. Chief Justice Is Acquitted by State Senate," *Washington Post,* October 11, 2000, 7.

18. Edward Lazarus, *Closed Chambers* (New York: Times Books, 1998), 196–197; Linda Greenhouse, "William Brennan, 91, Dies," *New York Times,* July 25, 1997, 1.

19. Lee Epstein and Jack Knight, *The Choices Justices Make* (Washington, D.C.: CQ Press, 1997), 95–107.

20. Kathleen Sullivan, "A Thousand Opinions, One Voice," *New York Times,* July 25, 1997, 29.

21. Hughes denounced Roosevelt's plan in a calm but forceful letter to Sen. Burton Wheeler. The letter is credited with weakening congressional support for the court-packing plan.

22. Henry Glick, *Supreme Courts in State Politics* (New York: Basic Books, 1971).

23. Herbert Jacob, *Urban Justice: Law and Order in American Cities* (Englewood Cliffs, N.J.: Prentice-Hall, 1973).

24. Epstein and Knight, *The Choices Justices Make,* 176.

25. *Daubert et al. v. Merrell Dow Pharmaceuticals, Inc.,* 509 U.S. 579 (1993).

26. Marc Galanter, "Why the 'Haves' Come Out Ahead: Speculations on the Limits of Legal Change," *Law and Society Review* 9 (fall 1974): 95–160.

27. Glendon Schubert, *Quantitative Analysis of Judicial Behavior* (Glencoe, Ill.: Free Press, 1959); S. Sidney Ulmer, "The Political Party Variable in the Michigan Supreme Court," in *Judicial Behavior,* ed. Glendon Schubert (Chicago: Rand McNally, 1964), 279–286; Malcolm Feeley, "Another Look at the 'Party Variable' in Judicial Decision-Making: An Analysis of the Michigan Supreme Court," *Polity* 4 (fall 1971): 91–104.

28. Philip Dubois, *From Ballot to Bench: Judicial Elections and the Quest for Accountability* (Austin: University of Texas Press, 1980), 231.

29. C. Neal Tate, "Personal Attribute Models of the Voting Behavior of U.S. Supreme Court Justices: Liberalism in Civil Liberties and Economics Decisions, 1946–1978," *American Political Science Review* 75 (June 1981): 355–367; Sheldon Goldman, "Voting Behavior on the U.S. Court of Appeals Revisited," *American Political Science Review* 69 (June 1975): 491–506; and Robert Carp and C. K. Rowland, *Policymaking and Politics in the Federal District Courts* (Knoxville: University of Tennessee Press, 1983).

30. Robert Carp and Ronald Stidham, *Federal Courts,* 3d ed. (Washington, D.C.: CQ Press, 1998), 126–127.

31. David Whitman, "Reagan's Conservative Judges Are Singing a Different Tune Now," *Washington Post,* national weekly edition, August 24, 1987, 23.

32. Bernard Schwartz, *Super Chief: Earl Warren and the Supreme Court* (New York: New York University Press, 1983), 40–44.

33. Lawrence Baum, *The Supreme Court* (Washington, D.C.: CQ Press, 1981), 156–162.

34. Martin Shapiro, "On Predicting the Future of Administrative Law," *Regulation* 6 (May–June 1982): 18–25; R. Shep Melnick, *Regulation and the Courts: The Case of the Clean Air Act* (Washington, D.C.: Brookings Institution, 1983); and William Gormley, *Taming the Bureaucracy: Muscles, Prayers, and Other Strategies* (Princeton: Princeton University Press, 1989), chap. 4.

35. On the Court's activism, see Edward Walsh, "An Activist Court Mixes Its High-Profile Messages," *Washington Post,* July 2, 2000, 6. On the 2000 election controversy, see Jeffrey Rosen, "Disgrace," *The New Republic,* December 25, 2000, 18–21; and Ronald Dworkin, "A Badly Flawed Election," *The New York Review of Books,* January 11, 2001, 53–55.

36. Much of the credit for the unanimous decisions goes to Earl Warren, a remarkably adroit political leader. Warren's handling of the *Brown v. Board of Education* decision is a good case in point. When Warren took over as chief justice, the *Brown* case had already been argued, and the Court was prepared to vote 5–4 in favor of desegregation. In a clever ploy, Warren suggested that the justices postpone the vote. Instead, Warren led a freewheeling discussion that ultimately revealed some common ground on which they could agree. The process was not easy. Three separate conferences and numerous private conversations between Warren and individual justices were required before Warren's efforts were successful. In 1954 the Supreme Court issued a unanimous opinion in a case that is doubtlessly one of the most important in U.S. history. See Schwartz, *Super Chief,* 72–127.

37. Archibald Cox, *The Role of the Supreme Court in American Government* (New York: Oxford University Press, 1976), 38–39.

38. Vincent Blasi, "The Rootless Activism of the Burger Court," in *The Burger Court: The Counter-Revolution That Wasn't,* ed. Vincent Blasi (New Haven, Conn.: Yale University Press, 1983), 198–217.

39. Robert Greenberger, "Firms Had Mixed Success in High Court," *Wall Street Journal,* June 25, 1999, 2.

40. For an excellent discussion of leading cases, see Douglas Reed, *On Equal Terms: The Constitutional Politics of Educational Opportunity* (Princeton: Princeton University Press, 2001).

41. A. E. "Dick" Howard, "State Courts and Constitutional Rights in the Days of the Burger Court," *Virginia Law Review* 62 (June 1976): 873–944; Mary Porter, "State Supreme Courts and the Legacy of the Warren Court: Some Old Inquiries for a New Situation," in *State Supreme Courts: Policymakers in the Federal System,* ed. Mary Porter and G. Alan Tarr (Westport, Conn.: Greenwood, 1982), 3–21; and Robert Pear, "State Courts Surpass U.S. Bench in Cases on Rights of Individuals," *New York Times,* May 4, 1986, A1.

42. John Kincaid and Robert Williams, cited in Staci Beavers and Jeffrey Walz, "Modeling Judicial Federalism: Predictors of State Court Protections of Defendants' Rights under State Constitutions, 1969–1989," *Publius* 28 (spring 1998): 45.

43. Beavers and Walz, "Modeling Judicial Federalism," 58.

44. Charlotte Carter, *Media in the Courts* (Williamsburg, Va.: National Center for State Courts, 1981).

45. Michael Fletcher, "Court Camera Measure Rolls," *Washington Post,* June 1, 2000, 23.

46. Norman Davis, "Television in Our Courts: The Proven Advantages, the Unproven Dangers," *Judicature* 64 (August 1980): 85–92.

47. Fletcher, "Court Camera Measure Rolls," 23.

48. Jonathan Casper, "The Supreme Court and National Policy Making," *American Political Science Review* 70 (March 1976): 50–63; Baum, *The Supreme Court;* and Harold Spaeth, "Burger Court Review of State Court Civil Liberties Decisions," *Judicature* 68 (February–March 1985): 285–291.

49. Casper, "The Supreme Court and National Policy Making."

50. Reginald Sheehan, William Mishler, and Donald Songer, "Ideology, Status, and the Differential Success of Direct Parties before the Supreme Court," *American Political Science Review* 86 (June 1992): 464–471.

51. Robert Dahl, "Decision Making in a Democracy: The Supreme Court as a National Policy-Maker," *Journal of Public Law* 6 (fall 1957): 279–295.

52. Geoffrey Stone, *Individual Rights and Majoritarianism: The Supreme Court in Transition* (Washington, D.C.: Cato Institute, 1985).

53. Michael Rebell and Arthur Block, *Educational Policy Making and the Courts: An Empirical Study of Judicial Activism* (Chicago: University of Chicago Press, 1982), 36.

54. Martin Shapiro, *The Supreme Court and Administrative Agencies* (New York: Free Press, 1968); Jerry Mashaw et al., *Social Security Hearings and Appeals* (Lexington, Mass.: D. C. Heath, 1978), 125–150; Craig Wanner, "The Public Ordering of Private Relations, Part Two: Winning Civil Court Cases," *Law and Society Review* 9 (winter 1975): 293–306; Stephen Frank, "The Oversight of Administrative Agencies by State Supreme Courts: Some Macro Findings," *Administrative Law Review* 32 (summer 1980): 477–499; and Donald Crowley, "Judicial Review of Administrative Agencies: Does the Type of Agency Matter?" *Western Political Quarterly* 40 (June 1987): 265–284.

55. Galanter, "Why the 'Haves' Come Out Ahead."

56. Frank, "The Oversight of Administrative Agencies."

57. Reginald Sheehan, "Administrative Agencies and the Court: A Reexamination of the Impact of Agency Type on Decisional Outcomes," *Western Political Quarterly* 43 (December 1990): 875–886.

58. Ibid.

59. It also depends on the court. For example, the District of Columbia Circuit Court of Appeals, during the 1970s, was much more supportive of environmental protection than other circuit courts of appeals. See Lettie Wenner, *The Environmental Decade in Court* (Bloomington: Indiana University Press, 1982), 35–63.

60. Mashaw et al., *Social Security Hearings and Appeals,* 125–150.

61. William Gormley Jr., *The Politics of Public Utility Regulation* (Pittsburgh: University of Pittsburgh Press, 1983), 94.

62. Frank, "The Oversight of Administrative Agencies."

63. The gap has narrowed as industry plaintiffs have become more common. Also, industry groups are more likely than environmental groups to file appeals in appeals courts. See Wenner, *The Environmental Decade in Court,* 35–63.

64. Ibid., 94.

65. Lettie McSpadden, "Environmental Policy in the Courts," in *Environmental Policy,* ed. Norman Vig and Michael Kraft, 4th ed. (Washington, D.C.: CQ Press, 2000), 154.

66. According to Mashaw, this is the practice of the Social Security Administration, the National Labor Relations Board, and the Internal Revenue Service, as well as

other agencies. See Jerry Mashaw, *Bureaucratic Justice* (New Haven, Conn.: Yale University Press, 1983), 186. The SSA's refusal to follow precedents set by lower federal courts aroused considerable controversy during the Reagan years, when the agency cut financial awards to disabled workers. There is no evidence that this policy of selective adherence to precedent (or nonacquiescence) is changing, however.

67. Donald Van Meter and Carl Van Horn, "The Policy Implementation Process: A Conceptual Framework," *Administration and Society* 6 (February 1975): 445–488; Carl Van Horn, *Policy Implementation in the Federal System* (Lexington, Mass.: D. C. Heath, 1979); and George Edwards III, *Implementing Public Policy* (Washington, D.C.: CQ Press, 1980).

68. Bob Woodward and Scott Armstrong, *The Brethren: Inside the Supreme Court* (New York: Simon and Schuster, 1979), 112.

69. Neal Milner, *The Court and Local Law Enforcement: The Impact of Miranda* (Beverly Hills, Calif.: Sage, 1971), 225.

70. Horowitz, *The Courts and Social Policy,* 226.

71. Henry Lufler, "The Supreme Court Goes to School: *Goss v. Lopez* and Student Suspensions" (Ph.D. diss., University of Wisconsin–Madison, 1982).

72. Horowitz, *The Courts and Social Policy,* 234.

73. *Bush v. Vera,* 517 U.S. 985 (1996).

74. Edward Walsh, "High Court Upholds Miranda Rights, 7–2," *Washington Post,* June 27, 2000, 1.

75. Daniel Mazmanian and Jeanne Nienaber, *Can Organizations Change?* (Washington, D.C.: Brookings Institution, 1979), 37–60.

76. Jennifer Hochschild, *The New American Dilemma: Liberal Democracy and School Desegregation* (New Haven, Conn.: Yale University Press, 1984), 180.

77. Leslie McAneny and Lydia Saad, "America's Public Schools: Still Separate? Still Unequal?" *Gallup Poll Monthly,* no. 344, May 1994, 28–29.

78. Kenneth Dolbeare and Phillip Hammond, *The School Prayer Decisions: From Court Policy to Local Practice* (Chicago: University of Chicago Press, 1971); Milner, *The Court and Local Law Enforcement;* Baum, *The Supreme Court;* Charles Johnson and Bradley Canon, *Judicial Policies: Implementation and Impact* (Washington, D.C.: CQ Press, 1984); and Gerald Rosenberg, *The Hollow Hope: Can Courts Bring About Social Change?* (Chicago: University of Chicago Press, 1991).

79. Baum, *The Supreme Court,* 211.

80. Rosenberg, *The Hollow Hope.*

81. Ibid., 187.

82. Charles Bullock III, "Equal Education Opportunity," in *Implementation of Civil Rights Policy,* ed. Charles Bullock III and Charles Lamb (Monterey, Calif.: Brooks/Cole, 1984), 68–69.

83. Richard Scher and James Button, "Voting Rights Act: Implementation and Impact," in Bullock and Lamb, *Implementation of Civil Rights Policy,* 40.

84. Albert Karnig and Susan Welch, *Black Representation and Urban Policy* (Chicago: University of Chicago Press, 1980); and Peter Eisinger, "Black Employment in Municipal Jobs: The Impact of Black Political Power," *American Political Science Review* 76 (June 1982): 380–392.

85. Michael Danielson, *The Politics of Exclusion* (New York: Columbia University Press, 1976).

86. The fairness doctrine, abolished by the Federal Communications Commission in 1987, required broadcasters to devote a reasonable amount of time to the discussion of issues of public importance. When covering such issues, broadcasters did not need to provide equal time to all points of view, but their coverage had to be balanced and fair.
87. Fred Friendly, *The Good Guys, the Bad Guys, and the First Amendment* (New York: Random House, 1975), 89–102.
88. Mazmanian and Nienaber, *Can Organizations Change?*
89. David Rothman and Sheila Rothman, *The Willowbrook Wars* (New York: Harper and Row, 1984).
90. Horowitz, *The Courts and Social Policy.*
91. Lufler, "The Supreme Court Goes to School."
92. Horowitz, *The Courts and Social Policy.*
93. Matthew Wald, "After Years of Turmoil, Judge Is Yielding Job of Integrating Boston Schools," *New York Times,* August 22, 1985, A16.
94. Melnick, *Regulation and the Courts.*
95. Colin Diver, "The Judge as Political Powerbroker: Superintending Structural Change in Public Institutions," *Virginia Law Review* 65 (February 1979): 43–106; Abram Chayes, "Public Law Litigation and the Burger Court," *Harvard Law Review* 96 (November 1982): 4–60.
96. Tinsley Yarbrough, "The Judge as Manager: The Case of Judge Frank Johnson," *Journal of Policy Analysis and Management* 1 (spring 1982): 386–400.
97. Rothman and Rothman, *The Willowbrook Wars.*
98. J. Anthony Lukas, *Common Ground* (New York: Alfred Knopf, 1985).
99. Vernon Loeb, "Mission Accomplished: How One Man's Receivership Turned D.C. Public Housing Around," *Washington Post,* July 30, 2000, B1.
100. Ibid.
101. Malcolm Feeley and Edward Rubin, *Judicial Policy Making and the Modern State* (Cambridge: Cambridge University Press, 1998), 15.
102. John Sullivan, "States and Cities Removing Prisons from Courts' Grip," *New York Times,* January 30, 2000, 1.

Chapter 8 Living Room Politics

The United States is a representative democracy. American grade school children are taught that government and public policy are based on the consent of the governed. President Abraham Lincoln said that American government is "of the people, by the people, and for the people," and every national leader before and after him has cited the "will of the people" to justify particular courses of action.

Debates about the proper role of citizens in guiding public policy date back to the founding of the nation. James Madison and other authors of the Constitution were strong advocates of democracy, but they did not believe that elected representatives should slavishly follow mass opinion in determining public policy. Many of the Founders feared that the public could be unstable, tyrannical, and even dangerous to liberal democracy.[1] They believed that periodic elections give citizens sufficient safeguards against elected representatives who served them poorly. Between elections, leaders should govern as they saw fit. This concept of democracy was perhaps best summed up by the British political philosopher and statesman Edmund Burke. In a treatise on representative democracy, Burke said: "Your representative owes you, not his industry only, but his judgment; and he betrays instead of serving you if he sacrifices it to your opinion."[2]

The fact that thousands of elected officials must face the voters every so often keeps many citizens involved in government at the most basic level. But for the most part, public policy is not made and implemented by the public. Instead, elected officials, bureaucrats, judges, and corporate leaders determine public policies. They are attentive to, not ruled by, the concerns of the public—a point underscored throughout this book. Yet, people's opinions influence the course of public affairs, and occasionally, when aroused, people do play a central role in politics. This chapter on living room politics explores how public opinion, the mass media, and public officials interact in the making of public policy choices between elections.

Public opinion is a potent weapon of democracy, but it is not something one can visit, like a building, or read, like a book. There are many publics, many opinions, and many voices in American society. Public opinion is defined and channeled into the policy process by groups such as the media, public officials, and citizen activists.[3] Elected officials gauge public opinion by scrutinizing public opinion polls and television and newspaper reports and by talking with interest group representatives, friends and coworkers, and perhaps the local gas station attendant.

The mass media—television, radio, and newspapers—are the principal vehicles through which public opinion is expressed and manipulated.[4] Policymakers, the press, and interest groups attempt to shape the view of reality that is presented to the people. Journalists influence the public's understanding of politics and public policy and then inform public officials about what the "public" thinks. Perhaps most important, the media frame political and policy discussions, telling people what issues are important and who favors each position. When the media or public officials succeed in defining the parameters of the policy debate, they are exercising what E. E. Schattschneider called "the supreme instrument of political power."[5]

The public does not make policy directly, but citizens *can be* more than just an audience watching contests between political elites. Citizens who are angered by government decisions or frustrated by inaction can go beyond passive forms of democratic participation and organize grassroots political movements to attempt to achieve their objectives. Citizens can choose among policy options that affect their states and communities. Through ballot initiatives and referenda—devices of direct democracy available to citizens in most states—voters can force state legislators to write new laws or to eliminate old ones.

Bystanders and Activists

Although public opinion is involved in virtually everything that government institutions do, most citizens are typically little more than bystanders.[6] The public policy enterprise occurs in the background of their lives: they hear noise, but they seldom listen. A much smaller "attentive public," probably no more than one American in ten, closely follows public affairs. They read newspapers carefully, write letters, and call elected officials; they have opinions and they express them. On rare occasions, the bystanders are drawn into the fray. When large segments of the public become concerned about issues, their preferences can become a powerful force and living room politics dominates the policy process.

Real Opinions, Soft Opinions, and Nonopinions

A sizable industry is devoted to surveying the public's thoughts on every subject from baseball players' salaries to the morality of public figures. All the major television networks, newspapers, and news magazines regularly commission public opinion polls or report public attitudes toward political officials, government institutions, and policy issues. Are the concerns that are measured in public opinion polls what people are really thinking about or merely pale imitations of preferences expressed by public officials through the media? Sometimes it seems that Americans are like the hapless couple depicted in the cartoon who tell a poll taker, "We don't have any opinions today. Our television is busted."

When people have little or no personal experience or stake in the outcome of a policy debate, public attitudes are likely to reflect views expressed by public officials and reported in the media. For people to hold real opinions, the issue must be important to them and they must have information on which to base a conclusion. On many policy questions, people have either no opinion or what might be called "soft" opinions, which may change rapidly in response to events or new information. When the public holds real opinions—about issues that touch basic values or arouse strong preferences or fears—news reporters and public officials are far less persuasive. The public is also less malleable when the policy remedies under debate are controversial.

Opinion polls suggest that many Americans are deeply troubled about abortion and drug abuse, but the polls show differences in their responses. The vast majority agree that drug abuse should be curtailed quickly and by whatever means necessary, even if certain constitutional protections for citizens must be bent to enforce the laws. The public is easily riled to righteous indignation about crack cocaine dealers and the devastating effects of drug abuse on people's lives. In short, although few people favor drug abuse, the intensity of feelings about the drug issue can be influenced by the efforts of public officials and news organizations.

Abortion is another matter. People believe that abortion is an important issue, but they are deeply divided about the proper course for public policy to take. The increasing political and media attention paid to late-term abortions, which opponents label "partial birth" abortion, illustrates how divided the American people are on this issue. Some believe that abortions constitute the taking of a human life and should be outlawed. Others believe that a woman has an absolute right to determine whether to complete a pregnancy and that government should not interfere in this intensely private decision. News organizations do not attempt to shape people's attitudes about outlawing or guaranteeing abortions, perhaps because taking either position would cost them public support.

When large segments of the public have direct personal experience with a problem, pollsters are more likely to measure genuine concerns than to reveal media-manipulated sentiment. Public anxiety about unemployment is a good example. During the early 1990s millions of American workers were unemployed, and millions more had jobless relatives or friends.[7] Thus, the attitudes they expressed about unemployment were grounded in personal experience and not easily influenced by politicians and journalists.

A poll taken in June 1998 by the PEW Research Center for the People and the Press found that potential regulation of health maintenance organizations (HMOs) was an issue the public saw as very important. When asked to rank a series of policy issues, 69 percent of those interviewed said the debate over HMO regulation was very important to the nation and they were following it closely. By way of comparison, in that same poll, only 9 percent said they were following news about elections and candidates in their states and only 36 percent said they followed politics and government most of the time.[8] Thus, pollsters tap genuine concerns when they quiz people about problems affecting their health and the well-being of their families. Today, public fears about managed care systems are palpable. An October 1999 poll found that 70 percent of respondents felt that the practice of health maintenance organizations denying some medical services to patients was a very serious problem. A poll taken in April 2000 found that the most commonly cited health care reform priority was dealing with the problem of HMOs and insurance companies limiting medical treatment because of cost. This same poll revealed that 67 percent of respondents felt that the government should guarantee health insurance coverage for every American.[9] Well-informed, strongly held public opinions limit the freedom of politicians.

When pollsters and journalists venture into subjects that are unfamiliar to the public, they often discover, and then communicate, soft opinions or nonopinions to policymakers. Out of politeness or fear of appearing ignorant, many people will answer questions about policy issues even when they have no knowledge or opinions. When this happens, public officials and journalists are more likely to draw false conclusions about what the public really wants. Public opinion jells only when the issue becomes sufficiently important for people to pay attention to it. Until then, public moods can swing widely.

On many public issues Americans hold ambiguous and contradictory opinions, and on such issues public officials are free to interpret what the sentiment is. One might suppose that on important perennial issues such as taxes, spending, and the budget, the public would hold rational views. Yet most polls show that the public wants lower taxes, more spending, and a balanced budget, too. People are unwilling to accept the logic that all three cannot be done simultaneously. A survey taken in August 1999 reported that 68 percent of the American public favored legislation to cut the federal income tax. Yet, when asked about funding specific programs, Americans would prefer spending more money on education, defense, and Medicare rather than cutting taxes.[10] Elected officials and pollsters, therefore, are free to argue over what the polls mean, but they cannot ignore them because these kinds of bread-and-butter issues tap more than nonopinions. Even inconsistent and confusing public attitudes play a role in establishing policy options.

Polls and pollsters affect the understanding and impact of public opinion simply by asking certain questions and phrasing them in certain ways. When pollsters use the term *crises* in seeking opinions on matters such as drugs, energy, crime, drunk driving, and garbage, the results they report may be magnifying concerns that exist primarily in the minds of pollsters, journalists, and public officials. By asking respondents whether President Clinton committed perjury or not while testifying under oath about his relationship with Monica Lewinsky, pollsters were forcing citizens to confront the issue of whether the president of the United States might be a liar. When people were asked during the 1988 presidential campaign whether it was important to know whether presidential candidates had committed adultery, pollsters and journalists were implying that personal moral conduct is an important criterion for judging potential presidents.

Interestingly, such a criterion was not as important in forming public opinion during the Clinton/Lewinsky scandal. Polls showed that the majority of Americans believed that Clinton was wrong for having an affair with an aide and for lying about it during questioning by the independent counsel, Kenneth Starr. Clinton's approval ratings were not seriously harmed by the scandal. When asked if Clinton should resign or be impeached, most Americans answered that he should be allowed to finish out his term and that the incident did not greatly affect his ability to fulfill his duties as president.[11]

Despite their limitations, public opinion polls perform valuable functions in democracies. They are the only mechanism, outside of elections, through which the concerns of the ordinary citizen are expressed to political elites. The results of public opinion polls are often more representative of public sentiment than elections because voter turnout, even for presidential elections, is only slightly more than 50 percent. Turnout for congressional elections is even lower, about 45 percent during a year of a presidential race and less than 35 percent during off-year elections.[12] Polls can put issues on the public agenda that go beyond the wish lists of special interest groups. And finally, polls provide some feedback about public satisfaction with the direction and performance of government. One such poll is the University of Michigan's American Customer Satisfaction Index (ACSI), which provides data concerning consumer attitudes about government services. ACSI is contracted by the federal government to measure public satisfaction with thirty government agencies on a 100-point scale.

Top-Down Public Opinion

Contrary to the civics book notion that the public will drives elected officials to carry out the public's wishes, political elites usually decide what public opinion is, what it means, and whether to use it or ignore it. This does not mean that opinions of the public are unimportant, only that they are defined by public officials. In this view, such opinions should be thought of as ammunition used by political elites to support their point of view and to advance policy positions.

The creation, interpretation, and use of public sentiment by public officials, the media, and interest groups in the policy process has been called "top-down public opinion."[13] Political elites "construct" a notion of what the "public" wants by listening to a variety of individuals and to reports on public sentiment.[14] According to political scientist V. O. Key Jr., public opinion is "private opinions which government finds it prudent to heed."[15] Nevertheless, policy formulation and implementation occur within the boundaries of political culture established by public opinion. The nation's political culture comprises "the enduring beliefs, values and behaviors that organize social communication and make common interpretations of life experience possible."[16] According to political scientist Robert Weissberg, "Virtually all the alternatives . . . considered [during policy debates] will be at least tolerable . . . by the vast majority. Thus although the precise preferences of 50 percent plus one may not be satisfied by the policy outcome, the losers would not regard the results as completely unacceptable."[17]

Under these circumstances, the public's greatest power is as a deterrent. Just as massive nuclear arsenals presumably deter the United States and Russia from starting a nuclear war, public opinion constrains what government institutions can accomplish or even propose. A "law of anticipated consequences" usually checks public officials, preventing them from implementing policies that offend fundamental values in the political culture. Elected officials know that if the public is ignored or offended, it can be mobilized by political opponents.

Political elites also wield interpretations of public sentiment in day-to-day struggles for power and policy advantage. Legislators and chief executives cite public support as the rationale for policy innovation, such as tough new laws against criminals. Governors and legislators also use public opinion as a shield against modification of existing policies, such as tax rates. Even when reliable and up-to-date public opinion polls are available, each side in a policy debate will claim public support.

Chief executives are especially dependent on the mobilization of public support for their positions; they must maintain the perception that the majority stands with them. Scholar Richard Neustadt argues that the principal power of the presidency is the "power to persuade."[18] Legislators try to read the tea leaves of public opinion to see how well the president or governor is doing before deciding whether to lend their support. If the public seems to favor the president's or a governor's policies, legislators may be reluctant to criticize.[19]

The record of the Clinton administration illustrates both sides of this point. During his 1992 campaign Clinton focused on national health care reform as a primary issue for the first term of his presidency. When he took office, public support for health care coverage for every family reached a forty-year high of 66 percent.[20] But his decision to create a task force of experts, headed by his wife, Hillary, to draft a comprehensive health care reform proposal drew criticism from both Democrats and Republicans on Capitol Hill. The group of five hundred experts worked mainly in closed-door meetings, and the eventual plan never gained much support among members of Congress or the public. Despite plenty of speeches and advertisements by the administration about health care, the general public never really truly understood the complex plan.[21] Clinton's efforts to rally congressional support for his health care plan were countered by the health care industry. One memorable feature of the battle for public opinion on health care reform was the "Harry and Louise" advertisements that the Health Insurance Association of America paid to put on television. These ads depicted a sympathetic middle-class couple worrying about whether the president's plan would limit their choice of doctors and cost them money. After he failed to obtain congressional support for national health care reform, Clinton's approval rating dropped, as did public support for many of his other initiatives.[22] Indeed, the Republicans went on to make health care reform a central focus of their 1994 election campaign, winning both houses of Congress and delivering a devastating blow to Clinton.

It wasn't long, however, before Clinton was able to turn the tables on congressional Republicans. After the 1994 elections, conventional wisdom held that Clinton would not be able to push any of his major initiatives through a strongly partisan, Republican-controlled Congress. But the president was able to mobilize public support for his budget priorities— education, environment, Medicare, and Medicaid—and prevent deep cuts in these programs. The refusal of congressional Republicans to provide temporary funding to avert a government-wide shutdown while the budget was under discussion in 1995–1996 was widely perceived as the turning point in this struggle for control over national policy. The public viewed the Republican action as unwise and excessively partisan, and this helped to boost Clinton's standing. Voices from the living rooms helped Clinton win the battle of the budget and eventually the election in 1996.

Most politicians work hard to build and maintain public support for their policy agenda. Gov. George W. Bush used the mass media and public events to build support for his education reform agenda. Claiming it to be the "clearest and most profound goal for Texas," Bush committed massive state resources to promoting a reading initiative. In "Reading Summits" he sponsored in cities statewide, Bush enlisted the help of celebrities and athletes to advocate his proposals. In this way he communicated directly with the public to promote his agenda.[23]

Bottom-Up Public Opinion

The public is not always passive. Large segments of the public, marginally interested or even disinterested in politics, may be awakened gradually.[24] Salient issues, such as war, civil rights, morality, public health, or economic hardship, can stir the passions of ordinary citizens, causing people to abandon their bystander status and vote on policy issues or even become active participants. When this happens, public opinion may exert significant pressure on political institutions and public officials from the bottom up. Bottom-up politics is closely aligned with what is sometimes called "grassroots politics." The idea is that citizens and/or communities take direct responsibility for defining the issues that are important to them rather than relying on politicians to perform this task.

A classic example of grassroots politics is the New England town meeting. This system of local government, present in hundreds of small communities, invites every citizen to have a say in the making of public policy. Although town meetings are often tedious and sometimes confrontational, they have maintained a niche in the political life of New England over several centuries.

Throughout the course of American history, grassroots political movements have sprung up to demand reform—sometimes with striking success, and at other times with stunning failure. For decades prior to the Civil War, for example, abolitionists sought the end of slavery. In the middle of the nineteenth century, suffragettes began to press for the right to vote for women, which was granted by ratification of the Nineteenth Amendment to the Constitution in 1920. Agrarian populists and labor unionists at the turn of the twentieth century demanded economic justice for low-income Americans.

Since World War II, American politics has witnessed strong public movements to secure civil rights for African Americans, to stop the war in Southeast Asia, to clean up the nation's air and water, to end the deployment of nuclear weapons, to crack down on drunk drivers, to curb utility rate hikes, and to stop abortions. The 1990s saw a resurgence of strong public movements, such as the Million Man March for self-empowerment of African American males, the Million Mom March to endorse stricter gun control laws, protests on college campuses against the use of sweatshop labor in the production of college apparel, and mass street protests by numerous organizations in Seattle against the World Trade Organization's free trade agreement. Each of these political movements emerged outside of conventional political arenas, was sparked by unelected leaders, and was characterized by large, vocal, and active participation by citizens who previously may have played little or no role in politics.[25]

What makes citizens stop relying on the voting booth and march in the streets? What makes people switch from watchers to central players? Grassroots movements spring up when citizens become impatient with the pace of decision making, frustrated by the unwillingness of public officials to address their concerns, or angered by laws that infringe on basic rights or fundamental interests. When public opinion is "carried through from conversation to action [it] almost always carries with it a sense of outrage or injustice. At this point it is no longer opinion at all . . . but rather a state of emotional shock . . . a feeling of deprivation."[26] Often citizens are drawn into political conflicts when they believe their health, safety, or property is threatened by government policies. The issue could be a proposed toxic waste site, a new professional sports stadium, the introduction of charter schools, or a new condominium development that alarms people sufficiently to spur them to act. Under these conditions, a small group of citizens, who normally eschew politics, can be motivated to attend meetings, join protest marches, contribute money, and become political animals. Intense local opposition to public policy decisions has come to be known as the "Not in My Back Yard," or NIMBY, syndrome. For example, citizens have strenuously opposed the construction of nuclear waste dumps in their communities.[27] Public opinion is expressed from the bottom up when communities mobilize to protect their vital interests.

Citizens, Politicians, and Journalists

Living room politics consists of the interaction of political leaders, who want to control and manipulate public opinion; citizens, who want to bring about changes in government policy; and the media, which serve as conduits of important political information about the public. On rare occasions citizens join together to fight the White House, the capitol, or city hall, but even "spontaneous" outbursts of public concern are unlikely to occur or succeed without the drumbeat of newspaper and television coverage and strong political leadership.

The instruments of mass communication—television, radio, newspapers, the Internet, and magazines—are the most important weapons in the battle for public opinion. Whether public opinion influences policies from the top down or citizens agitate from the bottom up, the mass media are involved. The media not only keep the attentive public informed but also prominently feature stories that may eventually stir the normally apathetic mass of citizens.

Public officials and citizens can communicate face to face, but probably not on a regular basis. The media have become the principal intermediaries and therefore exercise enormous power.[28] The media influence people's perception of what is important, frame the terms of debate on many questions, and magnify the voice of a few political figures. From time to time, the media switch from an information "channel" to an information "source" to promote particular policy concerns. When network news programs focused intensely on the Kosovo bombing campaign, their coverage was not just a conduit of facts and opinions, but a source of information with powerful consequences for the conduct of American foreign policy. Extensive coverage of the Serbian aggression in Kosovo built increased support for the air strike among the American public. Similarly, when stories about the inadequate treatment of patients insured by HMOs aired during the 1990s, the coverage did more than just convey facts; it forced the Clinton administration to propose reforms concerning patients' rights.

Living room politics, like all politics, is dominated by political elites, rather than by the public or even by journalists. Journalists usually take their cues about policy issues from public officials. News organizations are not neutral, but the media seldom create policy debates on their own. Media criticism of U.S. policy in the Persian Gulf, for example, evaporated when the air and ground war against Iraq began and when public officials on Capitol Hill muted their criticisms. President Bush was successful in the Persian Gulf War in part because he recognized that the war would be fought simultaneously in the deserts of the Middle East and in America's living rooms. The president and his close advisers had obviously learned many lessons from that military and political debacle, the Vietnam War. They devoted considerable attention to public relations.

Policymakers use the press and television to build public support for their policy preferences. They depend on the media for feedback about policy initiatives and programs. But what officials read in the press and see on television is not an independent measure of public concern. Media critic Leon V. Sigal observed: "Listening to the news for the sound of public opinion, officials hear echoes of their own voices. Looking for pictures of the world outside, they see reflections of their own images."[29] What elected officials regard as public opinion is often derived from what other political actors say, rather than from systematic evidence gathered through reliable public opinion polls.

Citizen activists are also adept at using the media to pursue living room politics. They have learned that when one is losing a political battle, one "expands the scope of conflict" and tries to draw in members of the "audience who might support your cause."[30] The process goes something like this. A group is upset about an issue such as high state taxes. The group members collect signatures on petitions, hold press conferences, march to the state capitol, release public opinion polls, make speeches, appear at editorial board meetings, give interviews to newspapers, and appear on public affairs programs. If they are skillful, diligent, and a little lucky, they can garner millions of dollars' worth of publicity. The press and television give more exposure to their issue; the public becomes more aware and more interested; support builds; the media report that public support is building. Eventually, policymakers, sensing a groundswell of public concern, respond by cutting taxes.

Bringing Issues to the Living Room

The media magnify issues and promote them to the top of the agenda by their choice of what to highlight in the limited space and time available. The media may not tell people what to think, but they tell people what to think about.[31] The nation's leading newspapers—the *New York Times* and the *Washington Post*—can each present only about ten stories on the front page; the network news shows have time for only fifteen to twenty stories in their half-hour shows.[32] Thus, at any point in time relatively few policy issues are receiving major media attention. Because most citizens have no personal contact with the political process, it is not surprising that they are dependent on the media for interpretations of the world around them.

Elected officials gravitate to issues that are salient to the public. Reports in the media tell them and the public what is important.[33] Elected officials know that issues so identified by the media are likely to become priorities for the public.[34] In this way the media enhance the importance of the issues they cover and diminish the political significance of the problems they ignore.[35] Media attention also enhances or detracts from the political power of individuals. Because presidents and governors receive by far the greatest attention from television, they have considerably more power than other political actors to set agendas, frame policy debates, and influence public sentiment. Conversely, ordinary citizens, even if they represent a widely held view, have trouble gaining access to the public airwaves and to newspaper columns.

Media surveillance of the political process helps keep issues on the agenda, especially if a president or governor addresses a policy question.[36] The public's agenda is not set in a single stroke; rather, it is built in a cycle of activity that elevates issues that are initially of interest to a few to issues that concern a broader public. The process through which the media, the government, and the citizenry influence one another has been labeled "agenda building" by scholars Gladys Engel Lang and Kurt Lang.[37] Intense media attention to issues such as tax reform or the Watergate break-in or to the struggles between Congress and the president over the federal budget transforms intramural squabbles into public controversies. A press secretary to a member of Congress has described agenda building on Capitol Hill:

If I leak a story . . . in the *New York Times* on asbestos and the name Y is attached, what happens is an immediate phenomenal reaction. The calls come cascading in, and the name Y and asbestos in schools are intertwined. Suddenly, he's nationally known because of asbestos compensation and asbestos in schools. Then other members are calling Y asking about the report, asking for more information. . . . Then he can introduce a bill. He kicks the tail of the administration and gets lots of cosponsors who go out and get [media] hits themselves.[38]

Once Bill Clinton raised the issue of Social Security reform in his 1998 State of the Union address, the Republican Congress found it difficult to ignore the issue. Clinton argued that in a period of budget surplus, we need to make the fiscal commitment to save "Social Security first." He urged the Congress to shore up the Social Security system before allocating the budget surplus to other causes. This made the reform a high priority issue for both Republicans and Democrats, even though it is a complicated and difficult issue. His framing of the issue helped to undercut the Republicans' desire for a broad-scale tax cut—something Clinton and his fellow Democrats opposed. It also helped to ensure that Social Security, a policy that Democrats have generally benefited from having at the forefront, would be a major issue in the 2000 election cycle.

Issues ignored by the national media seldom generate the sustained attention of elected officials and ranking administrative officials. Consider the case of highway traffic fatalities. In the United States, more than 43,000 people die in motor vehicle accidents every year. They are the leading cause of accidental death of Americans under the age of seventy-four. Car accidents cause 32 percent of all fatalities and 76 percent of the accidental deaths of young Americans—those fifteen to twenty-four years of age. Yet because motor vehicle deaths are so commonplace, they are seldom covered by the national media.[39]

Contrast media reporting on motor vehicle deaths with the media's reaction to deaths caused by airplane accidents. Air traffic accidents typically result in fewer than 500 deaths per year, but they receive enormous attention in the national press. If the media reported cumulative statistics on automobile accidents and their causes each day or week, would they focus public attention and political debate on finding methods to reduce them? Without media attention, this yearly loss of thousands of American lives is all but ignored by senior officials of federal and state governments.

In the 1990s twenty-four-hour news programs, such as the Cable News Network (CNN), became more common, allowing for more extensive coverage of top stories. Such programs brought the details of the Clinton impeachment, the O. J. Simpson murder trial, gun violence at Columbine High School in Colorado, and the custody battle for a Cuban child, Elian Gonzales, into America's living rooms many times per day. These battles were portrayed endlessly on television, but such coverage would seem to narrow the public's policy attention span rather than expand it. The proliferation of around-the-clock news shows and Internet news coverage means that Americans now have multiple sources of information; the immediacy of much of this news means that viewers receive a lot more "unfiltered" information. On the one hand, this means that people who are interested get more news than ever before; on the other hand, many of the first impressions conveyed by these programs turn out later to be incorrect and misleading. Indeed, the line between professional journalism and rumormongering has never been more difficult to discern.

A troubling example of the new media rumor mill came with the charges that President Clinton and his staff were either involved in or covered up the suicide death of Vincent Foster, a deputy chief counsel in the White House. Despite credible, independent police reports and investigations by independent prosecutors, many organizations opposed to President Clinton continued to post stories on their Web pages purporting to have new evidence linking the president or his staff to Foster's death. Some of these reports eventually found their way into the mainstream media and thus registered an impression on the public at large.

The Myth of the Neutral Media

Just as public officials claim they are not trying to manipulate the press, journalists perpetrate the myth that they are merely reporting what they see. Walter Cronkite, the former CBS News anchorman, closed his nightly broadcast by saying, "That's the way it is," implying that he was merely letting people know what had happened that day. In fact, the media are not neutral observers of the passing scene; there is a difference between the news and the truth.[40] Newspapers, television networks, and local stations shape the news and thus influence public officials and public opinion.

Newspaper editors and television producers simplify complex issues, place them in common frames of reference, and explain new policies with familiar terms.[41] When the media organizations report on a public problem, an event, a speech, or a policy proposal, they not only describe it but also give the public a context within which to interpret it. According to media analyst Martin Linsky, "The way the press frames an issue is as important as whether or not it is covered at all. If the press characterizes a policy option one way early on in the decision-making process, it is very difficult for officials to turn that image around to their preferred perspective."[42]

Because the media's descriptions of a problem often influence public perceptions, they may narrow the options available to public administrators. A policy debate can be labeled a "partisan squabble" or a matter of "urgent public concern." A governor's speech can be characterized as a "fight for his (or her) political life" or a routine report to the public. If dangerous polychlorinated biphenyls (PCBs) are discovered in a local warehouse, news stories suggesting that the public's health is gravely threatened can provoke panic, forcing public officials to react to an emergency that may not exist.

The conventions of newspaper reporting and television news also influence the kinds of issues brought to the public's attention and the way they are dealt with by public officials.[43] Bureaucratic routines, organizational politics, competition, and economics distort the view mass media organizations present to the public. What reporters think is probably less important than how they work. "News is thus less a sampling of what is happening in the world than a selection of what officials think—or want the press to report— is happening."[44] Reporters often exhibit a "herd mentality," as they take their cues about what to report from their colleagues and superiors in their organization. Journalists and television crews position themselves where they decide news will be "made," and, in so doing, they make news. In the reports themselves, extreme viewpoints are often highlighted because provocative statements and actions make more interesting reading and better television. Complicated issues—international trade, the savings and loan crisis, health care costs, for example—that are hard to explain and impossible to depict with pictures are frequently eschewed in favor of events that can be filmed, such as families salvaging their belongings after a flood, or a videotape of police beating a suspect during an arrest. News reports often convey a heightened sense of alarm about policy problems. Issues are personalized and dramatized, and a crisis atmosphere is created. In many cases, however, the "crisis is a function of publicity."[45] Public officials then feel compelled to take some action in order to ward off more negative stories.

The media's power to create a mood of urgency and demands for action was reflected in the sudden emergence and disappearance of public concern about laws requiring residents to be notified when convicted sex offenders move into their neighborhoods. In 1994, after the murder of seven-year-old Megan Kanka by a twice-convicted sex offender who lived across the street, public concern fueled a nationwide campaign to pass legislation to protect children from such crimes. Widespread media attention provoked strong public reactions, eliciting strong support for new laws. Within a two-year period forty states adopted "Megan's Law," requiring convicted sex offenders to register with local authorities. President Clinton even signed the law into federal anticrime legislation in 1996. A few years later, however, the issue had virtually disappeared from the national media, America's living rooms, and Congress's agenda; even the people in the affected communities did not seem to be using the new information the laws made available to them.[46]

The media's portrayal of Saddam Hussein illustrates how time and historical context can lead the media to change their tune. When Saddam was an ally of the United States during the Iran-Iraq war, his mistreatment of Iraqi citizens was overlooked. But after Saddam's forces invaded Kuwait, newspapers and television news accounts likened his cold-blooded actions to the second coming of Adolf Hitler. By building up the image of a madman determined to destroy civilization, the media helped build support for the Persian Gulf War and for President Bush's policies. Similarly, the media's concentration on the limited extent of U.S. casualties and the near absence of reports on the deaths of Iraqi civilians and soldiers helped convince Americans that the Persian Gulf War was not only just but one without much cost.

Occasionally, journalists and news organizations also can become active participants in the policy process. Newspaper investigations of problems in a local police department or fraud in defense contracting practically force public officials to address the problems. Reporters from CNN have, at times, become important participants in the making of American foreign policy. When the Chinese government violently suppressed student protesters occupying Tiananmen Square in 1989, for example, CNN accounts of the event horrified the American public and helped move U.S. policy further in the direction away from supporting the repressive regime. Sometimes the media come under fire for their activism. During the Persian Gulf War, CNN reporters provided the most extensive accounts of civilian casualties in Iraq—a practice that led one U.S. senator to charge that CNN was sympathizing with the enemy.

Media organizations also play an active role in shaping public policy when they commission public opinion polls and then report new or controversial findings. Today, numerous polls are sponsored by news media, including the ABC News/*Wall Street Journal* Poll, the CBS News Poll, the *Los Angeles Times* Poll, the *New York Times* Poll, the *USA Today*/CNN Poll, and the *Washington Post* Poll. The results of these polls are reported frequently and are not easily ignored by politicians, even during times of apparent crisis. During the 1999 NATO air bombing in Kosovo, public opinion polls showed that only 51 percent of Americans approved of the way President Clinton handled the situation. Although the number of those who supported the air strikes increased during the first days, the majority of those polled opposed sending U.S. ground troops into Kosovo as part of a NATO peacekeeping force, despite increasing reports of Serbian aggression against Kosovar civilians. These polls may have bolstered Clinton's resistance to deploying ground troops as part of this military operation.[47]

Although they are less important than bureaucratic conditions that drive news reporting, the personal biases of journalists and media managers cannot be overlooked. Media watcher Herbert Gans pointed out that most journalists have a reformist/progressive attitude toward government.[48] They are deeply suspicious of government policymakers and the ability of political institutions to solve problems. These views lead to predictable, formulaic stories about incompetence, fraud, waste, and abuse. Stories about effective programs or the achievements of dedicated civil servants are scoffed at as "not newsworthy." In the shorthand of reporters, "Good news, bad story; bad news, good story."

Referenda and Initiatives

Citizens can select policies and structure government institutions by means of referenda and initiatives. There are no provisions in the U.S. Constitution for national referenda or initiatives, but forty-nine state constitutions authorize referenda, which give citizens a voice on measures approved by state legislatures.[49] Typically, referenda allow citizens to vote yes or no on amendments to state constitutions; on state capital spending projects, such as highways or new prisons; or even on major state laws, such as environmental protection and health care programs.

Initiatives—provided for in twenty-four state constitutions—give citizens the right to petition public officials to place issues on the ballot for approval or disapproval, without waiting for the state legislature to act.[50]

Before questions are put to the voters, a significant number of state residents must sign petitions, usually 5 percent to 10 percent of the number voting in the last statewide election. If the qualified initiative receives majority support, the legislature is expected to enact a law embodying the purpose of the initiative. Initiatives have been employed on a wide variety of policy questions, such as whether to raise the minimum wage, ban government-sponsored affirmative action, allow the use of marijuana for medical purposes, hike cigarette taxes, and prohibit same-sex marriage.[51]

Giving the public a vote on policies has a long tradition in American politics. Referenda were first used in 1778 when Massachusetts voters approved the state's first constitution. The initiative grew in importance during the late nineteenth and twentieth centuries as the Progressive political reform movement swept the country west of the Mississippi River. The influential Progressive reformer Robert M. La Follette summarized the rationale for referenda and initiatives:

> For years the American people have been engaged in a terrific struggle with the allied forces of organized wealth and political corruption. . . . The people must have in reserve new weapons for every emergency if they are to regain and preserve control of their governments. Through the initiative and referenda, people in an emergency can absolutely control. The initiative and referenda make it possible for them to demand a direct vote and repeal bad laws which have been enacted or to enact by direct vote good measures which their representatives refuse to consider.[52]

Since 1976 these instruments of "direct democracy" have been used with increasing frequency. The number of state ballot initiatives doubled between that year and 1986.[53] From 1991 to 1998, 323 initiatives were proposed by citizens and 149 were adopted.[54] In 1998 there were 235 ballot questions in forty-four states, including 61 citizen-proposed initiatives.[55] Initiatives also represent a wide range of issues (see Table 8-1).

In the 1990s nearly 30 percent of initiatives dealt with government or political reform, such as term limits or campaign finance reform; over 25 percent dealt with revenue and tax measures; 15 percent concerned "public morality" issues, such as abortion; almost 10 percent had to do with environmental issues; and about 16 percent dealt with the regulation of business.[56] In recent years, voters weighed important, complex, and controversial proposals, such as:

- requiring all public school instruction to be taught in English in California (passed)
- allowing the medical use of marijuana in Alaska, Nevada, Oregon, and Washington (passed)
- prohibiting the medical use of marijuana in Arizona (passed)

Table 8–1 Numbers of Initiatives by Type, 1976–1992

		Passed	
Issue	*Total*	*Number*	*Rate*
Abortion	12	3	25.0%
Beverage containers, recycling	15	1	6.7%
Budgets, spending, taxes, bonds	134	55	41.0%
Campaign, lobbying laws	10	8	80.0%
Consumer, auto insurance	11	2	18.2%
Crime and punishment	27	17	63.0%
Educational standards, operations	11	2	18.2%
English as official language	5	5	100.0%
Health care financing	10	1	10.0%
Lottery, gambling	31	11	35.5%
Nuclear weapons	10	7	70.0%
Nuclear power, hazardous waste	37	16	43.2%
Redistricting, legislative powers	20	11	55.0%
Sexuality and gender/AIDS	8	2	25.0%
Term limitations	20	18	90.0%
Voting rights, registration, elections	15	10	66.7%
Utilities: rates, commissions	16	7	43.7%
Other issues	103	40	38.8%
Total	495	216	43.6%

Source: Lisa Oakley and Thomas H. Neale, *Citizen Initiative Proposals Appearing on State Ballots, 1976–1992* (Washington, D.C.: Congressional Research Service, 1995), 3.

- banning government-sponsored affirmative action in the hiring of state workers in Washington (passed)
- establishing public funding of political campaigns in Arizona and Massachusetts (passed)
- banning the hunting of mourning doves in Ohio (failed)
- banning partial birth abortions in Colorado and Washington (failed)
- banning same-sex marriages in Alaska and Hawaii (failed)[57]

The Conduct of Direct Democracy

Most initiative and referenda campaigns rely on volunteers, but some have become costly public relations efforts requiring millions of dollars for television advertising.[58] For example, supporters and opponents of eleven propositions that appeared on California's November 1998 state ballot spent approximately $200 million. In the most expensive campaign—licensing Indian casinos—both advocates and opponents spent approximately $95 million.[59]

In 1994, local smoking regulations in California were defeated by Phillip Morris and associates, who wrote Proposition 188 and spent $20 million in favor of it.[60] In the 1980s initiatives that would have required deposits on bottles in Arizona, California, and Montana were defeated as a result of heavy spending by out-of-state beverage interests. Ninety-seven percent of the funds used to successfully oppose an antismoking initiative in California were contributed by out-of-state tobacco firms.[61]

Initiative and referenda campaigns have spawned an industry that collects signatures and mounts public awareness advertising campaigns. These services are available for hire, but they are expensive, and only groups with money can afford them. The Florida Medical Association organized an initiative drive to impose ceilings on financial awards in negligence suits. The doctors dished out $8 million in fees for canvassers who went door to door in "friendly" neighborhoods seeking signatures to place the question on the ballot. The canvassers assured citizens that passing the initiative would reduce medical costs, but they did not mention that their ability to sue for damages would be curtailed. The Florida Supreme Court refused to qualify the issue for the ballot because of the misleading campaign.[62] Reacting to tactics that undermine the democratic nature of the process, Colorado, Massachusetts, and Nebraska now prohibit paid solicitors in initiative and referenda campaigns.

Governors, state legislators, and others aspiring to elected office are using ballot questions to gain political visibility and attain policy objectives. In several states, legislative and gubernatorial candidates are backing ballot initiatives, hoping that their support will bring sympathetic voters to the polls on election day. As David Magleby, a leading student of the initiative process, pointed out, elected officials see referenda and initiatives as another tool in their political arsenal. If they win, initiatives allow legislators and governors to bypass the lengthy, arduous, and chancy legislative process. Even if they lose, politicians can gain political visibility through free media time.[63]

The line between show business and politics has been blurred in the controversy surrounding some ballot initiatives in California. A complex and far-reaching environmental initiative, Proposition 128, known as Big Green, went down to defeat in 1990. But it attracted dozens of well-known show business personalities, including Chevy Chase, Jane Fonda, Gregory Peck, and Cybill Shepherd. The supporters of the proposition produced a thirty-minute television commercial with fifteen celebrities, which accompanied a fast-paced program that resembled an MTV video.[64]

Another example is the 1998 California initiative, Proposition 10, which was designed to raise taxes on cigarettes in order to pay for children's health care. Sponsors included the actor Charlton Heston, the millionaire Michael

Huffington, and the well-known movie director Rob Reiner. The proposition would raise funds for early childhood development, prenatal care programs, and programs to discourage smoking among teenagers. Although the tobacco industry outspent proponents $28.5 million to $7.8 million, bipartisan support and celebrity endorsements resulted in the approval of Proposition 10.[65]

Not all initiatives and referenda are endorsed by big business and statewide political candidates; many feature household names as supporters or opponents. Questions about civil rights and moral issues are often raised by grassroots organizations whose volunteers collect signatures and operate on shoestring budgets. Large corporations are not interested in spending their money or risking their credibility on campaigns about the regulation of pornography, funding for abortions, or civil rights for disabled Americans.

Battles over the insertion of equal rights amendments (ERAs)—amendments that would guarantee equal rights or equal protection under the law to women—in state constitutions are an example of low-cost, door-to-door campaigns waged with intensity by citizen organizations. Since 1973, twelve states have voted on ERA referenda. Voters have approved them in five states and rejected them in seven. No state ERA has passed since Massachusetts amended its constitution in 1976. Typically, the pro-ERA forces have included state chapters of the National Organization for Women, the League of Women Voters, and labor organizations with large numbers of women. The anti-ERA coalition has encompassed the Eagle Forum, founded by Phyllis Schlafly; the Daughters of the American Revolution (DAR); the Federation of Women's Clubs; and assorted conservative organizations. The costs of ERA ballot fights have been considerably less than the costs of statewide campaigns on issues in which business and industry have been involved. Pro- and anti-ERA groups spent a combined total of $60,000 in Florida and $68,000 in Massachusetts, for example.[66]

Popular Leaders

Elected officials, media elites, and large corporations play central roles in living room politics. Public officials and private business leaders attempt to manipulate public opinion to suit their specific purposes. Journalists and pollsters shape public opinion in policy debates. The public, however, does not follow only elected officials and media personalities. Many leaders of initiative and referenda drives and grassroots citizen campaigns come from the ranks of ordinary citizens. These individuals, who have the power to persuade, have transformed national, state, and local politics by mobilizing citizens to take political action.

With regard to state ballot questions, the name Howard Jarvis is associated with Proposition 13, one of the most influential citizen campaigns in recent times. This tax and spending initiative, which was approved overwhelmingly by California voters in 1978, launched a drive to cut taxes and spending in many other states. Jarvis became so identified with government tax reform and spending limitations that subsequent California initiative campaigns have revolved around positive and negative campaign advertisements about Jarvis himself, rather than about the policy choices.[67]

Less well known, but more typical of the citizen activist, is Ray Phillips, an octogenarian who, with his volunteers, led a tax reduction movement known as Oregon Taxpayers United in the 1980s. Phillips describes his motivation:

> I like being a rabble rouser. If the legislature did what it was supposed to do, we would not have to be out collecting signatures. The legislators spend too much time listening to lobbyists and not enough time listening to the people. Taxpayers don't control taxes anymore. That's what our measure would do— give power back to the people.[68]

Important grassroots political movements have been led by individuals who emerged from nonpolitical roles into the limelight and became identified with their cause. Dr. Martin Luther King Jr., a charismatic preacher, developed a large, loyal following as he organized demonstrations, marches, and other efforts to secure the full rights of citizenship for black Americans. Ralph Nader, a shy, ascetic lawyer, raised the consciousness of the American consumer and helped secure passage of new consumer protection laws. His nationwide network of state and local organizations continues to monitor industry production and use of dangerous products. As mentioned earlier, Phyllis Schlafly, a self-described housewife, energized a large conservative movement in dozens of states to prevent passage of the ERA. Bill Sizemore, the successor of Ray Phillips and current executive director of Oregon Taxpayers United, was a small businessman who has become a household name in that state.

The Power of Public Opinion

Living room politics has been the catalyst for significant and startling changes in government policies. Public opinion—whether it originated at the top or at the bottom—played a critical role in forcing a president from office, halting the growth of nuclear power, cracking down on drunk drivers, slowing the growth of government spending, and limiting the number of terms that state legislators may serve. Citizens exert a powerful policy influence in the voting booth, on the streets of America, and perhaps most significantly, in the minds of elected and appointed leaders.

Public Opinion and the Media

Shifts in public support for government policies, often stimulated by media coverage, have brought about important changes. Extensive television coverage of the civil rights marches in the South during the 1960s exposed racism and the use of excessive force against peaceful individuals protesting racial discrimination.[69] Television scenes of the Vietnam War, showing bloody battles and the destruction of a country, crystallized public opposition to America's involvement.[70] Coverage of the nuclear accidents at Three Mile Island and Chernobyl undermined public support for nuclear power and halted the construction of nuclear power plants.[71] Government funding for research to find a cure for AIDS jumped by more than 200 percent after public opinion polls revealed widespread fear about the epidemic.[72] Extensive coverage of the violence and deaths caused by drug use influenced public opinion and brought about more stringent criminal penalties for drug users and suppliers. Media coverage of high school gun violence, such as the Columbine shootings, fueled intense public support for stricter gun control laws.

The power of public opinion—and the role media organizations and political elites play in shaping it—was evident during the Clinton/Lewinsky scandal. Congressional Republicans thought they could use the issue of President Clinton's affair with a young White House aide, and his apparent lies about it, to drive the president from office. However, after the House voted articles of impeachment, Republicans leaders were not able to muster the two-thirds vote needed for conviction in the Senate, and the president completed his second term. Public opinion played an important role.

In this case, media attention did have a negative effect on the way the public viewed Clinton's behavior and character, but it also drew attention to the president's enemies. Polls showed that the public disapproved of the time and money Congress spent on the impeachment hearings and trial.[73] More important, Clinton's job approval ratings remained very high throughout the scandal and impeachment process. Even while the hearings were under way Clinton registered a 65 percent job approval rating—the highest in his career—because the vast majority of citizens believed he was doing a good job as president.[74] These high job approval ratings continued despite the fact that eight in ten Americans questioned in a December 1998 poll said they believed the president lied under oath about his affair, and six in ten thought he obstructed justice in concealing his relationship with Lewinsky.[75] According to Gallup Polls, the percentage of respondents who believed honesty and trustworthiness did not apply to Clinton increased 10 percentage points between January and August of 1998.[76] Clinton won the battle for public opinion because most people believed he was doing a good job during an era of unprecedented economic expansion, negative feeling about his personal behavior notwithstanding.

Passionate public responses to issues are unusual, but they have far-reaching effects. Public policies may be changed quickly when large segments of the public rally to support or oppose issues of high salience. Politicians feel compelled to act rather than face a disgruntled, even angry, citizenry. One reason the public seldom becomes aroused is that public officials are adept at anticipating serious problems and responding to them before people get angry.

Given the weight assigned to public opinion in the myth and reality of American politics, it is perhaps surprising that strongly held public preferences are sometimes ignored. Politicians are known to use public opinion polls when they support their point of view and to ignore or denounce them as unreliable when they bring unfavorable, unwanted, or inconvenient news. Public officials often believe that poll results put them in an embarrassing position. If they follow public opinion as recorded in the surveys, cherished positions may have to be abandoned. If they ignore the polls, their opponents or journalists may chastise them for disregarding the will of the people. Fortunately for politicians, journalists are not particularly vigilant about calling attention to public officials who fail to respond to sentiment expressed in public opinion polls.

As intermediaries between the public and political leaders, the media influence policy choices and the evaluation of programs. Policymakers are preoccupied with managing the news because the media command public attention in a way that no elected officials or interest group possibly can. More than half of the senior federal government policymakers contacted in a recent survey reported that the press had substantial effects on federal policy. One official in ten believed the press to be the dominant influence on policy. To some extent, press influence has become a self-fulfilling prophecy: "If policymakers themselves believe the press is influential, then by definition it is."[77]

Managing the press and responding to it often becomes a surrogate for managing public opinion and responding to it. Interactions among the media, public opinion, and public officials affect public policies in subtle ways. According to Linsky, extensive press coverage oversimplifies and nationalizes stories, forces quick responses, pushes decisions up the bureaucratic chain of command, and creates supportive climates for some options and excludes others.[78] Two case studies illustrate the dynamic relationships that are part of living room politics and their influence on government policies.

Love Canal

In the late 1970s state and local health officials discovered that between 1942 and 1952, Hooker Chemical Company had deposited 21,000 tons of hazardous chemicals in an abandoned canal in Love Canal, New York.[79] The Environmental Protection Agency (EPA) commissioned pilot studies to ascertain the possible health and environmental threats posed by chemicals that were leaching into the groundwater, yards, and basements of homes around the canal. President Jimmy Carter declared the Hooker site at Love Canal a national emergency, and hundreds of residents were evacuated from the area. Media attention to the problems at Love Canal influenced these decisions.

After Love Canal became a national issue, a consultant was hired by the EPA to examine the possible genetic effects of the leaking chemicals. The consultant examined individuals who had experienced serious health problems, such as cancer or birth defects. By first selecting people with known health problems, the consultant hoped to determine whether a more thorough investigation was warranted. Research uncovered chromosomal aberrations in twelve of the thirty-six people tested. Without more rigorous and comprehensive tests, however, it was not possible to establish a definite link between the chemicals dumped in the canal and the health problems experienced by people in the pilot study.

Fearing that the preliminary study would be leaked to the press, White House officials decided they would release the report and promise further investigation. But before they could act, the report was published in the *New York Times*. Love Canal was hot news. In the ten days following the publication of the findings, the *Times* printed thirty-one articles on Love Canal, including eight front-page stories and three editorials. Other newspapers and the television networks ran dozens of related stories describing serious threats to health from the uncontrolled dumping of hazardous wastes.

To put an end to stories about government insensitivity to the problems of Love Canal's residents, the White House decided to relocate 710 individuals. The pressure to respond so as not to appear callous and indifferent had been intensified by media coverage. Ironically, the complete review of the EPA pilot study was finished the same day that the relocation decision was announced. It concluded that there was "inadequate basis for any scientific or medical inferences from the data (even of a tentative or preliminary nature) concerning exposure to mutagenic substances because of residence in Love Canal." If the Love Canal story had not been framed by the media as a dangerous health threat to hapless victims, the government might have undertaken a lengthier investigation and might not have spent millions to relocate the families.

Like many instances of press and public involvement in the policy process, the Love Canal story had far-reaching effects. The spotlight was focused on one example of a national problem—the cleanup of abandoned hazardous waste dumps. The publicity that resulted from the Love Canal incident helped focus public attention on this lingering problem. Soon after, new environmental legislation to clean up abandoned waste dumps was enacted by Congress.

Welfare Reform

The powerful influence of the media on public opinion and public policy is also illustrated by the media's handling of welfare fraud and the cutbacks it has spawned in the past three decades. The derogatory term *welfare queen* as a reference for welfare recipients emerged in the midst of an economic crisis in the United States as the Vietnam War came to an end. Public tension was high and the 1980 presidential elections were around the corner. Candidates were looking for new policies and platforms to get the attention of the American voters. Then governor, Ronald Reagan had won approval for his drastic welfare reforms in California that required women to work in public sector jobs in return for their welfare assistance and for his tough stance against welfare fraud.

Reagan drew upon his "success" in California during his 1980 presidential campaign. One such story involved a Chicago woman by the name of Linda Taylor, who had cheated the system by claiming benefits under multiple names, addresses, and social security numbers. Reagan dubbed her the "welfare queen," and the stereotype of low-income people cheating the system became the cornerstone of Reagan's proposal to cut welfare spending. The welfare queen image spurred intense, negative reactions to alleged welfare fraud. Stories about "cheaters" splashed the headlines all over the country. Polls at the time showed that high percentages of the American public believed welfare fraud to be rampant and a serious problem. Actual studies revealed that welfare fraud was uncommon, that it was mostly confined to the underreporting of income, and that even with such underreporting recipients rarely exceeded poverty-level incomes. Nevertheless, during his two terms as president, Reagan succeeded in making major cuts in welfare spending because of the unpopularity of the program.

By the 1990s the new welfare mantra was that recipients could and should work, rather than stay at home and receive benefits. This belief was held by a large percentage of the public and eventually attracted bipartisan support in Congress, which led to the enactment of welfare reform in 1996. The Personal Responsibility and Work Opportunity Reconciliation Act of 1996 eliminated the entitlement program that supported low-income families with young children and replaced it with a temporary assistance program that requires recipients to work.

Choosing Policies in the Voting Booth

Referenda and initiatives give millions of Americans a direct say on policy issues, and liberal and conservative groups have been equally successful with the voters. A study of nearly 200 initiatives approved between 1977 and 1984 revealed that 44 percent of the 79 proposals backed by liberals were approved, and 45 percent of the 74 conservative-sponsored initiatives were approved. (The remainder were classified as not having ideological content.)[80]

The longest and most instructive story of statewide initiatives and public policy involves tax and government spending limitations. "No other issue cluster . . . has faced popular scrutiny more often. Win or lose, the tax cut movement has . . . been deciding the bounds of political debate on tax and fiscal policy," wrote Patrick McGuigan, the author of an authoritative newsletter on referenda and initiatives.[81] The modern tax revolt began with California's Proposition 13, which reduced property tax revenues by 57 percent and limited future tax increases to no more than 2 percent annually.

In 1965 less than half of the electorate thought that taxes were too high. By 1983 nearly 75 percent were complaining that taxes are excessive. And eight Americans in ten thought that government funds were often wasted.[82] Between 1976 and 1984, however, only three states of the nine that voted on Proposition 13–type initiatives approved them. But voters in eleven states approved moderate tax and spending measures referred to them by state legislatures that were trying to head off more Draconian revenue cuts. Alaskans dropped the income tax; North Dakotans reduced the income tax bite; and Washingtonians eliminated the state inheritance tax.[83]

In the 1990 elections, initiatives proposing government spending and tax limitations did not fare very well. Voters in Colorado, Massachusetts, Montana, and Utah said no to proposals that would have required legislators to roll back or curtail taxes. Public officials, public employees and teachers, and others who would be negatively affected by budget cuts rallied enough voter support to defeat efforts to further shrink state and local governments.[84] But such propositions continued to appear on ballots in the 1990s with mixed results. In 1992 Colorado voters approved a proposition that puts limits on income and property taxes and requires voter approval for state tax increases. A 1996 proposition in Oklahoma to reduce property taxes to their 1993 level was rejected by voters, whereas Montana voters approved an amendment forbidding state legislatures to increase taxes without voter approval.[85]

The history of government tax and spending measures also shows that a state need not have a strong initiative process to be affected by initiatives passed in other states.[86] In fact, legislators in states without the initiative process interpreted the rash of tax and spending initiatives as a message they must heed. They thought voters wanted lower taxes and changes in the methods of taxation, and they responded with policies that spoke to these preferences.

Even a defeated initiative may trigger a remedial or preemptive policy response. In South Dakota the Public Utilities Commission approved special rates for the elderly and the poor two years after the defeat of a similar but more comprehensive rate initiative.[87] The California state legislature responded to an antinuclear initiative while the campaign for it was still under way. One week before the scheduled election, the legislature approved a weaker version of the antinuclear initiative, which was subsequently rejected by the voters. The defeated initiative had served as a catalyst, prodding politicians to act before the voters took matters into their own hands.

According to most observers, policymaking through initiatives and referenda has reached its most advanced level in California. Indeed, many would argue that the focus of policy debate in the state has shifted from the legislature to the initiative process. During the 1980s California citizens set major policy directions on insurance rates, the environment, and the levels of spending for education. In the 1990 election California voters were asked to weigh twenty-eight ballot issues, ranging from sweeping environmental policy changes to taxes on alcohol. In this election Californians passed a marine resource conservation initiative but voted down an initiative to regulate the use of pesticides. They also rejected a new surtax on alcohol. In the 1998 general election California had twelve statewide ballot questions, ranging from raising taxes on cigarettes to animal rights.[88] "It [the initiative] is a force that has produced occasional benefits, but at enormous cost—an erosion of responsibility in the executive and legislative branches," says Eugene C. Lee of the University of California.[89]

Public ballot proposals have also given voters a voice on issues of social policy.[90] Voters cut abortion funding in Colorado, but similar proposals in Arkansas, Oregon, Rhode Island, and Washington were defeated. Following the 1989 Supreme Court decision that gave states more latitude in regulating abortions, Oregon voters rejected a proposal that would have required parents to be notified when teenagers sought an abortion. Citizens rejected stricter regulations on the sale of pornographic materials in Maine and Utah, endorsed prayer in the public schools in West Virginia, and repealed the Massachusetts law requiring the use of seat belts. Laws restricting the disposal of radioactive waste were strengthened in Montana, Oregon, and Washington. Maine voters rejected a proposal to shut down a nuclear power plant and threw out laws requiring large stores to close on Sunday. More stringent environmental protection laws were endorsed by voters in California, Massachusetts, and New Jersey. California voters declared English the state's official language and rejected a plan to quarantine victims of AIDS. In the 1998 cycle California voters approved Proposition 207, which requires all public school instruction to be taught in English. A ban of so-called partial birth abortions was rejected by voters in Colorado and Washington. Citizens in Michigan defeated a proposition to legalize physician-assisted suicide. Californians voted to raise the tax on cigarettes fifty cents a package to discourage smoking and raise funds for prenatal care and youth development programs. Florida citizens voted to preserve the death penalty and make it easier for third party candidates to get on the ballot. At the same time that all these states took advantage of the process, voters in Mississippi, Missouri, Utah, and Wyoming voted to make it more difficult for citizens to utilize initiatives.[91] Citizens have also used the ballot box to register dismay over U.S. foreign and defense policies, even though state and local governments have no control over foreign policy and the result of such ballot measures are not binding on the federal government. Nevertheless, activists frustrated with U.S. foreign policy have used this tactic to goad the president and Congress to halt the production and deployment of nuclear weapons.[92] With nearly 20 million people voting, the so-called nuclear freeze referenda were the closest the nation has come to a national referendum on a policy issue. Similarly worded proposals calling for a halt to the arms race were approved by comfortable margins—averaging 60 percent—in ten of the eleven states and thirty-one of thirty-two communities where balloting occurred in 1982. Perhaps the measure won easily because freeze supporters encountered almost no organized opposition (except in Arizona, where the measure failed) and outspent their opponents thirteen to one nationwide. Still, the vote can be considered a measure of the desire for reduced tensions in the arms race.

Policy from the Grass Roots

Grassroots political movements grow out of the frustration citizens feel about the pace of reform or their outrage at decisions that threaten their way of life. Seeking relief from the government, citizen groups have denounced U.S. foreign policy and pestered legislators, administrators, and judges to alter policies on a host of social, moral, and environmental issues, including prayer in public schools, abortion, the sale of pornographic materials, the death penalty, the disposal of radioactive waste, and the citing of garbage incinerators.

The success of minority groups in quickening the pace of change is noteworthy. What began as an effort to secure basic rights evolved into a broad-based effort to increase economic opportunities. The ability of leaders to mobilize minorities beyond protest and get them into the voting booth had positive effects on the appointment and election of minority officeholders, expanded employment opportunities for minorities in city governments, and enlarged programs for the minority community.[93]

Since the late 1960s, hundreds of national and local environmental groups have also achieved considerable success in translating widespread public support for environmental conservation and protection into political action and policy changes. Statutes have been passed governing air and water quality, control of toxic pollution, and the disposal of industrial, agricultural, and urban wastes. Regulatory agencies have been established at the state and national levels. Billions of dollars have been allocated to environmental protection and cleanup. Environmental interest groups are represented in Washington and in state capitals. Obviously, these sweeping reforms were not stimulated entirely by ordinary citizens, but grassroots environmental organizations were powerful agents for change.[94]

Student-based groups effectively organized in 1999 to stop the sale of university products produced by companies that employ individuals at low wages, often in horrendous working conditions in less developed countries. These practices are often referred to as "sweatshops." Students enrolled at more than sixty universities nationwide protested manufacturers such as Nike who produce college apparel and other products. Student sit-ins at college and university offices forced many university presidents to respond to student demands. For example, the president of Duke University, Nannerl Keohane, required companies making products that used the university's name to disclose their factory locations in order to have their contracts with the school renewed. Nike was forced to permit independent inspections of its factories and eventually increased wages for workers in its manufacturing facilities.[95] Student protests also persuaded universities and colleges to contract with manufacturing companies that do not use foreign labor.

Majority Rule and Minority Rights

Who benefits from living room politics? Who are the winners and the losers? Because living room politics concerns issues that arouse the public and galvanize ordinary citizens into action, one might glibly conclude that the public wins. Unfortunately, figuring out who benefits from living room politics is considerably more complicated than that.

Living room politics can be the expression of majority sentiments, and public officials are inclined to heed the will of the people when public preferences are clear and reflect a broad-based consensus. When the majority of the public supports a controversial course of action, however, policymakers may ignore it, especially if the public's wishes would infringe on minority interests. Suppose that public opinion polls showed that most people favored isolating AIDS victims from the rest of the population. It is unlikely that political institutions, especially the courts, would be guided by such opinions because the basic rights of a disadvantaged minority would be violated in an attempt to allay the fears of the majority.

Well-organized and well-financed groups are more likely to have their views heeded than are those who are economically disadvantaged. Those who are better off are generally more successful in directing media and public attention to their concerns. It is no accident that many ballot initiatives are of greater interest to white, middle-class voters than they are to minorities and the poor. Disadvantaged Americans are more likely to go to the courts for help than to the ballot box (see Chapter 7).

A central dilemma of democracy is the clash of majority rule and minority rights. Basic issues, such as war, civil rights, morality, and public health and safety, are most likely to stimulate public concern and foster intense, divergent beliefs. Individuals with diametrically opposed positions on controversial issues, such as abortion, women's rights, and nuclear plant safety, usually do not find the alternative point of view acceptable.

When people are divided over an issue that arouses strong feelings, public officials search for Solomonic compromises that might satisfy the losers as well as the winners. However, finding such answers is often impossible. When accommodation fails, the public policy process grinds to a halt because neither side is willing to compromise. Elected officials and government administrators either ignore the problem as long as they possibly can or pass the buck to another institution—the judiciary or the president. They may even pass the buck to the voters, hoping to find an answer in the majority will expressed via referenda.

When majority preferences are honored, the losers may be angry, feel alienated, and resort to unconventional methods, including civil disobedience and violence. Indeed, many of the most violent or potentially violent episodes in American political history took place when the losers felt the political system no longer cared about them. Riots and violence over racial segregation and injustice in the 1950s and 1960s and demonstrations against the Vietnam War that ended in violent confrontations between marchers and police and national guardsmen are but two vivid examples. More recently, individuals opposed to the U.S. Supreme Court's legalization of abortions have bombed abortion clinics. Environmental activists have sabotaged chemical plants and physically blocked the construction of nuclear power plants and hazardous waste disposal facilities. Some individuals who were extremely disgruntled with the U.S. government contributed to the rise of militia activity in the 1990s that resulted in terrorism in many states. Bombings of state and federal government buildings have been linked to such groups.

Well-organized, sophisticated segments of the citizenry benefit most from living room politics, but when minority concerns are trampled on, the potential for political instability increases. It is perhaps for this reason that politicians fear citizen participation in the government process. Once citizens are drawn into the conflict, they demand satisfaction, and once the genie is out of the bottle, it is hard to get it back in again.

A Potent Weapon of Democracy

Whether through the informal plebiscite of public opinion polls or through active participation, citizens can have a powerful influence on the implementation and impact of public policies. Public pressure may be brought to bear concerning the tactics and pace of program administration. The public's evaluation of government policies, institutions, and political actors, which is shaped by the media, may influence financial support for a program or cause its cancellation. Public perceptions of a specific leader's popularity may embolden or intimidate other political leaders. Finally, angry citizens can force radical changes in public policy.

Public and Media Evaluations of Government Policy

Americans are generally skeptical about government programs and institutions. Such perceptions are based partly on personal experience, such as frustration with the Internal Revenue Service (IRS), a state department of motor vehicles, or the local building code enforcement officer. For the most part, however, the public's understanding of politics and policy comes to it via newspapers and television, which not only reflect this skeptical attitude about government but also encourage it.

As messengers of public concern and guardians of the public interest, reporters often deserve high praise. Journalists criticize weak government policies and inform the public about crises and conflicts, fraud and corruption. Journalists root out corrupt public officials and call attention to the insensitivity and injustice of public institutions. Media scrutiny, followed by public anger, can spur an indifferent, cautious, or incompetent agency or legislature to positive action in the public interest.

The contributions of media organizations and journalists to policy implementation can be a mixed blessing, however. Media publicity can divert administrators from important tasks and induce them to attend to relatively trivial matters. In the fall of 1999, for example, New York City mayor Rudolph Giuliani launched a huge campaign against an art exhibit at the Brooklyn Museum of Art. The exhibit, by a young British artist, featured a painting of the Virgin Mary with elephant dung on it. After media attention to the content of the upcoming exhibit publicized this piece of art, the mayor released several public statements condemning the exhibit and the museum. He went so far as to threaten cuts in public funding to the Brooklyn Museum, dismissal of its board of trustees, and eviction from its city-owned building if the painting was not removed and the exhibit cancelled.[96]

As the controversy escalated, Giuliani became the number one spokesperson opposing the exhibit. Meanwhile, public opinion polls began to show that the residents of New York City viewed the mayor's efforts against the museum as a trivial waste of his time and the city's resources. One poll showed that 59 percent of respondents believed the museum should show the exhibit, whereas only 35 percent believed it should not. Only 27 percent agreed that the government should cut funding to the museum compared with 69 percent who felt government funding should not be reduced. New Yorkers overwhelmingly supported artistic freedom and the First Amendment regardless of whether or not they agreed with the content of the exhibit itself. Giuliani's handling of the museum controversy left him with a negative 31 percent approval rating among New Yorkers.[97]

According to some analysts, the media's influence on elected officials and the public is pernicious. Timothy E. Cook argued that members of Congress are less concerned with the public interest than with what will sell with the media.[98] Obsession with the way things appear in the press, he maintained, drives elected officials to search for overly simple answers to complicated questions. The need to explain one's position on television in thirty seconds encourages legislators to latch onto symbols and slogans, rather than to seek carefully crafted solutions.

A case in point is the federal "three strikes and you're out" laws passed as part of the 1994 Omnibus Crime Bill. The simplicity and potential impact of the "three strikes" approach appealed to the public: anyone who has been successfully prosecuted for three violent crimes is subject to a sentence of twenty-five years to life in federal prison. But the effectiveness of these laws is suspect, to say the least. First, very few violent crimes are prosecuted in federal courts. Second, judges are more likely to use the repeat-offender than the "three strikes" provisions in such cases, precisely because they give the judges more flexibility in sentencing.[99] Third, the "three strikes" laws have been used more often to target nonviolent offenders and have been used disproportionately against minorities. Finally, these laws have contributed to the backlog in the court system. Although the law received great approval among officials and voters during its passage, it has proven to be somewhat weak in actual results.[100]

The pervasive role of the media in shaping the public's view of politics helps explain why it is difficult to galvanize the public to support some issues. People trust and understand what they can see more than what they hear.[101] Thus identifiable villains and scenes of destruction help to make good stories. In the 1980s, government policies and the financial practices of hundreds of banking institutions led to a near collapse of the savings and loan industry and the costliest government financial rescue in the history of this country. Still, despite the enormous consequences, the mass media were very late in grasping the significance of what was going on. This seemed to be a classic example of how the media falter when a political and policy story cannot be reduced to the bare essentials of good guys and bad guys. According to one observer, "given its complexity and its lack of identifiable heroes, the S&L debacle may have become the inert issue of the 1990s."[102]

In contrast, when the media can readily sensationalize administrative shortcomings and the foibles of public officials, otherwise effective programs may be damaged and their base of public and political support eroded. Consider the media's role in the implementation of the Comprehensive Employment and Training Act.[103] The law called for CETA administrators to take on some nearly impossible tasks. Press accounts criticized the hiring of ineligible workers, blatant political patronage, and programs of doubtful value. Although such practices were the exception rather than the rule, the public and political officials responsible for its administration believed the program to be riddled with fraud, waste, and abuse. In reality CETA's problems were caused as much by congressional pressure to spend money too rapidly as they were by unscrupulous or incompetent administrators. Nevertheless, a negative image plagued CETA, and its public service jobs component was ultimately terminated.

The attitudes news organizations have toward government institutions and programs color their reporting. According to Lewis Wolfson, a former reporter and editor, the press is "not inherently interested in what's involved in developing a policy or administering a program or what impacts these decisions may have at the grass roots." If a policy fails, journalists "rush to discover what went wrong, looking more for incompetence or corruption than for shortcomings of the policy-making process that may have compromised the approach from the start."[104] In consequence, the public may be led down the path to ignorance rather than understanding.

Sometimes the consequences of this approach can be dire. By ridiculing the National Aeronautics and Space Administration (NASA) for failing to launch on schedule, the media may have contributed to the space shuttle disaster in 1986. Elected and appointed officials bristle at media criticism and try to avoid it. At times their thin skins cause irresponsible behavior, such as the decision to launch the *Challenger* despite warnings about faulty O-rings and inclement weather. On the evening of January 27, 1986, the television news networks announced that the launch had been delayed for a third time. Following are the remarks of Dan Rather of CBS on the decision to "scrub" the flight:

> Yet another costly, red-faces-all-around-space-shuttle-launch delay. This time a bad bolt on a hatch and bad weather bolt from the blue are being blamed. What's more, a rescheduled launch for tomorrow doesn't look good either. Bruce Hall has the latest on today's hi-tech low comedy.[105]

The other networks were equally harsh. And the *New York Times* described the situation as a "comedy of errors." The following morning NASA launched the space shuttle and seven astronauts perished. Ultimately, NASA must accept responsibility for the disaster. Its flight schedule was unrealistic, and it should have resisted pressure for a premature launch. The reality of media pressure is undeniable, however. As one NASA official put it:

> Every time there was a delay, the press would say, "Look, there's another delay. . . . Here's a bunch of idiots who can't even handle a launch schedule. . . ." You think that doesn't have an impact? If you think it doesn't, you're stupid.[106]

The media's relentless unfavorable portrayal of political institutions, public officials, and government programs fosters negative public attitudes about the public sector.[107] Media analyst Michael Robinson calls these feelings about the political world "video-malaise."[108] Cynical views about government and political figures are conveyed not only by news and public affairs programs but by soap operas and drama series as well.

Contempt for the political world is pervasive on entertainment television. There are very few television series in which political figures are cast in positive roles. Television regularly portrays "heroes" doing battle with evil politicians.

The Impacts of Initiatives and Referenda

In earlier sections we discussed the politics of getting proposals on the ballot and voted upon. Now we turn our attention to assessing the impact that initiatives and referenda have on public policy. Initiatives and referenda probably have had profound effects on the shape of social, political, and economic change. Voters have spoken against nuclear arms, nuclear waste, the sale of pornographic literature, crime, and drug use; and they have spoken in favor of stronger criminal penalties for the use of illegal substances, environmental protections, and term limits for public officials. Initiatives and the political fallout generated by them have restrained public spending. Voters have mandated expenditure limitations and tax policies that have altered the economies of more than a dozen states. Resources for public institutions, the poor, and minority groups have been cut, while property owners have retained a larger portion of their income. Voters in California have removed bilingual education from the state's public schools and abolished the use of affirmative action policies in the hiring of state employees and selecting applicants for college; voters in Alaska, Arizona, California, Nevada, and Oregon utilized the initiative to legalize the use of marijuana for medical purposes. Voters in many states have imposed campaign finance reform and term limits on their public officials. In recent years amendments concerning same-sex marriages have become prominent in many states.

Nuclear freeze referenda and initiatives clearly revealed the public's anxieties about a nuclear holocaust, but the measures have had little practical effect. Most freeze propositions required state and local officials to communicate with the president and Congress about the deployment of nuclear weapons. The initiatives did constitute a symbolic victory, however, and may have had some impact on the cold war debate.

Public officials often are unable to implement public ballot decisions because the decisions are not clear or call for significant policy adjustments.[109] In 1986 California's Proposition 65 required the state government to reduce substantially the flow of toxic chemicals into the state's water supply. During implementation, administrators found it extremely difficult to identify and classify all the chemicals that might harm the water supply, to determine safe standards, and finally to establish a system for monitoring thousands of chemical manufacturers and users. After more than five years of costly lawsuits to determine which substances the state would list as toxic, the impact of Proposition 65 finally began to be felt in California in the early 1990s.[110]

Like any other method of decision making, initiatives and referenda have their strengths and weaknesses.[111] On the positive side, initiatives give citizens an opportunity to raise issues that elected leaders and interest groups might just as soon ignore. Initiatives can also help overcome stalemates in the legislative process. Taking policy choices to the voters can be an effective method of legitimating controversial decisions. In the late 1990s initiatives were used to propose amendments concerning same-sex marriages in many states, to deal with the late-term abortion issue, and to confront the subject of the right to die or assisted suicide.

On the negative side, initiatives and referenda are blunt instruments. It is not possible to reduce complicated questions to one-line statements. Ballot questions—with the choices restricted to yes or no—lack the deliberation and accommodation of legislative institutions and administrative agencies. For example, California voters approved a proposition in 1987 that requires that at least 40 percent of the state's general funds go to the public schools. As a result, the flexibility of the legislature and the governor to respond to changing priorities is severely limited.

Moreover, initiatives and referenda may not be as sensitive to minorities as the courts might be. Evidence suggests that interest groups and political officials are seizing the tools of direct democracy to seek victories that they were unable to gain through mainstream institutions. The practice of direct democracy is becoming professionalized and costly and, therefore, may be moving beyond the reach of volunteers. Finally, the opportunity to evade difficult decisions may encourage irresponsible behavior by public officials. Rather than assume duties they were elected to perform, they may wait for voters to send a clear signal. By then it may be too late.

Summary

Living room politics is a unique, important, but often misunderstood part of democratic government. High school civics books and Independence Day speeches may exaggerate citizen control of the policy process, but many sophisticated observers also may underestimate the power the public wields in policymaking.

For most ordinary citizens, politics and public policy are another form of entertainment. They find it interesting to tune in now and then but not to stay tuned. From time to time, however, large segments of the public hold strong opinions on public issues, and an enraged, out-of-control public is a formidable threat to political stability. In full force, the power of public opinion and citizen participation has driven high officials from office, changed the course of American foreign and domestic policy, and stopped countless government proposals from ever getting off the ground.

The mass media are particularly important players in living room politics. Newspapers, television, and radio are the principal sources of information about politics and government for most Americans. The power of the media derives not from a conspiracy to lead American policy in a particular direction but from the fact that most people have no other way of conjuring up a political reality.

Legislators, chief executives, bureaucrats, corporate leaders, and even judges are sensitive to the need for public understanding and support because without it government can lose its legitimacy—the very foundation of governance. Public officials must not only understand but also manage public opinion in order to build support for their cherished programs and to maintain control of the political process.

Notes

1. W. Lance Bennett, *Public Opinion in American Politics* (New York: Harcourt Brace Jovanovich, 1980).
2. As quoted in Leo Bogart, *Polls and the Awareness of Public Opinion*, 2d ed. (New Brunswick, N.J.: Transaction Books, 1985), 3.
3. See, for example, W. Russell Neuman, *The Paradox of Mass Politics* (Cambridge: Harvard University Press, 1986); and Benjamin Ginsberg, *The Captive Public* (New York: Basic Books, 1986).
4. Martin Linsky, *Impact: How the Press Affects Federal Policymaking* (New York: W. W. Norton, 1986), 36–37.
5. E. E. Schattschneider, *The Semi-Sovereign People* (New York: Holt, Rinehart and Winston, 1960).
6. Neuman, *The Paradox of Mass Politics.*
7. Bureau of Labor Statistics, "Unemployment Rate, 1989–2000," online at http://www/bls.gov/wh/cpsbref3.htm, May 24, 2000.
8. The PEW Research Center for the People and the Press, "Compared to 1994: Voters Not So Angry, Not So Interested," June 1998, online at http://www.people-press.org/june98mor.htm, May 31, 2000.
9. "Health Care," *Polling Report,* May 24, 2000, online at http://www.pollingreport.com/health1.htm, May 24, 2000.
10. Gallup Organization, "Gallup Poll Topics: A–Z," online at http://www.gallup.com/poll/indicators/indtaxes.asp, May 24, 2000.
11. Richard A. Brody, "The Lewinsky Affair and Popular Support for Clinton," *Polling Report,* November 16, 1998, online at http://www.pollingreport.com/brody.htm, May 30, 2000.
12. Bureau of the Census, "Participation in Elections for President and U.S. Representatives: 1932 to 1998," *Current Population Reports,* Washington, D.C., 1999, P25–1085, online at http://www.lexis-nexis.com/statuniv, May 31, 2000.
13. The concepts of top-down and bottom-up public opinion are borrowed from Cliff Zukin of the Eagleton Institute of Politics at Rutgers University.
14. Bennett, *Public Opinion in American Politics.*
15. V. O. Key Jr., *Public Opinion and American Democracy* (New York: Knopf, 1961), 14.
16. Bennett, *Public Opinion in American Politics,* 367.
17. Robert Weissberg, *Public Opinion and Popular Government* (Englewood Cliffs, N.J.: Prentice-Hall, 1976), 213.

18. Richard E. Neustadt, *Presidential Power: The Politics of Leadership from FDR to Carter* (New York: John Wiley, 1980). See also Samuel Kernell, *Going Public* (Washington, D.C.: CQ Press, 1986).

19. See for example, George C. Edwards, Andrew Barrett, and Jeffrey Peake, "The Legislative Impact of Divided Government," *American Journal of Political Science* 41 (April 1997): 545.

20. Jennie Jacobs Kronenfeld, *The Changing Federal Role in U.S. Health Care Policy* (Westport, Conn.: Greenwood Publishing, Praeger, 1997), 15.

21. Haynes Johnson and David S. Broder, *The System: The American Way of Politics at the Breaking Point,* (Boston: Little, Brown, 1996), 623–633.

22. Kronenfeld, *The Changing Federal Role in U.S. Health Care Policy,* 120–133; Margaret Carlson, "Another Dose of Harry and Louise," *Time,* November 24, 1997, 24.

23. Office of the Governor, "Governor Outlines Progress in Fighting Illiteracy," May 2, 1997, online at http://www.governor.state.tx.us/message/records97/05-02-97illiteracy.html, May 22, 2000.

24. Neuman, *The Paradox of Mass Politics.*

25. Barry Commoner, "A Reporter at Large: The Environment," *New Yorker,* June 15, 1987, 46–71.

26. Bogart, *Polls and the Awareness of Public Opinion,* 198.

27. See Barry George Rabe, *Beyond NIMBY: Hazardous Waste Siting in Canada and the United States* (Washington, D.C.: Brookings Institution, 1994).

28. See, for example, Linsky, *Impact;* Stephen Hess, *The Ultimate Insiders: U.S. Senators and the National Media* (Washington, D.C.: Brookings Institution, 1986); and Austin Ranney, *Channels of Power: The Impact of Television on American Politics* (New York: Basic Books, 1985).

29. Leon V. Sigal, *Reporters and Officials: The Organization and Politics of Newsmaking* (Lexington, Mass.: D. C. Heath, 1973), 186.

30. Schattschneider, *The Semi-Sovereign People,* 2–3.

31. Donald L. Shaw and Maxwell E. McCombs, *The Emergence of American Political Issues: The Agenda-Setting Function of the Press* (St. Paul, Minn.: West Publishing, 1977).

32. Sigal, *Reporters and Officials,* 12.

33. See, for example, David E. Price, "Policymaking in Congressional Committees: The Impact of Environmental Factors," *American Political Science Review* 72 (June 1978): 548–574.

34. Linsky, *Impact,* 90.

35. Sigal, *Reporters and Officials;* Shaw and McCombs, *The Emergence of American Political Issues.*

36. Timothy E. Cook, "P.R. on the Hill: The Evolution of Congressional Press Operations," in *Legislative Politics,* ed. Chris Deering (Homewood, Ill.: Dorsey Press, 1989).

37. Gladys Engel Lang and Kurt Lang, *The Battle for Public Opinion: The President, the Press, and the Polls during Watergate* (New York: Columbia University Press, 1983), 58–61.

38. As quoted by Timothy E. Cook, "Marketing the Members: The Ascent of the Congressional Press Secretary" (paper presented at the annual meeting of the Midwest Political Science Association, Chicago, April 1985), 15.

39. Centers for Disease Control and Prevention, "Deaths: Final Data for 1997," *National Vital Statistics Reports,* June 30, 1999, http:www.cdc.gov/nchs/data/nvs47_19.pdf, May 30, 2000.

40. Edward Jay Epstein, *Between Fact and Fiction: The Problem of Journalism* (New York: Vintage Books, 1975).

41. Linsky, *Impact;* Sigal, *Reporters and Officials.*

42. Linsky, *Impact,* 94.

43. See, for example, Edward Jay Epstein, *News from Nowhere: Television and the News* (New York: Vintage Books, 1983); W. Lance Bennett, *News: The Politics of Illusion* (New York: Longman, 1983); and Sigal, *Reporters and Officials.*

44. Sigal, *Reporters and Officials,* 188.

45. Ibid., 186.

46. See, for example, "A Crusade Won, Then Forgotten," *Los Angeles Times,* August 27, 1999, B2.

47. Charles Babington, "Slim Majority Backs Clinton's Battle Plan," *Washington Post,* March 30, 1999, online at http://www.washingtonpost.com/wp-srv/politics/daily/march99/clinton30.htm, May 30, 2000.

48. Herbert J. Gans, *Deciding What's News* (New York: Pantheon Books, 1979).

49. Initiative and Referendum Institute (I&R Institute), "I&R Factsheet," online at http://www.iandrinstitute.org/factsheets/fs1.htm, May 18, 2000.

50. Ibid.

51. James K. Glassman, "Making Law at the Ballot Box," *Washington Post,* A17, November 3, 1998.

52. Ellen Torelle, comp., *The Political Philosophy of Robert M. La Follette* (Westport, Conn.: Hyperion, 1975), 173–174.

53. Michael Nelson, "Power to the People: The Crusade for Direct Democracy," in *The Clash of Issues,* 7th ed., ed. James Burkhart, Samuel Krislov, and Raymond L. Lee (Englewood Cliffs, N.J.: Prentice-Hall, 1981), 25–28.

54. I&R Institute, "I&R Factsheet."

55. Glassman, "Making Law at the Ballot Box."

56. Shaun Bowler, Todd Donovan, and Caroline J. Tolbert, eds., *Citizens as Legislators* (Columbus: Ohio State University Press, 1998), 7.

57. I&R Institute, "Initiatives and Referendum on the 1998 Ballot: Report Summary," *1998 Post Election Synopsis,* online at http://www.iandrinstitute.org/98post.htm, May 18, 2000.

58. Reported in "Liberals, Conservatives Share Initiative Success," *Public Administration Times,* February 15, 1985, 1, 12.

59. Joseph F. Zimmerman, *The Initiative: Citizen Law-Making* (Westport, Conn.: Greenwood Publishing, Praeger, 1999), 92.

60. Bowler, Donovan, and Tolbert, *Citizens as Legislators,* 91.

61. Ruth S. Jones, "Financing State Elections," in *Money and Politics in the United States,* ed. Michael J. Malbin (Chatham, N.J.: Chatham House, 1984), 206–207.

62. Manning J. Dauer and Mark Sievers, "The Constitutional Initiative: Problems in Florida Politics," in *State Government: CQ's Guide to Current Issues and Activities, 1986–1987,* ed. Thad Beyle (Washington, D.C.: Congressional Quarterly, 1986), 29–82.

63. David B. Magleby, *Direct Legislation: Voting on Ballot Propositions in the United States* (Baltimore: Johns Hopkins University Press, 1984).

268   **Politics and Public Policy**

64. Barnes, "Losing the Initiative," 2050–2051.
65. Zimmerman, *The Initiative*, 111.
66. Patrick B. McGuigan, *The Politics of Direct Democracy in the 1980s* (Washington, D.C.: Free Congress Research and Education Foundation, 1985), 93–106.
67. Ibid., 58–59.
68. Ibid., 63.
69. Doris Graber, "Say It with Pictures: The Impact of Audio-Visual News on Public Opinion Formation" (paper presented at the annual meeting of the Midwest Political Science Association, Chicago, April 1987).
70. David Halberstam, *The Powers That Be* (New York: Knopf, 1979); Peter Braestrup, *Big Story* (New York: Doubleday Anchor, 1978).
71. Peter M. Sandman and Mary Paden, "At Three Mile Island," in *Media Power in Politics,* ed. Doris Graber (Washington, D.C.: CQ Press, 1984), 267; Christopher Flavin, "Reassessing Nuclear Power," in *The State of the World, 1987,* ed. Lester R. Brown et al. (New York: W. W. Norton, 1987), 57–80.
72. Victor Cohn, "Fear of AIDS Is Spreading Faster than the Disease," *Washington Post,* national weekly edition, September 16, 1985, 37.
73. Dan Balz and Claudia Deane, "Poll: Most Oppose Continuing Trial," January 31, 1999, online at http://www.Washingtonpost.com/wp-sr...cial/clinton/stories/poll013199.htm, May 24, 2000.
74. Brody, "The Lewinsky Affair."
75. Richard Morin and Claudia Deane, "Public against Impeachment, but Clinton Support Has Limits," *Washingtonpost.com,* December 14, 1998, online at http://www.washingtonpost.com/wp-srv/po. . . cial/clinton/stories/poll121598.htm, May 30, 2000.
76. Brody, "The Lewinsky Affair."
77. Linsky, *Impact,* 84; see also David L. Protess et al., "The Impact of Investigative Reporting on Public Opinion and Policymaking Targeting Toxic Waste," *Public Opinion Quarterly* 51 (summer 1987): 166–185.
78. Linsky, *Impact,* 86.
79. This case study is adapted from Linsky, *Impact,* 71–78.
80. "Liberals, Conservatives Share Initiative Success," 1.
81. McGuigan, *The Politics of Direct Democracy,* 46.
82. Susan Hansen, "Extraction: The Politics of State Taxation," in *Politics in the American States,* ed. Virginia Gray, Herbert Jacob, and Kenneth N. Vines (Boston: Little, Brown, 1983), 441–442.
83. Ibid., 45–66.
84. Carol Matlack, "Where the Big Winner Was the Status Quo," *National Journal,* November 10, 1990, 2748–2749.
85. Zimmerman, *The Initiative*, 105–106.
86. David B. Magleby, "Legislatures and the Initiative: The Politics of Direct Democracy," *State Government,* spring 1986, 31–39.
87. William Gormley Jr., *The Politics of Public Utility Regulation* (Pittsburgh: University of Pittsburgh Press, 1983), 208.
88. I&R Institute, "Initiatives and Referendum on the 1998 Ballot, 1998," online at http://www.iandrinstitute.org/98post.htm, May 18, 2000.
89. As quoted in Barnes, "Losing the Initiative," 2047.

90. McGuigan, *The Politics of Direct Democracy;* and Patrick B. McGuigan, *Initiative and Referendum Report* (Washington, D.C.: Free Congress Education and Research Foundation, 1987).

91. I&R Institute, "Initiatives and Referendum on the 1998 Ballot."

92. McGuigan, *The Politics of Direct Democracy,* 67–92.

93. See, for example, Rufus P. Browning, Dale Rogers Marshall, and David H. Tabb, *Protest Is Not Enough: The Struggle of Blacks and Hispanics for Equality in Urban Politics* (Berkeley: University of California Press, 1984).

94. Commoner, "A Reporter at Large"; Daniel A. Mazmanian and Jeanne Nienaber, *Can Organizations Change? Environmental Protection, Citizen Participation, and the Corps of Engineers* (Washington, D.C.: Brookings Institution, 1979); and Lynton Caldwell, Lynton R. Hayes, and Isabel M. MacWhirter, *Citizens and the Environment* (Bloomington: Indiana University Press, 1976).

95. Margaret Loftus, "A Swoosh under Siege," *U.S. News & World Report,* April 12, 1999, 40.

96. Stephanie Cash, "'Sensation' Battle Erupts in Brooklyn," *Art in America,* November 1999, 37.

97. Quinnipiac University Polling Institute, "New York City Voters Solidly Back Artistic Freedom," *New York City Surveys,* October 20, 1999, online at http://www.quinnipiac.edu/news/polls/nycpolls.html, May 31, 2000.

98. Cook, "P.R. on the Hill."

99. Kelly McCurry, "'Three-Strikes' Laws Proving More Show than Go," *Trial,* January 1997.

100. Marc Mauer, "Three Strikes Policy Is Just a Quick-Fix Solution," *Corrections Today,* July 1996.

101. Graber, "Say It with Pictures."

102. James A. Barnes, "Pinning the Blame," *National Journal,* September 22, 1990, 2259–2263.

103. See Donald C. Baumer and Carl E. Van Horn, *The Politics of Unemployment* (Washington, D.C.: CQ Press, 1989), 198–199.

104. Lewis Wolfson, *The Untapped Power of the Press: Explaining Government to People* (New York: Praeger, 1986).

105. As quoted by David Ignatius, "Maybe the Media Did Push NASA to Launch the Challenger," *Washington Post,* national weekly edition, April 14, 1986, 19.

106. Ibid.

107. Linsky, *Impact,* 146–147.

108. Michael J. Robinson, "Public Affairs Television and the Growth of Political Malaise: The Case of the 'Selling of the Pentagon,'" *American Political Science Review* 70 (June 1976): 409–432.

109. Magleby, "Legislatures and the Initiative."

110. Robert Guskind, "Big Green Light," *National Journal,* October 6, 1990, 2403.

111. Magleby, *Direct Legislation.*

Chapter 9 Institutional Performance

Politicians and ordinary citizens in the United States believe that properly structured political institutions are essential to freedom, democracy, and prosperity. The Constitution reflects this view in that it prescribes certain relationships among these institutions and between them and the citizens. Characteristic of the political culture of the United States is an unquestioning support for the election of legislatures and chief executives, an independent judiciary, and federalism. Despite the symbolic reverence for government institutions, they are continually examined and criticized by citizens and politicians alike. Explanations and evaluations of the government's performance are another political tradition.

The principal observations and conclusions offered in Chapters 3 through 8 provide a useful starting point for an explanation of institutional performance.

1. Corporations focus primarily on one goal, company profits, and boardroom politics is highly centralized—dominated by top executive officers—although pressure is growing to increase the number of actors involved and to consider other goals. Corporate decisions, made privately, have far-reaching consequences for society.

2. Bureaucracies like to define issues so that they are compatible with standard methods of operation. Policy decisions are made at various levels in the organization by administrative officials who are subject to many outside influences, including legislative committees, interest groups, chief executives, and courts. The standards for bureaucratic decisions are often explicit, but they can be quickly and dramatically changed by outsiders.

3. Legislatures react to many issues but are often slow to make decisions. Decision making is decentralized and subject to many influences, most notably well-organized, well-financed interests. Majorities rule when they are assembled, but the institutional structure of most American legislatures does not encourage the formation of decisive working majorities. Issue characteristics and contextual factors have a great impact on whether decisions are incremental, innovative, gridlocked, or symbolic, and on whether the decision-making process is slow or rapid, decentralized or centralized.

4. Chief executives address highly visible issues and dominate public perceptions about government, but the policy significance of a chief executive's term may be quite different from its image. The essence of chief executive leadership is the ability to persuade other policymakers, especially

legislators, to transform chief executive priorities into policy. This part of the policy process is always difficult, even for presidents making foreign policy.

5. Courts consider a more restricted range of issues but are capable of taking decisive policy actions that sometimes have significant effects on society. The politics of judicial policymaking is controlled by clear, specific procedures and criteria. The independence of the courts is rarely challenged.

6. Public opinions are influential in American politics. When highly salient issues are the subject of debate, the public may directly change public policy by acting through grassroots organizations and expressing opinions via initiatives or referenda. But there are also instances in which public opinions are manipulated by media elites and government officials. The public, therefore, can be an active agent of democracy or a fairly weak, passive part of the policy process. Although it would be going too far to assert that media and governmental elites conspire to keep the public passive, political elites enjoy much more latitude in their policy actions when the public is passive.

Do these disparate observations form some larger picture? The answer is that American political institutions reflect rather faithfully their historical and philosophical roots. Their performance can be explained fairly well by reference to the free market/procedural democracy model of politics discussed in Chapter 2. American political institutions perform different roles in striving to uphold the basic principles of the market paradigm and the ideals of procedural democracy. Understanding these differences is the key to explaining institutional behavior. Boardroom politics and living room politics expand the system's repertoire of policymaking processes in interesting and important ways, some of which push the political process beyond the limits of procedural democracy.

An Analysis of Conventional Political Institutions

Most political scientists would agree that the legislative, executive, and judicial branches of government represent core political institutions. In thinking about the executive branch, it is useful to distinguish between chief executives and the bureaucracy. Indeed, some argue that the bureaucracy represents a de facto "fourth branch" of government. But we have warned that it is not enough to consider the branches of government. Both corporations and citizens exercise considerable influence in American politics, and much of that influence has been institutionalized. Thus our appraisal of America's political institutions encompasses both conventional and unconventional political institutions.

Courts and Legislatures

This analysis begins with a comparison of two very different political institutions: the Supreme Court and Congress. The Court acts on the basis of a philosophical view of procedural democracy; Congress understands procedural democracy on a more personal level. Why has the Court been the political institution most inclined to act decisively to secure the rights of disadvantaged minorities? The reason is that the Supreme Court justices, in their role as interpreters of the Constitution, have been forced to define in legal terms what the main principles of this document mean in specific circumstances. The nature of the judicial process—using written opinions to establish precedents that guide future decisions—induces justices to take a philosophical look at constitutional principles. The logic of the Constitution is derived from a school of thought that places importance on certain procedural values. In the case of disadvantaged minorities, the guiding principle is equality of opportunity, and the specific means to achieve equality of opportunity are the equal protection and due process clauses of the Fourteenth Amendment. The context in which the Court makes decisions, and the process employed, encourage it to be decisive about the core principles of procedural democracy.

Supreme Court interpretations of constitutional principles have done a great deal for advantaged minorities as well as the disadvantaged. This outcome of Court decision making can be seen as another indication of the pervasiveness of the market paradigm, which discourages a distinction between market participants. An interesting example of the Court's adherence to market principles is the freedom granted to the press. The press has continually invoked the Constitution on behalf of its right to publish or display all sorts of misleading and distasteful material. Anyone who has stood in a check-out line at a grocery store can testify to the alluring, but false, headlines used by some newspapers and magazines. By defining libel and slander restrictively, the Court has allowed the press to continue printing sensational material. The courts believe there should be a marketplace of ideas in a free society and that valid ideas persist and invalid ideas perish in such a setting. Therefore, the Court protects and promotes economic and information markets.

The Court's strength depends on its adherence to the central principles of the Constitution, and the Court is generally reluctant to increase the number or expand the meaning of these principles. When the Court breaks new constitutional ground, however, as it has on civil rights and abortion, it is difficult for it to ignore subsequent cases pursuing related questions. Despite a tradition of deference to the political branches, the Court has shown an increasing willingness to overturn laws enacted by Congress and signed by the president. In the past five years alone, the Court invalidated twenty-four acts of Congress.[1] The overturned laws include gun control legislation, the Violence Against Women Act, and legislation granting the line-item veto to the president. When the Court strikes down legislation of this magnitude, it sends a powerful message to the political branches of the federal government. In effect, that message is that the Court is the ultimate arbiter of what can and cannot be done in government.

The Court must understand the rules of procedural democracy because it is its principal guardian. To perform this guardianship well, it must be somewhat removed from popular passions. Citizens and politicians often fail to grasp some of the unpleasant nuances of procedural democracy—for example, that angry Americans have the right to burn their nation's flag to protest policies they oppose. The Court is not a very good vehicle for popular participation, although class action suits and other advocacy efforts have made it a forum in which some popular causes have been advanced. The Court will never lead the way to radical social changes such as wealth redistribution, public ownership of industry, or income guarantees, but it sometimes forces the system to live up to its ideals, as when it required that public schools admit children of all racial backgrounds.

The market paradigm fits well with cloakroom politics. Citizens register their preferences for representatives who then try to give their constituents what they want at the lowest political cost. Those who are successful in retaining elected offices are, in most cases, efficient producers of political goods. Citizen preferences can be expressed individually or through political parties or interest groups. It is not surprising that citizens are wary of political parties. So were our Founding Fathers. But congressional political parties reasserted themselves in the 1990s, when both parties became more cohesive. During the brief tenure of Newt Gingrich as Speaker of the House, the House Republican Party resembled the parties of western Europe in its emphasis on orthodoxy, loyalty, and discipline. In general, however, Congress remains more receptive to interest groups than to political parties. Interest groups are effective, aggressive, and persistent; they operate as if politics were a market in which each person's pursuit of self-interest is justified because it is part of a system that maximizes collective welfare. The idea that interest group competition produces policies that serve the public interest is accepted by some political scientists.[2] But some interests, it seems, will always be unrepresented or underrepresented. Unfortunately, broad, diffuse interests are less likely to be represented because they are more difficult to organize.[3]

Why does Congress specialize in policies that carry particularized benefits, created in decentralized settings where interest groups are accepted participants? Why is meaningful congressional policy action difficult to bring about on matters that do not carry clear benefits for constituents? One answer is that the legislative version of the market paradigm encourages such behavior. Like businesses in a market, legislators like to make a profit, and their profits are measured in votes. To secure comfortable electoral margins, they hand out benefits. Who gets the benefits? Those who can pay with money or votes. Another answer is that the very organization of Congress facilitates responsiveness to relatively narrow geographic or policy interests. Always decentralized, Congress became even more so during the 1970s. Decentralization provides multiple opportunities for special interests to plead their case. If the head of one congressional subcommittee won't listen, perhaps the head of another will. Nor is strong party leadership necessarily an antidote to such behavior. Parties can advance their cause by promoting some version of the public interest or by defining the public interest as the sum total of diverse special interests. When the latter happens, strong party leadership and strong interest group politics become indistinguishable in practice.

It is alleged that one of the advantages of a free market economic system is its self-correcting tendency. If producers churn out too much of a product, its price falls; then new buyers are attracted, and eventually the price stabilizes. If only a little is produced of a product people want, its high price attracts the interest of potential producers. Periods of vigorous consumer spending generate rising prices and high levels of production, which eventually result in overstocked inventories and falling prices. These self-correcting factors are not purely automatic; rather, they are linked to government monetary and fiscal policies. But what about political markets? Are they self-correcting?

Recent American history suggests that congressional self-correction mechanisms do not function very well. Congress practiced dispensing benefits in exchange for votes from the 1950s through the late 1970s. Federal spending and taxes grew to the point that they became highly salient issues. Deficit spending provided a temporary refuge, but soon the deficits ballooned and threatened our nation's economy. Various reforms were tried, but most of them failed, leaving a legacy of bitterness and frustration. In 1993 President Bill Clinton persuaded Congress to take the first significant steps toward eliminating the budget deficit. Eight years later, as Clinton left office, the federal government at long last was enjoying a robust surplus. But Congress was dragged kicking and screaming to this outcome. For example, the historic deficit reduction legislation of 1993 became law only after Vice President Al Gore cast a tie-breaking vote in the Senate. Just as free markets do not always work as they are supposed to because entry is restricted, or because consumer knowledge is imperfect, political markets also have flaws. Voter knowledge of issues and candidates is not what it should be. Some groups, such as the poor, are not represented in a way that reflects their numerical significance. Some politicians engage in deceptive advertising and get away with it. Because elected politicians establish the rules of politics, it is not surprising that they use the rules for their own advantage and distort political markets. Political reform is always needed in a system that depends on periodic corrections of destructive tendencies.

Chief Executives and the Bureaucracy

The bureaucracy resembles the courts in some ways and the legislatures in others. It resembles the courts in having formal and specific decision-making criteria, although not so specific or complete as to eliminate discretion. The courts have laws, the Constitution, and legal precedents to guide their decisions, and bureaucratic agencies have written statutes and rules. The agencies resemble legislatures because they are highly vulnerable to politics. Agencies can be battered by interest groups, legislators, chief executives, or judges, and their vulnerability has led them to assume a defensive posture toward the outside world. Standard operating procedures, public hearings, advisory committees, and cost-benefit analyses are all forms of defense. Even innovation is usually a response to a threatening political environment.

American bureaucracies are highly political, not because they want to be, but because they are forced to be in order to defend themselves against stronger political institutions. Many political scientists have confirmed the vitality of principal-agent theory, which postulates that bureaucratic agents respond favorably to political principals.[4] Bureaucratic officials know they cannot succeed if they offend powerful interests, and they need to know where they stand with the legislature and the office of the chief executive. Agencies are increasingly conscious of their public image, but administrative policymakers cannot depend on voter satisfaction alone. They must be prepared—with defensible procedures and services—in case political head-hunters demand action or accountability. Even mighty agencies, such as the Internal Revenue Service, are quickly humbled when political principals decide to flex their muscles.

Chief executives are the principal promoters of majoritarian rule in American politics. They are the main corrective force against the potentially harmful effects of fragmentation toward which legislatures drift if left to their own devices. Chief executives often try to define a public interest that is separate and distinguishable from the sum of the parochial interests. They set certain goals—a cleaner environment, better schools, less poverty—and try to figure out ways to achieve them. The problem is that they have limited authority to act on their own, and persuading legislators to follow a clear and consistent policy path is extremely difficult.

The nature of this difficulty should be apparent by now. Legislators have their own relationships with voters and they do not like having them disrupted by chief executives. Legislators sometimes can be convinced that departure from their cherished mode of operation—giving subsidies to those who are organized—is necessary if a crisis is to be avoided, but they require a good deal of proof that conditions warrant such extraordinary action; they also need to be skillfully coaxed and made aware of public pressure. Some chief executives are able to provide the proof, the coaxing, and the pressure; others are not.

The strength of chief executives lies in their ability to command attention. Their efforts to assemble ruling coalitions and resolve crises provide much of the action and drama in politics, and the mass media find action and drama irresistible. People identify with chief executives and, for the most part, with their legislators, but not with the legislature as a whole. This interest and loyalty give chief executives a certain amount of leverage that can be used to pursue policy objectives. The greatest weakness of chief executives is their lack of power, influence, and authority over other political elites, which stems from the independence of government institutions and the weak party system. Although chief executives have some ability to act independently, through executive orders, they must usually exercise their power to persuade.[5]

The strength of the bureaucracy lies in its staying power. Bureaucracies are essential to the operation of government, and elected officials recognize this when they stop to think about it. Bureaucracies can be decisive, even innovative, but most show a marked preference for stability and continuity. The weakness of bureaucratic agencies is their formal and informal subservience to political institutions and interests. They can usually defend themselves against abolition, but they have to be constantly on their guard. The Reagan administration was unable to eliminate two cabinet-level departments, but the Clinton administration successfully reduced the size of the federal bureaucracy by 17 percent. Some critics, such as political scientist Donald Kettl, doubt that a leaner bureaucracy is necessarily a better bureaucracy.[6] If the size of the federal bureaucracy is reduced, the odds are that key functions will be performed by state bureaucracies and private contractors. When bureaucratic agents depend on other agents to carry out vital tasks, their performance may suffer unless they become adept at oversight and contract management.[7]

Alternatives to Conventional Politics

Politics and public policies are not simply produced by government institutions. Private institutions also shape public policy, as do individual citizens and grassroots organizations. Boardroom politics and living room politics reflect contrasting philosophical principles and cultural values.

For most corporate decision makers the market paradigm is the world view of utmost importance. They have no doubt about the value of the pursuit of private gain because it is accepted as an essential part of a system that maximizes social welfare by translating free market competition into overall economic efficiency and productivity. This world view is part of what enables corporate decision makers to lay off thousands of reliable, skilled workers in Michigan, Pennsylvania, and Texas while they commit funds to new automobile and steel plants in Mexico, Taiwan, and South Korea. They argue that market forces should dictate wages, plant locations, and, ultimately, living patterns. Many corporate leaders understand that markets can be cruel to human beings, and they sympathize with the plight of their workers.

Rhetoric and reality are frequently at odds in the boardroom. Government intervention is abhorred when it costs money, but eloquently defended when it protects or subsidizes. Herbert Simon's pioneering work on corporate decision making demonstrates that private sector decision making is neither simple nor automatic.[8] Economic theory holds that businesses attempt to maximize their profits. Simon showed that in practice, large corporations with many decision makers normally choose options that satisfy as many interests as possible, rather than seek optimal profits in every circumstance. In this way, corporations resemble legislatures and public bureaucracies because bargaining and accommodation figure in their decision making. This kind of decision making is found particularly in publicly owned corporations, those that are subject to a great deal of government regulation, and those that are controlled by public officials. In such institutions decision makers are sometimes forced to confront the fact that the pursuit of private gain and the enhancement of society's well-being may not be synonymous.

"We the people," the opening phrase of the Constitution, conveys an unmistakable message: government should be controlled by the citizenry. Certain Americans throughout the nation's existence have taken this message seriously. They have attempted to make the public an active instrument of policymaking, to establish a more participatory mode of democracy. Their successes—town meetings, initiatives, referenda, recall, grassroots movements—add important elements to American politics. Clearly, many Americans believe there is an important difference between pursuing private gain and serving organized interests, and the achievement of collective well-being. Because of this belief, living room politics is very much alive.

Living room politics, in its ideal form, comprises those occasions when politicians take a back seat to citizens, when popular feelings are registered in a clear, unmistakable way. This activism is what Jean-Jacques Rousseau saw as essential to democracy, and what contemporary advocates of participatory democracy would like to see strengthened in American politics. It would be naive to think that the dominant forces could be removed from any arena of politics, however. The mass media and communication technology have shown themselves to be both friend and foe of democratic reformers and activists. The media reach people, but they also bring their own priorities, procedures, and prejudices to the information they transmit. Grassroots leaders and mainstream politicians sometimes find, to their mutual surprise, that they have much in common because they both have to deal with the media to succeed, and they at times find this difficult and frustrating.

Direct democracy is easily perverted by demagoguery or captured by elite interests because symbolism and showmanship are so much a part of its practice in modern societies. Living room politics springs from the genuinely democratic impulse to allow people to determine the rules under which they will live. But we must be ever mindful of the gap between the ideal and reality in politics. Just as real markets are often woefully inadequate representations of the free market paradigm, initiatives, referenda, and grassroots movements can be a far cry from the ideals of unitary or strong democracy.[9]

Performance Appraisal

The preceding brief analysis of American political institutions shows that these institutions are driven by philosophical principles, constitutional prescriptions, cultural traditions, and economic forces. Here the focus shifts to evaluation. How well do American political institutions work? Should Americans be satisfied with their performance? One way of approaching these questions is to take a broad look at society and examine how satisfied people are with it. American society has both positive and negative characteristics:

- individual freedom of thought, movement, religion, lifestyle, and consumption
- widespread prosperity, but a persistent underclass
- real and symbolic violence
- great cultural, educational, residential, and aesthetic diversity
- a materialistic, pragmatic value orientation
- a pervasive belief in the importance of individual and group competition
- a tradition that people have a recognized right to participate in politics

Some positive aspects of institutional behavior were pointed out in Chapters 3 through 8. Corporate boards are more representative and less incestuous than they used to be; some companies are innovative and public-spirited. Modern bureaucracies are seldom "captured" by narrow interests, and most listen to a wide variety of interests. Chief executives can be powerful agents of change and usually are given the leeway they need to be effective in crises. Even legislatures are capable of achieving major breakthroughs when political and economic conditions are ripe. The courts address some of society's most troublesome controversies in a forthright and reasonable manner, and they can, over time, foster significant changes. Public opinion, once aroused, has played a constructive role in disputes over foreign involvement, environmental protection, and presidential impeachment.

Those who want a society that is more cohesive, peaceful, humanistic, cooperative, and democratic would be inclined to give American political institutions a less favorable overall evaluation. But such critics would acknowledge that the dominant forces in society—legal, social, political, and economic—have been pushing in a direction that is quite different from one they advocate; that is, toward a strong private sector and a government that acts cautiously to correct the problems that private sector competition leaves behind. American political institutions were not designed to be strong enough to chart an independent course for national development because the Founders feared what unchecked political institutions might do.

Nevertheless, Americans generally impose high standards of performance on their political institutions. They expect them to be open, efficient, and caring, in part because politicians make inflated claims about what government can accomplish. When the institutions fail to live up to these expectations (as they frequently do), citizens become disappointed, cynical, and distrustful.

These attitudes are reinforced by media attention to corruption in government. Coverage of allegations, investigations, indictments, and convictions conveys the sense that corruption is widespread in American government. In the 1980s some top officials of the Reagan administration were investigated, and in some cases removed, for committing improprieties or illegalities. Two Clinton administration cabinet members were accused of felonies, and one, Henry Cisneros, admitted to one of the accusations.[10] Republican Speaker of the House Newt Gingrich was rebuked by his colleagues for improprieties involving a lucrative book contract; weakened, he later resigned. Ironically, Gingrich had played a major role in toppling Democratic Speaker of the House Jim Wright, who resigned in 1989 because of questionable financial arrangements and practices. Although there is far less corruption in the United States than in, for example, China, corruption persists and can have significant effects on government.

In addition to facing a demanding audience, government institutions confront many difficult problems. Some of these problems, such as poverty, unemployment, pollution, and crime, may be virtually unsolvable in a society with a dominant private sector and an ever-changing economy. But these are matters with which government is expected to grapple. The number of intractable problems at the top of the agenda seems to be increasing rather than decreasing, however. The New Deal bit off some of the easier problems: providing a reasonable income for the elderly and the disabled, guaranteeing worker rights, and building a physical infrastructure for economic development. Since the 1960s, the government has directed attention and money to the more difficult problems, such as poverty, but the returns have been disappointing. Although poverty declined during the Johnson administration, it increased during the Reagan and Bush administrations.[11] Fortunately, it declined under President Clinton.[12] As policymakers have become more committed to balanced budgets, they find themselves less able to attack such social problems as poverty, inadequate health care, and global warming.

Americans are fixers. If something is not working properly, the American instinct is to find a cure, usually through technology. This fix-it mentality is evident in almost every aspect of American life, including government and politics. Perceived malfunctions of government generate suggestions for reform. Americans, therefore, have established a civil service to correct the evils of the spoils system; created regulatory agencies to curb private sector abuses; reorganized the executive branch to make departments more responsive to chief executive preferences; and instituted initiative and referendum procedures to make government more responsive to citizens. There is an obvious and natural link between performance assessments and proposals for institutional reform.

Assessing institutional performance on the basis of broad societal outcomes—how healthy, wealthy, and wise a society is—leads to endless debates of questions that are difficult to answer with any precision. For this reason, it is necessary to introduce some guidelines and standards into an evaluative discussion. Six criteria of political institutions—stability, representativeness, responsiveness, public awareness, efficiency, and competence—are identified as positive characteristics in the discussion that follows.

Stability

Government stability may be the most important standard by which to judge the success or failure of political institutions, and the American system would get high marks on anyone's stability scale. From a world perspective, the peaceful transfer of power from one regime, usually defined by its leader, to the next is still one of the most difficult problems for countries to solve. The U.S. constitutional prescriptions regarding presidential succession have passed all tests, including the Watergate crisis, with flying colors. Furthermore, when the institutions are unresponsive to strongly felt public desires, there are other mechanisms, such as living room politics, through which discontent can be expressed without threatening the stability of the system. The Founders believed that having a stable government was more important than having an enlightened one, and the performance of American institutions has generally reflected this priority.

State constitutions have also proved quite durable. For example, the Colorado constitution dates back to 1876, and the Kansas constitution was ratified in 1859.[13] And many newer constitutions bear a close resemblance to their predecessors. At the state level, as at the federal level, the basics of institutional design, such as three branches of government and a bicameral legislature (except in Nebraska), remain intact.

Economic markets are not expected to be stable in the same way that governments are. Indeed, the private sector is supposed to be dynamic, innovative, and ever changing. But changing private sector markets can have profoundly painful human consequences, and liberal reformers have sought to smooth the rough edges of business cycles through economic planning and joint public and private ventures. Few of these reforms have ever been implemented. Instead the federal government provides modest and temporary financial assistance to individuals and communities who suffer when the economy changes. Thus the worker who loses his or her job as a bank teller when two banks consolidate may receive up to six months of unemployment insurance—partial income replacement. Or the truck driver who loses his or her job when a manufacturing business moves from Texas to Mexico may receive assistance in preparing for another job. Such policies are also appreciated by community leaders and businesses because they have a stabilizing effect. In other words, they encourage people to stay in their communities rather than to move elsewhere.

Stability, of course, can be a mixed blessing. The same political and cultural factors that facilitate constitutional stability also discourage policy change. Still, it is useful to distinguish between regime stability and other forms of continuity. Most students of comparative politics would agree that the United States is fortunate to have avoided the frequent political upheavals that have wracked countries in Africa, Asia, Europe, and Latin America.

Representativeness

A simple way of approaching the representativeness of political institutions is to ask: Who gets into policymaking circles and who does not? The answer to this question has been that well-educated white professional men, especially lawyers, tend to get in; women, blacks, the poor, and those with limited education do not. Despite years of effort to change the skewed demographic composition of policymaking groups, limited progress has been made. That public officials are better educated than the average citizen is not surprising, and it is not a primary concern of most critics. But other aspects of the leadership profile are troubling.

Women are underrepresented in every institutional arena. They constitute 13 percent of the U.S. Senate and 13.5 percent of the U.S. House of Representatives.[14] Only three of our nation's governors are women. In the private sector, women hold only 11 percent of the seats on boards of directors in the Fortune 500.[15] On the positive side, female representation has improved in both the public and private sectors. For example, the number of Fortune 500 companies with at least one woman board director increased by 21 percent from 1993 to 1999, and the number of Fortune 500 companies with multiple women directors grew by 34 percent from 1994 to 1999.[16] In politics, women have made substantial gains in state legislatures and city councils. In 2000, 22.5 percent of the nation's state legislators were women, a sharp increase from 4 percent in 1969.[17] Women are also better represented in state bureaucracies and as the heads of state bureaucracies. In 1994, 22 percent of state agency heads were female, a dramatic increase from 2 percent in 1964.[18]

Blacks (12 percent of the population) and Hispanics (also 12 percent) have made some progress, although some glaring representation gaps persist. Blacks have been elected to 5 percent of the state legislative seats.[19] Blacks constitute 5 percent of state agency heads, better than thirty years earlier, not better than ten years earlier.[20] In 1999, Hispanics represented fewer than 1 percent of all elected officials in the United States, although they did constitute 4 percent of the membership of the House of Representatives.[21] Like women, blacks and Hispanics are still virtually absent from the tops of corporate hierarchies, but they have made significant advances in middle management; about one-third of all corporate boards have a minority member. A bright spot in minority representation is the steady election of black and Hispanic mayors. Michael White of Cleveland, Ronald Kirk of Dallas, Dennis Archer of Detroit, Lee Brown of Houston, Marc Morial of New Orleans, Willie Brown of San Francisco, and Anthony Williams of Washington, D.C., are among the nation's black mayors. Interestingly, there is no black governor today.

Women and ethnic minorities still face an uphill struggle in obtaining policymaking positions. This situation is long-standing and will likely improve as the pool of women and minorities with the qualifications traditionally sought for top institutional positions—advanced degrees, relevant work experience, and favorable references—gradually expands.[22] Still, the preferences and commitments of those making appointments can make a big difference. Jimmy Carter made the appointment of more women and blacks to the federal courts a priority, and 30 percent of his appointments went to these groups. Ronald Reagan did not share this commitment; less than 15 percent of his court appointments went to women and blacks, although he did appoint the first woman to the Supreme Court.[23] On average, George Bush appointed more blacks to the federal bench than Ronald Reagan (including Clarence Thomas, whom he appointed to the Supreme Court), but fewer than Jimmy Carter. Like Carter, Bill Clinton appointed a substantial number of women and blacks to the federal bench. As of June 1999, 18 percent of Clinton's district court appointees and 10 percent of his circuit court appointees were black.[24]

The selection processes are obviously different for elected officials. A critical problem for women is recruitment—getting women into state and local party organizations, getting some of them elected to state and local offices, and then supporting female candidacies for more visible, powerful offices. Racial prejudice seems an important reason blacks are not selected. White voters have shown a clear, sustained disinclination to vote for black candidates at all levels of government. For the most part, black candidates win only where blacks are the majority or near majority of voters, as in certain big cities.

Responsiveness

Democratic political systems are supposed to be responsive to popular needs and preferences. Critics fault the U.S. government for not being more responsive to problems such as the spread of AIDS, ozone depletion, soaring medical costs, and homelessness. Many would argue that the government has a responsibility to take the lead in diagnosing and making plans to avert potential catastrophes because the private sector cannot be relied on to do so. Judgments about which problems are the most important at any given time are difficult to make with certainty, however. Some problems turn out to be less serious than they first appeared, and government institutions are seen as justified in having given them scant attention. Moreover, small steps may eventually yield substantial returns. Still, it seems to many that major American institutions often ignore problems for which no popular and easy solution is apparent, and they do so to the detriment of society as a whole.

Political scientists disagree on just how responsive governments have been, partly because of differences in how responsiveness is defined. If responsiveness is defined in broad ideological terms, then governments do tend to be responsive to public opinion. For example, Robert Erikson, Gerald Wright, and John McIver found that state governments with more liberal voters tend to adopt more liberal policies.[25] Similarly, shifts in public opinion at the national level often result in changes in national policy that are roughly consistent with such shifts. According to Benjamin Page and Robert Shapiro, public opinion and public policy are congruent at the national level for approximately two-thirds of all domestic and foreign issues.[26] According to James Stimson, Michael MacKuen, and Robert Erikson, national public policy has shifted in a liberal direction as the electorate has become more liberal, in a conservative direction as the electorate has become more conservative.[27] As Stimson and his colleagues put it, "When the public asks for a more activist or a more conservative government, politicians oblige."[28]

Still, it is easy enough to cite gross disparities between the public's policy preferences and public policy at any given point in time. For example, the public has long supported tough national gun control legislation, and by wide margins, but has seldom gotten it. When Congress did pass significant gun control legislation, known as the Brady Bill, that law was invalidated by the Supreme Court.[29] More broadly, Alan Monroe has argued that national government policies were less consistent with public opinion during the 1980s and the 1990s than they were during the preceding two decades.[30] At the state level, the voters of many states support school vouchers, but only a handful of states have adopted them. In most instances, limited responsiveness to public opinion means substantial responsiveness to powerful interest groups. Which is more legitimate? Political scientists disagree. Although public opinion polls capture the views of all Americans, they do not take preference intensity into account.

Where gaps exist between public opinion and public policy, one explanation is our campaign finance system. Critics allege that politicians have to spend so much of their time attending to money matters—giving speeches to donor groups, attending fund-raisers, meeting with contributors, planning media promotions—that they have little time for the public's business. This problem is prevalent at the national and state levels. For most politicians, simply maintaining their positions in the highly competitive political world is almost a full-time job. In such an environment, politicians may be responsive to money, but to little else.

A variety of campaign finance reform proposals have been advanced and considered by Congress since the mid-1980s, but only one fairly modest measure has been enacted into law. In 2000, after waging a spirited but unsuccessful bid for the presidency, Sen. John McCain, R-Ariz., was able to persuade his colleagues in Congress to pass a campaign disclosure bill, which requires that the names of contributors to organizations operating under Section 527 of the federal tax code be disclosed.[31] That legislation in effect forces organizations that spend soft money to support a particular political campaign to disclose expenditures larger than $500 and donations larger than $200. But it neither eliminates nor limits soft money, as the more significant McCain-Feingold bill would do. Even without unreported expenditures, the Federal Election Commission estimated that $3 billion would be spent on federal election campaigns in 2000.[32]

If one of the principal concerns about campaign financing is the advantage incumbents have in raising money and getting reelected, then imposing limitations on the number of terms members of Congress can serve might be an attractive reform. Indeed, this idea gained popularity in the early 1990s, as several states (California, Colorado, and Oklahoma) passed term limitation proposals in referenda and President Bush publicly endorsed it.[33] A potential disadvantage of this reform is the possibility that Congress would be less able to compete with presidents in battles over public policy because of a lack of seasoned legislators. Indeed, such concerns have already arisen at the state level, where eighteen states have authorized term limits for state legislators. In each of these states, legislative turnover has deprived the state legislature (and the public) of knowledgeable, experienced policymakers who were not permitted to run for another term.

Efforts to make corporations more responsive have included citizen protests and lobbying efforts by unions, churches, public interest groups, and grassroots organizations. These protests have brought to the attention of corporate managers and boards, politicians, and the public such examples of corporate abuse and social irresponsibility as conduct of business operations in South Africa, discrimination against blacks and women, and the exposure of workers and the public to dangerous chemicals. Many of these efforts have stimulated changes in corporate policy and, perhaps more important, have served to politicize corporations. The once sedate stockholder meetings have been turned into forums for discussions of a wide range of political and social issues and of shareholder or proxy resolutions.

This movement has spawned numerous corporate reform proposals, most of which aim to make managers more accountable to individual and institutional investors and to the public. These proposals include giving all shareholders, regardless of the size of their investment, one vote on proxy resolutions; taking the selection of directors out of the hands of management and putting it into the hands of shareholders; and requiring that corporate boards include government or other outside representatives.[34] Although there have been a limited number of clear victories, the accountability movement has made corporate decision makers more aware of their public responsibilities. Because they are sympathetic to genuine expressions of public sentiment, some corporate managers willingly make policy changes, as long as the changes do not threaten profitability.

Public Awareness

The picture of the public's role in the political process presented thus far has not been entirely complimentary. Public opinion is often manipulated by political and media elites. Many expressions of public opinion suggest that Americans are concerned mainly about the economic well-being of their families and communities, that they are unreasonably impatient with government, and that they are ignorant of many aspects of national and international politics.

In a masterful study of what Americans know about politics, political scientists Michael Delli Carpini and Scott Keeter found enormous gaps in the public's knowledge of how the political process works, who our political leaders are, and what public policies they have approved. Unfortunately, trivia often made more lasting impressions than facts that matter. For example, during the early 1990s, the overwhelming majority of Americans knew that President Bush hated broccoli, whereas only half knew that he had vetoed a plant-closing bill.[35] Although one might hope that political knowledge would improve over time, that does not appear to have happened. Compared with the 1950s and the late 1940s, the American people in 1989 were no better informed politically.[36] As Delli Carpini and Keeter put it, "In spite of an unprecedented expansion in public education, a communications revolution that has shattered national and international boundaries, and the increasing relevance of national and international events and policies to the daily lives of Americans, citizens appear no more informed about politics."[37]

Another worrisome trend has been an apparent decline in what social scientists call "social capital," or the formation of social connections that can promote trust and mutual support. According to political scientist Robert Putnam, Americans are less connected to family, friends, neighbors, and other social institutions than they were a generation ago. They are also less likely to belong to organizations or groups, which, according to Putnam, means a regrettable decline in social capital.[38] An obvious cure would be for America to become once again, in Alexis de Tocqueville's famous phrase, "a nation of joiners." But political scientist Mark Warren cautions that associations differ in their ability to make a positive contribution to democratic life. For example, Warren argues, advocacy groups, consumer cooperatives, and public schools are more likely to develop a sense of political efficacy among members than social clubs, fraternal orders, or sports associations.[39] If Warren is right, then what matters is not just how many groups we belong to but which groups they turn out to be.

Over the years many reforms have been advanced that are aimed at increasing the quantity and quality of citizen participation in American government. Political scientist Benjamin Barber and others believe that a comprehensive system of citizen education is needed to make American democracy work. He has proposed extensive reforms that begin with institutionalized neighborhood assemblies. According to Barber, Americans have no place to meet where they can learn about and discuss issues. Therefore, all neighborhood groups ranging from 5,000 to 25,000 citizens should have a facility that can be used for regular public meetings to discuss local and national issues. Once established, these assemblies could vote on local issues and choose local officials (in some cases by lot), be tied in to a national civic education electronic network, and eventually vote on national issues through electronic referenda. Barber also would establish universal citizen service requirements, democratize the workplace, and generally reorient society to focus on communal concerns and civic responsibilities.[40]

A more modest proposal would be to encourage the development of "organizational report cards" that enable citizens to evaluate governments, government agencies, and public or private organizations that deliver social services, such as schools, hospitals, and health maintenance organizations.[41] By condensing and simplifying large amounts of data, report cards can shed considerable light on the performance of organizations in and around government. Armed with such information, citizens and citizens' groups would be better able to evaluate public officials and those who serve them under contractual arrangements. As William Gormley and David Weimer put it, "Report cards can be thought of as mechanisms for reducing information asymmetries between organizations and those who consume their services."[42] At their best, organizational report cards help to make government more accountable to the citizenry.

Having more television coverage of court proceedings might be another means of encouraging civic education. The presence of television cameras in Congress is now accepted, and they have not disrupted or fundamentally altered the legislative process. The audience usually is small, but not insignificant. Court proceedings in Florida have been televised since the late 1970s. The results have been generally positive—lawyers and judges do not play to the camera, and witnesses and jurors are not confused or intimidated by the camera's presence. The response from citizens indicates a genuine fascination in seeing how the judicial process really works, a development that advocates of participatory democracy would no doubt applaud.[43]

Efficiency

American government is far from efficient in the way it makes and implements policies; many of the inefficiencies stem from basic tenets of the Constitution such as the separation of powers, bicameralism, and federalism. If stability is the strongest virtue of American government, inefficiency is probably its greatest vice.

That inefficiency is demonstrated by the difficulty Congress has in making controversial policy decisions and its penchant for policies that are symbolic, vague, weakened by compromise, and internally inconsistent. When Congress cannot decide, problems are either left unresolved or settled by the courts or the state governments. Bureaucratic implementation of ambiguous statutes frequently leads to new problems, and then to ongoing cycles of legislative patchwork, discretionary enforcement, public or interest group complaints, and more patchwork. Chief executives have trouble making government more efficient because legislatures often refuse to cooperate. Chief executives cannot force cooperation because legislators have independent bases of political power. National and state policy is all too often a mishmash of statutory actions taken by small groups of legislators whose principal aim in formulating the statutes is to serve the interests of organized groups or of the localities they represent. Almost everyone gets something, but there is no clear policy direction and a great deal of duplication and lack of coordination occurs.

The solution? Students of the problem suggest some combination of discipline and central control. They see strong political parties, such as those found in western Europe, as the best source of discipline. Political scientist Leon D. Epstein, however, believes that truly disciplined parties are unlikely ever to take hold in the United States because candidate-centered elections are deeply rooted in the culture and supported by elected officials. He does see value in reforms that would increase the role of parties in the control of campaign financing because raising money and providing campaign services are functions that American parties could potentially perform well.[44] Invigorated national parties might also push the government to act more efficiently.

Another approach to discipline is what political scientist Theodore Lowi has called "juridical democracy."[45] What Lowi had in mind was that Congress should be prevented from passing so many ambiguous laws. The Supreme Court could take the first step by resurrecting the reasoning it used in declaring unconstitutional Franklin Roosevelt's National Industrial Recovery Act. The Court said that policies that delegate power to administrative agencies without defining the precise standards that should be used during implementation are invalid under the Constitution.[46] The problem with this remedy, however, is that it ignores both technical and political complexity. Many issues involving health care, environmental protection, telecommunications, banking, and other policy sectors have become so complex that it is difficult for Congress to specify solutions with precision. Even if Congress knew what ought to be done, it would face the political challenge of forging a winning coalition in support of a definitive allocation of resources.

Another reform proposal that would complement the strengthening of parties by enhancing the power of presidents is to increase the term of House members from two years to four and possibly to decrease Senate terms to four years. The idea is to tie congressional electoral fortunes more directly to those of presidents, who have an obvious stake in emphasizing party loyalty. Perhaps more important, it would do away with midterm elections, which almost invariably contribute to gridlock among policymakers, because the president's party tends to lose seats. Such a change would encourage a more national outlook among House members and should reduce their obsession with reelection, casework, and pork-barrel policies.

Competence

In evaluating the competence of institutional actors, we ask whether American policymakers are knowledgeable and skilled enough to accomplish their tasks. Most elected officials are lawyers or businesspeople, which means that, on average, they are well educated. State and local politics traditionally serve as the first test of aspiring politicians' interest and ability; the more successful ones move on to Congress or state executive positions. Those who make it that far tend to stay in politics a long time. They are career politicians and policymakers.

Legislatures. The U.S. Congress stands out among the national legislatures in the world for the low turnover of its members and its preponderance of lawyers. Nearly 40 percent of the members of Congress were lawyers in 1999, whereas in most western European countries lawyers constitute about 20 percent of the legislators.[47] Most western European legislatures include more journalists, teachers, intellectuals, and blue-collar workers than does the U.S. Congress.[48] Low turnover among legislators would seem to earn Congress low marks for representativeness and accountability but high marks for competence, although much depends upon what kind of competence is sought. American legislators know a good deal about their specialized committee decisions, but they tend to be weak when it comes to formulating long-term answers to major national or international questions. At the state level, legislative turnover has increased in recent years, at least in the eighteen states that have mandatory term limits.

Bureaucracies. The U.S. federal bureaucracy has sometimes been criticized for inadequate competence, professionalism, and common sense.[49] That charge has been vigorously rebutted by Charles Goodsell and others.[50] Even defenders concede that civil servants in the United States lack the status and prestige of their counterparts in Great Britain, France, and Germany. For example, civil servants in these three countries are extremely well paid, whereas civil servants in the United States are simply well paid.[51] Ever since the Reagan years, scholars have worried about the morale of the federal civil service. It is difficult to encourage young people to choose the civil service as a vocation when politicians treat bureaucrats as punching bags and when their private-sector counterparts are earning far more money.

The situation is somewhat different for the political and career executives who actually run federal and state agencies. The political executives, most of whom leave for other jobs after two to three years of service, can endure challenging work conditions because they expect to escape before long. As for career executives, they must simply learn to develop thick skins. Both political and career executives take pride in being able to manage and reform important government programs that promote clean air, good health, safe roads, secure investments, and protection from discrimination.

In a recent study, Cynthia Bowling and Deil Wright found that state agency heads have impressive educational backgrounds, which have improved over time. In 1994, 60 percent of state agency heads had a graduate degree, a substantial increase from 40 percent in 1964.[52] At the federal level, educational backgrounds are even more impressive. According to Joel Aberbach and Bert Rockman, top federal executives are 80 percent more likely to have attended graduate school than top private-sector executives and are three to four times more likely to have professional degrees.[53]

Bureaucratic reforms at the national and state levels typically revolve around similar themes: providing incentives for better performance, making it easier for managers to fire unproductive employees, establishing clear lines of authority, encouraging creative solutions to difficult problems, improving coordination within and between agencies, and bolstering the image of public employees. Unfortunately, these reforms do not always point in the same direction. For example, "hierarchical" accountability encourages bureaucrats to do what they are told, whereas "professional" accountability encourages them to think for themselves.[54]

Courts. The power and prestige of American courts are unrivaled in the world. They do far more than merely apply laws to specific cases; the courts often make policy, especially when other institutions are unwilling to do so. One way to ensure judicial competence is to improve the quality of appointments to the bench. Chief executives can appoint advisory panels to make recommendations; groups of citizens and legal professionals then can narrow the list of potential nominees to candidates with outstanding records and abilities. The use of advisory panels would not eliminate partisan considerations, but it could ensure that only truly competent individuals are considered. President Carter created panels of this sort to assist him in making circuit court appointments, but the panels were dropped by President Reagan. President Bush relied on the Justice Department to help him screen nominees, and his slowness in filling vacancies was criticized by several members of the Senate Judiciary Committee.[55] President Clinton, too, was slow to nominate federal judges, but the Senate also moved ponderously to confirm them. In at least one instance, President Clinton was able to expedite judicial confirmations by offering concessions on otherwise unrelated appropriations bills.

The proper connection between the law and science is increasingly of interest in modern society, and the competence of judges is tested when they confront highly technical questions. Agencies like the Environmental Protection Agency make complex scientific assessments about what industries can and should do to comply with environmental statutes, and their assessments are often contested in court. These cases can be difficult for judges. Although they are inclined to defer to agency expertise on technical matters, they maintain a role for themselves in taking a "hard look" at the evidence and the procedures an agency employed in making its assessment.[56] The late appeals court judge Harold Leventhal, who had extensive experience with such matters, proposed that judges hire scientific experts in highly technical cases. The experts would not judge the adequacy of agency rulings but would assist judges "in understanding problems of scientific methodology and in assessing the reliability of tests conducted by the agency in light of specific criticisms."[57] Such individuals would be similar to special consultants or law clerks, in that their advice to judges would not be a matter of legal record, and they would not normally be cross-examined.[58] Similar proposals have been made with regard to the interpretation and use of social science evidence to help judges make informed decisions about conditions in mental health facilities, prisons, and schools.[59]

Chief executives. If national politics are the leading edge of American politics, then presidential experiences should shed some light on the future for governors and mayors. One problem is that the public relations aspects of the job have become so dominant in the media age that competence is now what good looks used to be—a desirable quality but not necessary. Chief executives can be, and are, packaged and sold all over the country. The more salient the politics, the more likely it is that public relations specialists will dominate. In the United States, chief executive politics is the most visible form of politics and, therefore, the most prone to deceptive appearances.

Successful chief executives must be able to perform their many difficult political and administrative tasks with the knowledge that many people are watching and waiting to exploit every failing, both public and private. Furthermore, because they lack the authority to do everything they would like, their leadership is often more a matter of symbolism than substance. The ability to utter symbolic rhetoric convincingly in front of huge, but usually remote, audiences is rapidly becoming the primary qualification for chief executives.

Thus far, most states and localities have benefited from more visible and competitive politics. It was not all that long ago—prior to 1940—that state governments were weak and, in many cases, corrupt. Governors' powers were limited; their offices were poorly staffed; money and favor-trading pervaded legislatures; and the bureaucracy was filled with patronage appointees who did more political work than government work. A good deal of progress has been made since then. Governors have been granted broader powers, and they exercise them more vigorously. State legislatures sit longer, and legislators are better paid and less corrupt. Bureaucracies have been enlarged and revamped, with most appointees governed by merit systems. Innovative policies are coming from the states: education reform, far-reaching environmental statutes, welfare-to-work programs, financial incentives to encourage day care centers to improve their quality, joint public and private economic development efforts, and others. Most big-city governments have also become more professional in outlook and practice. Some mayors, such as Stephen Goldsmith of Indianapolis and John Norquist of Milwaukee, have even written books about their many innovations and accomplishments.[60]

Boardrooms. Private sector competence and effectiveness are difficult to characterize in general terms. The nation has experienced a steady stream of economic difficulties since the 1960s, and at least some of these problems can be attributed to private sector decisions and practices. The most important recent example was the creation of the junk bond market and the freewheeling practices of deregulated savings and loan executives, which together led to the rapid escalation of real estate prices and then to the collapse of real estate markets in many parts of the country. These ill-advised private sector activities have cost the public, and especially many individual investors, billions of dollars. Still, in comparison with most of the rest of the world, Americans enjoy a very high standard of living, and there are consistent signs of innovation and vitality in the private sector.

American industry has depended for years on the high-volume manufacture of standardized products by workers who performed repetitive tasks for union-negotiated wages. Consensus is growing that this production style cannot compete effectively against western European and Japanese systems that are more flexible and yield higher-quality products, or against cheaper systems, organized along American lines, in developing countries. The difficulties of the American steel and auto industries are attributed by most analysts to the failure of corporate leaders to modernize plants and change their product orientation soon enough to avert disaster. Problems of this sort are to be expected in market economies, however, and they can even provide valuable lessons for the future.

The experience of the steel and automobile industries, for example, seems to have led to a new consensus about the importance of investment in infrastructure, research and development, and methods to improve worker productivity. By the early 1990s, manufacturing accounted for 23 percent of the gross national product, up from 20 percent in 1982. This increase was attributable to very high productivity rates in the 1980s because the number of jobs in manufacturing did not increase.[61] Most Americans believe the future of U.S. industry rests with high-technology products, precision manufacturing, telecommunications, and farming, in which the United States has what economists call a "comparative advantage." The private sector has become much more attentive to international markets, a fitting development because that is where the fate of American industry will be determined.

Summary

The competence of American policymakers is not the main issue with regard to institutional performance. The more fundamental issue is political will or the lack thereof. Overall, one of the greatest failings of American public institutions is their indecisiveness. This failing is obvious to anyone who has studied the workings of Congress, where indecision in the form of stalling, ambiguous statutory language, symbolic responsiveness, and passing the buck has been raised to an art. Former Ohio State football coach Woody Hayes always explained his reluctance to use the forward pass by saying, "There are three things that can happen when you pass—completion, incompletion, and interception—and two of them are bad." This philosophy captures the essence of legislators' attitudes: faced with the choice between taking forceful action to resolve a problem, which could be ineffective or unpopular, or using one of their polished methods of delay, obfuscation, and pacification, they will invariably choose the latter.

Indecisiveness is not simply a product of the fear of making mistakes. It also stems from the fixation that elected officials have with public opinion and the extraordinary role played by interest groups in American politics. The socialization of conflict and increased public and group participation in decision making have produced, in a political system of fragmented power, more gridlock than direction, which is another way of saying that democratic decision making is cumbersome. Powerful groups in society often disagree about the steps that should be taken to resolve problems. The government apparatus is designed to reflect such disagreement, and it does, in the form of inaction. This inaction then becomes the target of reformers and other critics because chief executives are almost always unsuccessful in charting a clear course of government policy, bureaucrats are paranoid because they never know when elected officials are going to turn on them, and the public is confused and disillusioned.

At the beginning of the twenty-first century the effects of gridlock and indecision at the national level are placing increasing demands on the states. The inability of presidents and Congresses to chart a clear course for national policy is forcing states to make tough decisions about everything from social welfare and taxes to the environment. Inaction by representative institutions at all levels of government has also increased the significance of living room politics (initiatives, referenda, and grassroots movements) and courtroom politics. The growing conservativism of the U.S. Supreme Court further adds to the importance of state-level politics, particularly the importance of state supreme court decisions.

But overly harsh judgments about the performance of American political institutions may not be fully justified. In this postindustrial age, government institutions of all sorts face vastly expanded policy agendas. The rapidity of change in society denies policymaking institutions any opportunity to rest on their laurels. A steady stream of demands can be heard from groups who want more or less from government, as technological and social developments alter the environment within which they operate. As the government has taken on new tasks and sought to satisfy more demands, its old responsibilities have not withered away. Instead, the earlier commitments usually have become permanent. The inability to shed old baggage is another reason why government institutions are reluctant to take on new problems. This reluctance to act has a positive side: it reduces the chances of making serious mistakes.

The reform impulse enjoys continuing popularity in the United States because it offers methods for overcoming governmental problems that will not cause a great deal of pain. Americans are always searching for a "quick fix." But the reality of change is that it is slow and that it is a cumulative process rather than a single decisive act. Some of the most significant reforms, such as equal rights for women and minorities, have followed a long, painful course.

In many ways the question is whether private sector performance is rewarding enough to justify a government that is so timid that it rarely acts in a disruptive way. Whenever such a question is posed, the answer that almost invariably comes forward is that "the people" should decide. But are the people in any position to decide? Are alternatives stated in a way that people can understand and make reasoned judgments about what is in society's best interest? In general, the answer to these questions is no, primarily because a good deal of what the people know has been packaged for them by people who have a vested interest in keeping things much as they are. Nevertheless, history makes clear that when conditions get bad enough, decisive popular action is likely. In a free society, widespread suffering can lead to strong expressions of citizen preference and significant changes in institutions and policies. Citizen inattentiveness to politics and government and policy gridlock are an indication of relative prosperity. Perhaps there is some wisdom in letting peoples' sense of economic well-being, or lack of it, determine the government's policy.

Notes

1. Edward Walsh, "An Activist Court Mixes Its High-Profile Messages," *Washington Post,* July 2, 2000, 6.
2. For the classic statements of pluralist theory, see Robert A. Dahl, *Who Governs?* (New Haven, Conn.: Yale University Press, 1963); or Nelson W. Polsby, *Community Power and Political Theory* (New Haven, Conn.: Yale University Press, 1963). For the classic critiques of the pluralist position, see Peter Bachrach and Morton S. Baratz, "Two Faces of Power," *American Political Science Review* 56 (December 1962); or Theodore J. Lowi, *The End of Liberalism,* 2d ed. (New York: W. W. Norton, 1979).
3. Mancur Olson, *The Logic of Collective Action* (Cambridge: Harvard University Press, 1973).
4. Terry Moe, "Regulatory Performance and Presidential Administration," *American Journal of Political Science* 26 (May 1982): 197–224; Terry Moe, "Control and Feedback in Economic Regulation: The Case of the NLRB," *American Political Science Review* 79 (December 1985): 1094–1117; B. Dan Wood, "Does Politics Make a Difference at the EEOC?" *American Journal of Political Science* 34 (May 1990): 503–530; B. Dan Wood and Richard Waterman, "The Dynamics of Political Control of the Bureaucracy," *American Political Science Review* 85 (September 1991): 801–828.
5. Kenneth Mayer, "Executive Orders and Presidential Power," *Journal of Politics* 61 (May 1999): 445–466.
6. Donald Kettl, "Building Lasting Reform: Enduring Questions, Missing Answers," in *Inside the Reinvention Machine,* ed. Donald Kettl and John DiIulio Jr. (Washington, D.C.: Brookings Institution, 1995), 9–83.
7. Donald Kettl, *Sharing Power: Public Governance and Private Markets* (Washington, D.C.: Brookings Institution, 1993).
8. See Herbert A. Simon, *Administrative Behavior: A Study of Decision Making Processes in Administrative Organizations* (New York: Macmillan, 1957); or James G. March and Herbert A. Simon, *Organizations* (New York: Wiley, 1964).
9. Jane Mansbridge, *Beyond Adversary Democracy* (Chicago: University of Chicago Press, 1983); Benjamin R. Barber, *Strong Democracy: Participatory Politics for a New Age* (Berkeley: University of California Press, 1984).
10. Cisneros, who served as secretary of housing and urban development, eventually pleaded guilty to a charge of lying to the FBI about payments to a former mistress. Michael Espy, who served as secretary of agriculture, was acquitted by a jury on charges that he received $35,000 in illegal gifts from companies regulated by his agency. See Robert Jackson, "Cisneros Heads Off Trial, Pleads Guilty to Lying," *Los Angeles Times,* September 8, 1999, 1.
11. U.S. House of Representatives, Committee on Ways and Means, *1998 Green Book* (Washington, D.C.: Government Printing Office, 1998), 1303.

12. Ibid., 1303. During President Clinton's first term, the poverty rate declined from 14.8 percent in 1992 to 13.7 percent in 1996.

13. Christopher Hammons, "Was James Madison Wrong? Rethinking the American Preference for Short, Framework-Oriented Constitutions," *American Political Science Review* 93 (December 1999): 847.

14. "Women Who Will Serve in the 107th Congress, 2001–2003," online at http://www.cawp.rutgers.edu, December 2000.

15. "Fact Sheet: The 1999 Catalyst Census of Women Board of Directors of the Fortune 1000," online at http://www.catalystwomen.org/press/factswbd99.html, September 25, 2000.

16. Ibid.

17. "Fact Sheets: Women in State Legislative Office," May 12, 2000, online at http://www.cawp.rutgers.edu, November 29, 2000.

18. Cynthia Bowling and Deil Wright, "Change and Continuity in State Administration: Administrative Leadership across Four Decades," *Public Administration Review* 58 (September/October 1998): 432.

19. Figures were taken from Randall B. Ripley and Grace A. Franklin, *Congress, the Bureaucracy, and Public Policy,* 5th ed. (Pacific Grove, Calif.: Brooks/Cole, 1991), 30; *Congressional Quarterly Weekly Report,* November 10, 1990, 3835; Sheldon Goldman and Thomas Jahnige, *The Federal Courts as a Political System,* 3d ed. (New York: W. W. Norton, 1987), 55; and *The State of Black America* (New York: National Urban League, 1987).

20. Bowling and Wright, "Change and Continuity in State Administration," 431.

21. Rodney Hero et al., "Latino Participation, Partisanship, and Office Holding," *PS* (September 2000): 533.

22. See *Business Week,* June 22, 1987, 72–78.

23. See Goldman and Jahnige, *The Federal Courts,* 55.

24. Jennifer Segal, "Representative Decision Making on the Federal Bench: Clinton's District Court Appointees," *Political Research Quarterly* 53 (March 2000): 139.

25. Robert Erikson, Gerald Wright, and John McIver, *Statehouse Democracy* (Cambridge: Cambridge University Press, 1993).

26. Page and Shapiro found somewhat higher congruence for domestic issues than for foreign issues. See Benjamin Page and Robert Shapiro, "Effects of Public Opinion on Public Policy," *American Political Science Review* 77 (March 1983): 182. See also Benjamin Page and Robert Shapiro, *The Rational Public: Fifty Years of Trends in Americans' Policy Preferences* (Chicago: University of Chicago Press, 1992).

27. James Stimson, Michael MacKuen, and Robert Erikson, "Dynamic Representation," *American Political Science Review* 89 (September 1995): 543–565.

28. Ibid., 559.

29. *Printz v. United States,* 521 U.S. 898 (1997).

30. Alan Monroe, "Public Opinion and Public Policy 1980–1993," *Public Opinion Quarterly* 62 (spring 1998): 6–28. See also Lawrence Jacobs and Robert Shapiro, *Politicians Don't Pander: Political Manipulation and the Loss of Democratic Responsiveness* (Chicago: University of Chicago Press, 2000).

31. Sen. John McCain, "McCain Moves to Close 527 Tax Loophole," press release, Washington, D.C., June 7, 2000; Sen. John McCain, "527 Reformers Clarify Intentions, Send Letters to IRS, Treasury," press release, Washington, D.C., July 26, 2000.

32. Karen Foerstel and Peter Wallsten, "Campaign Overhaul Mired in Money and Loopholes," *CQ Weekly,* May 13, 2000, 1084–1093.

33. The term limitation measures passed in California and Oklahoma apply only to state legislators, but members of Congress were included in the Colorado measure. Legal scholars doubt that it is constitutional for states to limit the terms of federal officials in this way.

34. See David Vogel, *Lobbying the Corporation* (New York: Basic Books, 1978), 219–220.

35. Michael Delli Carpini and Scott Keeter, *What Americans Know about Politics and Why It Matters* (New Haven, Conn.: Yale University Press, 1996), 62–104.

36. Ibid., 105–134.

37. Ibid., 133.

38. Robert Putnam, *Bowling Alone: The Collapse and Revival of American Community* (New York: Simon and Schuster, 2000).

39. Mark Warren, *Democracy and Association* (Princeton, N.J.: Princeton University Press, 2000), 142–162.

40. Benjamin R. Barber, *Strong Democracy* (Berkeley: University of California Press, 1984), chap. 10; Benjamin R. Barber, *A Place for Us* (New York: Hill and Wang, 1998), 75.

41. William Gormley Jr. and David Weimer, *Organizational Report Cards* (Cambridge: Harvard University Press, 1999).

42. Ibid., 24.

43. See Norman Davis, "Television in Our Courts: The Proven Advantages, the Unproven Disadvantages," *Judicature* 64 (August 1980): 85–92.

44. Leon D. Epstein, *Political Parties in the American Mold* (Madison: University of Wisconsin Press, 1986), chap. 9.

45. Lowi, *The End of Liberalism,* 298.

46. *Schechter Poultry Co. v. United States,* 295 U.S. 495 (1935).

47. Roger Davidson and Walter Oleszek, *Congress and Its Members,* 7th ed. (Washington, D.C.: CQ Press, 2000), 128.

48. Lawyers and businessmen usually make up a large percentage of western European conservative party legislators; the other parties have many educators, journalists, and political organizers as candidates. See J. Blondel, *Comparative Legislatures* (Englewood Cliffs, N.J.: Prentice-Hall, 1973), 76–91; and *Guardian* (London) May 29, 1987.

49. See, for example, E. S. Savas, *Privatization and Public-Private Partnerships* (Chatham, N.J.: Chatham House, 2000); Philip Howard, *The Death of Common Sense* (New York: Random House, 1994).

50. Charles Goodsell, *The Case for Bureaucracy,* 3d ed. (Chatham, N.J.: Chatham House, 1994).

51. B. Guy Peters, *The Politics of Bureaucracy,* 4th ed. (White Plains, N.Y.: Longman, 1995), 109.

52. Cynthia Bowling and Deil Wright, "Change and Continuity in State Administration," 431.

53. Joel Aberbach and Bert Rockman, *In the Web of Politics: Three Decades of the U.S. Federal Executive* (Washington, D.C.: Brookings Institution, 2000).

54. Barbara Romzek, "Where the Buck Stops: Accountability in Reformed Public Organizations," in *Transforming Government: Lessons from the Reinvention Lab-*

oratories, ed. Patricia Ingraham, James Thompson, and Ronald Sanders (San Francisco: Jossey-Bass Publishers, 1998), 193–219.

55. See Joan Biskupic, "Bush Lags in Appointments to the Federal Judiciary," *Congressional Quarterly Weekly Report,* January 6, 1990, 38–42.

56. Harold Leventhal, "Environmental Decision-making and the Role of the Courts," *University of Pennsylvania Law Review* 122 (January 1974): 514.

57. Ibid., 550.

58. Ibid., 550–555.

59. See Peter W. Sperlich, "Social Science Evidence in the Courts: Reaching beyond the Adversary Process," *Judicature* 63 (December 1979–January 1980): 280–289; David M. O'Brien, "The Seduction of the Judiciary: Social Science and the Courts," *Judicature* 44 (June–July 1980): 8–21.

60. John Norquist, *The Wealth of Cities* (Reading, Mass.: Addison-Wesley, 1998); Stephen Goldsmith, *The Twenty-First Century City* (Lanham, Md.: Rowman and Littlefield, 1999).

61. Sylvia Nasar, "American Revival in Manufacturing Seen in U.S. Report," *New York Times,* February 5, 1991, Al, D8.

Chapter 10 **Assessing American Public Policy**

The political struggle that yields public policies is not just a game about the exercise and maintenance of power. Whether governments and private corporations produce effective policies and programs profoundly affects the nation and its citizens. At stake are national survival, the quality of life, and the nature of justice in society.

Public policies are developed and implemented by private corporations, courts, legislatures, chief executives, administrative agencies, and citizens. In this chapter we consider fundamental questions of governmental performance. How well do public policies serve the needs and wants of the American people? Does the United States live up to the ideals proclaimed by elected leaders and set forth in the Constitution? Is the nation better off or worse off in the first decade of the new century than it was fifty, twenty-five, or ten years ago? What pressing problems has the nation failed to grapple with effectively? These are difficult questions to answer. A selective report card on the nation's policy accomplishments and failures is offered here; more questions are raised than answered.

Choosing Yardsticks

What criteria should be applied in an assessment of public policy? What evidence is available to measure policy performance? Against what standards can progress and failure be judged? The question is not just whether the public policy "glass" is half full or half empty, but which glasses should be examined. There are many inherent difficulties in assessing public policy. Following is a discussion of a few of them and how they might be handled.

Principal Policy Goals

Before evaluating any public policy, one must decide what questions to ask, which is not as simple as it sounds. What is important to one observer may not be important to another. People in different circumstances have distinct views of the world and its problems. The inner-city resident and the suburban homeowner whose dwellings may be less than an hour apart have different expectations about what government should do to help them. The city dweller is more likely to be concerned about crime, public transportation, air quality, overcrowding, and housing. The suburban homeowner is more interested in the state highway system, the availability of safe drinking water, and recreational opportunities.[1]

Public policy concerns are also shaped by the nature of the times. Some goals, such as peace and prosperity, always command attention. Issues such as drug abuse or education may seem urgent one year but less pressing the next. Circumstances change; policies change; new problems arise, or new aspects of old problems are recognized. During the late 1950s, for example, policymakers debated whether black Americans had the right to enjoy the same public facilities, schools, mass transportation, restaurants, and parks as white Americans. In the first decade of 2000 the policy issues center on how far the government should go in promoting economic and social opportunities for minority groups.

Conceptions of the proper role of government in the lives of American citizens are highly controversial and provide a framework for evaluations of public policy. Should the government permit employers to require individuals to stop smoking, even if they smoke only when they are not on the job? Should the government be able to require individuals to use mass transportation and stop using outdoor grills in order to cut air pollution? Should government provide subsidies for families whose children attend private elementary and secondary schools, when public schools are available? Should the United States continue to play a central role in policing the "new world order," or should other nations begin to play a larger role in defending the interests of Western democracies? Should the government require employers to provide health insurance to their workers, or should it provide coverage for all Americans through a national program? Should governments have the right to tax and control transactions through the Internet, when it has no real geographical boundaries? Because people disagree about what government ought to do, they often disagree about what governments actually accomplish.

Despite disagreement about whether government should increase its involvement, expand its reform programs, or get out of the way, there is fundamental agreement on the nation's principal public policy aspirations.[2] They are (1) to defend the nation, (2) to achieve sustained economic growth, (3) to ensure equal opportunity, (4) to provide a "safety net" for the disadvantaged and senior citizens, and (5) to protect the environment. The stability of these central policy goals over the last several decades reflects a widespread consensus about government responsibilities in American political culture. In the United States, in contrast to other nations, political battles usually take place over means, not ends. Public officials fight fiercely about how basic values will be expressed and defined in practice, but almost always there is little conflict over core values.

What is at stake in these struggles is not whether public policies should help the poor, for example, but how much and in what way. Lawmakers often fight over subtle differences in the language of a statute or a bill because they know that their decisions may one day have profound consequences. Only in rare instances, such as the New Deal of President Franklin Roosevelt, do major changes occur quickly. The 1990s also saw one of these rare major changes with the passage of the Personal Responsibility and Work Opportunity Reconciliation Act in 1996, which changed welfare by removing its entitlement status and dismantling many of the programs instituted during earlier reform eras, like the New Deal.

Weighing Evidence

How does one know whether government policies and programs are effective? Reliable, objective information is available for the evaluation of many policies. Government agencies and public and private analysts monitor unemployment, inflation, trade balances, life expectancy, race relations, the quality of the environment, and so on. Knowledge about the effectiveness of public policies has increased substantially since the 1960s. Policymakers can be better informed than ever before about conditions in society and the possible effects of their actions.[3]

In spite of these gains, policymakers still may not know enough about the effectiveness of public policies to reach sound conclusions. Too often they are unwilling to use the information that is available. It is embarrassing to discover that a once-ballyhooed policy does not work; therefore, many lawmakers are more likely to ask probing questions than to authorize careful evaluations or listen to disconcerting evidence, unless it serves their short-term political agenda. Politicians usually are more concerned about who gets what, when, and how than with evaluations of program performance. In divided government they are also more concerned with making their party or institution look good than they are with careful evaluations of public policy outcomes.

Establishing cause-and-effect relationships between a government action and a societal consequence is difficult. If millions of Americans suffer from heart disease and high blood pressure, is the U.S. health care system to blame, or is it because Americans refuse to eat properly, quit smoking, and take care of themselves? If minorities increase their membership in the professions, should credit accrue to civil rights laws, or are there simply more minority applicants who are better prepared? Because a single government policy cannot be isolated from other events, trends, or policies, the specific effects of government decisions may go undetected.

Welfare reform of the 1990s is a good example. Welfare caseloads fell by more than 50 percent from 1994 to 2000. Politicians have been quick to claim credit for this drop by attributing it to the 1996 welfare reform law. But the reduction in welfare rolls is more likely a result of the expanding economy during the mid- and late-1990s, the creation of millions of new jobs in the United States, and the negative connotations surrounding the welfare debates, which may have prevented many poor people from seeking assistance. The true source of the smaller welfare caseloads today is hard to pinpoint and most likely a result of several contributing factors, not just welfare reform policies.[4]

Making Judgments

After evidence is gathered about the effects of a particular policy, standards must be applied to judge success or failure. For example, the unemployment rate among Americans is carefully calculated and reported each month, but the raw data do not speak for themselves. Is a 6 percent unemployment rate alarming or acceptable? Sound public policy conclusions should not be based on the optimism or pessimism of the observer, but where do analysts turn for standards that yield reasonable judgments?

The determination of standards begins with an examination of the objectives of governmental policy. One must be careful to distinguish between pronouncements and results, however. Public laws, regulations, and judicial decrees state objectives; they are not automatically translated into positive outcomes. Political leaders frequently engage in hyperbole, claiming that new laws and policies will solve long-standing problems. But the proposed solution may not work in practice, or the problem may be much more difficult than originally envisioned. Therefore, careful observers ignore the rhetoric and examine the effects of policies on people, institutions, and society.

A thorough evaluation of public policy also requires looking beyond contemporary policy debates. Policymakers should anticipate and address problems before they become unmanageable crises or potential catastrophes. Only governments have the broad powers to act on behalf of an entire state or nation. Scientists warn, for example, that the ozone layer that shields the earth from harmful ultraviolet rays is gradually diminishing, causing the earth's temperature to rise. They predict that unless the use of ozone-depleting chemicals is curtailed, the earth's fragile ecology may be severely damaged. Since 1987, more than 170 nations, including the United States, have signed the "Montreal Protocol on Substances That Deplete the Ozone Layer" and pledged to reduce and eventually eliminate the production and use of man-made ozone-depleting substances, particularly chlorofluorocarbons (CFCs). In addition to this, the U.S. Congress amended the Clean Air Act to include provisions concerning ozone depletion. Although progress has been made, many individuals and corporations are prosecuted and fined by the U.S. Environmental Protection Agency (EPA) each year for violations of the law.[5]

Public perceptions should be carefully considered in judging policy performance, but it is misleading to rely solely on public satisfaction. Public opinions about government policies are often based on fragmentary or unreliable information. Policies should not be judged exclusively according to whether an individual feels personally better off than before. The perspective of most citizens is narrow, limited to their families, jobs, and neighborhoods. What is good for one family may not be good for another family or for the community as a whole. Majority preferences may be insensitive to minority rights and needs. Indeed, disadvantaged minorities often receive benefits they would probably be denied if public policies were based exclusively on majority sentiment.

Perspectives on the effectiveness of public policy are possible when meaningful comparisons can be made to put the naked evidence into perspective. Placing current policy performance in historical perspective is particularly valuable. Taken as a raw number, a 4 percent unemployment rate does not reveal much. Its significance is established only by comparison with peak levels of nearly 10 percent in 1991 and with the lower than 4 percent rate in the mid-1960s. The 4 percent unemployment rate in 2000 is lower than at any time in the last thirty years, but based on the experience in the 1960s it may be possible to lower it even more.

Comparing U.S. policy performance with experiences in other countries may also be useful, if handled with care. For instance, the fact that infant mortality rates are higher in the United States than in twenty-four other countries suggests that Americans have inadequate access to health care.[6] Conversely, there may be little comfort from the fact that U.S. toxic waste cleanup efforts lead in comparison with those of other nations, because most would still judge U.S. efforts inadequate.

Comparisons of different states, communities, and population subgroups may also yield insights. Ideally, analysts would like to know what conditions would have been like without a public policy or program. Because such knowledge is often unattainable, analysts compare states that have programs with those that do not or compare groups in the population that have received services with those that have not. In this way, it may be possible to understand what difference the program made in people's lives.

In the following review of five principal policy goals, we examine how the United States measures up by comparing current performance with announced objectives and by looking at historical and cross-national comparisons where appropriate. The effects of public policies on different groups of Americans are highlighted. In each section we consider accomplishments, failures, and unanswered questions. The summary is a discussion of the challenges facing the nation and its leaders in the years ahead.

Defending the Nation

The U.S. Constitution declares that a primary purpose of government is to "provide for the common defense." Nothing could be more fundamental than ensuring the survival of the nation, protecting its vital economic interests, and preserving the freedom of its citizens. Americans and their leaders have had grave concerns about the nation's security since World War II. These anxieties derive from the perception that in the age of nuclear weapons and dependence on foreign oil supplies, foreign powers are potential adversaries capable of seriously threatening U.S. economic interests and national security.

Consequently, since the late 1940s, a bipartisan consensus has existed in favor of maintaining sufficient military power to deter nations from pursuing hostile intentions.[7] The American commitment extends beyond defending U.S. soil, citizens, and overseas investments. U.S. policymakers believe that military force and the threat of nuclear retaliation must be used to protect allies and to counter attempts by hostile nations to expand their influence. American lives and military resources were spent defending Korea and Vietnam from Communist regimes and in protecting Middle East oil supplies during the Persian Gulf War. In 1991 more than $14.8 billion in U.S. foreign and military aid was distributed throughout the world—to Afghanistan, Egypt, Israel, Nicaragua, Saudi Arabia, and dozens of other countries.

With the collapse of the Soviet Union and the spread of democracy to previously Communist nations, the United States has reassessed its military position. President Clinton reduced the military budget significantly during his first term. Although no longer facing a threat from one large adversary, the Soviet Union, the U.S. military has been deployed many times in the past decade in other countries and at home. For example, terrorism at home and abroad has demanded military attention. The bombing of a government building in Oklahoma as well as terrorist attacks on U.S. citizens and sailors in the Middle East and Africa have created a new threat.

During the 1990s the U.S. military, in cooperation with forces of the North Atlantic Treaty Organization (NATO), was deployed to quell regional conflicts, such as the internal conflicts in Kosovo and Bosnia, and to enforce democratic elections in Haiti. The military has since played the part of peacekeeper and protector of exploited peoples in these areas of domestic conflict. Finally, the military has been called in when the proliferation of nuclear and chemical weapons by foreign countries, such as India, Iraq, North Korea, and Pakistan, have threatened the nation's interests directly or indirectly.

Soldiers and Dollars

Disputes over national security policy have often been heated. When should U.S. military forces be involved in hostile actions? American involvement in Vietnam provoked one of the most damaging internal political conflicts in the nation's history, and it has had lasting effects. How much conventional military and nuclear weaponry does the country need? Critics argue that the military establishment and many U.S. politicians exaggerate the threats posed by other countries such as Iraq and North Korea and that the defense budget is larger than necessary. Supporters of a large defense budget maintain that it is the price that must be paid to protect U.S. interests at home and abroad. The swift military victories in Grenada, Iraq, and Panama helped vindicate U.S. defense policymakers who argued that overwhelming U.S. military power could be used effectively without great cost in American lives. In stark contrast to this, the 1990s and the early years of the new century have seen a profound reluctance on the part of military leaders and chief executives to use extensive military force, unless it is clear that we have a vital interest, overwhelming force at our disposal, and an "exit" strategy. This so-called Powell Doctrine, after Secretary of State Colin Powell, former general and chairman of the Joint Chiefs of Staff, stems from costly failures, humiliating withdrawals, and organizational disintegration following military interventions in places such as Beirut, Somalia, and Vietnam. Thus, recent conflicts, such as those in Haiti and Bosnia, have resulted in a slower and less significant response from U.S. leaders than would have occurred in the past.[8]

National security policy not only affects the nation's survival and prosperity, it also influences domestic priorities and is influenced by them. The funds that remain after defense spending requirements have been met determine what else the government can do; defense spending consumed more than $275 billion of the $1.8 trillion federal budget in 2000.[9] Strong national security requires the fostering of industries to design and manufacture ships, submarines, tanks, airplanes, and nuclear weapons. Today, the cost of constructing an aircraft carrier, like the U.S.S. *Truman,* commissioned in 1998, is approximately $4.5 billion. The construction takes about five years and at its height employs more than 4,000 workers.[10]

The strength and self-reliance of a nation's economy shapes the strategies that must be taken to defend it. The United States is one of the most independent and self-sustaining nations in the world; it has abundant raw materials necessary for survival and adequate food supplies for the entire population. Yet the United States depends on other nations for oil and other materials, and it sells its products and services around the world. Hence, U.S. policymakers must be concerned with the political, military, and economic situations in dozens of other nations. The U.S. reaction to Iraq's invasion of Kuwait with its possible threat to oil supplies was swift and decisive. In contrast, the United States did not confront the Soviet Union when it invaded Afghanistan, a relatively resource-poor nation.

Unlike inflation, air pollution, or crime, national security problems are not "experienced" by large segments of the American public, except in times of war. A segment of the population also must serve in the military. Since the mid-1970s, U.S. armed forces personnel have been volunteers—a change that reshaped the composition of the military substantially. Soldiers in the modern volunteer army are more likely than in the past to come from low-income, poorly educated, and minority backgrounds.[11]

The size of the defense budget is based on perceptions of risk and assumptions about the strategies that will be most effective in minimizing those risks. Unlike the planning of government entitlement programs, in which needy populations can be precisely defined and spending determined accordingly, the task of constructing defense budgets is a deadly guessing game. If military power is inadequate to protect vital economic interests, the problem may not be apparent until it is too late to do anything about it. How serious is the military threat posed by foreign powers? To what extent should the United States shield other nations against military attack? Should the United States respond to all situations in which potential adversaries wield military power? Should the United States attempt to resolve ethnic conflicts in other nations?

The ups and downs of U.S. military expenditures since the end of World War II reflect changing perceptions of the threat to U.S. interests at home and abroad. From 1945 through the 1960s, military spending constituted nearly 9 percent of the gross domestic product (GDP). By the 1970s the defense budget had dropped to 6 percent of the GDP, despite the expenses connected with the Vietnam War. By 1980, the end of Jimmy Carter's administration, defense spending had fallen to 5.3 percent of the GDP.[12] President Clinton made a campaign promise to cut defense spending if elected. By the end of his second term, defense spending had declined to about 3 percent of the GDP.[13] Defense spending accounted for more than 50 percent of the federal budget in 1960, 42 percent in 1970, and only 23 percent in 1980.[14] For the year 2000 only 16 percent of the federal budget was earmarked for defense spending.[15]

During Reagan's presidency, the United States accomplished the largest sustained peacetime expansion of military spending in its history. By fiscal year 1988 the military budget was more than double the fiscal 1980 outlays. The military's share of the federal budget rose from 28 percent in 1980 to 32 percent in 1988; in the same period, its share of the GDP jumped from 5.3 percent to 6.4 percent.[16] In fiscal year 1990, following improvements in relations with the Soviet Union in the late 1980s, defense spending fell slightly to 22 percent of overall federal spending. These outlays were 24 percent lower than 1985 outlays for defense programs in real terms.[17] President Clinton's campaign promise to reduce defense spending has resulted in defense outlays for the year 2000 that are about 29 percent lower than in 1990.[18]

How Much Is Enough?

Is the United States more capable of protecting itself and projecting its influence around the world than it was before the military expansion? Were the benefits worth the costs? Officials of the Reagan and Bush administrations have argued that the massive military buildup of the 1980s brought the former Soviet Union to the bargaining table and resulted in an arms control agreement—the first to result in the destruction of an entire class of nuclear weapons. They have further argued that U.S. military dominance allowed the United States to conduct the war effectively in the Persian Gulf with few American casualties.

Critics maintain, however, that the former Soviet Union was willing to bargain because of its need to reduce defense spending and to improve relations with the rest of the industrial world. Despite the reductions in intermediate-range nuclear weapons, the strategic nuclear defense arsenal on the ground, in submarines, and in bombers remains incredibly destructive. They also argue that the massive military buildup of the 1980s increased the likelihood that U.S. policymakers would resort to deadly force in situations when diplomacy and economic sanctions would work just as effectively and without great loss of lives. Finally, military might does little or nothing to deter suicidal terrorist attacks on U.S. citizens and military personnel.

American politicians are always reluctant to engage U.S. forces in armed conflict. President Clinton and the public were reluctant to send troops into Kosovo as part of a NATO peacekeeping force despite increasing reports of Serbian aggression against Kosovar civilians.[19] U.S. intervention in the Persian Gulf was favorably received by the public largely because Americans perceived that a vital economic interest—the supply of oil—was at stake and because the war lasted less than two months. Public opinion ran strongly against military involvement when World War II began in Europe; U.S. troops were not committed until after the Japanese attacked Pearl Harbor in December 1941. Large segments of the public opposed subsequent military actions involving American armed forces in Korea and Vietnam, as well as the Persian Gulf.[20] In fact, one legacy of the war in Southeast Asia is the so-called Vietnam syndrome—a deep distrust of U.S. military involvement in other nations. Such concerns have continued to shape public opposition to U.S. involvement in Lebanon, Nicaragua, and the Persian Gulf.[21] President Bush claimed that this skepticism was removed by successful conduct of the Persian Gulf War. As the experience during the NATO bombings of Kosovo has shown us, it is more likely, however, that public distrust of U.S. troop commitments in armed conflicts will continue to shape U.S. foreign policy.

Achieving Sustained Economic Growth

Sustained economic growth, like national security, is a central policy goal of all governments. This broad goal subsumes several specific economic objectives: rising standards of living and wealth, low levels of unemployment and inflation, increasing productivity of the workforce, and expanding exports. Policymakers of all stripes want to promote economic growth and vitality. For more than a decade, the sharpest partisan and ideological disputes have revolved around the extent to which the government can and should manage the economy. Today this partisan division on economic issues can be seen between Democrats and Republicans in Congress. Republicans favor less regulation and lower taxes, especially for upper-income taxpayers. Democrats, in contrast, support more regulation, more extensive public services, and lower taxes, but for middle-income and working-class taxpayers.

The achievement of economic goals depends, perhaps more than any other policy objective, on the policies and financial resources of both the government and the private sector. In general, government involvement in fostering a healthy economy takes two forms: *macroeconomic policy* decisions and decisions about *investment* in human capital and the nation's physical infrastructure. Macroeconomic policy encompasses matters such as the government's spending and tax policy, the supply and cost of money, and trading policies with other nations. When the economy is functioning at less than full employment, the government can increase public and private spending through fiscal and monetary stimulation, which in turn generates greater demand for goods and services and puts more people to work.[22] Federal Reserve Board decisions that establish the size of the money supply and the level of interest rates profoundly influence the rate of inflation in the price of goods and services and the ability of individuals and corporations to raise capital.

Government-sponsored education and research strategies also affect the ability of the nation to achieve its economic goals. Education and training programs translate directly into improvement in the quality and productivity of the workforce. America's colleges and universities have produced one of the most highly educated populations in the world, but the supply of qualified individuals is not meeting the demand in some fields. The American Electronics Association estimates, for example, that between 1996 and 2006 the demand for trained specialists in the computer industry, such as computer engineers and systems analysts, will more than double in the United States. Unfortunately, this demand will not be met by American workers because there have been large decreases in the number of students graduating from U.S. universities with high-tech degrees. For example, the number of bachelor degrees in electrical engineering and computer and informational sciences decreased 33 percent and 27 percent, respectively, between 1990 and 1996.[23]

Government-sponsored research and development activities often generate new products and increase economic growth. More than half of the money spent on research and development in the United States is supplied by the federal government—the sum was more than $80 billion in 1999.[24] Since 1962, government research in the aerospace industry has yielded numerous products and productivity improvements. For example, the demand for lightweight, reliable circuitry helped spawn the development of microchips, which eventually led to the development of the personal computer. Historically, countries with the highest rates of growth in research and development expenditures have also experienced greater gains in productivity and had higher GDPs.[25]

Finally, the quality of the nation's infrastructure is vital to a prosperous economy. As a percentage of GDP, federal investment in infrastructure has fallen to 0.7 percent, its lowest point since 1949.[26] Bridges, roads, and water systems are simply wearing out. The Rebuild America Coalition, a nonpartisan group dedicated to bringing infrastructure issues to the nation's agenda, estimates that planned government spending on infrastructure should equal over $400 billion a year in order to meet the demands of our decaying roadways, water systems, public schools, and airports.[27] Most of the funds for this massive undertaking will be raised and spent by state governments.[28]

Effective government policies promote a prosperous, competitive economy, but many factors are beyond government control. Private sector decisions have a direct influence on the size and health of the U.S. economy (see Chapter 3). Private businesses generate nearly two-thirds of the nation's gross domestic product and control virtually all major industrial activities. Therefore, the cumulative impact of corporate decisions is significant. If General Motors decides to locate a plant to manufacture automobiles for the U.S. market in Mexico rather than in Atlanta, the decision costs Americans thousands of high-paying jobs. Because IBM is the leading manufacturer of computers, its decision to develop faster computer-processing equipment enhances the ability of the U.S.-based manufacturers to make faster, more reliable computers that can compete effectively in the world market.

Economic growth also depends on the behavior of investors, workers, and consumers. Workers' productivity and wage demands are important factors in economic expansion. The preference of American consumers for imported products, such as Japanese automobiles and electronic equipment, means that billions of American dollars flow to other nations. Japanese consumers also prefer Japanese-manufactured products, even when U.S. products are superior.[29]

Progress and Challenges

The United States has been the world's dominant economic power since the 1950s. American living standards have risen substantially during this period; the per capita income of Americans has more than doubled.[30] Americans are enjoying more leisure time, and they are retiring at a younger age than previous generations. By many standards the United States remains an economic powerhouse. Nevertheless, it seems proper to conclude that the record is mixed and the future is uncertain.

Despite its strong showing, the U.S. economy has not always outperformed those of other nations. From the mid-1960s to the 1990s, the economies of several countries, including Austria, France, Italy, Japan,

Norway, and the former West Germany, grew at faster rates than the U.S. economy.[31] Japan's economy expanded at roughly twice the U.S. growth rate. This trend changed during the 1990s, with growth in the United States exceeding that in Japan, which experienced a slower rate of growth than in the previous decade.[32] The first quarter of 2000 saw an improvement in Japan's GDP, once again surpassing the U.S. growth rate. The spendable earnings of American workers have been declining since 1960.[33] By the mid-1980s, the wages of workers' employed in the manufacturing sector in Belgium, the Netherlands, Sweden, and West Germany had surpassed the earnings of American workers in the same industries.[34]

Although the American standard of living remains high in absolute terms, it is gradually declining relative to that of other industrial countries. Life expectancy is lower in the United States than in fifteen other nations. Infant mortality rates are higher in the United States than in twenty-four other countries,[35] although they have improved in this country since the early 1960s as a result of the introduction of medical assistance for the poor. The U.S. economy has been plagued by several recessions—periods of either no growth or decline. Severe recessions, bringing high levels of unemployment, occurred in 1954, 1958, 1975, 1979, 1982, and 1991. Since the late 1960s, U.S. unemployment levels, on average, have exceeded those of several other nations, including Germany and the United Kingdom.[36] Although this trend changed in the 1990s as the U.S. economy improved, resulting in low rates of unemployment, it is difficult to determine if these new conditions will continue or if the United States will again fall behind other nations. Furthermore, although the sustained economic growth of the 1990s has benefited many in the United States, large portions of society have been left behind. There continues to be a growing bifurcation of the economic classes, with increasing disparity between the six- to seven-digit incomes of corporate executives and the minimum wage of a growing number of service workers. To compound this, capital flight from the major cities (as well as from U.S. soil altogether) has contributed to the degradation of the nation's urban centers, where the increasing difficulty of the poor to move out of poverty has left whole communities trapped in its grip.[37]

Since 1992, more than 20 million new jobs have been created to absorb the expanding workforce, but despite that impressive record, not everyone who has wanted to work has been able to find a job.[38] During the 1950s and 1960s unemployment averaged 4.6 percent; during the 1970s the average climbed to 6.2 percent. The average for the 1980s was 7.3 percent. During the 1982 recession, unemployment reached 10.8 percent—the highest level since World War II. More than 12 million Americans were unable to find jobs.[39] During the recession of the early 1990s unemployment, although not as high as in the 1980s, rose sharply to 7.8 percent.[40] Unemployment rates dropped to a record low of under 4 percent in the late 1990s.

The aggregate figures do not reveal all the underlying problems. Not counted in the official unemployment statistics are the more than 325,000 "discouraged workers"—people who have given up looking for work because they do not believe any jobs are available—and 3.5 million part-time workers who would rather be working full time.[41] The reported unemployment figures therefore understate the magnitude of the real demand for jobs by Americans.

Older workers who have lost long-term stable jobs because of changes in the structure of the U.S. economy present another vexing problem. Although the service sector (telecommunications, insurance, banking, and restaurants) grew during the 1980s, the manufacturing sector did not. As a result, many workers have been displaced—that is, they lost their jobs permanently. It has not been uncommon for displaced workers to take positions offering lower pay, longer hours, and reduced benefits. Steel, automobile, textile, and machinery workers account for more than half of the estimated 2 million displaced workers. Most of these people live in one of the eight states where the economy is dominated by heavy industry—Illinois, Indiana, Michigan, New Jersey, New York, Ohio, Pennsylvania, and Wisconsin.[42] Although some of these areas, such as Michigan, New Jersey, and Wisconsin, have bounced back by attracting large numbers of jobs in the new high-tech and computer industries, the others continue to lag behind as a result of the devastation caused by the changing economy.

The United States has also struggled with inflation in the prices of goods and services for several decades. From 1950 to the mid-1960s prices increased, on average, no more than 2 percent or 3 percent annually. From 1968 to 1973, prices rose at a 4.6 percent average rate; from 1973 to 1980 the average rate was 8.9 percent.[43] Double-digit annual inflation rates were reached in 1974 and 1975 and in 1980 and 1981.[44] An average car cost approximately 25 percent of the median annual income in 1968. By 1997 an automobile purchase consumed more than 50 percent of the median annual income.

After reaching peak levels, inflation rates dropped significantly in the late 1990s, hovering around 3 percent for the end of that decade and into the first decade of 2000.[45] The underlying factors contributing to higher prices include the price of fossil fuels and agricultural commodities, mortgage interest rates, and wage demands. The collapse of the oil cartel and the rapid decline in the price of crude oil accounted for nearly half of the decline in inflation from 1980 to 1985.[46] When Middle East oil-exporting countries increase prices or become embroiled in war, energy prices and inflation shoot up again.

The New Economic Agenda

Prior to President Clinton's first term the nation was facing a burgeoning federal budget deficit. When Clinton entered office it stood at $290 billion; by the end of his second term, the deficit had been abolished and the federal government was running an annual surplus of more than $120 billion.[47]

When Clinton entered office in 1992, he proposed to reduce the deficit mainly by increasing taxes on higher incomes and secondarily by reducing spending. The proposal included a stimulus package to get the lagging economy back on its feet, but this spending faced serious opposition by Republicans in Congress. After much deliberation and negotiation, a budget deal was finally passed that included deep cuts in Clinton's stimulus package, lower taxes on the wealthy than had been proposed, and reduced spending on many social programs. This deal would achieve Clinton's goal of a $500 billion, five-year deficit reduction package.

Another balanced budget battle occurred toward the end of Clinton's first term in 1995. With Clinton arguing that the budget could be balanced without cuts in program spending and the Republican majority in the House resisting any tax increases and pushing for decreased social spending, the president and Congress came to a showdown in December 1995 that resulted in the shutdown of the federal government for several days. The shutdown brought heightened public support for Clinton's economic priorities and forced a balanced budget act through Congress in 1996 that reflected the president's priorities in program spending levels.

The expanding economy in the mid-1990s helped to eliminate the deficit and balance the budget before the legislated deadline of seven years. This positive economic performance also produced a growth of budget surpluses for the first time in forty years, which resulted in increased tax cuts and spending in areas such as education and health care at the federal level.

The booming economy and government surpluses affected the status of some entitlement programs. For example, new government surpluses were used to "shore up" the Social Security system, which was previously predicted to run dry as a result of the increased number of recipients from the baby-boomer generation. Surpluses also generated demand for new entitlements, such as prescription drug benefits for the elderly.

The United States is at the fore of the "dot-com" economy. It is leading the world in science and information technology. Although its share of heavy manufacturing has declined significantly since the 1970s, the United States has replaced much of this heavy industry with new high-tech industries. For the first time in decades, U.S. economic growth has surpassed other leading industrial countries such as Japan.

The Organization for Economic Cooperation and Development (OECD) argues that much of the U.S. success has come from investments in its workforce training and skills as well as investment in technology infrastructure.[48] Productivity in the United States increased during the 1990s, and export revenues from high-tech goods and services also increased. A large share of U.S. productivity growth in the 1990s was due to growth in the information and communication technology sector alone. The OECD attributes much of this growth to U.S. economic practices that encourage venture finance and competition in the new technology industries.

Expanding trade agreements championed by Clinton, such as the North American Free Trade Agreement (NAFTA) and the General Agreement on Tariffs and Trade (GATT), have opened new markets for U.S. goods but have also increased the ability of U.S. companies to move their operations overseas in search of cheaper labor. Although workers in the high-tech industries in the United States are benefiting from the current state of the U.S. economy, many workers, especially in the manufacturing sector, have been displaced by low-cost foreign labor. It is safe to argue that although the United States has made many positive changes in order to improve the economy, not everyone has been included in those changes. Continued and increased investment in the U.S. workforce is necessary to ensure the proper training and skills essential to success in the "new economy."

Ensuring Equal Opportunity

Since the founding of the nation, America's leaders have espoused a commitment to equality of opportunity. But when Thomas Jefferson, a slave owner himself, wrote in the Declaration of Independence that "all men are created equal," he did not include African Americans, women, or Native Americans. Over time, government policies have gradually extended political, social, and economic opportunities to groups originally denied them. The Constitution has been amended to ensure political rights for African Americans and women. Statutes prohibiting discrimination on the basis of race, gender, ethnicity, age, disability, and sexual orientation have been applied to education, employment, housing, voting, and public accommodations.

The nation's moral credo rejects discrimination and advocates equal opportunity, but living up to this code and giving it practical meaning have been as difficult to accomplish as any aspect of American public policy. The battle over racial equality was marked by lynchings, bombings of black churches, and other ugly incidents. The uncomfortable chasm between American ideals and the actual distribution of opportunities and benefits has properly been called an American dilemma.[49] Americans place a high value on individual initiative and self-reliance. But there is a growing awareness that even in a democracy, prosperity that is not shared is prosperity soon disdained. Working toward and giving people a sense of fairness is the glue that holds a democratic society together. The late economist Arthur Okun commented that U.S. society awards prizes that allow the big winners to feed their pets better than the losers can feed their children. For example, in the late 1990s the average income of U.S. families in the top 20 percent of the income distribution was $137,500, or more than ten times that of the poorest 20 percent of families, which averaged $13,000.[50] In 1998, CEOs made 419 times the pay of workers, with the average annual salary package for a CEO, including stock options and bonuses, totaling $10.6 million.[51] Such is the double standard of a capitalist democracy, professing and pursuing an egalitarian political and social system and simultaneously generating gaping disparities in economic well-being.[52]

The achievement of equal opportunity raises four difficult questions about what equal opportunity means and how the government should promote it:

1. Should government guarantees of equal opportunities encompass both the political system and the economic system?
2. To what extent is the government obligated to redress past discrimination against particular groups of Americans?
3. Should government promote greater equality in the distribution of wealth and other social benefits?
4. Does meaningful affirmative action require a quota system?

Unfulfilled Promises

The United States has made significant strides, especially since the early 1960s. Women, blacks, and other minorities are no longer denied the right to vote or hold office. The U.S. armed forces no longer places black and white Americans in separate fighting units. The Supreme Court has declared that all children in a particular community should be educated in the same schools, regardless of race. Congress has determined that Americans must not be discriminated against because of their race, gender, disabilities, or ethnic origin when they apply to colleges and universities, seek employment or housing, and apply for insurance and bank loans. White Americans have become more racially tolerant.[53]

Despite these significant accomplishments, America remains a society in which millions do not fully enjoy the nation's political, social, and economic benefits.[54] Poverty, homelessness, and hunger remain serious problems in one of the world's most affluent nations. After dropping to 11 percent in 1973 from 22 percent in 1960, poverty gradually increased in the 1980s. In 1989 more than 31 million people, or 13 percent of the population, could not afford the basic necessities of life as defined by government standards. The poverty rate for children was even higher.[55] The overall poverty rate dropped to 12.7 percent of the population in 1998, but this still means that 34.5 million Americans were below the poverty level for that year. The number of poor children was 13.5 million in 1998, or 18.9 percent of people in the United States under the age of eighteen.[56]

Income and wealth are unequally distributed. The bottom 20 percent of all U.S. families received only 3.6 percent of the aggregate household income in 1998; the top 20 percent received more than thirteen times that much, or 49.2 percent of the total.[57] Inequities in the distribution of income have not improved since World War II.[58] "There has been an increase in income inequality in the United States during the last decade and a half," according to Census Bureau official Gordon Green.[59] The equity of income distribution in America ranks eighth among the eleven members of the OECD, which includes Australia, Canada, Japan, Sweden, and the United Kingdom, among other nations.[60] The ownership of wealth is even more unevenly distributed than income; the top 1 percent of all U.S. families held 35.6 percent of the wealth in 1998, whereas the bottom 90 percent held only 30.5 percent.[61]

Federal, state, and local tax systems do little to redistribute income, and in some ways they increase inequities. According to political scientist Benjamin Page:

> The federal income tax is more egalitarian than other taxes. But the progressivity of the actual effective rates—as contrasted with the nominal schedule rates—is rather mild and has been eroded over time. Taxes on the rich are not very high. . . . Various exclusions and exemptions and deductions from taxable income greatly benefit the rich.[62]

The tax code revision of 1986 eliminated millions of poor and near-poor Americans from the tax rolls, but even after these major changes tax laws remained inequitable. To address this problem, in 1993 President Clinton signed the largest expansion of the Earned Income Tax Credit into law; it provided a tax cut for 15 million working families. This expansion is expected to continue and has been cited as a partial cause of the reduction in poverty and welfare caseloads since the mid-1990s.[63]

People earning the same income often pay very different amounts in federal taxes. High-income Americans may pay less in taxes than people who earn a great deal less. Inequities persist because the tax code contains a host of exclusions, preferences, and deductions. For example, homeowners are permitted to deduct all of the interest they pay on mortgages for their primary residence and for a vacation home. The owner of a $60,000 house and the owner of a $5 million mansion can deduct the entire amount of their interest payments from their tax liability. The home mortgage deduction amounts to a direct subsidy of more than $40 billion to high-income individuals. People who rent or have modest mortgage payments receive little or no tax benefits.[64]

If federal income taxes do little to redistribute income from the rich to the poor, payroll taxes and state and local income taxes accomplish the opposite: the more money a person is paid, the lower the percentage of income paid to the government. Social Security taxes, for example, are withheld at a flat rate and only on $65,000 in income. The $250,000-a-year investment banker on Wall Street pays the same amount in Social Security taxes as the $65,000-a-year civil engineer. State and local taxes, which rely heavily on the sales tax, are regressive. People with low incomes pay the same tax rate as those with high incomes. But a larger share of the poor person's income is used to purchase the goods and services necessary for survival.[65]

These disparities are especially difficult to justify in a society where economic hardship is not random. Minorities are much more likely to be poor, unemployed, and otherwise disadvantaged than white Americans. In 1998 the poverty rate for African Americans was 26.1 percent and for Hispanics 25.6 percent, but it was only 8.2 percent for whites.[66] Unemployment rates follow a similar pattern. In June 2000, for example, the unemployment rate for white adults was 3.4 percent, but it was 7.9 percent for African Americans and 5.6 percent for Hispanics. The picture is even bleaker for young people. In June 2000, 9.4 percent of white teens were unemployed, as opposed to 25.4 percent of African American teenagers.[67]

More than half of female-headed families live below the poverty level, continuing a trend that has been called the feminization of poverty. Of all poor adults, two-thirds are women.[68] Most poor women are widowed or divorced and have been left without economic support for themselves and their children. Many are unwed mothers. Many receive no financial support from the child's father; almost 40 percent of custodial mothers do not receive awards for child support payments and about 30 percent of those awarded support do not receive the payments from the child's father.[69] Teen pregnancy rates jumped 20 percent between 1970 and 1990 but have actually decreased about 12 percent since 1991[70]; two-thirds of those young mothers will spend at least some time in poverty. Many women are poor even though they work at full-time, year-round jobs. Two-thirds of minimum-wage earners are women. Because of inflation, the purchasing power of their minimum-wage jobs eroded since the early 1980s. The 1996 increase in the minimum wage from $4.25 to $5.15 hour did not restore the minimum wage to its 1981 purchasing power.[71]

Progress for minorities has been slow because in many ways the United States remains a racially segregated society. Minority groups are concentrated in cities; they may be kept from living in suburban communities by discriminatory real estate sales practices or the lack of affordable housing for moderate- and low-income individuals. Efforts to desegregate the schools have had limited success. Seven in ten African Americans attended schools that were at least 50 percent African American in the 1996–1997 school year, and nearly four in ten African Americans attended schools at least 90 percent African American. The typical white student attended a school that was 81 percent white.[72]

Women have not achieved economic and political parity with men. Women have increased their participation in the workforce from 42 percent in 1970 to over 60 percent of all women in 1999, and laws guaranteeing equal pay for equal work have been passed in many states.[73] But women earn on average seventy cents for every dollar earned by men.[74] Women are concentrated in several occupations (teaching, nursing, child care, and clerical positions) that pay less than occupations predominantly held by men (accountants, salespeople, and laborers), even though the female-dominated jobs require similar levels of skill and training. Although women constitute more than half of the U.S. population, there are few women in leadership positions in business and industry or government.

Prospects for Change

Strategies promoting social, political, and economic equity have been highly controversial and only moderately successful. The women's movement has failed to obtain ratification of an equal rights amendment to the Constitution. Although the Supreme Court has endorsed the strategy of affirmative action, the practice is still subject to legal challenge and to resistance by many institutions. Affirmative action has been challenged in several court cases since its inception, the most notable being the landmark Supreme Court case of *Regents of the University of California v. Bakke* (1978), which imposed limitations on affirmative action in professional school admissions by ruling that the use of inflexible quotas was not a legitimate practice. This precedent was followed by *Hopwood v. University of Texas Law School* (1996), in which the U.S. Court of Appeals for the Fifth Circuit suspended the university's affirmative action program, asserting that race could not serve as a factor in admissions. The anti–affirmative action atmosphere heightened during the last decade of the twentieth century with two states, California and Washington, banning all affirmative action programs.[75] The tax policy changes of the Reagan and Bush administrations did not address inequities in the distribution of income and wealth, and the Democratic Party has not advanced any bold or promising initiatives to redistribute income in America. Although President Clinton enacted policies that addressed this unequal distribution by allowing working families to keep more of their income through the Earned Income Tax Credit and by increasing taxes for the richest of Americans, data from the late 1990s still illustrate a huge income gap between the rich and the poor.

A major impetus for change may come from the desire of American business and industry to remain competitive in the world economy. Business and political leaders are beginning to realize that the nation must fully use available human resources. The tight labor market and low unemployment rates of the late 1990s and early 2000s made human resources even more scarce and valuable to U.S. business. For the foreseeable future a significant portion of entry-level workers will consist of minorities, immigrants for whom English is a second language, and other low-income individuals.[76] Many of these new workers will come from the population of previous welfare recipients, who must meet strict work requirements mandated in the welfare reform of 1996. The work emphasis of this reform means millions of new workers will be entering the labor market, many without any previous work experience, training, or skills. This surge of disadvantaged workers, as well as the high demand for all workers in the tight labor market, may prompt greater efforts to bring them into the mainstream of the American economy.

Providing a Safety Net

The power of government has not been exercised in an attempt to achieve a radical redistribution of income and wealth, but American policymakers have erected a network of programs that provide financial support and health care to millions of citizens. These measures may not always lift the poor out of poverty, but they keep people from falling farther into it. Initiated by liberal Democratic president Franklin D. Roosevelt in the 1930s, these New Deal social insurance and welfare programs were considered an essential social "safety net" even by conservative Republican president Ronald Reagan.[77]

The vast array of programs that support elderly, poor, unemployed, and disabled Americans consume the largest proportion of the federal budget. It has grown so quickly since the 1950s that politicians are beginning to ask some very tough questions. Can Americans afford these programs? Can the country afford to be without them? How can these programs be made more efficient and equitable?

Income-Support Programs

Since the New Deal, the basic structure of the American welfare state has expanded to encompass new classes of beneficiaries and to authorize more generous benefits. Once a small fraction of the budget, income-support programs now account for approximately 35 percent of federal outlays and constitute a huge portion of state and local spending. Income-support programs amounted to less than 3 percent of the GDP in 1960; by 1990 they amounted to nearly three times as much. Federal expenditures have increased tenfold in less than thirty years.[78] During the 1980s, the trend of extending eligibility and expanding benefits slowed, but safety net spending continued its upward trend.[79]

President Clinton entered office in 1992 with plans to expand the safety net with the addition of a universal health care program. After his appointed task force composed a 1,300-page proposal, Clinton ultimately failed to pass legislation for a national plan. Opposition from the health care and insurance industries and Republicans in Congress combined with inept political strategizing to derail these attempts. Congressional Republicans attempted to roll back entitlement programs in the mid-1990s and these attempts eventually provoked a showdown with the president in 1995. The resulting government shutdown created public support for the president's spending priorities on some entitlements and defeated the Republican proposals for cutbacks.

The number of Americans benefiting from the safety net has grown by leaps and bounds. Social Security—which aids retirees, the children of deceased workers, and disabled workers—is the largest federal program, with expenditures of $372 billion in 1998.[80] In 1990 one American in six received Social Security retirement checks, and 90 percent of the working population contributed through payroll tax deductions to the program. An average of 7.1 million Americans received unemployment compensation during 1998 that averaged $191 weekly, and most of the nation's more than 100 million workers are employed by companies that contribute to the insurance system.[81] Approximately 19.8 million people received food stamps in a given month during 1998 for a total of $17 billion in benefits that year.[82] During fiscal year 1999, nearly 2.5 million American families received public assistance.[83]

Income-support programs come in two forms: programs dispensed according to need and programs distributed without regard to need. Many income-support programs are called "entitlement" programs because people receive benefits as a matter of statutory right. The largest income-support programs, including Social Security and unemployment insurance, are available to eligible recipients no matter what their income or assets may be. Therefore, most income-support programs are not subject to a means test: full benefits are extended to rich and poor alike. About 90 percent of the funds reserved for older Americans do not require applicants to demonstrate financial need.[84]

Social Security and unemployment insurance replace part of the income lost due to retirement, disability, or unemployment. Retirees who made $1,000 per month during their working years receive about a 60 percent replacement.[85] A typical unemployed worker is paid about $764 per month, or between 50 and 60 percent replacement of income. Unemployment insurance lasts only a few months and is open only to those workers who lost their jobs through "no fault of their own"; the "insured unemployed" represented about 36 percent of the total number of unemployed workers in 1998.[86]

Social Security and unemployment insurance are based on the concept of social insurance. During their working years, individuals contribute about 7 percent of their income into the Social Security trust fund to help cover the cost of benefits they may eventually receive. Employers pay into an insurance trust fund from which workers receive benefits during periods of unemployment.

Intended as a partial supplement to private pension plans and family incomes, Social Security provides a financial base for those who could not adequately prepare for retirement. Social Security is the nation's strongest antipoverty program and, along with medical insurance for senior citizens, it has contributed substantially to reducing the number of older Americans who are poor. Once, the elderly were a disadvantaged group: in 1960 more than 25 percent of the nation's senior citizens lived in poverty. Today, fewer than 10 percent of the elderly are poor.[87] Median family incomes of the elderly have more than doubled since 1960. In fact, their incomes have increased faster than the incomes of the rest of the population. The average Social Security check for a retired couple in 2000 was higher than $1,300 per month, which by itself provides sufficient income to live above government-defined poverty levels.[88]

The biggest challenges for administrators of the Social Security program have been controlling growth and keeping the system solvent. The earlier retirements and longer life spans of Americans have imposed new strains on the Social Security trust fund. Since the mid-1970s, benefit payments have increased at regular intervals as a result of legislated cost-of-living adjustments and thus roughly keep pace with inflation.

Proposals for trimming Social Security benefits in the early 1980s met a firestorm of criticism from Democrats and senior citizen groups, who form a large, politically powerful constituency. A bipartisan reform commission made several short- and long-term changes in the program, but virtually all the modifications increased the funds for distribution, rather than curtailed existing benefits.[89] With the elimination of the annual deficits that prevailed for most of the 1990s, President Clinton and other politicians called for the use of budget surpluses to "shore up" the future of Social Security. Proposals for increased government investment of tax revenues in the Social Security trust fund dominated the agenda of the late 1990s. Another proposal was the creation of personal retirement accounts to save the program. Regardless, President Clinton's message, "Social Security first," ruled expenditures of the new budget surpluses.

The balance of the federal and state income-support programs are reserved for poor Americans. Aid to Families with Dependent Children (AFDC), the welfare entitlement program that had existed for thirty years, was replaced with block grants to states through the welfare legislation called the Personal Responsibility and Work Opportunity Reconciliation Act, passed in 1996. The new welfare program institutes many changes, including the end of the entitlement status of aid to the poor, strict work requirements, lifetime eligibility limits, and new teen parent provisions (see Table 10-1). Temporary Assistance to Needy Families (TANF) and food stamps are made available only after individuals have proved they need assistance. A woman must have young children and no support from her family or the father of her children in order to be considered for TANF payments. States receive wide discretion in determining eligibility rules.

The TANF program is paid for by the states and the federal government and administered by states and localities. Benefit levels vary widely. For example, in 1998 the monthly payment for a family of four in Alabama was $147, whereas in Alaska it was $833.[90] Benefits are below the poverty line in all fifty states, ranging from Mississippi, where benefits are a low 13 percent of the poverty line, to Alaska, where they amount to 79 percent.[91] The typical

Table 10-1 Comparison of Aid to Families with Dependent Children (AFDC) and the 1996 Welfare Reform Legislation

Provision	Prior law (AFDC)	Personal Responsibility and Work Opportunity Reconciliation Act of 1996 (P.L.104-193) (PRWORA)
Funding	Open-ended categorical grant funding requiring state matching grant.	Block grant to states estimated at $16.4 billion for each year from FY1996 to FY2003. Each state receives a fixed amount based upon historical expenditures for AFDC.
Entitlement	Entitlement to states. Benefits were guaranteed to eligible individuals at state-established benefit levels. States received federal matching dollars, without a cap.	End of entitlement status. No individual guarantee of benefits. States have discretion in setting "objective criteria for delivery of benefits and determining eligibility."
Time limits for assistance	Recipients remained eligible for benefits as long as they met program eligibility requirements.	Five-year lifetime limit on benefits. States are permitted to exempt 20 percent of their caseload from the time limit. Non-cash assistance may be made available to families after the federal limit.
Work requirements	For FY1994, 15 percent of the non-exempt caseload was required to participate in JOBS activities for at least twenty hours per week.	States must require families to work after two years on assistance. By FY2002, a minimum of 50 percent of single-parent family cases and 95 percent of two-parent families must be working a minimum of thirty hours per week. Individuals who receive assistance for two months are required to participate in community service.
Work activities	States were required to provide basic and secondary education, ESL, job skills training, job development and placement, and job readiness.	No education or training component for recipients over eighteen. To count toward the work requirement, recipients must participate in subsidized or unsubsidized employment, on-the-job training, work experience, community service, or provide child care services to individuals who are participating in community service.
Teen parent provisions	No federal regulation, so state option.	Unmarried minor parents are required to live with an adult or in an adult-supervised setting and participate in training and educational activities to receive assistance.
Family cap	Families on AFDC received additional benefits whenever they had another child.	States are given the option to impose family caps, wherein families do not receive extra benefits for children born while they are receiving assistance.
Illegitimacy issue	States required to provide family planning services to any AFDC recipient who requested the service.	Establishes a bonus to states that demonstrate that the number of out-of-wedlock births and abortions decreased over the past two years in comparison to the prior two-year period.

Source: Adapted from U.S. Department of Health and Human Services, "Comparison of Prior Law and the Personal Responsibility and Work Opportunity Reconciliation Act of 1996," online at http://www.aspe.os.dhhs.gov/hsp/isp/reform.htm, March 10, 1999.

welfare recipient is a white female who remains on welfare for less than two years and works part time.

Welfare and food stamps consume fewer federal dollars and constitute much smaller portions of the federal budget—less than 5 percent—than the non–means-tested entitlement programs. Welfare and nutrition aid for the poor cost the federal government approximately $33 billion in fiscal year 1998—less than 10 percent of the cost of Social Security alone.[92] Food stamps were the fastest-growing component of these programs. From the 1970s to the 1990s the cost of food stamps increased nearly twentyfold.[93] But the Personal Responsibility and Work Opportunity Reconciliation Act of 1996 placed several new restrictions on food stamp eligibility for legal immigrants and able-bodied adults without dependents. Although almost $16 billion was paid out in food stamp benefits in 1999, caseloads declined 33 percent, from 27.5 million cases in 1994 to 18.5 million cases in 1999.[94]

Unlike Social Security, which is widely regarded as a successful, but expensive, program, AFDC was disliked by taxpayers and recipients alike. Even though only a small percentage of funds was spent on ineligible people, opinion polls consistently showed that the public perceived the program as awash in corruption and abuse. Welfare recipients and others complained that AFDC payments were stingy and that the system encouraged recipients to remain poor and discouraged their self-reliance.

The widespread perception that the welfare system was "broken" led to significant welfare reform, first in 1988 and then in 1996.[95] Congress endorsed a major overhaul of the system, modeled after successful state initiatives.[96] Under the Personal Responsibility and Work Opportunity Reconciliation Act of 1996, welfare no longer penalizes those who want to work their way off welfare. The new programs are designed to require recipients to seek full-time employment and get off welfare by providing them with extended health benefits and child care assistance after they find jobs, as well as sanction those who do not comply with the work requirements.

Health Care

America's income-support programs were spawned primarily by the New Deal. The health care programs—Medicare for the elderly and Medicaid for the poor—were the offspring of Lyndon Johnson's War on Poverty. When Medicare was adopted in 1965, the Social Security Administration estimated that it would cost the federal government $8.2 billion in 1983. It actually cost $38 billion in 1983. The estimate was terribly wrong. Medicare cost the federal government more than $192 billion in 1998; Medicaid cost the federal government another $101 billion.[97] Government health insurance pays nearly half of the hospital costs and doctor bills for the entire nation.[98] Although government support for health care in the United States still trails that of other industrial nations, the commitment has increased rapidly. When private contributions to health care spending are included, the United States leads the world in the amount of its GDP devoted to health care.[99]

Elderly and poor Americans are the principal beneficiaries of government health care programs. Medicare serves all Americans over the age of sixty-five regardless of need. Program participants pay for part of the cost of physician visits and hospital care, but most of the tab is picked up by the government. Medicaid is reserved for the poorest of the poor. Over one-third of America's poor population is not poor enough to qualify for Medicaid.[100] More than 40 million Americans who are not old or not very poor have inadequate medical insurance or none at all.[101]

Health care costs and government expenditures for health programs have skyrocketed, driven by three factors: demographics, third-party reimbursement, and the complexity of medical care. Increases in the aging and poor populations have resulted in greater outlays in these entitlement programs. Medical consumers and medical professionals are not motivated to keep costs down because three-fourths of all medical bills are borne by third parties, namely, the government or private insurance companies.[102] National health care expenditures represented only 5.1 percent of the GDP in 1960 but grew to represent a 13.6 percent share of the GDP by 1993.[103] The enormous increase in government outlays for medical procedures and hospitalization has generated demands for a less costly health care system.

Although President Clinton's attempt to establish a national health care plan in 1993 failed, the health care industry has undergone several market-driven changes that have altered the face of the system. Managed care, a core component of Clinton's proposal that was voted down, became much more common in the mid- and late-1990s. This shift was due in part to concerns of employers and patients over rising costs as well as pressures in the political arena for some sort of change. New concerns have arisen because of the increasing prevalence of managed care.[104] During the mid-1990s health care expenditures stabilized, partly as a result of the growing managed care industry, but concerns over quality of care grew. Such concerns generated legislative proposals for a patient's bill of rights to protect patients in the changed world of health care. Although a national plan failed, concerns over the rising costs of health care in the 1990s and early 2000s have resulted in other new proposals. The rising cost of prescription drugs has led to bills advocating a prescription drug plan for the elderly to reduce their out-of-pocket costs for expensive medicines.

In many ways Medicare and Medicaid meet their legislative objectives. Medicare provides financial assistance for a critical need of elderly citizens. Medicaid serves as an adjunct to food stamps and public assistance for the poor, the blind, and the disabled. Despite these accomplishments and burgeoning budgets, government health care programs have not substantially reduced many serious health care problems. Simply increasing health care expenditures does not necessarily lead to better health.[105] Infant mortality rates have declined, but they still exceed those in many other industrial nations. For black Americans, the number of deaths per 1,000 births is higher than in Malaysia, Cuba, Brunei, and thirty-six other countries.[106] Access to affordable, high-quality medical care remains a serious problem for millions of Americans, including many covered by Medicare and Medicaid. Medicare, for example, does not fund extended care in nursing homes—one of the most serious problems of the elderly. Older persons must exhaust their financial resources before they can turn to Medicaid for help.[107]

Most important, American health insurance programs do little to help prevent serious health problems.[108] Significant public health gains were realized in the first half of the twentieth century through government-sponsored measures to improve sanitation, water quality, and immunization against communicable diseases. Government-sponsored research contributes significantly to the treatment of serious diseases, but many health policy analysts argue that government policy should be changed to encourage Americans to take more responsibility for their own health. Some of the leading causes of death—smoking, alcohol consumption, and faulty diet—are influenced by personal choices. According to the surgeon general of the United States, smoking is "the chief, single avoidable cause of death in our society and the most important public health problem of our time."[109] Not only does the government do little to stop smoking (such as banning cigarettes and cigars), it actually subsidizes the production of tobacco in several states. The Food and Drug Administration case against the tobacco industry in 1995 brought the issue of smoking-related health problems to the front of the national agenda. Prior to this, several states had attempted to sue the industry to receive compensation for state Medicaid funds that had been used to treat tobacco-related illnesses. The federal case spawned regulation of tobacco advertising as well as vending machine sales. It also established a national program, funded by the tobacco industry, to prevent youth from smoking. Many other lawsuits have followed, some with success, such as the record class-action suit filed in Florida that ended in an order to tobacco manufacturers to pay $145 billion in punitive damages to Florida smokers.[110] However, in March 2000, the Supreme Court ruled in *FDA v. Brown & Williamson* that the FDA does not have the power to regulate tobacco.[111]

Protecting the Environment

Conserving the nation's resources and protecting its environment yield immediate, tangible benefits and long-term, intangible benefits. The primary purpose of environmental controls is improved public health, which means lower mortality and morbidity rates and reduced medical expenses. The long-term benefits derived from protecting the environment are less tangible and more diffuse, but they are critically important. President Carter's Commission for a National Agenda for the Eighties posed this question: "What value can be placed on public enjoyment of purer air, cleaner water, or protected wilderness, or more importantly, on preserving the long-term integrity of natural life support systems?"[112]

Preserving and protecting the environment has been a central policy goal in the United States for a short period of time. Prior to the 1960s, concern for the environment centered on preserving the natural environment. Land-mark policies adopted during the early decades of the twentieth century established national parks, forests, and wilderness refuges. The federal gov-ernment is the nation's largest landholder: it owns 660 million acres, or 29 percent, of the entire country.[113] Environmental measures—such as the Refuse Act of 1899, which brought into being basic sanitation and sewage disposal practices—were adopted to blunt the most egregious results of urbanization.

Although conservation goals have not been abandoned, environmental policies since the early 1960s have constituted reactions to the consequences of an industrial, chemically dependent society. For decades, American con-sumers and businesses took environmental quality for granted. Vast quanti-ties of hazardous and toxic wastes and chemicals were dumped on the land and in the water and released into the air. Perhaps more than any other sin-gle event, the publication of Rachel Carson's *Silent Spring* in 1962 pro-moted an awareness of the fragility of the environment. Carson's book doc-umented that the use of the chemical DDT in farming destroyed wildlife and threatened humans. Ten years later, the production of DDT was banned for use on American soil.

Concern over the deterioration of the environment generated widespread public support (marked by the first Earth Day 1970) for stronger environ-mental laws. Americans are frequently reminded of potentially harmful sub-stances lurking in the air and water. The poisoning of the food chain with cancer-causing PCB (polychlorinated biphenyl), the presence of noxious fumes and smog in urban communities, and the contamination of water from leaking toxic waste dumps are the price exacted for the casual attitudes of the past. According to environmental scholar Walter Rosenbaum, "We are practically the first generation in the world's history with the certain technical capacity to alter and even to destroy the fundamental biochemical and geophysical conditions for societies living centuries after ours."[114]

More than twenty major environmental protection laws were enacted at the federal level during the 1970s—the "environmental decade." Among the landmarks were the National Environmental Protection Act, which established a process of assessing the environmental impact of federal proj-ects; the Water Pollution Control Act; the Clean Water Act; the Clean Air Act; the Insecticide, Fungicide, and Rodenticide Act; the Toxic Substances Control Act, which regulates the production and handling of toxic waste; the Resource Conservation and Recovery Act, which regulates the dispos-al of solid waste; and the Comprehensive Environmental Response,

Compensation, and Liability Act, commonly called the Superfund, which established procedures for cleaning up toxic waste dumps. Hundreds of state and local laws were also adopted during this period. Standards for improving the quality of the air, water, and land were established, along with government agencies to monitor and enforce compliance. Driving this surge of government regulation was the need to correct the harmful practices of private businesses and individuals.

Several policies have been added to this extensive list since the 1970s. The Superfund was revised in the 1980s to increase federal funding, to emphasize citizen participation in decisions concerning local toxic waste cleanup, and to strengthen state involvement in Superfund actions. Congress amended the Clean Air Act in 1990 to include regulations on ozone-depleting chemicals, which have been blamed for the global warming effect. It also created a national market for sulfur emissions, allowing polluters to buy and sell pollution permits, a policy long recommended by economists.[115] Through so-called Brownfields initiatives, federal, state, and local government funds have been dedicated to redeveloping contaminated and abandoned land in urban areas.

A Legacy of Contempt

The laws and agencies created during America's environmental awakening set ambitious goals, but decades of contempt for the environment have proved difficult and costly to rectify. Citizens and policymakers began to realize by the late 1980s that improving environmental quality would require years of sustained effort, billions of dollars, and profound changes in the way Americans do business and live. The United States has stepped up its attack on environmental problems, but much remains to be done.

Water Quality

Water quality laws enacted during the 1960s and 1970s were supposed to ensure safe drinking water and to clean up polluted rivers, streams, and lakes. The National Technical Advisory Committee on Water Quality Controls reported, however, that measurements of five standard pollutants revealed little improvement in water quality during the 1980s.[116] Pollution generated by individuals and industry continues to flow into surface and ground waters at alarming rates. The $100 billion spent on water pollution control measures has not significantly cut dangerous levels of toxic chemicals, bacteria, nitrates, and phosphorus in the water supply. A national survey of the nation's harbors and lakes in the late 1990s revealed almost no improvement since 1992, and very little before that. Forty percent of the nation's waterways do not meet EPA standards for fishing and swimming.[117]

Air Quality

Lawmakers hoped that the standards and enforcement mechanisms established by the Clean Air Act of 1970 would significantly reduce air pollution in five years. Despite some progress, those hopes are yet to be fulfilled. On the positive side, by the mid-1980s, dangerous lead emissions had dropped 86 percent, largely as a result of a ban on the use of high-lead gasoline. Between 1986 and 1995 lead emissions decreased another 32 percent.[118] Particulate and dust pollution declined by about 33 percent between the early 1960s and the 1980s and another 22 percent between 1988 and 1995. Overall, however, air quality improved by only 13 percent between 1975 and 1985. The air is still fouled with sulfur dioxide and carbon monoxide, which harm the respiratory system. These persistent problems finally resulted in new air pollution legislation in 1990. However, the EPA's efforts to implement that law have met with resistance, including an unfavorable decision by the District of Columbia Circuit Court of Appeals.[119]

Toxic Waste

Notable success in protecting the public from the negative effects of toxic chemicals has been achieved by imposing sharp restrictions on the production and use of several cancer-causing products, including DDT, PCBs, and dioxin. Federal laws governing the handling of toxic wastes established procedures for assessing chemical hazards and disposing of them properly. Government agencies responsible for cleaning up abandoned toxic waste dumps have identified hundreds of dangerous situations and eliminated or curtailed many threats to the environment and public health.

Unfortunately, toxic waste problems are growing in complexity and scope. Many possibly toxic chemicals are being introduced so fast that the government is unable to test them all for potential hazards. American industry generates 265 million metric tons of hazardous waste every year—more than one ton for each citizen. Up to one-third of these wastes, most often in the form of "dirty water," are released untreated into the environment.[120] In 1990 Congress passed the Pollution Prevention Act (PPA), which expanded the Toxics Release Inventory (TRI), a national database that identifies for public information the annual amount of chemicals released from manufacturing facilities. Since the TRI program began in 1987, industries have reduced their releases of chemicals by more than 45 percent, or 1.5 billion pounds.[121] A key reason for this is that investors have reacted negatively to firms with higher reported toxic releases.[122]

Progress in implementing the Superfund cleanup program has been slow and disappointing. According to the EPA, there are over 37,000 toxic waste dumps in the United States, thousands of which pose serious health threats. The Office of Technology Assessment estimated that cleanup measures could cost more than $50 billion.[123] The Environmental Protection Agency has identified more than 1,400 priority toxic dumps for remedial action, but only about 35 percent of them have been completely cleaned up.[124] The $13 billion fund available under the Superfund program will not be adequate to complete the task. Often the health effects of toxic chemicals are impossible to detect accurately; the technology for defusing toxic bombs and neutralizing toxic soups is still in its infancy.

From React and Cure to Anticipate and Prevent

America's first two decades of serious environmental regulation were marked by uneven progress. Much effort and billions of dollars have yielded important but modest improvements. The problems that have been discovered and addressed await resolution, but the environmental threats in the immediate future may be even more intractable. An EPA task force reported that "newer" environmental problems, such as "indoor radon, global climatic change, . . . acid precipitation, and hazardous waste," will be difficult to evaluate and may "involve persistent contaminants that move from one environmental medium to another, causing further damage even after controls have been applied."[125]

Enormous expenditures and upheavals in industrial production practices will be needed to clean up and preserve the environment, as will serious changes in our personal behavior. Americans' preoccupation with automobiles, especially gas-guzzling Sport Utility Vehicles, or SUVs, and our current living arrangements that require commuting between home and work, must be altered to reduce environmental stress. These economic and social costs must be borne today, but most of the benefits will accrue to future generations. Thus far, private and public policymakers have been unwilling to take the necessary steps. The pressures for immediate economic growth have been too powerful to resist. The so-called greenhouse effect illustrates the trade-offs. Increased accumulation of carbon dioxide and other gases in the upper atmosphere has caused global temperatures to rise by three to four degrees in the last hundred years. Scientists project that similar temperature increases could occur by the year 2100, causing drastic changes in the earth's climate, severe flooding, drought, and famine on a scale unparalleled in human history. Reversing or slowing this trend will require reductions in the use of fossil fuels and unprecedented cooperation among the nations of the world.[126]

Compared with many other parts of the world, the United States has an admirable environmental protection record. The industrial Communist nations have relatively poor environmental records. Levels of sulfur dioxide emissions from the former Soviet Union are three times greater than the levels emitted from the United States. Hundreds of thousands of people were exposed to dangerous radiation levels in the aftermath of the world's worst nuclear power plant disaster at Chernobyl in the former Soviet Union.[127] Environmental degradation is widespread in developing countries, where the pressures for development to support exploding populations are intense. Thirty-three million acres of ecologically valuable rain forests—more than the combined total area of the New England states of Connecticut, Massachusetts, New Hampshire, Rhode Island, and Vermont plus Delaware and New Jersey—are destroyed every year.[128] If this destruction continues unchecked, the loss of the rain forests could become "an ecological disaster of major proportions."[129]

Clearly, public policymakers in this country and around the world must do better. The World Commission on Environment and Development concluded that

> many present development trends leave increasing numbers of people poor and vulnerable while at the same time degrading the environment. How can such development serve next century's world of twice as many people relying on the same environment? . . . [T]he react and cure environmental policies that governments have pursued are bankrupt. . . . Anticipate and prevent is the only realistic approach.[130]

Achieving a sustainable environment in the face of enormous worldwide development pressures will be extremely difficult, but the very survival of the planet depends on it.

Summary

Any fair assessment of American public policy would conclude that great progress has been made toward fulfilling the nation's goals and values. At the writing of this book, unemployment is near its lowest ever, the U.S. economy is booming, the country leads the world in science and technology, and many Americans are pretty comfortable and content with their lives. The United States is, in many ways, better off than it was fifty, twenty, or ten years ago. Some significant arms control agreements have been signed, and the prospects for farther-reaching controls look better than they have in many years. Despite several difficult recessions in the 1980s and in 1991, the economy experienced a strong revitalization in the 1990s and remains strong at the beginning of the new century. What this prosperity will bring in the future or whether it will continue is uncertain. The most egregious forms of racial and gender-based discrimination have been curtailed or at least identified. The social safety net of income support and health care for the elderly and disadvantaged has survived attempted reductions, and new proposals to strengthen Medicare through prescription drug benefits have emerged. The first steps have been taken to preserve and protect the air, water, and land necessary for survival.

But U.S. public policies are not as effective as they should be. Massive increases in defense spending have not produced a country that is significantly less vulnerable to terrorist attacks. The rising tide of economic recovery has failed to lift all boats. In one of the world's most affluent nations, with an unprecedented booming economy in the 1990s and early 2000s, millions are unemployed, homeless, and hungry. The gaps between rich and poor, black and white, have grown wider. Discrimination based on race, gender, age, and disability is still pervasive. The costs of income security and health care programs have risen so rapidly that their solvency is threatened, yet benefits for poor people are barely adequate for their survival, and the health of Americans has not improved significantly. The water and air remain dangerously polluted by automobile exhaust, industrial waste, and toxic chemicals. Much, therefore, remains to be done. The problems facing policymakers and citizens are as intractable as any the nation has faced. Among the most pressing are:

- keeping America competitive in the world economy
- redressing discrimination against minorities and women
- bringing poor people into the mainstream of society
- improving the social safety net
- meeting unprecedented threats to the environment, such as global warming
- accommodating an increasingly diverse population.

If the past is prologue, there is reason to be deeply concerned about the willingness and ability of American political institutions and their leaders to meet these challenges. Extraordinary skills, leadership, and cooperation will be required in the years ahead.

Notes

1. Center for Public Interest Polling, *Images 111: The Quality of Life in New Jersey* (New Brunswick, N.J.: Eagleton Institute of Politics, Rutgers University, 1985).
2. See, for example, President's Commission for a National Agenda for the Eighties, *A National Agenda for the Eighties* (Englewood Cliffs, N.J.: Prentice-Hall, 1980).
3. See, for example, Carol Weiss, *Evaluation Research* (Englewood Cliffs, N.J.: Prentice-Hall, 1972); Arnold J. Meltsner, *Policy Analysts in the Bureaucracy* (Berkeley: University of California Press, 1976); and Peter Rossi and Howard E. Freeman, *Evaluation: A Systematic Approach,* 8th ed. (Thousand Oaks, Calif.: Sage, 1999).
4. Alberto Martini and Michael Wiseman, *Explaining the Recent Decline in Welfare Caseloads: Is the Council of Economic Advisors Right?* (Washington, D.C.: Urban Institute, 1997), and online at http://www.urban.org1/welfare/cea.html, August 10, 2000; Daniel P. McMurrer and Isabel V. Sawhill, "Planning for the Best of Times," *Washington Post,* August 18, 1997, A19.
5. Environmental Protection Agency, "What Has the EPA Done about Ozone Depletion?" April 14, 1999, online at http://www.epa.gov/ozone/geninfo/

actions.html, June 29, 2000.

6. World Bank, "2000 World Development Indicators: Mortality," online at http://www.worldbank.org/data/wdi20.pdf, June 30, 2000.

7. John D. Steinbruner, "Security Policy," in *The New Direction in American Politics*, ed. John E. Chubb and Paul E. Peterson (Washington, D.C.: Brookings Institution, 1985), 343–364.

8. Kenneth J. Campbell, "Once Burned, Twice Cautious: Explaining the Weinberger-Powell Doctrine," *Armed Forces & Society* 24 (Spring 1998): 357–374.

9. Executive Office of the President, Office of Management and Budget, *A Citizen's Guide to the Federal Budget: Budget of the United States Government for the Fiscal Year 2000* (Washington, D.C.: Government Printing Office, 2000), online at http://www.access.gpo.gov/usbudget/fy2000/guide02.html, June 29, 2000 (hereafter cited as *Citizen's Guide to the Budget, 2000.*

10. Frank McCleary, "USS *Harry S. Truman* Commissioned," *Independence (Mo.) Examiner*, July 28, 1998, and online at http://www.examiner.net/ussharrytrumen/shipservice.html, July 12, 2000.

11. B. Guy Peters, *American Public Policy: Promise and Performance* (Chatham, N.J.: Chatham House, 1986), 287–289.

12. Henry J. Aaron et al., *Economic Choices, 1987* (Washington, D.C.: Brookings Institution, 1986), 75.

13. *Citizen's Guide to the Budget, 2000.*

14. *Economic Report of the President* (Washington, D.C.: Government Printing Office, 1985); John L. Palmer and Isabel V. Sawhill, *The Reagan Record: An Assessment of Changing Domestic Priorities* (Cambridge, Mass.: Ballinger, 1984), 8.

15. *A Citizen's Guide to the Budget, 2000.*

16. Steinbruner, "Security Policy," 349.

17. Executive Office of the President, Office of Management and Budget, *Budget of the United States Government, Fiscal Year 1991* (Washington, D.C.: Government Printing Office, 1990), 183.

18. Executive Office of the President, Office of Management and Budget, *Historical Tables: Budget of the United States Government, Fiscal Year 2000* (Washington, D.C.: Government Printing Office, 1999), 107–109.

19. Charles Babbington, "Slim Majority Backs Clinton Plan," *Washington Post*, March 30, 1999, online at http://www.washingtonpost.com/wp-srv/politics/daily/march99/clinton30.html, May 30, 2000.

20. Leo Bogart, *Polls and the Awareness of Public Opinion*, 2d ed. (New Brunswick, N.J.: Transaction Books, 1985), 89–96.

21. W. Lance Bennett, "Marginalizing the Majority: Conditioning Public Opinion to Accept Managerial Democracy" (paper presented at the annual meeting of the Midwest Political Science Association, Chicago, April 1987), 16.

22. Joseph A. Pechman, *Federal Tax Policy*, 4th ed. (Washington, D.C.: Brookings Institution, 1983), 27–28.

23. Senate Judiciary Committee, Subcommittee on Immigration, *Workforce Shortages in the High-Tech Employment Market: Hearing before the Subcommittee on Immigration*, testimony of William T. Archey, American Electronics Association, 106th Cong., 1st sess., October 21, 1999, online at http://www.aeanet.org/aeanet/Public/public_policy/, July 7, 2000.

24. Executive Office of the President, Office of Management and Budget, *Budget of the United States Government, Fiscal Year 2001* (Washington, D.C.: Government Printing Office, 2000), 99.

25. Executive Office of the President, Office of Management and Budget, *Budget of the United States Government, Fiscal Year 1992* (Washington, D.C.: Government Printing Office, 1991), 35.

26. Associated General Contractors of America, "Increased Funding for Critical Infrastructure Investment," 1999, http://www.agc.org/legislative_Info/position_papers/incr_fund.inc, July 13, 2000.

27. Rebuild America Coalition, "Infrastructure Investment Recommendations," *The American Public Works Association,* http://www.rebuildamerica.org/reports/rebuildpricetagfinal.pdf, July 13, 2000.

28. U.S. Congress, Joint Economic Committee, *The 1985 Joint Economic Report* (Washington, D.C.: Government Printing Office, 1985), 70–71; Bureau of the Census, "State and Local Government Finances," in *Statistical Abstract of the U.S.: 1999* (Washington, D.C.: Government Printing Office, 1999).

29. Bruce R. Scott, "U.S. Competitiveness: Concepts, Performance, and Implications," in *U.S. Competitiveness in the World Economy,* ed. Bruce R. Scott and George C. Lodge (Boston: Harvard Business School Press, 1985), 61.

30. Ibid., 38.

31. Ibid., 36–37; Robert Kuttner, *The Economic Illusion: False Choices between Prosperity and Social Justice* (Boston: Houghton Mifflin, 1984), 291.

32. Organization for Economic Cooperation and Development, *Is There a New Economy? First Report on the OECD Growth Project* (Paris: OECD Publications, 2000), 4–5.

33. Scott, "U.S. Competitiveness," 35–36.

34. Ibid., 39; Robert B. Reich, *The Next American Frontier* (New York: Times Books, 1983), 118.

35. World Bank, "2000 World Development Indicators: Mortality," online at http://www.worldbank.org/data/wdi20.pdf, June 30, 2000.

36. Kuttner, *The Economic Illusion,* 291.

37. See William Julius Wilson, *When Work Disappears: The World of the New Urban Poor* (New York: Knopf, 1996).

38. Robert E. Scott, "The Facts about Trade and Job Creation," *EPI Issue Brief #139* (Washington, D.C.: EPI, 2000), online at http://www.epinet.org/Issuebriefs/Ib139.html, July 10, 2000.

39. Donald C. Baumer and Carl E. Van Horn, *The Politics of Unemployment* (Washington, D.C.: CQ Press, 1985), 2–3.

40. Department of Labor, Bureau of Labor Statistics, "Labor Statistics from the Current Population Survey," online at http://www.stats.bls.gov/eag/eag.map.html, July 5, 2000.

41. *Economic Report of the President* (Washington, D.C.: Government Printing Office, 1999), 100; Department of Labor, Bureau of Labor Statistics, "The Employment Situation: July 2000," August 4, 2000, online at http://www.bls.gov/news.release/pdf/empsit.pdf, August 11, 2000.

42. Joint Economic Committee, *The 1985 Joint Economic Report,* 36.

43. Kenneth M. Dolbeare, *Democracy at Risk: The Politics of Economic Renewal,* rev. ed. (Chatham, N.J.: Chatham House, 1986), 60.

44. Joint Economic Committee, *The 1985 Joint Economic Report,* 97.
45. *Economic Report of the President* (Washington, D.C.: Government Printing Office, 2000), 64.
46. Joint Economic Committee, *The 1985 Joint Economic Report,* 25. Inflation rates for 1980–1990 are from the *Economic Report of the President* (Washington, D.C.: Government Printing Office, 1991), table B-58. Figures are from the *New York Times,* August 15, 1991, D1.
47. *Economic Report of the President,* 2000, 3.
48. Organization for Economic Cooperation and Development, *Is There a New Economy? First Report on the OECD Growth Project* (Paris: OECD Publications, 2000).
49. Gunnar Myrdal, *An American Dilemma* (New York: Harper and Row, 1944).
50. Economic Policy Institute and Center on Budget Policy and Priorities, "State Income Inequality Continued to Grow in Most States in the 1990s, Despite Economic Growth and Tight Labor Markets," January 18, 2000, online at http://www.cbpp.org/1-18-00sfp.html, July 13, 2000.
51. Chuck Collins, Chris Hartman, and Holly Sklar, "Divided Decade: Economic Disparity at the Century's Turn," *United for a Fair Economy,* December 15, 1999, online at http://www.ufenet.org/press/DivDec.pdf, July 14, 2000.
52. Arthur M. Okun, *Equality and Efficiency: The Big Tradeoff* (Washington, D.C.: Brookings Institution, 1975), 1.
53. William Schneider, "People Watching," *National Journal,* January 12, 1985, 63.
54. See, for example, Okun, *Equality and Efficiency;* Dolbeare, *Democracy at Risk;* and Kuttner, *The Economic Illusion.*
55. *Economic Report of the President,* 1991, 320.
56. Joseph Delaker, Bureau of the Census, *Poverty in the United States, 1998,* Current Population Reports, series P60-207 (Washington, D.C.: Government Printing Office, 1999), v.
57. Bureau of the Census, *Money Income in the United States: 1998,* Current Population Reports, series P60-2-6 (Washington, D.C.: Government Printing Office, 1999), 18.
58. Harrell R. Rodgers Jr., *The Cost of Human Neglect* (Armonk, N.Y.: M. E. Sharpe, 1982), 29.
59. Robert Pear, "Poverty Rate Dips as the Median Family Income Rises," *New York Times,* July 31, 1987, A12.
60. Benjamin I. Page, *Who Gets What from Government* (Berkeley: University of California Press, 1983), 191.
61. Gene Koretz, "Surprise—The Rich Get Richer," *Business Week,* June 19, 2000, 38.
62. Page, *Who Gets What from Government,* 22–23.
63. The White House, Office of the Press Secretary, "President Clinton Proposes to Expand the Earned Income Tax Credit in Order to Increase the Reward for Work and Family," press release, January 12, 2000, online at http://www.whitehouse.gov/WH/New/html/20000112_2.html, July 12, 2000.
64. Pechman, *Federal Tax Policy,* 60–128.
65. Page, *Who Gets What from Government,* 35–41.
66. Delaker, *Poverty in the United States, 1998,* v.

67. Department of Labor, Bureau of Labor Statistics, "The Employment Situation: June 2000," July 7, 2000, online at http://stats.bls.gov/newsrels.html, July 13, 2000.

68. Randy Albelda and Chris Tilly, *Glass Ceilings and Bottomless Pits: Women's Work, Women's Poverty* (Boston: South End Press, 1997), 36, 8.

69. Lydia Scoon-Rogers, "Child Support for Custodial Mothers and Fathers: 1995," report of the Bureau of the Census (Washington, D.C.: Government Printing Office, 1999).

70. Wendy Castro, "Welfare Reform and Abstinence Education: An Issue Brief," (Washington, D.C.: Child Welfare League of America Press, 1998), 4.

71. Frank Levy, *The New Dollars and Dreams* (New York: Russell Sage Foundation, 1998), 183.

72. Michael W. Lynch, "The Dream Is Gone," *Reason Magazine,* December 1999, online at http://www.reasonmag.com/9912/bk.ml.the.html, July 14, 2000.

73. On increased participation of women, *Economic Report of the President,* 2000, 168; on equal pay, Renee Cherow-O'Leary, *The State-by-State Guide to Women's Legal Rights* (New York: McGraw-Hill, 1987).

74. Teresa L. Ammot and Julie Matthei, *Race, Gender, and Work: A Multicultural Economic History of Women in the United States* (Boston: South End Press, 1996).

75. Borgna Brunner, "Timeline of Affirmative Action Milestones," online at http://infoplease.com/spot/affirmativetimeline1.html, July 14, 2000.

76. National Alliance of Business, "Employment Policy Issues for the End of the Century and the Year 2000" (National Alliance of Business, Washington, D.C., November 22, 1985, photocopy).

77. David Stockman, *The Triumph of Politics* (New York: Harper and Row, 1986), 8.

78. James B. Storey, "Income Security," in *The Reagan Experiment,* ed. John L. Palmer and Isabel V. Sawhill (Washington, D.C.: Urban Institute Press, 1982), 864–865.

79. R. Kent Weaver, "Controlling Entitlements," in Chubb and Peterson, *The New Direction in American Politics,* 308.

80. Executive Office of the President, Office of Management and Budget, *Budget of the United States Government, Fiscal Year 2000* (Washington, D.C.: Government Printing Office, 1999), 253.

81. Ibid., 250.

82. Ibid., 248.

83. U.S. Department of Health and Human Services, Administration for Children and Families, "Change in TANF Caseloads," June 2000, online at http://www.acf.dhhs.gov/news/stats/caseload.html, August 10, 2000.

84. *Economic Report of the President,* 1991, 167.

85. Peters, *American Public Policy,* 214.

86. Executive Office of the President, Office of Management and Budget, *Budget, 2001,* 250.

87. Albelda and Tilly, *Glass Ceilings and Bottomless Pits,* 28.

88. Department of Health and Human Services, Social Security Administration, *Social Security Questions,* no. 000406-0007 (Washington, D.C.: Government

Printing Office, 2000), online at http://www.ssa-custhelp.ssa.gov/, July 17, 2000.

89. Weaver, "Controlling Entitlements," 320.

90. Administration for Children and Families, "Total AFDC, Average Monthly Payment per Case, Fiscal Years 1987–1996," March 27, 1997, online at http://www.acf.dhhs.gov/programs/opre/timetren/ma_tca.html, July 17, 2000.

91. Ruth Sidel, *Keeping Women and Children Last* (New York: Penguin Books, 1996), 88.

92. Executive Office of the President, Office of Management and Budget, *Budget, 2000*, 248–253.

93. Executive Office of the President, Office of Management and Budget, *Budget of the United States Government, Fiscal Year 1986* (Washington, D.C.: Government Printing Office, 1985), pt. 5, p. 116.

94. Parke Wilde et al., U.S. Department of Agriculture, Economic Research Service, "The Decline in Food Stamp Program Participation in the 1990s," June 2000, online at http://www.ers.usda.gov/epubs/pdf/fanrr7/fanrr7.pdf, July 19, 2000.

95. Isabel V. Sawhill, "Anti-Poverty Strategies for the 1980s," discussion paper (Urban Institute, Washington, D.C., 1986, photocopy).

96. See, for example, Julie Kosterlitz, "Reforming Welfare," *National Journal*, December 6, 1986, 2926–2931.

97. Executive Office of the President, Office of Management and Budget, *Budget, 2000*, 238.

98. *Economic Report of the President*, 1991, 135–137 and 376–377, table B-77; and Executive Office of the President, Office of Management and Budget, *Budget, 1992*; and Jennie Jacobs Kronenfeld, *The Changing Federal Role in U.S. Health Care Policy* (Westport, Conn.: Greenwood Publishing, Praeger, 1997), 25.

99. Peters, *American Public Policy*, 188; and Kronenfeld, *The Changing Federal Role in U.S. Health Care Policy*, 7.

100. Kaiser Commission on Uninsured Facts, "Medicaid and the Uninsured: The Uninsured and Their Access to Health Care," Henry J. Kaiser Family Foundation, May 2000, online at http://www.kff.org/content/2000/1420/pub%201420.pdf, July 19, 2000.

101. Ibid.

102. Weaver, "Controlling Entitlements," 828.

103. Larry Levitt and Janet Lundy, "Trends and Indicators in the Changing Health Care Marketplace," Henry J. Kaiser Family Foundation, August 1998, online at http://www.kaiser.bitwtench.com/content/archive/1429/trends.pdf, July 19, 2000, 2.

104. For a discussion of the topic, see *Journal of Health Politics, Policy, and Law* 24 (October 1999). This is a special issue of the journal dedicated to a discussion of the backlash against managed care in the 1990s.

105. *Economic Report of the President*, 1991, 351–354.

106. World Bank, "2000 World Development Indicators: Mortality," online at http://www.worldbank.org/data/wdi20.pdf, June 30, 2000.

107. Peters, *American Public Policy*, 192.

108. *Economic Report of the President,* 1991, 139; and Kronenfeld, *The Changing Federal Role in U.S. Health Care Policy,* 44–45.

109. *Economic Report of the President,* 1991, 139.

110. Catherine Wilson, "Tobacco Industry Told to Pay $145 Billion," *Washington Post,* July 14, 2000, online at http://www.washingtonpost.com/wp-dyn/nation/specials/socialpolicy/tobacco/A45013–2000Jul14.html, July 19, 2000.

111. Legal Information Institute, "FDA v. Brown & Williamson Tobacco Corp.," online at http://www.supct.law.cornell.edu/supct/html/98–1152.ZS.html, August 10, 2000.

112. President's Commission for a National Agenda for the Eighties, *A National Agenda for the Eighties,* 49.

113. Department of the Interior, Bureau of Land Management, "Public Land Statistics—1996," online at http://www.blm.gov/nhp/landfacts/pls96.html, July 19, 2000.

114. Walter A. Rosenbaum, *Environmental Politics and Policy* (Washington, D.C.: CQ Press, 1985), 100.

115. Richard Andrews, *Managing the Environment, Managing Ourselves* (New Haven: Yale University Press, 1999), 271.

116. Barry Commoner, "A Reporter at Large: The Environment," *New Yorker,* June 15, 1987, 51.

117. U.S. Environmental Protection Agency, "Major Action Taken to Protect Rivers, Lakes, and Beaches," online at http://www.epa.gov/epahome/headline_0711.html, July 19, 2000.

118. Office of Air and Radiation, "1995 National Air Quality: Status and Trends," U.S. Environmental Protection Agency, December 12, 1996, online at http://epa/gov/oar/aqtrnd95/pb.html, July 19, 2000.

119. Joby Warrick and Bill McAllister, "New Air Pollution Limits Blocked," *Washington Post,* May 15, 1999, 1.

120. Commoner, "A Reporter at Large," 52.

121. U.S. Environmental Protection Agency, "Toxics Release Inventory: Community Right-to-Know," online at http://www.epa.gov/tri/tri98/98over.pdf, July 19, 2000.

122. James Hamilton, "Pollution as News: Media and Stock Market Reactions to the Toxic Release Inventory Data," *Journal of Environmental Economics and Management* 28 (1995): 98–113.

123. Office of Technology Assessment, *Technologies and Management Strategies for Hazardous Waste Control* (Washington, D.C.: Government Printing Office, 1983), 7n1.

124. Office of Emergency and Remedial Response, "Superfund Cleanup Figures," U.S. Environmental Protection Agency, June 22, 2000, online at http://www.epa/gov/superfund/whatisst/mgmtrpt.html, July 19, 2000.

125. Environmental Protection Agency, "Unfinished Business: A Comparative Assessment of Environmental Problems" (EPA, Washington, D.C., February 1987, photocopy), xiii.

126. U.S. Environmental Protection Agency, EPA Global Warming Site, "Climate," July 12, 2000, online at http://www.epa.gov/globalwarming/climate/index.html, July 19, 2000.

127. William U. Chandler, "Designing Sustainable Economies," in *The State of the World, 1987,* ed. Lester R. Brown et al. (New York: W. W. Norton, 1987), 187–190.

128. The Rainforest Alliance, "Rainforest Resources/Facts," April 1999, online at http://www.rainforest-alliance.org/resources/forest-facts.html, July 19, 2000.

129. Editorial Research Reports, *Earth's Threatened Resources* (Washington, D.C.: Congressional Quarterly, 1986), 163.

130. World Commission on Environment and Development, *Our Common Future: From One Earth to One World* (New York: Oxford University Press, 1987), 4.

Index